DOGMA AND PREACHING

BENEDICT XVI
Joseph Ratzinger

Dogma and Preaching

Applying Christian Doctrine to Daily Life

UNABRIDGED EDITION

Translated by Michael J. Miller
and Matthew J. O'Connell

Edited by Michael J. Miller

IGNATIUS PRESS   SAN FRANCISCO

From the fourth edition of the German original:

Dogma und Verkündigung

© 2005 by Erich Wewel Verlag, Donauwörth

Front cover art:
Saint Peter, detail from the facade. 1160–1180. Romanesque.
St. Trophime, Arles, France
© Andrea Jemolo/Scala/Art Resource, New York

Back cover photograph of Pope Benedict XVI by Stefano Spaziani

Cover design by Roxanne Mei Lum

Dedicated to Hans Urs von Balthasar
with respect and gratitude

Foreword

The path from dogma to preaching has become very difficult. There are no longer any patterns of thought and assumptions that carry the content of dogma into everyday life; it is too much to demand of the individual preacher, however, that he himself should figure out each time the entire path from the doctrinal formula to its core and from there back to contemporary language. Should we not instead leave out dogma entirely? With such a radical cure, which appears to many today to be the only way out, preaching becomes speaking in one's own name and loses all objective interest whatsoever, as Erik Peterson has strikingly and incontestably demonstrated from the painful experiences of crumbling liberal theology (*Was ist Theologie?* [Bonn, 1926]). The inner tension of preaching depends on the objective arch spanning and upheld by the pillars: Dogma-Scripture-Church-Today; not one of them can be taken away without the whole thing eventually collapsing.

If that is how matters stand, theology cannot be satisfied with reflecting on the faith in the Elysian fields of academe while otherwise leaving the preacher to his own devices. It has to provide everyday life with signposts and find paradigms for translating reflection into proclamation; thought is proved only when it can be expressed. This volume seeks to serve as a contribution to the development of a material kerygma. The fragmentary writings of which it is composed grew out of discussions with pastors or from my own attempt to speak pastorally in homilies, on radio, and in newspapers. This resulted in its structure: fundamental reflections on the path of proclamation, essays on particular subject areas, and attempts at practical application. This could amount to no more than an initial approach to a large task; still, perhaps the realism of the situations from which the whole thing grew may compensate somewhat for the lack of systematic method and completeness.

7

I am grateful to Miss Karin Bommes for preparing the index of names and biblical citations.

Regensburg, February 1973

Joseph Ratzinger

Contents

CHURCH

ESCHATOLOGY

PART THREE

Meditations and Sermons

THE LITURGICAL YEAR

THE COMMUNION OF SAINTS

PART ONE

Toward a Theory of Preaching

1. Church as the Place of Preaching

Talking about the crisis in preaching has already become commonplace today. The What, How, and Where of preaching have become, as it were, questionable; various kinds of attempts at reform are offered, from flight into strict biblicism to unadulterated congregational conversation in which those present merely exchange their opinions and possibly seek guidelines for action in common based on opinions they have worked out together.[1] The central fact behind all this is the crisis of ecclesial consciousness. Whereas formerly no one doubted that Church was the standard and locus of preaching, now she stands almost as an obstacle to it: preaching, it seems, must become a critical corrective to Church instead of being subordinate to her and allowing her to be normative. In this situation it might be necessary to inquire into the historical and material point of departure of Christian preaching in general, so as to reestablish its coherence on that basis. How, then, does preaching come about? What are its origin and its purpose?

1. The Development of the Basic Types of Preaching in the Old Testament

No sooner do we ask this question than it takes us back beyond the New Testament into the Old, for without the historical path of the latter, the New Testament message remains inexplicable. In the Old Testament, if I am looking at it correctly, we can find three principal roots of preaching. The first is found in the area of the Torah, Israel's ordinances for worship and living. The classical Old Testament liturgy, as portrayed paradigmatically in Exodus 24:5–8, includes two aspects:

Translated by Michael J. Miller.

[1] A survey of current discussion of the subject can be found in G. Biemer, ed., *Die Fremdsprache der Predigt* (Düsseldorf, 1970).

the burnt offering and the reading from the book of the covenant, the proclamation of the divine law for Israel. The saying about Levi in Deuteronomy 33:8ff. presupposes the same thing: the priests present the offerings and teach Israel God's law.[2] Here preaching as instruction for a life according to the ways of Yahweh is one part of the priestly ministry included in the form of divine worship that is shaped by God's law itself. The worship of God in Israel never has a merely cultic-sacrificial character; it is aimed at man as a covenant partner. Only in his living justice is service to Yahweh performed and worship complete. Preaching, as guiding all of life into the covenant and in terms of the covenant, is part of divine worship; it *is* divine worship. And conversely: divine worship takes place precisely in the act of bringing God's will to bear upon man, in the word that becomes for man the way.

In view of the extensive failure of priestly preaching, a second ministry of proclamation becomes increasingly prominent: that of the prophet who has been called and aroused by God himself, the prophet who inculcates precisely this character of word and reality of faith in Yahweh. Although the spontaneous and charismatic element becomes quite important here in comparison to the institutional element, the prophet nonetheless does not stand autonomous and aloof with regard to Israel's faith history. Prophecy, too, has a sort of institutional character; what really identifies it, however, is that it stands in the continuity of Israel's faith and sternly and unrelentingly asserts just this original covenant faith for Israel against all sorts of *aggiornamento*. Therefore even the prophet does not act outside of Israel but, rather, brings the true Israel to bear, as it is manifest in the faith of the fathers, against the distorted Israel of this or that present moment, and precisely thereby he upholds Israel's faith as something open to the future.[3]

We find a third component in the so-called vow psalms, for which we can regard Psalm 22 (21) as a model. The sorely oppressed righteous man pours out all his despair in the sight of Yahweh and begs him to rescue him. The psalm, which begins with the cry of distress of a man who has been forsaken by God and cast down already to the

---

[2] Cf. A. Deissler, "Das Priestertum im Alten Testament", in A. Deissler, H. Schlier, and P. Audet, *Der priesterliche Dienst*, vol. 1 (Freiburg, 1970), 9–80.

[3] On the concept and duty of the prophet, see in particular J. Scharbert, *Die Propheten Israels*, 2 vols. (Cologne, 1965–1967).

netherworld, then ends according to form with the promise to proclaim Yahweh's mighty deed "in the midst of the congregation". That is at first quite an anthropomorphic reason to urge Yahweh to grant his prayer: It is worthwhile, so to speak, for God to save the man, for if he should perish, that would mean the loss of a worshipper ("the dead do not praise you"), whereas in the case of a rescue, the saved man will proclaim Yahweh's might everywhere and continue to extol and spread abroad his glory. This anthropomorphic beginning then leads to a deeper meaning: the experience of God's benevolent might urges us to proclaim it, urges us to make a return. Like great good fortune, one cannot keep it to oneself. It urges one to give thanks by way of proclamation. One gives thanks to Yahweh's might by proclaiming it; man passes on the experience of his indebtedness and thus makes it possible for others, too, by adding their thanks, to become sharers in the saving power of Yahweh, to rejoice with him in Yahweh's might. Preaching as thanksgiving (*eucharistia*!) meshes here with the worship of God; as testimony to God's saving power, it is itself divine worship, and by its testimony it calls man into divine worship and yet at the same time gives him therein salvation and "redemption".[4]

This third type of preaching—the grateful account of God's saving deed in the midst of the assembly of the saints—is, from a New Testament perspective, especially important, inasmuch as the early Church from the very beginning identified with Jesus Christ and was partially defined by the cry of the dying Redeemer from the Cross, by the suffering just man of the psalms, who is called into life only by passing through death and in just this way testifies to the divine power. *He* is the one who prays these psalms; in him alone is actually fulfilled the destiny of those who pray. The communion of the brethren participates in his *eucharistia* for his resurrection from the dead, and therein is rooted their divine worship and likewise their preaching: that communion is basically nothing other than listening at his *eucharistia* and joyful entrance into it. This gathering of people into the listening and speaking of that word of thanksgiving is also preeminently the fulfillment of the anthropomorphic motive found at the beginning of this

---

[4] On the genres of the Psalms, see A. Weiser, *The Psalms: A Commentary*, trans. Herbert Hartwell (Philadelphia: Westminster Press, 1962), 52–91; H.-J. Kraus, *Psalmen*, vol. I (Neukirchen, 1960), xxxvii–lvi. I owe the observation about the vow structure above all to the lectures of Prof. F. Stummer on the Psalms (Munich, 1949).

path: all mankind becomes acquainted in this way with Yahweh and becomes the congregation of those who are privileged to hear about him and to give him thanks.

2. The New Testament Transformation

With that we have already made our transition to New Testament preaching; we are approaching the center of our topic, yet in order to understand it precisely, we still must examine once more the details of the path that we have just sketched roughly. In the case of the Old Testament, the listeners who form the locus of preaching are the "brethren", the "assembly of the holy ones", that is, the members of the people of Israel gathering for worship in the Temple. The sphere of preaching is already defined as the people Israel, and, practically speaking, it comes to pass precisely where this people gathers, in the Temple or also in the synagogue. Admittedly, there is already a universalistic feature to this whole picture: ultimately *everyone* should and will hear about it, since even the heavens tell about Yahweh.[5] But that remains a prospect that is fundamentally in the hands of Yahweh himself; it does not define the concrete present situation, in which the *ecclesia*, or perhaps the *ecclesia magna* (Ps 22 [21]:25) constitutes the audience. In the New Testament there is a change—necessarily so, inasmuch as now the psalm with its situation emerges from the hypothetical and indefinite form in which tradition presents it into a quite specific historical realization: Jesus is the one praying in this psalm. Thus the "all shall hear", the universalistic horizon to which the whole thing points, can no longer remain in its previous vagueness. If it has now come true that God *has* in fact brought his righteous one back from the netherworld, if the deed that affects the whole world and proves to the whole world that Yahweh is the true God *has been done*, then this is also the moment when all must

---

[5] Cf. Ps 19 [18]. The Vulgate has introduced this motif into Psalm 21 (Vulgate numbering) as well; verse 32 of that version reads: "Annuntiabitur Domino generatio ventura, et annuntiabunt caeli iustitiam eius, populo qui nascetur, quem fecit Dominus" [There shall be declared to the Lord a generation to come: and the heavens shall shew forth his justice to a people that shall be born, which the Lord hath made (Douay-Rheims)].

In the following discussion I do not translate the term *ecclesia* because the usual [German] translation, *Gemeinde* ["congregation"], has meanwhile taken on a fixed meaning that allows no room for the spectrum of connotations in the original text.

hear it, when not just the already existing *ecclesia* (which basically has always been presupposed) of the already constituted people Israel has to listen, but all mankind is to be called to that *ecclesia*, to that assembly which hearkens to the *eucharistia* of Jesus, to his thanksgiving.

The process in which the universalistic framework now necessarily ceases to be a hypothetical, eschatological expression and becomes an urgent task here and now could be even further illustrated by examining the history of tradition. The preaching of Jesus himself, indeed, still keeps completely to the framework of Israel, although of course in a series of parables it does incidentally and clearly allow a glimpse of the possibility of an exchange of roles.[6] Specifically, though, the fact that the *ecclesia* of Israel refuses to listen to the Eucharist of the Risen One is what actually leads to the fundamental opening up of the *ecclesia*, so that it is created anew by the Word as universal.[7]

This now results, however, in a very far-reaching transformation of the way in which *ecclesia* is subordinated to the preaching process. *Ecclesia* does not simply exist already, but, rather, it is created by the Word in the first place. The Word is constantly there in order to call people together to himself and thereby to make them into the *Ecclesia*. The New Testament *Ecclesia* is not something preexisting; it is an open-ended entity that comes into being through the word of proclamation, which is constantly commissioned to travel everywhere, to bring all mankind into the thanksgiving of Jesus Christ, and to make them thankful with him. Although we must speak then of a more dynamic concept of *ecclesia*, which follows from its universalistic character, we nevertheless must not suppose that this is an aimless dynamism. For the Word does not remain fruitless. Indeed, it actually creates *Ecclesia* and then is related to it otherwise than to the circle of those who still stand outside of the Word and are to be reached by it. That means, though, that in the domain of the New Testament Church, there are two fundamental forms of proclamation:

a. Preaching to those who are already gathered, who join in the

---

[6] Cf. J. Ratzinger, "Stellvertretung", in *Handbuch theologischer Grundbegriffe*, ed. H. Fries (Munich, 1963), 2:570f. To the passages mentioned there one could add, for instance, Mark 12:1–12 (parable of the vineyard tenants); Matthew 22:1–14 (parable of the marriage feast); Matthew 8:5–13 (the centurion in Capernaum); Mark 7:24–30 (the Syro-Phoenician woman).

[7] See especially E. Peterson, *Theologische Traktate* (Munich, 1951), 411–29; H. Schlier, *Die Zeit der Kirche* (Freiburg, 1965), 90–107.

eucharistia of Jesus and live on it, are led into it again and again and receive instruction from it.

b. The call that goes across boundaries, that seeks to make those standing outside into an assembly and gathers them in to the *Ecclesia* of those who listen and are thankful.

In both cases, *Ecclesia* is the point of reference of the proclamation, but in different ways: in the one instance, as the vital fulfillment of the Church that is already founded and already alive; in the other instance, as the act by which she goes beyond herself and is founded anew where she does not yet exist. It is of decisive importance for the proper life of the Church that both forms of preaching should be present in her and should stand in the proper relation to each other. On the one hand, there must be the interior self-fulfillment of the faith, in which it is perpetually received anew and at the same time becomes richer in a history of growth and life. On the other hand, there must be a constant surpassing of the closed circle and a proclamation of the faith to a new world, in which it must make itself comprehensible once again, so as to bring in people who are still foreign to it. The two are equally important: a Church that still preached but only internally, that always presupposed the faith as something given and passed it on and developed it further only within the circle of those who already believed and were taken for granted, would necessarily become sterile and lose her relevance; she would deprive herself of the impetus of "all shall hear" and thereby contradict the urgent realism of the Christ-event. Conversely, a Church that looked outward only, that tried only to take as her standard the abilities of the contemporaries of a given period to understand and no longer ventured to spend her own life joyfully and tranquilly in the interior of the faith, would die off from within and would finally have nothing left to say to the outside, either. There must be room for both; the Church must work hard for both, and the two must also interpenetrate in a meaningful way.

If we sum up what we have said thus far with respect to our topic, we can say: Church, in her twofold form as already founded and as to be founded, is the place of preaching. This is the basis for the inner openness and dynamic of preaching as well as for its definitiveness and reliability.

3. *Church as the Acting Subject of Preaching*

These reflections, admittedly, have outlined only one aspect of the problem of biblical preaching that we encountered: the identity and difference of *ecclesia* in the transition from the Old to the New Testament. Now we should inquire further as to how the remaining facts work out: we would then arrive at further distinctions with regard to the purpose of preaching and those responsible for preaching: we would come to one sort of proclamation that essentially has the function of moral instruction and to another that is essentially thanksgiving and the good news of God's grace; above all, to the question about the extent to which the corrective supplied in the Old Testament by prophetic preaching has to continue in the New Testament. Such a comprehensive categorical analysis of "preaching" cannot be the purpose of this little essay; instead, let us single out another aspect that supplements and rounds out what has been said thus far.

Until now we have considered the topic "Church as the place of preaching" from the listener's perspective; now, however, we must analyze it also from the preacher's side. I will attempt to do this in two series of theses that highlight the complementary aspects of this state of affairs and thus try to describe it as completely as possible from various angles, which nevertheless must always be correlated.

a. Two Theses concerning the Unity of Church and Word

1. The preacher does not preach on his own behalf or on behalf of any particular congregation or of any other group but, rather, on behalf of the Church, which is one in all places and at all times. Just as his own faith can only exist ecclesially, so also the word that awakens and supports this faith necessarily has an ecclesial character.

This point of view seems to have vanished to a great extent from contemporary consciousness: on the one hand, faith is understood purely as actual, as from above, continuing and modifying approaches taken by Bultmann and Barth; Church then appears as the organization of believers, or at best as the external cohesiveness that it needs, but as a concrete entity she has nothing to do with faith or is even perceived as an obstacle to it: "faith, yes; Church, no. Christ, yes; Church, no."

Alternatively, faith is reduced to theological scholarship, and the preacher appears then as the theological scholar, who with his expertise is at the service of the congregation. Here, too, the Church, being a non-academic authority, is thought to be inconvenient; whereas in the first case the preacher's legitimacy is derived from his personal decision of conscience, here it follows from his professional competence, for which the Church, in turn, can provide a sphere in which to operate, although she cannot interfere in that competence and by no means figures as the subject of that competence herself.

Or again, faith may appear as a predominantly social phenomenon, but then the Church is just one of the establishment powers, against which faith is to be used critically, and in this way faith is understood quite literally in opposition to the Church and not in union with her.

All of these notions contain an element of truth, yet they are fundamentally outside the reality "faith" that is disclosed by the New Testament evidence. For by its very nature, this faith is a process of gathering. To accept it means to allow oneself to be gathered in. It means becoming Church, for the word *ecclesia*, both etymologically and historically, means precisely this: assembly. We could demonstrate the same things in terms of the other fundamental New Testament designation for the Church: the Body of Christ. Faith means emerging from the isolation of one's own existence and becoming "one body" with Christ, that is, an existential unity with him. And this always means: existential unity of all who have become "one body". This "Body" alone is the abode of his "Spirit". The Body is the acting subject of the Word. The name given to those formulas in which the core of the proclamation was summarized points in this same direction: the symbol of faith. A *symbolon* is a divided token; when the parts are put together, the bearers recognize their own unity, and only when the parts are put together do they have the whole.

2. The Bible, too, being the basic form and basic norm of all preaching, is an ecclesial word and hence can be understood *as* Bible only within the context of Church. To construe Bible merely as something opposed to Church is ultimately a fiction: after all, the Bible comes into existence only as the expression of a common faith. It is becoming increasingly clear to us that inspiration is not an individual charismatic process but, rather, an essentially ecclesial and historical process embedded in the whole process of tradition, genre history, and redaction.

Only in the shared process of believing one after the other, of entering by faith into the faith history of Israel and into the turning point therein that occurs with Jesus does that tradition which is recorded in the Bible come about. And again, only through shared listening, critical views, and disputes do the most diverse pieces of literature become a canon, an ecclesial happening. The human subject of the Bible is the Church; she is at the same time the place of the transition from human spirit to *Pneuma*, to the Spirit of the common Body of Jesus Christ and, thus, generally the place in which inspiration is possible. Hence, although academic study of individual bits of Scripture can arrive at very important insights even apart from the Church, *as* Bible it can only be understood ecclesially and only in terms of its acting subject, without which it would not be Bible at all. . . .[8]

b. Two Theses concerning the Opposition of Church and Word

1. The Church herself is not God's Word but, rather, receives it. Thus God's Word is the counterpart of the Church and the basis that makes her possible at every moment; at the same time, it is also the critical authority for the Church in her concrete existential form; in all areas, it is for her the *krisis*, that is, the judgment from which she must take direction and according to which she must change herself.

Although there is no such thing as God's Word floating around outside of the Church—rather, it is always transmitted in Church and through her—the Church never coincides with the Word. It is in her and above her; not to be had without her and yet not to be identified with any one of her empirical stages. The Church of this time and this place must always be measured against the Church of all times and all places, but especially against the exemplary self-expression of the faith that is found in the Bible.

2. The Church is not the Word; she is the place where the Word dwells and in which it lives. That means, however, that she is obliged to be in reality the milieu or "living space" [*Lebens-raum*] and not the "dying space" [*Sterbe-raum*] of the Word. She must not let the Word degenerate into everyday talk or into the slogans of the changing times but, rather, must preserve it in its unmistakable identity. But in order

---

[8] On the formation of the canon, see the informative study by I. Frank, *Der Sinn der Kanonbildung* (Freiburg, 1971).

for it to be preserved, she must live it, she must suffer it. She must submit the vital energies of an era to the judgment of this Word, but she must likewise make new life, human flesh and blood, available to the Word. Mere preservation would be avoidance of suffering and would fail to carry the Word into today; somewhere between mummification and evaporation, the Church must find the way to serve the Word and to establish, based on the Word, unity among past, present, and future time.

Let us sum up. Preaching has to do with Church in a twofold manner. Church is, first, its point of reference, again in two ways: Church as already living, already believing, whose faith must grow deeper and more vibrant. And then Church as "to be created"—the universal outlook of the Psalms toward a listening, thanking world remains an intrinsic task of preaching. She is on the way to completing the Word of the psalm. This Word, which is fundamentally fulfilled in terms of Christ, must achieve its concrete fulfillment through the ministry of preaching.

This inner tension of preaching, which lives on the Yes to faith once it has been bestowed and yet knows that it is still unfulfilled, still open-ended, as long as it cannot make itself comprehensible to all— precisely this tension reoccurs in the second manner in which preaching and Church are related to each other: Church is, not only the point of reference for preaching, but at the same time its acting subject— those who have heard the Word about the exaltation [of Christ], the tidings that make us glad, and have been gathered into this Word are at the same time those who must carry it on farther. The tension between already gathered and yet to be gathered Church means here that the acting subject of preaching is that universal "I" that stands behind the Creed—I believe in the triune God—and supports it. But this means: preaching must, on the one hand, be genuinely "synchronic"; it must make what is unsuited to the times contemporary nonetheless, so that it is addressed to the here and now—this is required by the drive for *omnes* [all]; yet as a result of that same impulse, it must be radically diachronic, that is, not just the talk of today, and it must not reflect merely the present state of ecclesiastical opinion but, rather, give over today's opinions into the universal faith of the universal "I" of the whole Church, where they will be purified. And this, the true universality, could perhaps become again quite a concrete standard in today's confusion: what counts is not the separate opinion of this or that group, of this or that place, of this or that time; what is universal and has always belonged to the whole is the standard of authenticity. In a certain respect, one can even say that the reason why the Bible is the central standard is because it is the sole universal book of universal Christianity as a whole, just as the most central creed—the Resurrection of the Lord, the rescue of the truly Just Man from the pit of death —is at the same time the most universal. Stepping out into the whole, taking one's standard from the whole, is therefore the specific content of the decision to take one's standard from the *Ecclesia*. Taking one's standard from the whole *Ecclesia* in this way then always means also, at the same time and necessarily, being critical of today's *Ecclesia* whenever she latches onto what is merely of today: from the head to the members. . . . Accepting the *Ecclesia* as a diachronic entity means, finally, not just entering into the past history of the faith (which nevertheless was and is the proof of the true prophet); it means also to follow the drive for *omnes* and to accept the future of the Church as well by way of anticipation. From that vantage point, one could say: to be orthodox (or "right-believing") means to place one's faith in the faith of the whole Church and, thus, at the same time to keep it open to the coming path of the Church. Making what is diachronic synchronic, making what is perpetual and perpetually growing contemporary and, thus, at the same time opening the Now up critically to the Eternal, to the Truth—that would then be the real meaning of the ecclesial character of preaching. The true ecclesial character of preaching, which is really measured by what the Church authentically is, is far from being a mere determination of what is generally accepted today. It is the most decided protest against absolutizing the present moment. It demands of the preacher and of the listener a readiness to go beyond themselves. It advances into the crisis of today, the real sign of which is the crucified Just Man—the Just Man and the Cross, the Just Man and banishment into contradiction, into suffering, belong together. And yet the final perspective of preaching is optimistic, affirming: the crucified Just Man is at the same time the risen Just Man. Behind the condemnation by the world stands God's Yes. This Yes of God (which of course cannot be separated from the Cross, from the real experience of this world) is the central and universal content of preaching. This Yes is what prompts us, in the middle of the shadow of the Cross, to give thanks and to be glad.

2. Standards for Preaching the Gospel Today

What actually should be preached? What matters? What does not matter? This question, which not long ago Catholics could answer with apparently self-evident clarity, has become today a real predicament for the preacher. Of course, the old standards are still very much in existence, and so at first clear answers can be given with relative ease. But these standards, for their part, have lost their univocal character, and that is where the problem starts. I would like to proceed as follows: I will first list in four theses the permanent points of reference for all preaching, then outline the problems that have arisen for us in relation to these individual statements, and then try to indicate which path proves to be feasible today. Let us therefore list the standards for preaching that have been set by the faith.

1. The standard for all preaching is first and foremost Sacred Scripture: the interrelated unity of Old and New Testament.[1]

2. A second standard for preaching is provided by the Creeds, in which the universal Church has expressed her faith in a binding way; then come the dogmatic statements that supplement the Creeds, ranked according to the hierarchy of truths.[2]

Translated by Michael J. Miller.

[1] The fact that, essentially, Scripture exists only in this analogical unity is the fundamental state of affairs that is not infrequently overlooked in stating the scriptural principle. A fundamental study in this regard (for all its intellectual independence) is E. Przywara, *Alter und Neuer Bund* (Vienna, 1956), esp. 521–43; cf. also H. U. von Balthasar, *Spouse of the Word*, trans. A. V. Littledale with Alexander Dru, *Explorations in Theology*, vol. 2 (San Francisco: Ignatius Press, 1991), 289–98; von Balthasar, *The Glory of the Lord*, vol. 1, trans. Erasmo Leiva-Merikakis, 2nd ed. (San Francisco: Ignatius Press, 2009), 424–50; H. de Lubac, *History and Spirit: The Understanding of Scripture according to Origen*, trans. Anne Englund Nash (San Francisco: Ignatius Press, 2007).

[2] On the topic of the Creed, see my *Introduction to Christianity*, trans. J. R. Foster, rev. ed. (San Francisco: Ignatius Press, 2004), esp. 82–100; on the "hierarchy of truths", see H. Mühlen, "Die Lehre des Vaticanum II über die hierarchia veritatum und ihre Bedeutung für den ökumenischen Dialog", *Theologie und Glaube* 55 (1965): 329–66; U. Valeske, *Hierarchia veritatum* (Munich, 1968).

3. A third standard for preaching is the living Magisterium of the living Church.

4. A fourth standard for preaching is the concrete faith of the Church in her communities: this faith has the promise of *indefectibilitas*, abiding in the truth.

Every one of these four norms seems to be clear and seems to suffice; the fact that there are four of them points out a problem and raises the question of the relationship of the individual factors to one another. In fact, the mutual overlapping of the normative forces is based on the fact that each one taken alone would be insufficient: one calls for the other, and only all of them together fulfill their mission; on the other hand, it is likely that nowadays this very interrelationship is also the problem. Let us look more closely at this interrelationship.

1. The Scale of the Problems

a. Scripture as Norm

The norm for preaching is in the first place Scripture—patristic theology stated this quite emphatically in opposition to Gnosticism; Luther gave new force to this statement and spoke categorically about the *perspicuitas*, the transparent clarity of Sacred Scripture, which in his opinion is its own interpreter and has need of no other interpreter.[3] The biblical movement in our [twentieth] century was supported by a renewal of this awareness, and the sure progress of historical science seemed to put the thesis of the unequivocal nature of Scripture on solid ground once and for all. Today, disconcertingly, we have reached the other end, so to speak, of this state of affairs: the hermeneutical problem absorbs all of Scripture, and in the debate among historians and interpreters there is nothing left of its self-illuminating clarity.[4] The variety and many contrasts in a literature that developed over the course of centuries forces upon us the question of a canon within the canon—a question that can no longer be dealt with according to Luther's concise standard:

[3] The most important passages are compiled in H. Beintker, *Die evangelische Lehre von der hlg. Schrift und von der Tradition* (Lüneberg, 1961), 125–39.

[4] Cf., for example, the critique of J. Jeremias' position in E. Käsemann, *Exegetische Versuche und Besinnungen*, vol. 2 (Göttingen, 1964), 36f.; on this subject, see also my commentary on the Vatican II Constitution on Divine Revelation in *Das Zweite Vatikanische Konzil* (= *Lexikon für Theologie und Kirche*, supplementary volume 2 [Freiburg, 1967], 523ff.).

the inner canon is defined in terms of "what is impelled by Christ": Luther himself, in applying that standard, had identified Christology to a great extent with his understanding of the doctrine of justification and thus demonstrated precisely the ambiguity of his own criterion. If we were to continue listing the obfuscations, we could point out the differences between sources and redaction, between one exegesis and another; above all, overshadowing everything else, stands the question of the unity of then and now, within which lies the whole problem of world view and genuine preaching and so once again the problem of the standard. This problem is increasingly becoming the back door both for apologetic excuses and for venturesome modernizations, which all straighten out the discrepancy between presentation and message according to their own preferences, without feeling obliged to reflect on the standards for these distinctions.

Anyone who sees all this could give up hope of ever being able to receive any sort of direction from Scripture. I personally, nevertheless, am convinced, despite this primeval forest of problems, that there really is an unequivocal character to Scripture, its *Gestalt*, or significant form, as a self-illuminating, comprehensive statement: anyone who calmly and patiently reads the Bible as a whole may very well leave many questions about the details open, yet he soon learns to distinguish between where the path is leading and where it is not. But this unequivocal character is not a fact to be grasped by historical or abstract hermeneutical methods. In order to be perceived, it presupposes contemplation of the *Gestalt* as a whole and, thus, a way of looking in terms of the whole: within the living context of faith and Church . . .

b. Creed and Dogma

But with that we have already decisively gone beyond any *mere* Scripturism, which in this matter has failed as plainly as can be. The "self-evidence" of Scripture without presuppositions, in light of allegedly historical findings alone, is a mirage. There is no such thing. And this is just the reason why from the very beginning the Church's faith, in that same fundamental decision by which it found Scripture to be Scripture and decided in favor of it, has also identified the pivotal elements of this Scripture in the formula of the Symbol [or Creed] and thus pointed out the path of interpretation that leads to clarity.

Two things should be noted, therefore: the Creeds, as the fundamental form and the lasting crystallization point of what would later be called dogma, are not an addition to Scripture but, rather, the common thread leading through them; namely, the canon made within the canon; Ariadne's thread, so to speak, which allows Theseus to walk through the labyrinth and makes its plan recognizable. Consequently, neither are they an external clarification added to what is unclear; rather, they are precisely a reference to the self-illuminating *Gestalt*, the highlighting of the significant form that allows the reader to see the clarity of what is authentically scriptural.

Now the Symbol, too, was created at a particular point in place and time of human life and understanding and, hence, is always itself in need of fresh elaboration and supplementation, so as to maintain its function of clarification, but through this process it gradually becomes a tangled construct itself: it has been built in many historical stages, which in turn raise the question of order, unity, and relation to the whole. As a result, an oversimplified and isolated reference to dogma today initially grasps at thin air. For the once clear standard of the Creed (including the later formation of dogma) is—to put it more precisely —rendered uncertain today in two directions:

1. The relation between Symbol and Scripture has become problematic. The question is posed whether the Symbol really singles out the central elements of the Bible itself or is instead itself the canonization of a misunderstanding.[5] With such questions, of course, one separates oneself from the historical reality of Christianity and replaces it with a new creation out of the test tube of historical reason. So the more lenient critics admit that those interpretations may be quite meaningful for their respective times, but every age must have its own and cannot be bound by previous interpretations. Of course, then there is no telling where one could still draw the line between the spirit of the age and what is essential to the faith and makes it worth consideration in the first place.

2. A second problem seems to me more difficult in many respects. For anyone who dissolves the relation between Symbol and Scripture

---

[5] Theories about the "Hellenization" of Christianity see it this way, to varying degrees. For an objective study of the development of the Creed within the context of the formation of the Bible, see H. Schlier, "Die Anfänge des christologischen Credo", in *Zur Frühgeschichte der Christologie*, ed. B. Welte (Freiburg, 1970), 13–58.

actually ends up empty-handed. Once we have presupposed, however, the fundamental connections between Scripture, Creed, and dogma that have just been described, we soon find that the interpretation of Creed and of dogma itself has come into question as well. The problem of historicism and the problem of hermeneutics arise exactly as they did in relation to Scripture. "Dogma", too, has long been considered a historical process fraught with tension, in which further investigation of then and now, exegesis, redaction and source, and the form of the hierarchy of truths ("the canon within the canon") is required almost as urgently as in the case of the Bible.

c. The Magisterium

Awareness of this problem increased as the development of dogma advanced and the distance from the beginnings became noticeable along with the tension within the edifice itself. It was felt most acutely with the appearance of historicism. Hence, to the extent that the problem is posed, a third factor emerges, which admittedly has always been included in principle and objectively in the idea of the Creed. "Transparency" is ultimately derived, not from a text, but rather from something that is alive, from the living voice (*viva vox*) of the Church, which is the ever-living subject [that is, custodian] of Scripture and of the faith that is preserved therein. It seems to me no accident that as the age of historicism began, the First Vatican Council attempted to accomplish the same thing, as it were, for this new epoch that the formulation of the Creeds had been for the Church in antiquity: it created the authority in which the "I" of the Church is sure to be represented and can consequently settle concretely, according to the form, the endless quarrel among the texts. From then until the Second Vatican Council, this one factor in tradition increasingly became more prominent than all the others: the [Church's] teaching authority, which provides answers and thus makes the faith unambiguously present in its time. This formal principle seems to me to be almost more important than the individual declarations of the popes, since it is their strongest collective declaration: that the faith can be found here concretely and unambiguously at all times.

This principle, which is apparently quite univocal, gave the Church during the last hundred years an unprecedented clarity, security, uniformity, and singleness of purpose; yet we all know that this principle has been called into question and thus rendered largely ineffective: the history of the Magisterial statements of the past hundred years (but not just that) indicates all too clearly the limits of Magisterial competency. The errors in the decisions of the Biblical Commission, and also in many positions taken by the popes (for instance, in questions concerning the papal states, freedom of conscience, the importance of the historical-critical method), are in plain view of everyone today (though often in a very exaggerated and undifferentiated form); Vatican II was in many respects the collapse of a theology that was one-sidedly built in conformity with the latest encyclicals. And so today, in an unexpected yet understandable change of sentiments, an unvarnished skepticism about all Magisterial statements has broken out, which deprives the voice of the Magisterium of any effectiveness or perverts it into precisely the opposite. Many people seem hardly capable nowadays of reading statements that come from Rome with a halfway open mind; the mere fact that they originate from the Magisterium is held against them, and in this climate they certainly are not able to create uncontested clarity.

d. The Faith of the People of God

What is to be done? The obfuscation of Scripture and of dogma and the cutting off of the Magisterium have led to the rediscovery of the faith of the Christian communities as an authority. In a very contrary sense, admittedly. On the one hand, citing the victory of community faith over theological intellectualism and ecclesiastical diplomacy at Nicaea, one can see in the faith of the community the principle of continuity, consistency, and preservation, a faith that is ultimately immune to all intellectual games, which burn up like fireworks, leaving nothing behind. But a much more prevalent trend looks at the faith of the community in a completely different way: since it is no longer possible to establish and grasp anything common and objective, they say, faith in each case must be what the community in question thinks, what its members discover in dialogue to be their common conviction. "Community" replaces Church, and its religious experience is consulted instead of the Church's tradition. Such an attitude abandons, not only faith in the strict sense, but also and logically real preaching as well as the Church herself; the remaining "dialogue" is not proclamation at all but, rather, a form of talking to oneself amidst the echoes of old traditions.[6]

2. The Ladder in Reverse

Have we now landed in a void, or, if not, how should we proceed? In any case, it does little good merely to note the destruction of tradition and thus to consider the erroneous trains of thought that we encountered to be overcome. The fact that they can spread so far and wide signals a problem that demands an answer. Indeed, after all that we have been considering, one really cannot deny that there is a unique consistency in the ideas that have just been presented and that a path to the origins can be opened up again only if the underlying connection is illuminated as a whole. So we must try now to reverse the procedure and roll up the thread. Until now we have allowed ourselves to be led from authority to authority and at the same time from question to question, even though we saw several warning signals flashing to indicate that when issues become problematic, it is not always necessarily due to keen understanding but can also be the expression of intellectual laziness and weak generalizations and, therefore, that we must inspect these paths again before we can declare outright that they are impassable. This is precisely what we will try to do now in a second stage, starting from the other direction at the point where we stopped: at the faith of the communities, so as to explore the structure once more, this time from the bottom up.

a. The Faith of the People of God

It seems to me that a better answer can be found than the quite desperate theology of community we have just met when we reflect more

---

[6] This trend is represented by P. Siller, "Das Predigtgespräch", in *Die Fremdsprache der Predigt*, ed. G. Biemer (1970), 89–104, esp. 96ff. Siller does admit that in many liturgies "preaching" must occur, but in others, he says, it is anachronistic: "These people no longer want to play naïve" (99). He rejects discussion "when that is understood to mean stubborn and intolerant insistence on one position". Indeed, the dialogue should "not do violence to either party or silence them". The result is then: "Discussion as the community's search for a common truth and joint decisions should not be rejected, provided that opinions are expressed, listened to, accepted, and tolerated" (102). Nothing remains here of the "two-edged sword of God's word".

carefully and accurately on the reality around which everything here revolves—"community"—than is typically done in such theories; of course we must then also be ready to take into account the complicated nature of the reality, which cannot be captured in ready-made formulas. A community is a community of the Church, an entity with significance beyond that of a private club, only if it is not autonomous or self-enclosed. Its ecclesiality is based precisely on its standing within the whole.[7] Accordingly, however, it is community to the extent to which it divests itself and is free of self-will and united with the whole. It becomes community through its entrance into the faith of the universal Church, the latter being understood synchronically and diachronically. It is church within the Church by the fact that it places itself within the faith of the universal Church. But now this is the reason why the *sensus fidei*, or the "faith of the people", in fact has authoritative character in the Church: insofar as this faith, through the vicissitudes of intellectual speculation and in the clash of individual opinions, is a supporter of consistency and locus of commonality, in the power of the Holy Spirit, who by all means employs in such matters the natural prerequisites of human behavior. In my estimation this is important for preaching in two senses.

1. First we should mention a rather psychological fact, which of course also has its own theological depth. The simple faith of simple people deserves the respect, the reverence of the preacher, who has no right simply to play off his intellectual superiority against their still simple faith, which in some circumstances grasps the heart of the matter more surely as a simple overall intuition than does a reflection that is divided up into many separate steps and particular findings. Still fundamental here, in my opinion, is the insight that the transition from the Old to the New Testament took place in the faith of simple people: the *anawim* ("poor") were the ones who shared neither in the liberal views of the Sadducees nor in the letter-of-the-law orthodoxy of the Pharisees. In their simple basic intuition of the faith, they lived in terms of the core promise and teaching and thereby became the place in which Old Testament could be transformed into New Testament: Zechariah,

---

[7] Cf. J. Ratzinger and H. Maier, *Demokratie in der Kirche* (Limburg, 1970), 40ff.; J. Ratzinger, *Das neue Volk Gottes*, 2nd ed. (Düsseldorf, 1970), 122ff.

Elizabeth, Mary, Joseph, Jesus himself. . . .[8] The "faith of the poor" remains the central treasure of the Church; about it Jesus spoke the weighty words: "Whoever causes one of these little ones who believe in me to stumble [that is, destroys his faith through intellectual operations], it would be better for him if a great millstone were hung round his neck and he were thrown into the sea" (Mk 9:42). This verse is not (as the parallel passage in Matthew might suggest) speaking about children, declaring that no offense should be given to their innocence; and sexual scandal is certainly not the immediate theme of this saying. The "little ones who believe" are, rather, the simple people, who believe as simple persons and in their simplicity: the verse is talking about the faith of the little people, the ordinary folks, the poor. . . . I think this passage, which already in the Gospel tradition is addressed to the preacher, constitutes a warning of almost frightening seriousness. No preacher who acknowledges his responsibility before the Gospel can take it lightly. All too many today proceed rashly with their paltry intellectual discoveries; they would do well to let it frighten them.

2. The common faith of the communities that support the Church is, in its fundamental sense, a real authority, because in it the authentic acting subject "Church" has its say. It is a road sign that is binding also for the preacher, who does not stand above the Church, the *familia christianorum* [family of Christians], but rather in her. Here, I think, the theology of the laity is quite urgent—although admittedly, for all the accolades bestowed upon the layman, it is blatantly ignored at precisely this juncture. Today more than ever before, the preacher tends to place himself outside and above the believing Church—hardly ever in the name of his ordination, but all the more in the name of his learning—and to tell her how unenlightened she is and how different everything is in reality.[9] But precisely therein he is mistaken about his function. He stands, we repeat, *in* the Church, not over her, and hence he preaches *within* the common faith, which is binding on him as well and is the place that makes it possible for him to preach at all.

One thing should be noted in this connection: due to its whole na-

---

[8] Cf. J. Ratzinger, *Die letzte Sitzungsperiode des Konzils* (Cologne, 1966), 76f.; H. U. von Balthasar, "The Faith of the Simple Ones", in *Creator Spirit*, trans. Brian McNeil, C.R.V., *Explorations in Theology*, vol. 3 (San Francisco: Ignatius Press, 1993), 57–83.

[9] Cf. the references in J. Ratzinger and H. Maier, *Demokratie in der Kirche*, 45f.

ture and its function, the community's faith is not a productive but rather a conservative factor. When it becomes productive, it should be treated with suspicion, because then it is following the laws of folk imagination, as history clearly shows.[10] Its authoritative character resides in what it firmly holds in common, not in what it produces. This suggests the critical function of the preacher, to which we will have to return later. For now we can say: the simple faith of the living Church is an authority for preaching, insofar as and because it embodies the faith of the universal Church and gives a hearing to the authentic acting subject of the Creed: the one, whole Church of all ages.

b. The Magisterium

From this vantage point, it is possible now to return step by step to the other authorities that provide norms for faith and preaching, the ones that we encountered first. The Magisterium, as representative of the universal Church, can claim the respect, indeed, the obedience of the preacher. It is the normal source of direction: the "presumption of correctness", so to speak, is in favor of the Magisterium. That does not mean that the Christian conscience has been disengaged; in a specific case, it can very well come to the judgment that this directive or that declaration does not really represent the universal Church. Accordingly, it is true that the weight of Magisterial statements corresponds to the degree of the universality. Disagreement can more likely be appropriate, the more particular the directive in question is—particular, again, in the spatial and temporal sense, synchronically and diachronically. That states the limit of obedience to the Magisterium, which does in fact exist. But that does not mean that someone can in principle appoint himself judge over the Magisterium: it should cost something before one thinks he may decide otherwise. Skepticism about one's own reason and about ideas that are all too up to date is unfortunately quite underdeveloped in our profession; it should be our first response, and

---

[10] Cf., for example, the excessive proliferation of devotion to the Holy Souls, the exaggerations in the cult of the saints, and so on. It should be noted, nevertheless, that the mariological exaggerations analyzed by R. Laurentin, *La Question mariale* (Paris, 1963), 66–128, are chalked up almost exclusively to theologians. For an in-depth study of the problem of the sense of the faith, see W. Beinert, "Bedeutung und Begründung des Glaubenssinnes (*sensus fidei*) al seines dogmatischen Erkenntniskriteriums", *Catholica* 25 (1971): 271–303.

only when we have thoroughly and without prejudice investigated a matter in all directions can we meaningfully and responsibly set about criticizing the voice of those who are commissioned to preserve tradition.

The reference to the diachronic element that is necessarily inherent in ecclesial universality brings into focus yet another element that until now has probably received too little attention: anyone who speaks about diachronic universality should reflect that this includes not only the past but also the future, in its own way. To believe diachronically with the whole Church must also mean to accept the Church's faith as one that is open to and until the Second Coming of the Lord and that only then will arrive at its completeness. Let us look at an example so as to clarify what is meant by this. When the question of the meaning of the first chapters of Genesis is posed on the terms of historicism, on the one hand, and of modern science, on the other, then this is a new question, for which no universal answer yet exists. There are signposts: on the one hand, the fact of the Pneumatic (christological) interpretation of the Old Testament, which limits in advance its bare literalness; on the other hand, the conviction that the letter is really ordered to the Pneuma [Spirit], which stands in the way of a complete devaluation of the texts. But now what does that mean, when we have gained insights about the letter [that is, the literal interpretation] from two sharply contrasting sides that previously could not exist? How, under these conditions, does one remain faithful to the sense of the universal Creed? We must grope our way once more and go through it again. In this respect, there is also, no doubt, the danger of a false conservatism that wrongly makes an absolute out of the synchronic element. One is orthodox, then, when one enters into the faith of the universal Church and includes in this faith also the fact that the Church has a future in which the comprehensive form of her message can one day be revealed definitively. This means, in fact, that the ability of the faith and its boundaries to be fixed decreases, that a certain dynamic plasticity remains, and that for this very reason, of course, the faith becomes simpler in its core and approximates the "faith of the simple". In other words: only what is simple ultimately belongs to the core. . . .

c. Creed and Dogma

Let us continue in our retrograde reconsideration of the individual normative authorities of preaching: starting with the standard of universality, we have reflected on the authorities "faith of the community" and "Magisterium" and said that they are valid *because* they are representatives of the universal Church and *in the measure* in which they are such. That is valid now also for the normative sphere of Symbol and dogma: the Creed is a norm, because in it the universal Church declares herself in faith and prayer. And the "hierarchy of truths", too, can be defined in terms of the standard of universality. Of course we must still guard against one danger, or misunderstanding. It could appear that with this reference to universality everything was ultimately being shifted to a quantitative standard. One might be tempted to react to this with a radically christological norm for faith and preaching: the decisive thing is not the breadth of ecclesial tradition but, rather, the summit: He, he alone.

This contrast would be accurate if one were to regard Church and universality as purely statistical phenomena. But if it is true that Church is more than that, namely, the space in which *He* himself prevails, then she is present wherever she is really herself, that is, wherever she points to Him. Then the perspective from above, in terms of the christological standard, and the one from below, to which we were driven by the contemporary problem set, are only complementary aspects of one and the same reality. Their complementariness, of course, is indispensable: a merely ecclesial perspective that attempted to construe everything in terms of universality alone and gave no more thought to representing Christ in the Church and in her ministries would necessarily turn into a dogmatization of statistics; a merely christological perspective that dispensed with the concrete standard of what is ecclesial and universal easily becomes the dogmatization of a special theological opinion. The two belong together and point to each other.

In pointing out that the christological standard and the ecclesiological standard go together, we by no means need to be content with abstract assertions. This can easily be demonstrated with concrete examples. The most universal statements are at the same time the foundational statements of the faith: Jesus is risen; Jesus is the Christ, the Lord, the

Son of God. Around these fundamental statements the other contents
are gradually positioned.[11] This is how matters stand; the fact that the
greatest universality, the sharpest clarity of the speaking and praying
subject "Church" is found in the center is no accident, because, after
all, the Church is herself only on Christ's terms; she is most herself
where she is with him and where she originally comes from him. In
this respect, universality is identical with the stages of the christological
center and is the concrete signpost pointing to it.[12]

d. Scripture

Having reached this juncture, we can finally return to the point of departure of all our reflections and say: the Bible has such an absolutely
unique normative importance because it alone is really the sole book
of the Church as Church. But the Bible is this, not through some statistical accident, but rather because the Pneuma builds up the Church
and in so doing builds up her central and universal self-expression,
in which she does not express just herself but Him from whom she
comes. That clarifies again why one cannot *ultimately* understand the
Bible as opposed to the Church, however many details one may be
able to recognize without her.

   Once again here, at any rate, we must also oppose any fideistic oversimplification; precisely at this point, truly, the function of critical reflection, of the critical intellect in the Church and for the Church,
becomes evident. Faith must be made present. The fact that it exists
diachronically means that its reality must be thought and lived anew
into the present. Thus there are necessarily two functions in the Church
that supplement each other: the function of adhering to the one faith
and the function of opening it up, of making it present. On both sides
(the ecclesial teaching authority and the scholarly teaching authority)
there will be again and again hasty conclusions and failed experiments;
both offices can be tolerated and are salutary to the Church of God if

---

[11] On the development of the profession of faith in Christ, see Schlier, "Anfänge des
christologischen Credo".

[12] The fixation of christocentric theology on the doctrine of justification—a process that
is clearly evident in Luther's writings—shows how quickly the standard of christocentric
theology can be narrowed down otherwise.

they stay focused on the center of the Creed, which can exist only in a communal way and which wants to divest us so as to draw us into the Lord, who alone can truly give us ourselves as our very own.

Let us attempt to summarize our main conclusions. We can say: the real faith of the communities that abide in the faith and prayer of the Church of all ages is a signpost pointing to what matters. The standard of preaching lies in what the universal Church, the Church of all ages, testifies to communally. The judge of this testimony is the Magisterium, which can demand unconditional respect when it expressly speaks in the name of the whole Church and of her Lord. Scripture and dogma are to be read in the living faith of the universal Church and receive from her their univocal character, just as, conversely, the Church takes her direction from them. To contemplate the whole and thus to look to the Lord—that is the first direction to which the preacher must entrust himself, which then can lead him further, step by step, as he himself accompanies and prays with others.

3. Christocentrism in Preaching?

Preaching is always more than just a problem to be solved by theology. Theology is one of the components out of which it is constructed, indeed, a very important one, yet not the only one. In this respect there is something inherently inadequate and unsatisfactory about all theological discourse concerning the method and form of preaching: when genuine preaching occurs, in every instance it is ultimately a gift that cannot be forced by any theory but, rather, is either given or denied. For such preaching means that a bit of Pentecost comes to pass, in that people understand one another, find that they are being addressed in the word of another, and, indeed, hear God's Word in the word of a man. In this respect, the chances of theology attaining the status of preaching are always limited. But if it sees this limit, it still has an important task to carry out, by dealing with the question of the structure and content of what is doctrinal in preaching. I will try to make a few observations on this subject in the following pages, which for their part are intended only as an extremely incomplete attempt to trace a few lines of dogmatic thought in such a way as to make findings of more recent theological scholarship fruitful for the problem of preaching.

1. *The Fundamental Importance of Christocentrism*

The kerygmatic question about Christocentrism in preaching is logically dependent on the prior dogmatic problem of whether and in what sense it is correct at all to speak about Christocentrism. Indeed, one can raise the important objection that Jesus' own preaching was not "christocentric" but, rather, revolved entirely around the announcement that

Translated by Michael J. Miller.

the "reign and kingdom of God" was near.[1] The difficult problem that this poses is, as we have said, logically prior to the kerygmatic inquiry and, therefore, cannot be discussed in detail in this context. It must suffice here to mention immediately the solution that received its classic expression from Origen when he called Christ the αὐτοβασιλεία: the Lord himself is the coming of God's kingdom already begun in our midst.[2] This, however, is of decisive importance both for our understanding of the "kingdom" as well as for our comprehension of the biblical message about Christ. For if this is so, then, on the one hand, it is true that the reign of God in Jesus' message is no vague general concept but, rather, has in him its specific start and points to him as its genuine beginning; it is also true, conversely, that Christ is central for early apostolic preaching only because and in the sense that he signifies the irruption of God's reign into this world. In other words: in apostolic preaching Christ stands in the middle of the proclamation because he is the presence of divine action toward mankind.

We can deepen this insight and at the same time suggest its practical significance if we reformulate our starting question in yet another way: Is Christocentrism something that can actually be accomplished? It will always fail, ultimately, when it degenerates into the attempt to make a person from the past into a thrilling ideal for the present by dressing him up in contemporary garb. The Jesuanism of the youth movement, which attributed to the Lord the traits of a Germanic hero and depicted him as the most masculine of all men and celebrated his toughness and militancy, leaves nothing but a bad taste in the mouth today, even though it is understandable as a reaction to the feminized Jesus of the Nazarenes [a school of early nineteenth-century German painters], in which the ideal of infinite goodness found an expression

---

[1] Cf. R. Schnackenburg, *Gottes Herrschaft und Reich* (Freiburg, 1959), esp. 49ff. and 181ff.; Schnackenburg, *Die sittliche Botschaft des Neuen Testamentes* (Munich, 1954), 3ff.; on the theological problem that is broached by these works, see I. Backes, "Ist das 'Reich Gottes' oder Jesus Christus die Zentralidee unserer Verkündigung?" *TThZ* 62 (1953): 193–202. A groundbreaking work for the kerygmatic inquiry was J. A. Jungmann, *Die Frohbotschaft und unsere Glaubensverkündigung* (Regensburg, 1936); Jungmann continued to develop his thinking on this subject in his book *Glaubensverkündigung im Licht der Frohbotschaft* (Innsbruck, 1963).

[2] Origen, *in Mt tom XIV* 7 (commenting on Mt 18:23); cf. the comments by K. L. Schmidt in *ThWNT* I, 590f.; F. Mußner, "Die Bedeutung von Mk 1,14f. für die Reichsgottesverkündigung Jesu", *TThZ* 66 (1957): 257–75, esp. 272f.

that is repellent today. But is it any better for theology today to try to attract young people by making Jesus "relevant"? When we hear about a Jesus who seems to have spent his whole life at banquets with tax collectors and prostitutes, a Jesus who understood everything and (unlike the Church) judged nothing, can we take a Jesus like that seriously? Is he really so different from the Jesus of the Romantic Nazarenes from whom we have just turned away? And when we come to know Jesus as a revolutionary, as an outsider who stood up to society for the oppressed and was hanged by the powerful, is that enough to live on? Especially since there is still some doubt as to whether he really intended revolution. Especially since a political program that could be used today is not discernible. Especially since he, if he had one, was plainly much less successful than other Jewish freedom fighters before and after him. If you are merely looking for an ideal man—to suit one concept of the ideal or another—then is it not safer to look around in the present rather than in the twilight of a history that is long past? Do not Gandhi, Martin Luther King, Korczak, or Maximilian Kolbe offer more concrete examples for some, and Ho Chi-Minh and Che Guevara for others?

Allegiance to a merely historical Jesus is hopeless escapism, a poor copy of a kind of Christocentrism that misses its own mark. What makes Christ important is God, his Divine Sonship. If God really became man in him, then by all means he remains decisive for all times. Then and only then is he irreplaceable. And then, of course, his humanity becomes important, too. For then the fact that he is man shows who God is; then this man is a way. The Christ, the Son of God, makes Jesus the man precious and unique. To take him away is not to discover the man Jesus but, rather, to erase the latter as well for the sake of homemade ideals. Consequently, Christocentrism makes sense only if it acknowledges the Christ in Jesus, if it is theocentric. At the same time, this means that Chalcedon, the definitive ecclesial formulation of Jesus' Divine Sonship, is still, for preaching and piety as well, the pivotal truth that decides everything. Scholars used to like to contrast the being-Christology of Chalcedon and the event-Christology of the Bible and then to conclude that only the event can be of immediate interest to us, whereas being may still have some validity in the background as insurance. Today, in contrast to an empty Jesuanism, it is apparent that there was an event in the first place, that something happened, only if it is true that Jesus *is* the Son of God. Precisely this Being is the colossal event on which everything depends. To everything else—deeds, thoughts, programs—applies the resigned remark of Qoheleth the Preacher: "There is nothing new under the sun." But if this "Is" has taken place, if God really *became* man, then this is a dramatic break-through that nothing can surpass. In that case, the world and God are not just eternally alongside each other; only then has God *acted*. The fact that Jesus *is* God is God's deed, his act, which is the foundation for the "actuality" of what is preached; as long as it is based on this act, it maintains an objective interest. If preaching abandons this, it becomes irrelevant, even if it is decked out in a way that is subjectively interesting.

Hence we can formulate even more concretely the question of how Christocentrism should look in preaching. There is no such thing as a living relationship to a dead person. A dead man Jesus, who lived on only through the continuation of his cause, would be a dead person, and hence a relationship to him would be dead also. But if Jesus has risen, and if I can address God the Father in him, the Son, then a relationship to him can develop in prayer. In this respect, the question of Christocentrism is closely connected with the question of the possibility and importance of prayer. It has its intrinsic prerequisite in prayer.[3] At the same time, however, the Christ-question also clarifies the prayer-question. In meditative converse with the figure of Christ, it becomes clear who God is and what he is like. By getting to know Jesus, we become acquainted with God. His divinity makes it possible to address him in prayer as the all-seeing, all-hearing Lord. His human-ity makes it possible to speak to God, because it makes him a Thou who is tangible and comprehensible for us.

And a further consideration: God and man, each on his own terms, are separated from each other by an infinite distance. It seems impos-sible to bridge the gulf that divides eternity from time. Theological speculation to date has not been able to explain how the Eternal One, without renouncing eternity, can create and lovingly attend a tempo-ral creation, nor can anyone imagine how man is supposed to move from the limitations of his temporal state to the heart of the eternal. But neither can we press on to discover a merely historical Jesus: no

---

[3] On this subject, see the chapter in this volume entitled "Praying in Our Time".

hermeneutical method can really leap over the two thousand years and establish simultaneity between us and him. But there is another possibility: when the Church says "I believe" in the Creed, she is professing that she is a comprehensive "I" that spans and unifies the ages. There are certain parallels for this in the world of everyday experience as well: the "nation" outlasts the individuals who belong to it and through a common language and history fits them into a context of life that, like it or not, leaves a profound impression on them and even shapes their thoughts and desires. Church is not a nation, but she is a historical space that lives on the basis of very definite fundamental experiences and, in terms of them, keeps its identity down through the millennia.[4] These fundamental experiences are anchored in the sacraments, in which the Lord gives his very self. Thus the identity of the Church is founded on the identity of her Lord, who in the sacraments constantly creates her anew. But this again results in a twofold state of affairs: without Church, Christ recedes into the past; without Christ, the risen Lord, the Son of God, Church becomes a mere organization without inner unity.

For our inquiry this means: the Christian is not alone in his search for God and Christ; rather, he knows that he is supported by the comprehensive "I" of the Church, which makes him a contemporary of Jesus Christ and thereby conveys God into time and him into eternity. Paul depicted these connections in the bold image of the Church as Body of Christ: "Because there is one bread, we who are many are one body" (1 Cor 10:17), he says. "Following Christ", accordingly, demands over and over again the personal risk of searching for him, of walking with him,[5] but at the same time it means ceasing to build a wall around oneself, giving oneself over into the unity of the "whole Christ", the *totus Christus*, as Augustine beautifully puts it. "Having a personal relationship to Christ" means, first of all, emerging from the confinement of the ego. Out of the belief that we have become a new man in Jesus Christ grows the demand that we allow the self-

---

[4] Concerning Church as the communal subject of faith and prayer, compare the volume by the International Theological Commission on *Pluralismus in der Theologie* (Einsiedeln, 1973); see also H. U. von Balthasar, "Who Is the Church?", in *Spouse of the Word*, trans. A. V. Littledale with Alexander Dru, *Explorations in Theology*, vol. 2 (San Francisco: Ignatius Press, 1991), 143–91; H. de Lubac, *Geheimnis aus dem wir leben* (Einsiedeln, 1967), 49–82.

[5] See the chapter on "Following Christ" in this volume.

assertiveness of natural egotism to break up into the common interest of the new man Jesus Christ. That does not happen without a deep, personal relationship to him, without listening to his word, without seeking his way; it happens only by believing along with the Church, with the saints, in whom the true face of the Church becomes recognizable in every age.

Thus, as the result of this initial reflection on the fundamental importance of Christocentrism, we can formulate the following statements: *Christocentrism presupposes the event of God becoming man and is, therefore, at bottom nothing other than Theocentrism. It assumes the presence of the Risen Christ in the Church and, therefore, demands very personal obedience to Christ just as much as it requires unity with the faith, prayer, and liturgy of the Church.*

2. Christocentrism and Theocentrism

If God is to be preached in terms of Christ and Christ in terms of God, then this means that God must be preached in a trinitarian manner—for without the Spirit, who unites the historical Jesus with the historical Church and who is the unity of the Son with the Father, one cannot speak about Christ and God, either. Here we hesitate. Does the doctrine of the Trinity not demand too much of our listeners? As theological speculation, most certainly. In that form it does not belong in the pulpit. But as the historical reality in which God shows himself to us, it must be a theme of preaching. We will have to discuss this in more detail in the next section,[6] and so now a suggestion will suffice. Let us ask: In what way does the teaching of the Trinity appear in the New Testament? It appears, not in doctrinal form, but rather in the form of facts, from which the truth of the Trinity in God can be inferred. In the Old Covenant, it is simply "God" who acts toward his people; now, though, Christ appears and professes to be the "Son" of him who in the Old Covenant acted toward men. Christ in turn sends the Spirit, who is the inner life of God (1 Cor 2:10f.). In the New Testament, then, on the one hand, the fact remains that God is only one (1 Cor 8:4); at the same time, however, we encounter the further truth that there is a "Son of God", in whom God has become "God-with-us", and finally the fact that there is a "Spirit of God", who

[6] See the chapter on "Preaching God Today" in this volume.

acts toward and works in us, through whom we are drawn into the inner life of God. Reasoning back from this two-part series of facts, we can then conclude that the one God is tri-une and bears within himself the element of three-ness without abolishing his oneness. The New Testament, therefore, does not speak in a speculative way about the Trinity but, rather, speaks about it insofar as it has become the form of our existence, or, conversely, it deals with our existence insofar as it has become trinitarian, in the Spirit through Christ on the way to the Father. This means that the scriptural proclamation of the Trinity begins with the historical person of Jesus Christ and with the historical fact of the outpouring of the Holy Spirit. In other words: the scriptural proclamation of the Trinity is identical with its Christocentrism, with the message about God's action toward the world and mankind. Here, too, there is something analogous to what applies in Christology: the ontological character of the Trinity is central for the reality-content of Christianity, but it is not in opposition to the event; rather, it is revealed precisely in the event of God's action toward us.

When we recognize that Scripture is the foundation for all proclamation (and this will be discussed in even more detail in section 4a), then that implies for our inquiry that proclamation of the Trinity must be proclamation of salvation history. Our proclamation is trinitarian in the proper sense when it has as its object the factual certainty of Christian existence from the Trinity, that is, when it takes as its point of departure the fact that we are in Christ through the Holy Spirit and on the way to the Father through Christ Jesus. It is trinitarian when the structure of its composition agrees with the structure of Christian existence noted by Paul: "For through him we . . . have access in one Spirit to the Father" (Eph 2:18). In contrast, it would *not* be trinitarian if it knew how to say all sorts of speculative things about the Trinity and yet, beyond including the trinitarian life within itself, forgot about including the Christian in the Trinity. Here, too, there is something analogous to what applies in Christology: the ontological character of the Trinity is central for the reality-content of Christianity, but it is not in opposition to the event; rather, it is revealed precisely in the event of God's action toward us. A second thesis, accordingly, could read: *Trinitarian preaching means one and the same thing as christocentric preaching, namely, the exposition of the way of Christian existence through Christ in the Spirit to the Father.*

3. The Specific Starting Point for Christocentrism

The two fundamental deliberations on the importance of Christocentrism and Theocentrism in preaching that we have just carried out both eventually lead to the same reality, which thus proves to be the real starting point for all preaching. For the formula from the Letter to the Ephesians, "through Christ in the Spirit to the Father" (cf. 2:18), which we found to be the basic formula of trinitarian proclamation, does not intend to make a purely doctrinal statement but, rather, expresses the essential legitimacy of Christian divine worship.[7] Our reflections on Christocentrism led to the Pauline verse "Because there is one bread, we who are many are one body" (1 Cor 10:17), which in turn is a very specific indication of the place where the Christian encounters the action of the *Christus praesens*: the divine worship of the Church, which sits at table with the risen Lord.[8]

Consequently, if the specific starting point of all Christocentrism is reached in the Christian liturgy, then this means that preaching that intends to be christocentric must start out from this reality and lead back to it again and again. There is a table of God, at which people of all nations and all states of life sit and eat the one Bread, and this fact is the point where the message about the Body of Christ is a visible reality. It is the point from which the Christian mission sets out, from which Christian ethics is derived, and in which it is symbolically represented; it is the point in which the Christian faith in God's saving work is summarized and realized. Christian preaching is not the proclamation of a system of doctrines that follow from one another but, rather, guidance to a reality that is challenge, gift, and promise all in one. Neither is Christianity a "metaphysical system" to be set forth for people; it is a reality in which they are to be trained.

This means, furthermore, that Christian preaching is never purely doctrinal; rather, it has a *Sitz im Leben,* and this sociological setting,

---

[7] Cf. J. A. Jungmann, *Missarum sollemnia*, 3rd ed., vol. 1 (Freiburg, 1952), 486–92; J. Pascher, *Eucharistia* (Münster and Munich, 1947), 135–61, 243–54; on Ephesians 2:18, see H. Schlier, *Der Brief an die Epheser*, 2nd ed. (Düsseldorf, 1958), 122–40; K. L. Schmidt, *ThWNT* 1:133f.

[8] On liturgy as table fellowship with the risen Lord, see esp. J. Betz, *Die Eucharistie in der Zeit der griechischen Väter*, vol. 1, pt. 1 (Freiburg, 1955), 65–85.

with which it must stay in touch if it is not to die out, is the liturgy. This statement, of course, remains correct only if we keep in mind that the Christian liturgy is founded upon Jesus' real life and death and thus points beyond all that is merely liturgical: here the death of a man, of the God-man, is involved. This cannot be celebrated by rituals alone. Rather, the remembrance of him is the impetus to overcome thoughtlessness and to recognize him in those in whom he suffers. The Christian liturgy is called *agape*, and the discovery of Jesus in the suffering of this world belongs to it as really as the signs of bread and wine.

This approach to liturgical reality is quite clearly evident in the oldest Christian feasts, which are at the same time the crystallization points for preaching. *Easter* appears to most of us all too exclusively as the commemoration of the historical Resurrection of the Lord. That corresponds to an overly retrospective Christology that to a great extent consigns Christ to the past and overlooks his actual presence. Precisely because it recalls the historically real Resurrection of Jesus, Easter was originally at the same time a baptismal celebration and, thus, the realization of the Resurrection victory of Jesus Christ. When baptism is celebrated at the Easter Vigil, in the night when a new people is born to the Lord, when darkness turns to light, the Resurrection victory of Jesus Christ occurs today, here and now, and thus resurrection is proclaimed as something that once happened historically and, thus, became the source and foundation of the reality that takes place presently in our midst. Easter is, moreover, the endpoint of Lent, which for its part is a baptismal season, not because the baptismal candidates receive instruction in religious doctrine during it but, rather, because they are trained in Word and reality and are accustomed to Christianity.[9] Let no one say that this form of Lent is bound up with past historical circumstances! Alongside the catechumens even then stood the penitents, who had fallen back, as it were, to the level of the catechumenate. For are we not all sinners, who year after year have need once more of the catechumenate, of training, of becoming accustomed to what is Christian, and of outgrowing what is merely worldly? Are we not all sinners, who must accustom ourselves anew to the fact of being baptized? After all, no one enters fully into the spirit of being baptized until he has completely died with Christ and has been submerged with

---

[9] See the chapter "Lent" in this volume.

him in death, so as to be one with him and to live with him (Rom 6:1–12). In this process of advancing toward Christ and becoming free of oneself, this season is, of course, remembrance, too: real remembrance of the salvific suffering of the Lord, of his death and Resurrection.[10]

The situation is similar with the two other major feasts of Christianity. *Pentecost*, too, is not simply a commemoration of an event that happened long ago in Jerusalem; rather, it is, as a baptismal feast, the actual presence of the Pentecost event; *Epiphany*, also a baptismal feast, is the actual presence of the "enlightening of the Gentiles" that started in the adoration of the Magi and the baptism of Jesus; it is a present-day fulfillment of the gradual onset of God's glory, of his dominion in the world, as it began with the miracle at Cana (Jn 2:11).[11]

It is a different matter with Christmas. The "Hodie" [this day] at Christmas does not have the same reality content as the one at Easter. Christmas is connected, rather, to a natural event: the renewal of the world at the winter solstice, which appears as the symbolic depiction of the renewal of the world in the coming of Christ. In this respect, Christmas sets up the bridge between the order of creation and the order of salvation, which is very clearly expressed also in the fact that March 25, the day of Christ's conception, was also thought to be the day on which the world was created.[12] It indicates that the worship of the Christian does not create a little private world into which one retreats from hard realities; it indicates, rather, that the inconspicuous thing that began in Bethlehem and continues in the Church's liturgy is at the same time the decisive force in the world, which has no other Lord than the One who became man in Jesus Christ.

The Christmas celebration has of course another aspect, which is evident in the fact that the Marian feast days are subdivisions of Christmas. If Easter alludes to the breaking away from the world that should become a reality in the life of every Christian as a result of Christ's

---

[10] Cf. J. A. Jungmann, *Der Gottesdienst der Kirche* (Innsbruck, 1955), 199–223; A. W. Watts, *Easter: Its Story and Meaning* (London and New York, 1959); B. Fischer and J. Wagner, eds., *Paschatis Sollemnia: Studien zur Osterfeier und Osterfrömmigkeit* (1959). Important material can be found also in H. Rahner, *Griechische Mythen in Christlicher Deutung* (Darmstadt, 1957), 141–71.

[11] H. Frank, article "Epiphanie III (In der Liturgie)", in *LThK*, 2nd ed., 3:941–44.

[12] For summary treatments of Christmas, see Jungmann, *Der Gottesdienst der Kirche*, 228–38; H. Rahner, *Griechische Mythen*, 172–99. On the Annunciation, see E. Gößmann, *Die Verkündigung an Maria* (Munich, 1957), 23–26; A. G. Martimort, *Handbuch der Liturgiewissenschaft* II (Freiburg, 1965), 291ff.

Cross and Resurrection, then Christmas points to God's taking root in the world: he assumed a real human nature and "pitched his tent" among us, and in his saints and his Church he still dwells in the world today. If we can discern in theological thinking two major fundamental approaches—the theology of Incarnation and the theology of the Cross—then Christmas is devoted more to the first, and Easter to the second. We must not forget, however, that the Paschal perspective is the superior one. God's taking root in the world is not accomplished in order to canonize the world and to establish it permanently and definitively; the meaning of God's taking root in the world, rather, is the uprooting of the world for God. Therefore, the Paschal cycle also contains within itself the eschatological element: the prospect of the definitive overcoming of the world by God.[13] The saints of the liturgical year are ordered to both mysteries: they proclaim God's entrance into the world, but they proclaim no less the Paschal mystery of the overcoming of the world in Christ.

We conclude, therefore: the Christian liturgy has just one simple center: table fellowship with the glorified Lord in the Holy Sacrifice and Meal. But through the seasons of the Church year, this liturgy acquires its specific character and color, its place in the reality of the pilgrim way that is human life. If Christian preaching is related to its reality in the act of worship, then it is natural that it should also be based on the prescriptions for the holy year of the Church. This would result in the time before Easter being devoted to the themes of baptism, confirmation, and penance and to the doctrines of redemption and grace that lie behind them. Since Easter together with baptism at the same time means admission to the Eucharist, it is also obvious that Eucharist and Church should be placed in the foreground during the time between Easter and Pentecost and, thus, to point out during this essential time of the Church year the real center, the reality of the *Christus totus*. The interval between Pentecost and Advent remains available then for establishing the relation between the mystery of Christ and the various situations of people in today's world. Therefore, it can serve especially for ethical instruction, which is nevertheless still yoked to

---

[13] On Christianity as *mysterium crucis*, see H. de Lubac, *Catholicism: Christ and the Common Destiny of Man*, trans. Lancelot C. Sheppard and Sr. Elizabeth Englund, O.C.D. (San Francisco: Ignatius Press, 1988), 367ff.; J. Moltmann, *Der gekreuzigte Gott* (Munich, 1972); M.J. Le Guillou, *L'Innocent* (Paris, 1971).

the basic Paschal theme. The end of this period will furnish the occasion to broach the eschatological theme. The Christmas cycle then can be applied to the theme of creation and the doctrine about God, which in Christianity is not proclaimed in an abstract, philosophical way but, rather, is discerned from the figure of the incarnate Christ. One speaks quite differently about God's almighty power when one's concept of it is derived, not from a treatise *De Deo uno*, but rather from the crib! How differently one will speak about his faithfulness when one proclaims it on Epiphany or on the Feast of the Presentation![14]

A fundamental structure like this simultaneously offers such extensive material that one can use it over the course of a good three years and then start again with essentially the same material. It remains flexible and yet goes beyond a merely arbitrary or random selection of material and leads to a more meaningful connection with the given realities of the liturgy. If we attempt to formulate a thesis summarizing the results of this third cycle of reflections, it could read: *Christian preaching is not the presentation of a doctrinal system but, rather, training in Christian reality, the crystallization point of which is the eucharistic celebration.*

4. Word of God and Word of Man

a. Scripture and Dogma

Dogma is scriptural interpretation. Thus there is a necessary mutual relationship and a priority between Scripture and dogma. The interpreter ranks, not higher, but lower than what is interpreted. But that which is interpreted lives only through the interpretation. We cannot discuss that here; we are interested in another perspective—the difference in accent that can be noted between Scripture and dogma in terms of the different function of each. As far as Christology and trinitarian doctrine are concerned, dogma has put its finger on the ontological character of the event: the Bible depicts what happened; dogma indicates

---

[14] On preaching God in terms of the Christmas mystery, see G. Söhngen, "Die Offenbarung Gottes in Seiner Schöpfung und unsere Glaubensverkündigung", in *Die Einheit in der Theologie* (Munich, 1952), 212–34; concerning the ideas set forth here about preaching and the liturgical year, cf. Jungmann, *Die Frohbotschaft und unsere Glaubensverkündigung*, 127–41; L. Bopp, *Liturgie und Kerygma: Die liturgische Predigt nach Idee und Verwirklichung*, vols. 1–4 (Regensburg, 1952–1960).

the relative importance of what happened by uncovering the previously discussed root cause of the event—the fact that God *has* become man, that God himself is Father, Son, and Spirit and does not just appear that way.[15] Hence, one can understand the old Scholastic formula that dogma is the "closest and immediate rule of faith"; this means that the Catholic uses Scripture in the Church as the Church's book and so, also, according to the normative interpretation of the Church. Just as he has to deal, not with a *Christus historicus* from the past, but, rather, with the *Christus totus* who is now present, so too he has to deal, not with self-subsistent Scriptures as a primary source from the remote past, but, rather, with Sacred Scripture in the world of faith. He uses Scripture according to its normative interpretation by dogma. Once this is assumed, however, it follows that dogma per se is not already immediately kerygma, but, rather, the norm for kerygma. In contrast, Scripture understood according to the norm of dogma is itself kerygma, a thoroughly kerygmatic book. That means that there is a very special immediacy between Scripture and kerygma, which is essentially different from the relation of kerygma to dogma. Dogma in many instances is a rather negative norm: it marks off the *limits* of preaching. Scripture as a book of proclamation, in contrast, positively shows the *way* of preaching. One could formulate it somewhat schematically: Dogma is the norm for what is dogmatic about kerygma, while Scripture is the norm for what is kerygmatic about kerygma. The way of preaching is pointed out by Scripture as the normative original form of all proclamation.

b. The Salvation-Historical Structure of Preaching

Accordingly, although dogma and kerygma are in close agreement, albeit not simply identical, a real difference appears between the systematic reflection of dogma in theological scholarship and the concrete presentation of the faith in preaching: the systematic principle of dogmatic theology cannot in the same way be the organizational principle of preaching, also. The two approaches must look to one another, yet each one has its proper laws and, hence, its own method.[16] Dogmatic

---

[15] J. Ratzinger, *Introduction to Christianity*, trans. J. R. Foster, rev. ed. (San Francisco: Ignatius Press, 2004), 116–36, 151–61.

[16] In my opinion, the idea of a theology of preaching was right in this central in-

theology aims to unify the individual thoughts into the context of a logical structure of thought in view of the intellectual situation of the given era; preaching tries to seize upon the logic of human existence and, thus, to orient man toward faith and lead him into it. Because it speaks about reality in the call to faith and addresses itself also to man's understanding, which it wishes to lead to the truth, not to force into irrational decisions, it therefore needs the intellectual work of theology. But because it seeks man in his entirety and wants to help him to live, it does not strive to be intellectually systematic. Its goal, after all, is an event of a very radical sort: for a man to say Yes to the offer of God's love that he encounters in Christ. And it testifies to an event: this very entering of God into man and the new movement that it has created within mankind. Indeed, the fact that there is in mankind a "Body of Christ" unmistakably signifies that the process of the Incarnation, the inclusion of man in God, did not stop with the earthly Jesus but, rather, extends from him to all who bear a human countenance. The fact that a man has been elevated into personal unity with God concerns, not just this one man, but, rather, is an event involving human nature in its entirety, a nature that is only one in all men. This one, uniform human nature of all men has been touched by the Christ-event and set into motion toward God. The humanity of the man Jesus is, so to speak, the divine fishing-rod with which God the Fisherman has reached the humanity of all men. The existence of Jesus Christ and his message have carried a new dynamic into mankind, and the Church is, so to speak, this very dynamic, this ongoing movement of mankind toward God: she is by her very nature "Pascha", Passover, transformation of the

---

sight, the discussion of which should be resumed. Cf., finally, J. A. Jungmann, *Katechetik* (Freiburg, 1953), 299–305; Jungmann, *Glaubensverkündigung im Licht der Frohbotschaft* (Innsbruck, 1963); W. Nastainczyk, *Das alte Credo und die Glaubensunterweisung heute* (Freiburg, 1970); Arnold, Rahner, Schurr, and Weber, *Handbuch der Pastoraltheologie*, vol. 2, pt. 1 (Freiburg, 1966), 133–45 (Rahner); vol. 3 (Freiburg, 1968), 528–34 (Rahner), 535–48 (F. Wulf), and 653–64 (Lehmann). Unfortunately this voluminous handbook seems to be interested primarily in institutions and states of life and also in the pastoral administration of the sacraments, while the preaching of the Word is left in abject poverty; moreover, the few statements on the subject are often very theoretical and rather negative. So, for example, in vol. 2, p. 145, the basic themes treated previously are called into question, and to find out what should be required today as a "unifying and selective principle of preaching", the reader is referred to a later chapter, which, however, does not say a word about it.

body of mankind into the Body of Jesus Christ.[17] She is the concrete form of that event which we call salvation history, which starts with the choice of Abraham and continues until the moment when "God [will] be everything to every one" (1 Cor 15:28), when the process of passing over will be complete. Preaching revolves around this event when it revolves around Christ.

But then that also means that preaching, being christocentric, is also preaching about salvation history.[18] It is part of the ancient wisdom of preachers that stories [*Geschichten*] elicit a degree of attentiveness that is not shown toward mere instruction. Christian preaching does not just tell stories; rather, it proclaims a history [*Geschichte*], namely, the history of God with mankind, the process of *transitus*, of the holy Passover, which began with God's call to Abraham: "Go from your country and your kindred and your father's house to the land that I will show you" (Gen 12:1); the complete form of this history is the Church. Stories in Christian preaching are not just ornamentation for a non-narrative doctrine; rather, the core itself is history. That being said, it is also clear what sort of stories the preacher should primarily relate. The great history book of God, the Old and the New Testament, is his first source, even when he is looking for stories.[19] To this day, the Old Testament offers an unexhausted and inexhaustible wealth of stories that the preacher has to interpret as part of that one history which happens to mankind at God's bidding in Jesus Christ. However, since the entire Church, as we have shown, is a part of this real history, the preacher can also draw again and again from the rich treasury of the

---

[17] On this subject, see J. Ratzinger, *Die Einheit der Nationen: Eine Vision der Kirchenväter* (Salzburg, 1971), esp. 31–37.

[18] Moreover, in keeping with the previous discussion, "salvation history" presupposes Chalcedonian Christology, or, alternatively, the Council of Chalcedon, with its clarification of how God became man, designates the core of salvation history. For me, Chalcedonian Christology is at the same time the central definition of the term "salvation history". See my essay "Die Christologie im Spannungsfeld von altchristlicher Exegese und moderner Bibelauslegung", in *Urbild und Abglanz*, ed. J. Tenzler, Festgabe für H. Doms (Regensburg, 1972), 359–67; also "Heil und Geschichte", *Wort und Wahrheit* 25 (1970): 3–14. O. Cullmann, the most important proponent of salvation history theology at the present time, summarized his understanding of salvation history in his book *Heil als Geschichte* (Tübingen, 1965).

[19] Cf., for example, H. Thielicke, *Das Bilderbuch Gottes: Reden über die Gleichnisse Jesu* (Stuttgart, 1957). Moreover, I am glad that these comments, written in 1960, are to a great extent in accord with the demand made by J. B. Metz for a "narrative theology".

lives of the saints, in which history acquires exemplary form. There has been an impoverishment here in recent years, which we can only reject as a misunderstanding of "christocentric" preaching. Today in many places passages from Nietzsche and Marx are used instead of Scripture readings, which shows how quickly a false purism takes its revenge and how it has turned by now into its own opposite. The uniqueness of the Christ-event does not devalue the life of mankind; rather, it gives to that life a share in the strength of its own presence. The great figures of the faith, from Polycarp to Maximilian Kolbe, really demonstrate what a life of following Christ means; in them we can see the demands made by this life and the hope that it offers. They are all interpretations of Jesus Christ; in them he becomes concrete. Anyone who begins to look at the lives of the saints finds an inexhaustible wealth of stories that are more than homiletic examples: the testing of Christ's call in millennia of blood and tears. Only when we rediscover the saints will we also find the Church again. And therein we will find again that same one who is alive in the midst of all the darkness, who dies no more, who does not leave us orphans. Thus we have arrived at another thesis: *Christocentric preaching is preaching about salvation history against the background of God's actions on behalf of his saints, from Abraham down to the present day.*

5. A Concluding Remark: Truth and Truthfulness

In this chapter, which has been about Christocentrism in preaching, it is not necessary to go into detail about the various types of preaching, which include various accents and emphases in the structure of preaching: the method of missionary preaching is different from that of preaching within a liturgy, although, given the objective crisis of faith in our world today, no homily can be completely devoid of a missionary element.[20] It seems more important to me to note something else at the conclusion. Subjective truthfulness should accompany objective truth so that the latter may be effective. Now I do not agree with those who advocate a sort of Donatism of the word and act as though only a man completely filled with personal sanctity can ever preach effectively, indeed, almost as though a man may preach only what he himself

---

[20] Cf. what was said above in the chapter on "Church as the Place of Preaching".

lives. Certainly, personal holiness remains the obligatory goal of every preacher, as it is of every Christian; certainly, one will be able to tell from a man's word the extent to which it is fulfilled by his life and to what extent it is *merely* words. Nevertheless, God can work through unworthy instruments in the sacrament and in the word as well and has already done this quite often: ultimately, it is always God who works and not the subjective holiness of the preacher, however great it may be. It is plain heresy, however, to maintain that a preacher may say only what he himself has experienced; he *must* proclaim Christianity as a whole, including precisely what he has not yet put into action, and his own word, which judges and condemns him, should burn in his soul like fire and should become for him—as Scripture says about the Word of God—a two-edged sword (Heb 4:12) that cuts not only others but the preacher himself. What would have become of Christianity if so many popes, bishops, and priests had proclaimed only that part of the Christian reality which they themselves had been able to live? We preach, not ourselves, but rather Christ Jesus (2 Cor 4:5), even when this is at the same time a scathing judgment upon ourselves. The subjective holiness of the preacher will always fall short of the objective holiness of the message he has to convey.

What must be demanded, however, of this acting subject [that is, the preacher], who claims to preach the objective truth, is truthfulness. Someone who is plainly ready to speak against his own convictions cannot convince others. One may, or indeed must, preach what one does not live personally, but one must not pretend to be living it. One must place the guiding force of the Word on the side of justice, which is valid even when the servant of the Word is no less weak than his listeners. Furthermore, you must not say anything of which you yourself are not convinced. I recall a sermon preached to a large contingent of Catholic youth, in which the freedom of the Christian was praised eloquently and contrasted with the others' lack of freedom. But everyone sensed that neither the preacher nor the listeners believed it *in that form*, that they had a feeling, instead, that the freedom of the children of God in the Church was actually in a deplorable state, whereas those outside were basically the freer people. This is not infrequently the case with homilies that speak about the glory of the Christian state of life. No doubt the freedom of the children of God exists as a Christian reality; there is such a thing as the glory of the

Christian state of life, and we cannot be relieved of the responsibility to preach either one just because they are both under attack; but we cannot and must not remain silent about this opposition, either, if the great message that is at stake here is to be audible again at all to mankind today.[21] I remember another sermon in which the preacher, who had studied his dogmatic theology well, explained to his listeners that sin, death, and the devil had been conquered through the redemption. This victory was lauded and magnified, and it sounded nice; but who among those listeners was persuaded that sin, death, and the devil were really dead in the world? Did not this hymn to the Lord's victory necessarily remain ineffective, since the power of those powers is all too evident? Again, it is true that there is indeed such a thing as Christ's victory and that it is the sole hope of the Christian. But it is no less true that one cannot speak meaningfully about this victory without mentioning also the "not yet" that casts its gloomy shadow over Christian existence between this age and the next.

Perhaps nothing in recent decades or even centuries has done more harm to preaching than the loss of credibility that it incurred by merely handing on formulas that were no longer the living intellectual property of those who were proclaiming them. This is probably also the only way to comprehend the abrupt change in the Church during the postconciliar period, in which emphatically delivered dogmatic formulas were suddenly replaced by the same emphasis on secular slogans. There is no continuity of content to be found on this verbal marketplace. The only thing that has remained the same in this rapid external transformation seems to be, in quite a few cases, the zeal with which foreign formulas are repeated, without becoming any less foreign.

But that will not do. The first duty of the preacher is not to be on the look-out for foreign models and to expect relevance from them but, rather, to start by becoming personally a hearer of the Word and welcoming its reality. We will be able to be preachers of the Word only in the measure to which we have become its true hearers. Certainly every age and every individual man will have his blind spots. That does no definitive harm as long as the fundamental intention is still to believe the Word of God with the Church. No one has the

[21] Still worth reading on this subject is R. Egenter, *Von der Freiheit der Kinder Gottes*, 2nd ed. (Freiburg, 1947); important for the issues raised throughout this chapter is H. U. von Balthasar, *Wer ist ein Christ?* (Einsiedeln, 1965), esp. 87–91.

whole thing; only the Church has it wholly, and insofar as we dedicate ourselves to her, it belongs to us entirely in her. Such an outlook, which includes along with the whole Church the Church of yesterday and tomorrow, makes one generous and broadminded; the tolerance that develops from it remains fundamentally different, of course, from an attitude in which the individual sets himself up as judge of God's Word. Anyone who does this ultimately preaches only himself and, thus, always falls short.[22]

[22] On this matter, see the previous chapter on "Standards for Preaching the Gospel Today".

4. Theology and Preaching in the Dutch Catechism[1]

One is almost tempted to apply to the Dutch Catechism Schiller's famous remark about Wallenstein: "Von der Parteien Hass und Gunst verwirrt schwankt sein Bild durch die Geschichte" [Distorted by partisan hatred and favoritism, his image fluctuates through history]. For a long, long time it met exclusively with delighted enthusiasm or indignant rejection. Even though the waves have meanwhile become calm, until now no one has arrived at a sober, scholarly appraisal of the book's value or lack thereof.[2] During the course of the debate, it had become all too much of a banner waving over parties on the battlefield. Even though passions began to subside after peace was achieved by compromise, the situation continues to have repercussions. Characteristic of the partisan emotions in this matter is an incident at the Catholic

---

Translated by Michael J. Miller.

[1] Lecture given to the Catholic Student Union at the University of Tübingen on October 28, 1968, then repeated in Passau, Heidelberg, Ulm, and for an ecumenical discussion group in Tübingen.

[2] W. Bless and H. van Leeuwen, *Bildungsarbeit mit dem Holländischen Katechismus* (Freiburg, 1969), merely attempts to elucidate the Dutch Catechism for practical work in adult education. J. Dreißen, *Diagnose des Holländischen Katechismus* (Freiburg, 1968), aside from a few initial criticisms, offers an apologetic introduction to the work that contains much that is useful, yet glosses over the serious questions that have been raised by reducing the whole thing to problematic issues that arose during the theological renewal in Germany between the two World Wars. All that does play a part, but a whole generation has passed since then, so this approach cannot adequately explain the current state of those issues. Unfortunately, the information that served as the basis for the "Report über den Holländischen Katechismus", published in 1969 by Herder, is entirely inadequate. The fact that W. Dirks appears in it as a representative of the Lutheran Evangelical press (p. 211) . . . well, we can let that pass, but the fact that the reports on sessions in Nemi and Rome are based exclusively on rumors is a sign of a deeper problem; furthermore, the mentality and tone of the reportage is that of the current "cold war" in academic theology. Any critical voice whatsoever was inadmissible in this book. On the other hand, it is no less regrettable that Rome declared the sessions of the commission of cardinals and of theologians confidential, thus ensuring that available information would be one-sided and to a great extent preventing open discussion.

Congress in Essen: a participant at the major forum who threw out the question "Hasn't the Dutch Catechism found the right language for preaching today?" reaped thunderous applause, even though at that time (fall 1968) surely only an insignificantly small percentage of those present had ever had the book in their hands in the first place.[3]

1. Purpose and Form of Thought of the New Dutch Catechism

To understand the ripple effect that the Dutch Catechism triggered, we must start from the concept of "catechism", which contains a very definite claim. The literary genre "catechism" is a child of the Reformation; it goes without saying that precursors in the Late Middle Ages had prepared the way for it. The first "catechism" that bore this title was published in 1528 by the Protestant Althamer; in 1529 Luther's *Kleiner Katechismus* followed, which until the Dutch Catechism basically remained the model for the literary genre of the catechism and at the same time established its claim. In Evangelical Lutheran Christianity, the catechism is to a great extent the replacement for what dogma and Magisterium meant in the Catholic Church: it offers that standard scriptural exegesis which shows the way for kerygma and concretely defines for the individual Christian the coordinate system of his faith, the "hermeneutical horizon" of his interpretation of the Bible.[4] In their own way, Catholic catechisms adopt this claim, that is, to be the expression of Church doctrine and an application thereof to kerygma. Such a claim, of course, is possible only when one limits oneself to short questions and answers. As soon as one attempts a well-founded and foundational [*begründete und begründende*] presentation, theological thought necessarily must enter in much more forcefully with its helpful but not binding efforts, whereby specific views of theological groups or schools separated from the universal Church in no way shape the text. The opposition to the Dutch Catechism follows in large measure from the almost unavoidable discrepancy between the claim that its title makes for it and the completely different structure that it has in fact assumed.

---

[3] See the report in *Herderkorrespondenz* 22 (1968): 465.

[4] Cf. J. Hofinger, "Katechismus", in *LThK* 6:45–50, and especially the informative article "Katechismus" by E. Lohse and H. W. Surkau in *RGG* 3:1179–86, which clearly highlights Luther's connection with the ecclesiastical tradition as well as his creative accomplishment.

In any case, no one can deny that the Dutch bishops understood the book, which appeared as *The New Catechism*, to be making the lofty claim that that highly significant title suggests: to be a "creedal document" of the Catholic Church in the Netherlands, as reformed by the Second Vatican Council,[5] where it should be kept in mind that the changes brought about by this reform were a great deal more radical in Holland than elsewhere. Let us recall a few examples of the ghetto mentality that still prevailed in Holland shortly before the Council: In 1954 the Dutch episcopate forbade membership in Socialist political parties; anyone who regularly read Socialist newspapers and magazines or attended meetings of such parties was barred from receiving the sacraments and had to reckon with being denied a Catholic burial.[6] Thus the revolutionary change of the Council was felt much more acutely than in other countries, and the desire for a new overall presentation of the faith to correspond to the completely different situation was quite pronounced when it necessarily appeared.

Of course, even apart from this special situation of Dutch Catholicism, such a book was overdue. The systematic form of theology and preaching that has prevailed until now is being called into question in many ways. Scripture has been opened up anew by historical-critical scholarship and, I admit, locked up anew as well. It has been opened up anew: thanks to the labors of exegesis we hear the Word of the Bible in a completely new way in its historical originality, in the variety of a developing and growing history, with its tensions and oppositions, which are at the same time its unexpected richness. But in this way Scripture has also been locked up anew: it has become the object of specialists, and the layman, indeed even the professional theologian who is not an exegete, can no longer dare to speak about it at all, so that it plainly appears to be removed from the realm of spiritual reading and meditation as well, because anything that could result from that would necessarily smack of dilettantism. Scholarly erudition becomes a fence around Scripture, which is not accessible to the nonspecialist. At the same time, however, this Bible which is no longer read within the context of tradition but entirely on its own makes its all-encompassing

---

[5] I had selected this expression in 1968 without being able to foresee that the opposition at the Pastoral Council would arrive at a very similar formulation—in their case, of course, with a decided polemical intent.

[6] Dreißen, *Diagnose des Holländischen Katechismus*, 80, with further references.

demand on theology in a new way; the latter must prove itself in light of that demand, has to enter into it, and cannot emerge again without being changed. And then there is the whole shift of the historical horizon; but, above all, there is the fundamental change in the presuppositions of our thinking by the mathematical-scientific-technological world. The form in which the faith has been systematized until now presupposed the old, static, geocentric world view, which took ontological thinking for granted; this system no longer withstands the questions of a "post-metaphysical" age. Of course, anyone who looks farther into the matter will have to dispute the notion that man, who inquires about the meaning of his existence, can really ever be without metaphysics. The slogan about the post-metaphysical age is right about one thing, though: nowadays a common metaphysics accessible to all is nowhere to be found; the victory of "positivism" has largely deprived us of metaphysics, and thus there has been an inevitable and fundamental shift in our way of framing the religious question. The Dutch Catechism is now trying to produce what has become necessary in such a situation: a new organization of kerygma in keeping with the presuppositions of our way of thinking. This means two things for the catechism:

a. First, it says a decisive Yes to the continuity and unity of the faith —if it did not, it would no longer be "Catholic" but only "new". However, the fact that it deliberately includes the word "new" in the title and thereby burdens itself with what is almost a contradiction in terms with regard to "catechism" characterizes the way in which it understands continuity: as dynamic identity. In placing the term "catechism" side by side with the word "new", it expresses the experience of shock and change that Vatican II caused the Church of Holland.

In their foreword, the Dutch bishops characterize this understanding of continuity and unity, which forms the backdrop of the book, as follows: "Let us not misunderstand the expression 'new'! It does not mean that some bits of the faith have been changed. . . . Not a rigid system, but a living voice."[7] This sets a great and persuasive agenda, although of course it must be infinitely difficult to accomplish. For where does this "living voice" speak? How can we recognize it and distinguish

---

[7] As cited on p. 411 of the German edition. Cf. Dreißen, *Diagnose des Holländischen Katechismus,* 114.

it from other voices that set themselves up in its place? The concept of the living voice, indeed, is nothing new in theology: Luther used it to describe the perpetual vitality of self-interpreting Scripture, the Gospel, which needs no magisterial guarantees, because it is clear and unmistakable in itself; Catholic theology, in turn, used the expression precisely to maintain that the Gospel comes to us, not through Scripture alone, but above all through a living voice: that of the Magisterium, which at every moment creates a dynamic present for the testimony of Scripture. Neither approach is taken here; instead a path *between* the scriptural principle and magisterial theology is attempted, the contours of which remain unclear: here we already encounter the fundamental problem of this book, which strives for a new dynamism without reflecting clearly on its principles.

b. The catechism quite deliberately assumed the perspective of a "post-metaphysical" age. This means that throughout the book phenomenological, descriptive-narrative thinking predominates. There is an attempt to discover the question of meaning [*Sinnfrage*] and things that give meaning [*Sinngebung*] in the course of human life, in the events of history, and to situate the faith on the level of a meaningful answer [*Sinngebung*] that can be detected in the course of the events themselves. Closely connected with this "salvation-historical" orientation is a decided anthropocentrism that becomes clear, for example, when the chief editor of the catechism, Fr. Guus van Hemert, S.J., describes the outlook of the book by saying, "Human existence is never left behind. The whole catechism moves within human existence."[8] J. Dreißen, who did most of the work of translating it into German, intensifies this position when he writes, "Catechizing does not mean presenting to the child truths that it did not yet know. . . . The supply depends on the demand. . . . Life is believed, and the faith is lived."[9] The problems that radical anthropocentrism poses for theology thus become clear: Does Christian preaching really present nothing to us that we do not already know ourselves? And although it is true that the

---

[8] He says this in his instructive essay on the structure of the new catechism that is reprinted in Dreißen, *Diagnose des Holländischen Katechismus*, 9–20; citation at p. 9.

[9] Ibid., 25. See also 63: "The catechism intends to be anything but absolute. It is relative through and through. It means to reflect the 'status quo' of the Church in Holland." Should a catechism not intend more than that, without setting itself up as absolute? Should it not also try to be a corrective of the "status quo"?

faith is an answer to our human questioning, can we therefore fit cat-
echesis into the scheme of supply and demand? Or must it counteract
the superficial questions in which man is entangled by prevailing opinion so as to free him to face his real questions? Should it only affirm
and reinforce what already is, or should it aim at breaking through the
delusions of a situation and arriving at authenticity?

2. The Achievement of the New Catechism

Both the importance and the problematic character of the new catechism are rooted in the basic approach that is suggested with these
remarks. The importance: it really addresses man; it does not teach an
abstract system but, rather, takes up man's questioning and discovers
the place of faith in the midst of this questioning. In the refreshing
humanity of the catechism, I see its real strength and greatness, in a
humanity that is moved by a deep, true, and warm religiosity. This
is expressed especially well in the first part, in which the mystery of
existence, its uncertainty and its joyousness, is opened up step by step
without any artificiality toward a question that no this-worldly system
can answer: toward the call to the infinite, which arises indestructibly
out of man.[10] Only with difficulty can someone completely resist the
religious warmth and human sincerity that radiate from these pages—
one becomes aware of the spiritual climate of that land whose piety
found an inimitable expression in *The Imitation of Christ* and whose humanity became unforgettably apparent in Erasmus of Rotterdam, who
has been rediscovered by theology today. Among the most beautiful and
humanly impressive chapters I would include also the one on sin,[11] in
which none of the great seriousness of this theme is lost, but in which
the destructive moralism of casuistic morality is completely overcome
and decisive points are thereby presented anew to the reader's understanding. The depiction of the life of Jesus, which actually forms the
center of the book, is also marked by this joyful, simple devotion and
humanity. It acquires its immediacy and intimacy through the constant
connection with the Church year, with the liturgical representation of
this life: the origin of the Church's liturgical year is made completely
clear, and conversely, through this liturgical interpretation, what hap-

[10] Dutch Catechism, 3–22.
[11] Ibid., 449–54.

pened then is recognizable in its relevance to today. In my opinion there is no denying that, because of these merits, the book ranks among the milestones of the religious literature of this century. Its success is not only the result of a sensation but, rather, is objectively justified—and even Rome has always expressly admitted this.

3. Its Limitations

a. Problematic Organization

On the other hand, however, there is no disputing that the real problem of the new catechism lies at the same time in its anthropocentrism and its purely phenomenological thinking; the individual points in question that have been brought against it are at bottom merely symptoms of this deeper fundamental issue. This becomes clear, first of all, in the problem of its very organization. The fact that the catechism chooses no logical division into parts and chapters but, rather, is organized along historical, narrative lines need not be a reproach, although perhaps one may very well fear that a certain misunderstanding of the salvation-historical principle is at work here, probably the same one that is also the basis for the organization of the new dogmatic textbook *Mysterium salutis*.[12] The limitations of this historical approach become evident when it comes to fitting in the nonhistorical material.

The outline begins—very well—with the question posed to man by man himself. But then it simply continues in a historical-narrative manner: the prehistory of life and of mankind; pre-Christian history; the history of Israel; the history of Jesus; Church history. At this point, the story cuts to the story of the individual, which is depicted in the sacraments: baptism—confirmation—Eucharist—holy orders—marriage. In this context, the problems of moral theology are interpolated at various places, concluding with a treatment of sin and forgiveness (sacrament of reconciliation). After that, the narrative strand again comes to

[12] Cf. the critical remarks by M. Seckler in *ThQ* [*Theologische Quartalschrift*] 148 (1968): 232–35, esp. 234. An analysis of the outline followed by the Dutch Catechism is presented by van Hemert in Dreißen, *Diagnose des Holländischen Katechismus*, 9ff.; see especially the diagram on p. 10. The systematization offered there, however, seems to be somewhat artificial. Luther famously refrained from any attempt to be systematic and kept to a three-part structure: Ten Commandments, Creed, Our Father. Cf. Surkau, "Katechismus", 1180 and esp. 1183.

the fore: the anointing of the sick and the death of the individual are discussed; this leads to the description of death, resurrection, and the end times in general. The book ends with a chapter about God, who thus, judging from his place in the overall plan, appears as the "absolute future".

Much about this outline seems artificial, but that is unavoidable in any case. Nonetheless, the limitations of the merely narrative outline become especially conspicuous in the discussion of two fundamental themes of Christian theology: the doctrine of original sin and redemption (both are inserted after the treatment of baptism) and the theme of God. The presentation of the question about God at the end of the book is not without a certain logic, but the way it is carried out is not very convincing. There is no sense whatsoever of the importance that the question of God has acquired once again. The word "Trinity" is quite deliberately left out of the otherwise very thorough index; the one page in the text that discusses it (499) is excellent but inadequate, given the importance the question must have even for a historically oriented theology. Those thematic areas which are not historical narrative but rather expose the roots of human existence that run through the stages of history and point to being itself find no proper place in the phenomenological-historical outline of the Dutch Catechism.

b. Jesus and God

This external difficulty is, in turn, the sign of underlying limitations that result from the approach that has been chosen. One consequence of the narrative outline of the book, as already noted, is that the story of Jesus, presented in great detail, forms its real core, whereby the authors rely heavily on and frequently cite the book *Jesus of Nazareth* by G. Bornkamm for the particulars, just as they borrow several elements from studies by J. Jeremias.[13] For all that, there is no reflection whatsoever on what the life and message of the historical Jesus mean theologically, in what form and in what way they can or cannot define preaching. The book simply ignores the statement of the problem with which Bultmann emphatically and lastingly challenged theology: between the historical Jesus and the Church lie the Cross and Resur-

---

[13] G. Bornkamm, *Jesus von Nazareth* (Stuttgart, 1956; 7th ed., 1965); J. Jeremias, *Die Gleichnisse Jesu*, 4th ed. (Göttingen, 1956); Jeremias, *Abba* (Göttingen, 1966).

rection; these two events give expression to the rupture that occurred through the failure of Jesus' struggle for the faith of Israel. Certainly we will not be able to agree with Bultmann when he says that the historical Jesus does not belong in New Testament theology itself but, rather, is one of its presuppositions.[14] But the question that is linked with this observation prevents one from simply starting from the historical Jesus as the center of theology. Such an attempt, furthermore, is only possible if one blunts the keenness of the exegetical problem and draws a (thoroughly appealing) picture of Jesus that ignores the contradictions and uncertainties of modern exegesis and thereby is supposed to give the impression that only by the path of history does one have sure access to a picture of Jesus that can support the faith. Leaping over the hermeneutic problem in this way should be described, in scientific terms, as pre-critical, but at the same time it misses the opportunity to disclose meaningfully the function of dogma, which represents the ecclesiastical answer to the question of hermeneutics.[15] This gives the impression, however, that faith and history are basically the same and that faith is to be found merely on the level of the narrated story. Yet that diminishes both the seriousness of the historical inquiry and the seriousness of the claims made by faith. Exegesis and dogma exist alongside each other in a completely unconsidered compromise that is ultimately capable of doing justice to neither or of taking either one quite seriously. Despite all the detail in the account about Jesus, the christological question is left largely in a fog, which is unavoidable if one is unwilling to go beyond descriptive-phenomenological thinking, on the one hand, or to deal with Church tradition, on the other.

So the inquiry into Jesus ultimately remains as unsatisfactory as the inquiry into the Christ; this gives the impression of a harmonizing exegesis that leaves out anything dangerous and of a harmonizing dogmatic treatment that prefers not to press matters too far. Occasionally the reader can also find more or less tasteless statements, for instance, when it is said about the twelve-year-old Jesus in the Temple: "An

---

[14] R. Bultmann, *Theologie des Neuen Testaments*, 3rd ed. (Tübingen, 1958), 1; the extent to which this thesis of Bultmann is important for Catholic theology also is thoroughly considered by H. Schlier, *Besinnung auf das Neue Testament* (Freiburg, 1964), 12–20. After careful analysis, Schlier, too, formulates the problem as follows: "The story of Jesus Christ is a presupposition, not a part of New Testament theology" (p. 14).

[15] Cf. R. Marlé, *Das theologische Problem der Hermeneutik* (Mainz, 1965), 107–42.

intelligent boy discovers his vocation. That is the way in which God comes to his Temple."[16] Here the approach to Christ's humanity leads to banality; the attempt to keep just to the facts related in the Bible becomes uncritical psychologizing. Despite all the fine material that is offered, such an inadmissibly diluted view of Jesus' life can therefore not perform the function that the catechism intended for it: to replace the doctrine of divinity and to draw the picture of God concretely in the story of Jesus.

c. The Doctrine of Redemption

With that we have stated the decisive weakness of the Dutch Catechism. In order to illustrate further the importance and limitations of its approach, I would like to outline a few of the other points at which the problematic nature of the book becomes similarly evident. First, let us look at the most important question of Christian theology, after the doctrine of God: the doctrine of the redemption of man, which in turn provides the basic approach for the doctrine of the Eucharist. As a whole, the Dutch Catechism's teaching about redemption, which is entirely framed in terms of God's forgiving love, is impressive and convincing. Compared to a perspective that was widespread until recently, it surely brings the reader a good distance forward and does away with many a mistaken judgment: not God's anger, but God's love is the decisive center where Christian redemption is negotiated; man is not the one who appeases God, but, rather, God freely and lovingly forgives man. Yet this "katabatic" line of thought, which understands redemption wholly and entirely as a process from the top down, is developed so one-sidedly that again one part of the reality is concealed. Certainly, redemption is primarily an event from the top down; a wrathful God is not placated by human achievements, but, rather, the loving God overcomes human recalcitrance through the greater power of his love: he gives himself gratuitously. Jesus Christ is first and foremost the self-gift of God to mankind, not the work that men offer to God. His death is the self-sacrifice of God for us, not the price that groaning mankind renders to an offended God.

And yet Jesus is not only the God who descended; he is also the man who ascended. Jesus should be viewed and understood not only as the

---

[16] Dutch Catechism, 90.

epiphany or manifestation of divine love; he is also the representative of mankind, in whom human nature hands itself over to God in its most precious and purest form. His death on the Cross is not only God's self-surrender to us, it is also the unconditional self-abandonment of this man who is Jesus to God. In other words, this death is God's gracious gift and mankind's sacrifice combined. The "katabatic" (descending) and the "anabatic" (ascending) lines intersect. Both correspond to the biblical testimony; both correspond to the reality. God's gift of self to mankind is such that precisely therein he brings mankind to himself, that he enables it to be itself. That is why Jesus is not only God's epiphany but true man. And these two things are, not alongside or opposite each other, but in one another: the very fact that God shows himself in Jesus as the One who descends does not incapacitate man but gives him back to himself, so that in the descended God he becomes the co-ascendant, and in the gift-giving God he becomes the one who sacrifices and responds. But the Dutch Catechism here turned a necessary interpenetration into an opposition, an either-or. It basically allows only the katabatic view to be formulated and thus falls decisively short of the Christian reality. Indeed, the inevitable consequence of this is the horizontalization of piety on principle, for if only the descending line "God-to-man" is valid, the ascending line of prayer is dropped, and all that is left is the acceptance and handing on of what God has given. Fortunately the catechism did not proceed logically in this respect; what it says about prayer opens up a much broader perspective.[17]

d. Questions of Eucharistic Doctrine

Of course the consequences of this approach for eucharistic doctrine are clear: from this perspective there is no room left for the idea of sacrifice. Accordingly, the Dutch Catechism originally said on this topic: "Our sacrifice was offered two thousand years ago. For us all sacrifices are over." Following the discussions between papal theologians and theologians of the Dutch episcopate that took place April 8–10, 1967, in Gazzada in Northern Italy, the text of this passage was modified as

---

[17] On the convergence of the "ascending" and "descending" lines, see W. Averbeck, *Der Opfercharakter des Abendmahls in der neueren evangelischen Theologie* (Paderborn, 1967), 776–805; E. J. Lengeling, "Liturgie", in H. Fries, *Handbuch theologischer Grundbegriffe*, vol. 2 (Munich, 1963), 75–97, esp. 88f.

follows: "The sacrifice has already been offered. Strictly speaking we offer no other sacrifice than the sacrifice of Christ. No other offering is demanded of us."[18] But, even after this correction, the wording clings to an odd misunderstanding of the historicity of Christianity. For the uniqueness of the Christ-deed cannot mean that for us it is transported into the state of "having been" that characterizes things that happened once a very long time ago. What is essential to man cannot be forced into the limits of a historical given, especially not when it is "unique" and "definitive": for it is definitive precisely in that it continues to be valid, in that it remains in its decisiveness and cannot sink back into what merely has been. Thus Christ's sacrifice is never merely a fact of bygone history to which we now look back and whose result we accept; rather, it is the determining reality of human life here and now. Mankind lives on the sacrifice still, not just two thousand years ago; this sacrifice is no less "the present" for us than it was for those who were able to be there at its historical moment. But the almost exclusive "meal" concept [of the Eucharist] in the catechism shows once again the twofold weakness of its approach: persisting in a historical-descriptive way of thinking without adequate reflection on the problem of being and history; a one-sided katabatic approach that does not sufficiently take note of the two-sidedness of the dialogue between God and man or the empowering and call of mankind to make a countermove in response.

Things seem less clear-cut to me in the question about the Real Presence of the Lord in the eucharistic gifts. The difficulty here was that the catechism had to try to do without technical terminology and had the task of translating what was captured and encoded in the language of the Middle Ages into present-day language without that conven-

---

[18] Dutch Catechism, 340. Besides this concession, two other slight modifications resulted from the discussion in Gazzada. And so on the subject of original sin, the Gazzada statement reads as follows (296): "Thus the beginning is less important for us than it was earlier. This is also true as far as sin is concerned. The significance of the first sin, of course, is worth a more in-depth deliberation"; the original text, in contrast, said that we need not assign any particular importance to the "first sin". Moreover, in the chapter on family planning, a quotation from the Pastoral Constitution *Gaudium et spes* was inserted (450).

A whole raft of revisions was submitted to the "commission of theologians", that is, the commission of cardinals (published in German by Herder in 1968 as a manuscript), but those proposed changes merely offered new formulations of a position that remained substantially unchanged and hence could not settle the dispute.

tional vocabulary. The charge that the doctrine of the Real Presence has evaporated into a purely functional understanding was undeniably fueled by the fact that the delegates of the Dutch episcopate at the negotiations with the papal theologians in Gazzada declared, according to the minutes, that the eucharistic species *bring about* the *praesentia personalis et intima Christi* [the personal and interior presence of Christ] within the context of celebrating the eucharistic meal in the presence of the faithful who communicate and *offer* it outside of the eucharistic celebration, but in no case do they carry it *within themselves*. With those principles you would end up a Calvinist, practically speaking. It must be admitted, however, that the text of the catechism itself need not be understood in that way: anyone who reads it against the backdrop of the Church's faith can readily find that faith expressed here. Besides, it should be noted that the linguistic problem is especially difficult in this area, because even within theology itself the translation from the context of the medieval world view into ours has scarcely begun, and so we do not yet have the clarification in our own scholarly language that would be necessary for a translation into the language of preaching.

e. Particular Questions

Finally let us turn to a few more minor questions. Various formulas within the context of eschatology seem problematic to me. Does it mean anything to say that the dead "are about to rise"?[19] That the nearness of the saints perhaps points to the fact "that they are already farther on the way of resurrection"? Or is this not just fleeing from the specter of dualism right into new mythologies that will not be capable of convincing anyone? The debate about the Virgin Birth, which in Catholic circles was undeniably set in motion by the Dutch Catechism, need not be unrolled again here.[20] The impression cannot of course be entirely avoided that this suddenly became such a burning question in Holland because people coming from a self-contained Catholic environment were abruptly confronted with issues that are not new at

---

[19] Dutch Catechism, 474. Cf. 476.
[20] See my debate with W. Kasper and F. J. Steinmetz on this topic in *Hochland* 69 (1969): 539–42. The journal *Herderkorrespondenz* 24 (1970): 47 ridicules the fact that I resort to a hermeneutic of faith "that is beyond the scope of historical exegesis"; this strikes me as even more odd because the same anonymous critic on p. 45 praises a hermeneutic of modernity that abandons what is historical as a matter of course.

all outside of Catholic theology.[21] It is striking that the Virgin Birth is called into question despite the infancy narratives in Matthew and Luke, which clearly deal with the subject, while Mary's virginity after the birth of Jesus, which is much more difficult to square with Scripture, continues to be professed.[22] Also striking is the fact that, whereas the testimony of the ancient creeds is called into question, even though it can be substantiated biblically, the nineteenth- and twentieth-century Marian dogmas are taken for granted and left unchallenged. All this points to an intellectual imbalance and a lack of reflection in this matter that is alarming.[23]

The reader finds many inaccuracies in the section on Church history. In one passage this gives rise to a serious question: the chapter spends only a few lines describing the Reformation; the difference between the Catholic and the Reformation understanding of Christianity is treated on just *one* page. And yet the catechism cites the highly questionable information that the Dutch convert W. van de Pol has compiled on this subject, and even his testimony is once again considerably diluted. Van de Pol informs us that Catholicism addresses what is ontological, while Protestantism is oriented to the Word. The Dutch Catechism gives the following version: "Catholic Christianity believes more firmly that salvation is embodied in the most ordinary things. . . . The Reformation, in contrast, was certain from the start that God cannot be so palpably attained in the sacraments and in the authoritative word of the contemporary Church. Salvation for them is more spiritualized. . . . Special attention is paid throughout to the inner experience of the individual."[24] Now it is really not that simple. It would be better to say nothing at all on the subject. Besides, such

---

[21] Just compare the materials presented by H. M. Köster in J. J. Brosch and J. Hasenfuß, *Jungfrauengeburt gestern und heute* (Essen, 1969), 72–87, especially the texts from the debate about the *Apostolicum*. Above all the Harnack passage reprinted on 75f. should be heeded by all who intend to speak on this subject. It shows clearly that the hermeneutic question posed by the article [from the Apostles Creed] "natus ex Virgine", which refers to a historical fact, is quite different from the questions posed by the "descendit" and "ascendit" articles or even by the Resurrection or the Parousia.

[22] Dutch Catechism, 73.

[23] Ibid., 268 and 475f.

[24] Ibid., 225f. Cf. W. H. van de Pol, *Das reformatorische Christentum* (Einsiedeln, 1956), esp. 259: "because . . . the main difference consists precisely in the fact that revelation for the Reformed Christian has the character of a verbal revelation in the here and now, whereas for the Catholic Christian it has the character of a revelation of reality."

an inadequate treatment of the Reformation-Catholic problem is particularly odd in a book that is supposed to be promoting the new ecumenical movement.

Concluding Thought

To summarize: The Dutch Catechism is an important book. It has cleared new paths for preaching and in many cases given it a new language. Much about it, admittedly, is inadequate, and not just in peripheral matters. Some of this could have been avoided even without changing its approach. Other features clearly show the limitations of its concept: its attempt to stay within history that can be narrated, within human existence as it offers itself to our experience. Here one has to go beyond its framework for the sake of the content. Still other features reveal the dilemma that theology in general faces today; they are not a specific problem of this book but, rather, the manifestation of the problem that theology as a whole has become to itself today, in a world that has changed from the ground up and unceasingly continues to change. For example, the fact that the teaching on original sin is unsatisfactory in many respects, like the deficiencies of its teaching on redemption and the Eucharist, is only partly a failure of this book and of the particular path that it has chosen; to a considerable extent it is also simply an expression of the critical state of theology as a whole when faced with these problems, which demand a fundamentally new reflection and a new expression that has not yet been discovered in a convincing manner. Of course, one can repeat the classical formulas. But ultimately that accomplishes little. There has to be a new inquiry into what they mean, into the matter behind these formulas. That appears to be possible only by translating Then into Today, a process that must be carried out within the scholarly reflection of theology; but then that demands a further and separate step of translating what has been grasped through that reflection into the language of preaching. Thus two extremely difficult translation processes are required, in which there is more than one source of errors. But that does not relieve us of the duty to get to work. The particular difficulty of the Dutch Catechism lay in the fact that it had to attempt the second translation before the first was done; yet precisely in its efforts to find a language of preaching (something that is not yet readily available in academic theology), it was venturing into largely uncharted territory. In the past, all too often, preaching has been produced merely by simplifying theological reflection and its language, but in that way it could not come into its own. In this respect, the problem of "the theology of proclamation", which was discussed between the two World Wars, once again becomes urgent here. We have to say that, considered as a whole, the Dutch Catechism reflects the image of the Church in a time of transition, with its hopes and dangers. It is just as foolish to glorify it as it is wrong to reject the whole thing instead of allowing oneself to be enriched by its successes and challenged by its inadequacies: this is the only attitude that leads forward.

PART TWO

Some Major Themes of Preaching

GOD

5. Contemporary Man Facing
the Question of God

Man facing the question of God today finds himself in a situation of questioning and uncertainty, unless God is already reckoned as one of the outmoded questions that human consciousness has just shrugged off. If our discourse about God is to be comprehensible, if it is supposed to become for man an answer that clearly concerns him, it cannot ignore this situation. The crisis in Christian preaching, which we have experienced in growing proportions for a century, is based in no small part on the fact that the Christian answers have ignored man's questions; they were and remain right, but because they were not developed from and within the question, they remained ineffective. Hence to question along with man who seeks is an indispensable part of preaching itself, because only in this way can the Word [*Wort*] become an answer [*Ant-wort*].

I.

Accordingly, as a first step we must enter into this uncertainty of God, as contemporary man experiences it, so as to be able to rediscover and speak about God within it. Of course the average man is hardly conscious of the individual aspects of this uncertainty that are discussed here, yet together they define the intellectual climate, which has its formative influence even when the reasons for it are unseen. The withdrawal of God that distresses us today has roots going back to the change of world view that commences with the beginning of the modern era, although theology and Christian consciousness have still not

Translated by Michael J. Miller.

coped with it adequately. Until then God had his fixed place in the gradated structure of the world: the firmament; metaphysics was tangible, as it were, in the hierarchy that led from the nethermost and dullest level, the earth, to ever higher and more spiritual spheres and finally to the pure light, to the Mover of the universe. Dante's *Divine Comedy* remains the classic depiction of this world view, in which the faith had assumed a tangible form and could not be separated from the idea of the cosmos, which pointed to it on all sides. "Salvation history", too, centered on the Incarnation of God, could be understood graphically, for the earth was certainly, on the one hand, the lowest and basest link in the cosmic chain—the bottom of the universe, so to speak, over which the heavens towered. Yet as the bottom, it was also the very foundation of the structure, upon which everything rested, thus serving as the sensible theater for God's encounter with his creature, the right stage for the drama of God with his creation.

With the advent of the modern era, these reliable bearings, which until then had neatly subdivided the whole, disappeared. Another reference to Dante may be significant here: in hell the poet meets Ulysses (Odysseus) and learns from him that after returning home he set out once again with his companions, this time through the Straits of Gibraltar into the ocean. Dante anticipates the explorations of the late fifteenth and early sixteenth centuries by giving his Ulysses the traits of the later adventurers; the speech that Ulysses delivers to his frightened companions is surprisingly reminiscent of the speech that Columbus actually gave to his desperate crew. Only the outcome is quite different: according to Dante, Ulysses is shipwrecked on the mountain of Purgatory, at the Western limit of the earth; there is a direct transition from the earthly to the metaphysical.[1] The factual Ulysses, though, Columbus, discovers, not Purgatory, but America. The sudden change from medieval thinking that the discoveries of the modern era brought about could not be depicted more graphically than was done by history itself in this event. The world loses its metaphysical borders; wherever man may advance, it appears to be merely the world. What until now had been the heavens is unmasked now as the world, which has the same consistency all around, in which there is no Above and no Below but

---

[1] *Inferno* XXVI, 90–141; on this passage, see the excellent commentary by A. Rüegg, *Die Jenseitsvorstellungen vor Dante* (Einsiedeln, 1945), 2:108–17. See also the essay "Christliches Weltverständnis".

only the same construct of matter on all sides with the same laws in effect everywhere. The earth is neither a center nor a foundation, nor is the sky a heaven—everything is just "world". And the intelligent movers that had been postulated before, without which the even rotation of the stars was inexplicable (angels for the individual stars, God for the whole universe), become superfluous, because the movement can be explained by the laws of matter itself. The "God hypothesis" becomes superfluous—as the late eighteenth-century astronomer Laplace famously and ironically put it.

Behind these external facts there are shifts in the basic orientation of thought that lend new meaning to the whole. The successes in the progressive discovery of the material world and of its laws are achieved through an ever stricter and more refined application of that method which is characterized by the combination of observation, experiment, and the development of mathematical theories. Within this method, which limits itself to what is verifiable and falsifiable and from that acquires its generally binding certainty, there is no room for the question about the essential causes of things. Since God is not observable along the lines of a repeatable experiment and not calculable in terms of a mathematical theory, he cannot appear within this method—that is by its very nature impossible. From the perspective of faith, there is no objection to such a way of investigating reality; on the contrary, insofar as it reveals true knowledge to man and provides opportunities to shape a better existence for himself, it is in keeping with the Genesis commission that presents the world to man as the sphere of his investigation and activity. The situation becomes critical only when the positivistic method with its necessary methodological limitation turns into a positivistic world view which accepts as reality only what is accessible to this method and thus converts the methodological limitation into a fundamental one. The temptation to do so, however, becomes ever greater in the modern era and today appears almost insuperable. This is due, first of all, to the fact that the limits of this method cannot be gauged in advance; instead, the realm within which it can be successfully applied expands ever more in practice. Then, too, it is because in comparison to the sort of certainty and also measurable utility that is achieved thereby, all other forms of certainty appear questionable, so that one may easily be inclined to exclude them as inadequate and to wait until similarly certain results are forthcoming in those areas, which for the time being are bracketed off. What is done deliberately in science—making increasingly exclusive claims for the positivistic method—spreads crudely in less lucid forms in the general consciousness, which regards natural science as a panacea and theological findings as "medieval" and, therefore, unsuited to our modern thinking.

This touches on a further aspect, which I would like to call the "process character" of positivistic thinking. As we mentioned, the radius extends farther and farther, so that it occurs to anyone looking at the situation that someday this method should be able to comprehend all of reality. The areas reserved to theology and to a metaphysical-philosophical inquiry fuse together more and more, and even psychological and social processes become increasingly accessible to positivistic enlightenment. Thus theological statements almost necessarily appear to be prescientific, still possible for the time being because of the imperfections of positivistic research, but one day to be overtaken by it. We would do well, after all the setbacks that theology has experienced, to deal with this state of affairs promptly and not to wait until we are forced by new findings to do so against our will.

Corresponding to this development in the area of natural science there is a similar line of development in the area of history and anthropology. Just as "heaven" became "earth" through scientific research, so too historical research and the progressive encounter of religions and cultures is leading to an intellectual climate in which Christianity seems more and more to be sinking into a general history of religion. The Old Testament loses its absolute character; it presents itself to us completely embedded in the cultures of the Near East, and the story of Jesus is likewise taken back into the context of late Jewish religious history. Nothing seems unparalleled any more; mankind in its greatness and baseness, for all its changing forms, appears nevertheless to be one everywhere. Whereas it was always difficult to regard an individual, Jesus of Nazareth, as the one responsible for all of history and as the destiny of every human life, now, in light of the all-too-human elements in biblical history and in view of all that is honorable in other religions, it seems utterly impossible that any one form of religion could be absolute.

Add to all that the progressive disappearance of an independent philosophy that would give faith room in which to develop. There is no longer any generally accepted philosophy, unless you mean positivism, which has been widely adopted but does not even give faith a chance.

With that we have outlined in broad strokes the questions that make the reality of God increasingly inaccessible to contemporary man. What is left? How can we find answers? First we will have to admit that this is a task that will take generations. The self-evident way in which God seemed to be comprehensible in the Middle Ages was not something that happened overnight. Through a long process of thinking and living, the faith had stamped the form of Christian convictions upon the world view of antiquity, which had not been defined by the Creator God of Christianity at all. As this synthesis broke down bit by bit in the modern era, Christians persisted all too long in their efforts to save the old ways of thinking instead of dealing decisively with the new questions. Appropriating the faith anew in these new intellectual conditions thus remains a task that is to a great extent uncompleted.

That alone, of course, can never be a sufficient answer. For even though theology may have plenty of time, man must live *now* and ask about his path. What possibilities are offered to him? One can begin in various ways. One can point out that even today, and in a certain respect especially today, in light of all our knowledge about the mathematics of the universe, more than ever before the world that bears the hallmarks of mind points to the Creator-Spirit, without whom that mind which is objectively manifest therein remains inexplicable. One can point out that human freedom gives us a glimpse of the original creative freedom, of God; or that human seeking and questioning cannot come to rest in positivistic findings alone and urges us on to the creative "Thou" without whom the "I" remains inexplicable.

In the one case, we arrive at a more ontological picture of God, whereas, in the other, we find an image that is defined in more personal terms. Looking at both ways together would then point to the Christian image of God, to the synthesis of meaning and being [*Sinn und Sein*] that we call God.[2] Both aspects seem to me equally important, even though given the psychological situation the restriction of the positivistic outlook may seem more urgent: a man who tries to exist only in a positivistic way, in what is calculable and measurable, suffocates—the explosions in our present-day society basically demonstrate this with frightening clarity.

---

[2] Concerning these efforts, see J. Ratzinger, ed., *Die Frage nach Gott* (Freiburg, 1972), especially the essays by B. Welte and B. Casper (11–42) and by E. Biser (89–115). Another important study is H. Krings, "Freiheit: Ein Versuch, Gott zu denken", *Philosophisches Jahrbuch* 77 (1970): 225–37; R. Spaemann, "Die Frage nach der Bedeutung des Wortes 'Gott'", *Internationale katholische Zeitschrift* 1 (1972): 54–72.

Reinhard Raffalt recently pointed out these connections very impressively. He reports his impression that the Church is increasingly intent on improving the material situation of mankind first. A cardinal to whom he remarked (with reference to Latin America) that we have to look after mankind's need for salvation, too, replied, "Yes, a new proclamation of the Gospel must naturally be added sometime." When Raffalt suggested beginning with that, he smiled politely and said nothing.

> The Church, it seems to me, has arrived at the conviction that by exerting all her strength and through cooperation with like-minded people she can bring about a perfecting of temporal life. . . . One cannot deny the idealism in a plan like this. One just wonders: Is man in the imperfection of his nature capable in the first place of ever making the world into something other than what it has always been—the theater for the rampant powers of Evil, against which the Good can hope to defend itself only in silence, in faith, charity, and hope? Has there ever been in the history of mankind any situation at all in which it was in greater need than today of hearing the words of Christ: "My kingdom is *not* of this world"? It is certainly a lot to demand of the age of cynicism in which we live to take these words as a starting point. But is it demanded too often? Does not the exploited, oppressed, abused man basically want exactly the same thing as his brother who is ruined by comfort, sex, and drugs—namely, to be able to believe?[3]

Perhaps this is putting it too simply and directly, but it seems to me indisputable that a hunger for what no positivism can supply burns in contemporary man, along with the question of God (although the latter is quite often unrecognized). God is in fact today present in the form of this question in man, and we ought to recognize this very presence and call it by name.

II.

We could sketch here the initial lines of a new discourse about God, but I interrupt our reflection at this point so as to approach our topic once again from the other end: from the interior of the Christian image of God, which we want to try to look at just simply, in its own right.

---

[3] *Das Ende des römischen Prinzips* (Munich, 1970), 21.

How is God depicted in the Bible? Is there a question about God here, too, or only simple certainty about the God who reveals? What does access to God look like? It goes without saying that these questions cannot be pursued in detail here; a brief remark about access to God must suffice. The logical thought patterns of the Greeks are foreign to the Bible, which of course knows nothing about a "proof of God's existence"; there is in the Bible, however, increasing clarity about the transparency of creation toward the Creator, the resounding message that goes out through all the earth as the heavens tell the glory of God (Ps 19 [18]). This eloquence of creation still exists today, and we should persistently try to awaken the ability to see the world again as a meaningful figure that has something to say to us and not just as an assembly of functions that we can utilize. Besides God's actuality in creation, there is another way that is preeminent in the Bible: God is known through history. This corresponds to the concrete human experience that other peoples have had and that we still have today: we discover God at first, not through our own reflection, but rather by growing up in a religious environment that is aware that it was founded and is supported by God and thereby brings me also into a relation with God. Certainly a process of setting apart ensues in Israel in this regard. Rome distilled its experience of the God who rules over history in the formula of *Jupiter Conservator*. The Latin word for "redeemer", "savior", is *conservator*—salvation consists in the conservation of Rome, the preservation of the status quo from war, upheaval, and destruction. When the Christians proclaimed Jesus as the true bringer of salvation, it became evident that they could not use the earlier Latin word for this concept. For Jesus' salvation did not amount to a preservation of the earlier Rome at all. It meant renewal, transformation; it pointed to the *eschaton* and, thus, to what is completely Other. So they had to create their own language by forming the new word *salvator* to replace *conservator*.[4] This minor detail seems to me to be significant: in the Bible, the experience of God as the God of history is not related only to the past but, above all, bears within itself the character of hope and points to the future. This gives the Christian image of God its distinctive coloring, which in practice we had no doubt pushed too much into the background until now.

[4] H. U. Instinsky, *Die alte Kirche und das Heil des Staates* (Munich, 1963), 28ff.

The New Testament image of God, moreover, remains structurally in complete unity with that of the Old Testament. Only when one notices this can one understand correctly the figure of Jesus and the transformation that it does signify now for the image of God. Certainly, if one had to try to answer briefly the question "What does the New Testament mean by 'God'?" the answer could only be: "God" is the Father of Jesus Christ; "God" is the one to which or to whom Jesus said "Father". But that by no means constitutes a "christological overlapping" that is stuck in a narrow personalism and a purely historical way of thinking that forgets the breadth of reality; it is, rather, to adopt the fundamental approach of the Old Testament and, along with it, the breadth of human questioning about God. The Old Testament had begun by discovering God as the God of someone, as the God of men; it had defined him in terms of men: as the God of the fathers.[5] Jesus aligns himself with complete logical consistency with this faith tradition of Israel. For him, God is the God of someone, his God. He understands God as "his God", so much so that he consistently calls him his Father and views this God of "his", who is quite personally God to him, as being identical nevertheless with the God of the fathers: his God, whom he knows to be his Father, is the God of Abraham, Isaac, and Jacob, after all, and the Creator of heaven and earth.

Just as Moses, last but not least, received a definition of God in terms of men, that is, as God of the fathers, so too the question "who or what is God?" is defined for the New Testament once again in terms of a man, Jesus of Nazareth. It does not answer the question about God directly but, rather, by and through the man Jesus of Nazareth. It defines God in terms of him, or, rather, it does not define God but instead points to the one who said Father to God. We should meditate on this answer by considering the two sides of the relation that is thereby inaugurated. It signifies:

a. that the man Jesus, as the New Testament knows and sees him, can be understood only in relation to him whom he calls his Father and in terms of whom he understands himself as "Son". One cannot have Jesus if one is unwilling to have Jesus' Father—which is to contradict the many forms of a-theistic devotion to Jesus, from Marcion to Dorothee

---

[5] N. Lohfink, *Bibelauslegung im Wandel* (Frankfurt, 1967), 107–28; A. Deißler, *Die Grundbotschaft des Alten Testaments* (Freiburg, 1972), 43–47; 61–69.

Sölle (who in fact only adopts in her own way Marcion's primordial construct). The Father appears in the definition of Jesus; Jesus himself can be comprehended only in his constant relation to the Father. A Jesus without the Father has nothing, absolutely nothing in common with the historical Jesus, with the Jesus of the New Testament.

b. Conversely, this of course means also that the New Testament does not speak directly about God, not about God alone and as such, but rather knows him only concretely as the "God of someone": as the God and Father of Jesus, only by and through the Father-Son relation, mediated by and through the man who knew that he had access to God. It means that the New Testament does not know God apart from his relation of paternity or without the mediation of the man Jesus. It regards dialogue with God as possible only by and through his dialogue with Jesus. The New Testament speaks, not about God in himself, but about God-in relation-to. This relation is henceforth indissoluble on either side: Jesus cannot be cut off from the Father; that is the one side. Yet God, too, can no longer be thought of except in his relation to Jesus. That is the other side, and that is the novelty, the absolute importance of Jesus, who thereby steps out of [the line of] the "fathers" and enters directly into the concept of God and belongs to God essentially, belongs to God "divinely"—as man.

This means that knowledge of God and relation to God have a fundamental reference to the man Jesus: anyone who belongs to him can say to God "Father"—as the Our Father shows. According to Paul, glossolalia [speaking in tongues] interprets its ecstatic stammering as the cry "Abba" and thus as the empowerment of the Spirit of Jesus, who speaks in us and makes us share in Jesus' relation to God as child. The early Christian experience of Pneuma is thus altogether explained as participation in Jesus' relation to God and is attributed to the relation to God as his Father, which is mediated by Jesus. In John, this accessibility of God in Jesus can then be expressed in the formula: He who sees me sees the Father (cf. 14:9), whereby the answer to the "Hellenist" Philip is to be understood at the same time as an answer to the desire of the Greek Christians to see—meeting Jesus is "seeing" or "contemplating" the Father. The question about the knowledge of God is therefore answered by the call to follow Jesus. Knowledge of God is revealed in the measure in which one follows. The interrelationship—that from now on God can be known only as the Father of Jesus Christ, yet in this way is really accessible, and that, on the other hand, Jesus can be understood only as "Son"—appears in such radical form already in the New Testament itself that the New Testament does not merely see the bond between the knowledge of God and the Father-Jesus, Father-Son relation as a form of our knowledge, as something supplementary and external (or even insignificant) for God, but rather regards this relation as being essential for God himself, as something accomplished by him and inseparable from him, something not added on externally for our sake, but rather belonging properly to him: God in fact exists in the relation Father-Son; it belongs to him essentially. He is comprehensible only as relation—whereby the essential and fundamental core of the doctrine of the Trinity is already stated and becomes clear in its true, central content.

From here we could now feel our way into quite fundamental questions, for instance: If the New Testament describes God as Father of Jesus Christ (and is recognizable only as such), what kind of image of God does that present? What do we learn further about God thereby? We cannot attempt to consider this more in detail. Let us just indicate what direction an answer might take. Indeed, to start with, we could answer our question quite simply and say: About God we learn initially that he stands in the relation of Father to Son. But that means: God becomes recognizable first and foremost as Person. This is not self-evident, when one thinks of the Indian concept of God, of the Greek concept of God, of the unreasoned intimations of modern natural science, or of modern consciousness in general.

Naturally, one would have to ask more precisely here: What does it mean to say that "God is recognized as Person?" What is a "person"? If one attempts to formulate the concept of person from this juncture (and so it happened historically), the answer must be: Person is precisely what the New Testament brings to light in the reality of the Father-Son relation: a consciousness that is essentially relation, creative, loving, knowing relation. The God of the Bible is not only consciousness, but Word; not only knowledge, but relation; not only the ground of being, but the supporting strength of all meaning.[6]

---

[6] Cf. J. Ratzinger, *Introduction to Christianity*, trans. J. R. Foster, rev. ed. (San Francisco: Ignatius Press, 2004), 116–50.

III.

We really should take a third step now and ask: How can these findings and the fundamental understanding of life and world that they express be brought to bear on the situation of the modern mind that was described at the outset? How can one make them at home in that situation? To attempt even a sketch of an answer would far exceed the limits of this essay. Therefore let us be content to ascertain what insights come to us by way of the knowledge of God obtained from the New Testament data that we have described and, then, with what basic pattern we have to reckon, therefore, in our attempt to find the way to God and show it to others. I think that from what has been said thus far we can highlight three major statements on this subject:

1. God is made known through men who know him, place themselves at his disposal, and make room for him in the world. The path to God leads concretely again and again by way of the man who is already standing by God. It does not lead by way of pure reflection but, rather, through encounter, which of course is deepened with reflection and becomes more independent and thus at the same time communicable again. Whereas in this statement the importance of the preacher comes to the fore with its full gravity, a second statement makes the limit of our efforts visible as well:

2. God is made known through himself. He gives himself, on his own initiative, to be known in the man Jesus, who belongs divinely to God and is the active self-manifestation of God. God is not confined to our attempts, to our success or failure; he is (we repeat) made known by himself.

3. The knowledge of God is a way; it means discipleship. It is not revealed to an uncommitted, permanently neutral observer but, rather, is disclosed in the measure in which one sets out on the way. Therein lies once again the limit of all mere discourse; proclamation or preaching that is not also itself an expression of a way, an expression of following, in the final analysis remains mute.

6. Preaching God Today

No human discourse can adequately express the mystery of God, and yet we cannot remain silent about the one who underlies our discourse and makes it possible. The following pages are an attempt to offer in seven theses a guide to the essential aspects that should be kept in mind in speaking about God.

FIRST THESIS

God should be preached as Father, Son, and Holy Spirit

The first signpost for preaching is provided by the fundamental act of becoming a Christian: baptism, which is simultaneously an expression of faith. Baptism occurs in the name of the Father, of the Son, and of the Holy Spirit: this is more than a formula—it is the designation of a new position that man finds in and through baptism. The act of baptism is not only the formal incorporation into a community; it also indicates the content on which this community lives and thereby expresses at the same time the path the candidate is adopting in the act of baptism. To put it more pointedly: the goal of baptism is not the community, but the truth—mediated by the community.

For this reason, the baptismal formula is intended at the same time to mark the center of Christianity. This center is faith in the triune God. Baptism interprets being a Christian theocentrically. Being a Christian means above all else believing that God exists. This is the most fundamental option; this is what it is all about, even before any salvation history and ecclesiology. The core of the Christian profession of faith, the core of the Christian existential act lies in the statement: God is.[1]

Translated by Michael J. Miller.

[1] See on this subject the seminal comments by Henri de Lubac, *The Christian Faith: An Essay on the Structure of the Apostles' Creed*, trans. Richard Arnandez (San Francisco: Ignatius Press, 1986).

Leading people to this fundamental act is the first task of all preaching. The first word of the Christian message is God—and that is precisely what liberates man.[2]

God exists—this sentence can be analyzed into several facets. It means, first of all, that the Church abides by the creed of Israel. There is only one God. The world does not have many rulers. But again and again man creates them for himself, even when he does not call them gods: even today he sets up idols alongside God—money, sex, power, public opinion. He worships politics or history, expecting that it will develop into God. But there is only one God: the Creator who stands over the world and under whom we all stand.

God is—this sentence means, then: He really exists. Which means: He exists as someone who matters to us. He is an active power, not a heavenly body revolving around itself whose existence could ultimately be irrelevant to man. God is—which means: He has power over man and the world, even today; man matters to him, God can hear him, and God can speak with him. God can love him, and man can receive his love.

With that we have arrived at the trinitarian testimony, which is not a marginal feature of Christianity but rather represents its core. God exists as love, which means precisely that he exists as Trinity. As love, he is from everlasting, in himself and by his nature, the fruitful encounter of I and Thou and precisely in this way the highest unity.

God is Father. The experience of human fatherhood may give us here an inkling of what God himself is and how he is to us. Thus at the same time, in and through human language, all the reality of man himself is claimed for the knowledge of God. Where fatherhood no longer exists, where real fatherhood with its blend of manly strength, justice, dependability, and heartfelt kindness is no longer experienced, discourse about God the Father becomes empty, too. This is perhaps the real crisis of our image of God, the fact that to a great extent the analogous thing that is supposed to make him effable no longer exists. In this respect, being baptized into the Father and the Son with the Spirit is, of course, another very concrete claim along these lines: opening oneself up to the possibility of building human existence in such a

---

[2] See R. Spaemann, "Die Frage nach der Bedeutung des Wortes 'Gott'", *Internationale katholische Zeitschrift Communio* 1 (1972): 54–72. The necessity of a concept of God that does not take God to be somehow the function of man or of the world is strikingly set forth in that article.

way that it can become an analogy for God. If we consider, moreover, that the Bible quite deliberately includes in the image of the Father the idea of "Mother" also and means to present a Father in whom the true essence of motherhood is realized as well, then this reveals a demand of baptism that is as personal as it is social: to become, in terms of this Father, a father or a mother oneself and thus to make him visible and recognizable in the world; to preserve for it that basic social unit, "family", which is the first name of God.

Immediately we must add: no fatherhood on earth can sufficiently depict God's fatherly essence. It always remains more or less ambiguous: when the Greeks called their Zeus "Father", this was by no means striking a note primarily of love and trust; rather, it was saying: This Zeus is an unpredictable despot like human fathers. Calling God Father, in its Christian form, is not the projection of an earthly social (patriarchal) construct onto heaven, the heavenly duplicate of a particular earthly system, but, rather, the divine critique of all earthly states: what a father is, what he ought to be, we learn in the mutuality of this Father with his Son. This dialogue sets a new standard, which overturns all analogies.

Thus, an essential law of human discourse about God becomes evident here: the Bible takes up the analogy that presents itself, at first with all its human dross—many depictions of the Old Testament Yahweh are not all that far removed from the despotic image of the Greek father-god. But you have to begin that way in order to get the discussion going at all. Then gradually, however, this image of the Father is refined, broken down, and finally turned completely upside-down: now God himself sets the standard for the analogy that made the discourse possible. The main thing now is not that human fatherhood gives some notion of what God is, but vice versa: the dialogue of God as Father and Son defines what fatherhood is and sets a standard for it. This means: the revealing recasting of the human father-analogy, of the human understanding, into a discourse that God himself places on our lips arrives at its goal only at the moment when the whole reality of God's original fatherly essence comes to the fore in the mutuality of Father and Son—that is to say, at the moment when fatherhood is recognized as something belonging to God himself, as trinitarian.

Discourse about God the Father becomes complete only through discourse about God the Son. The Son, of course, cannot be mentioned apart from his becoming man: in Jesus Christ. In this respect, Christian discourse about God must open the way into salvation history. Another consequence is the proclamation of the Holy Spirit: God as fruitfulness, as communication, as unity, as love, and as peace.

Normally it cannot be the task of preaching to set out a speculative doctrine about the Trinity. It must, however, make God known specifically as Father, Son, and Holy Spirit and in so doing—indeed, precisely in this manner—proclaim the uniqueness and unity of God, who is one as fruitful love.

SECOND THESIS

God should be proclaimed as Creator and Lord

The baptismal formula, in which the direction of Christian existence is expressed, is in its formulaic brevity the utmost concentration of what the Christian decision entails. It sets forth unmistakably the theocentric structure of this existence and at the same time defines the Christian image of God as trinitarian. It is a framework that sets out the essential building blocks. Yet at the same time it points to more comprehensive statements and indicates their structure. Thus the individual elements of preaching can be drawn from the more elaborate creedal texts that stand in the background behind this authentic "covenant formula"— as one might call the baptismal formula.

This points the way, first of all, to two predicates of God: Creator and "might". God is Creator. This statement throws open the door to the proper field of human reason and to the province of world religions. There is a transparency of the world with respect to its Creator. Certainly, it is distorted in many ways, and his image appears only in dubious refractions, but it appears nevertheless. We must not allow this unity of Christianity with the presentiments of all peoples and with the reach of human reason beyond all that is measurable to be wrested away from us. Faith is not the ideology of a more or less important club but, rather, has to do with the whole of reality, with its ultimate foundation, and with the ultimate foundation of all human existence. It has to do with reason and with reality, the whole reality of the cosmos. Indeed, one of faith's tasks, when confronted with technical reason, is to keep in motion the kind of reason that listens, looks, and searches for meaning.[3] Faith, correctly understood, does not numb reason but, rather, awakens it: it is supposed to be on the lookout for the reason of things and for the creative reason that is reflected in them and that is at the same time our own Whence and Whither [our origin and destination]. One can speak about God only if one has not forgotten how to look, to wonder, to pause before the whole of reality, to listen to the deep foundations of being. And conversely: looking to God opens man's eyes and broadens his horizons—only the heart that has become broad can see him.

To preach God as Creator, then, means to proclaim him as the power of a universal Yes. Either way, Marcion's temptation, which is to pit creation against redemption, appears again and again in Christian history. Sometimes it happens that the crucified Savior is denied in favor of a supposedly pure, Dionysian nature that one wishes to espouse unrestrainedly so as to return to its pristine fullness. Other times it happens that the Creator is despised and redemption is expected only through the complete alteration of reality, which is demonized and discredited as "the status quo". In contrast, Christian faith is sure about the unity of Father and Son, of Creator and Redeemer. That means that although the world must be transformed, it must not be negated. It means trust, confidence, joy: the foundation of all reality is good, and there is no contrary force equal to God that could snatch the world definitively from his hands.

As Creator, God is the origin of things and their measure. The fact that all things come from God means at the same time that God rules over all things. As Creator, he is Lord. God's dominion is anchored in his creative might, and this has a very concrete significance: creation points to him, not only in the sphere of theoretical reason but also in the sphere of practical reason. One can criticize the way in which the concept of natural law and of the natural moral law has been used in history, but the thing itself continues to exist. Indeed, in the steady expansion of human power over creation, which threatens to turn into a lethal experiment for both man and the world, this standard asserts itself with new urgency. Created reality itself sets limits the transgression of which leads down the path to self-destruction.

---

[3] See my *Introduction to Christianity*, trans. J. R. Foster, rev. ed. (San Francisco: Ignatius Press, 2004), 74–79.

This is the point where what is universal about creation connects with what is quite personal about conscience: in the conscience, in the quiet knowledge that man shares with the inmost foundation of creation, the Creator is present as Creator to the man. The Christian God is a God of conscience: he is the completely interior God, because he is the completely Universal One. As Lord, he is at the same time the deepest center of our self. As Lord, he is salvation.

THIRD THESIS

God should be preached as Logos

This is just an extension of the concept "Creator": the New Testament creation account—John 1:1—summarizes the whole first chapter of Genesis in the one sentence, "In the beginning was the Word." It condenses creation theology into Logos theology. The images fall away, and the pure core remains: everything that exists comes from the "Word". The "Word" is mightier than the so-called facts. Or more precisely: it is the fact of all facts. Circumstances do not produce the Spirit; rather, it is the Spirit who creates things. He is the real power.

But what is it, this "Logos"? The word "Logos" means, first of all, the same thing as "mind" [*Sinn*]. To say that the world comes from the Logos, accordingly, means: the world is intelligible [*sinnvoll*]; it is the creature of the Mind that expresses itself. Even before we *make sense* [*Sinn machen*] of anything, meaning [*Sinn*] is there. It embraces us. We stand upon it. The intelligibility [*Sinn*] does not depend on our creative effort but, rather, precedes and enables it. This means that the question about our Wherefore [our reason for being] is answered in our Whence [our origin]. The Whence itself is the Wherefore. Creation is not just information about something that once happened; rather, it is an expression of the way the world is, here and now, and a statement about what its future will be like. The Whence of the world is at the same time the basis for its hope. God is Creator, the world is creation, I have been created: this sentence is not a hypothesis about the details of the origin of the world and the evolution of man—all this is opened up by the contraction of the creation account into the statement: "In the beginning was the Word." Thus, belief in the Creator ultimately has become a statement about what man is and what the world is by nature: the product of a creative Mind and thus empowered to bestow meaning that coexists with the meaning that is simply there.

In this connection, Romano Guardini has spoken about the primacy of Logos over Ethos: before Doing stands Being. In the beginning was not the "deed" but, rather, the Word; it is mightier than the deed. Doing does not create meaning; rather, meaning creates doing. This is connected, at the same time, with the fact that Christian faith has to do with reason, is not opposed to it but, rather, calls for it. Above all, however, this means that Christian faith essentially and originally has to do with the truth. What a man believes is not a matter of indifference to him; the truth cannot be replaced by a "good opinion". The loss of the truth corrupts even good opinions. It also corrupts love, which without truth is blind and, hence, cannot fulfill its real purpose [*Sinn*]: to will and to do for the other what is truly good. Only when I know what man is in truth and what the world is in truth can I also be truly good. Goodness without truth can bring about subjective justification but not salvation. God is the Truth—this statement is a program, a fundamental orientation for human existence, which finds verbal expression in the belief in creation.

In our first attempt at a definition, we translated Logos as "mind" or "meaning". In the Gospel of John, however, it means quite a lot more. It can be translated even more literally: Logos in the Johannine sense means not only *ratio*, but also *verbum*—not only "mind", but also "discourse". That is to say: the Christian God is not just reason, objective meaning, the geometry of the universe, but he is speech, relation, Word, and Love. He is sighted reason, which sees and hears, which can be called upon and has a personal character. The "objective" meaning of the world is a subject, in relation to me. As Logos, God is discourse—not just Creator, but revelation, which speaks to me and allows me to give answer. In the designation of God as "Logos", the genuine foundation for the Christian theology of prayer is revealed. The word replies to the Word. For this reason, the Logos of all things can encounter me with a human face, the face of Jesus of Nazareth.

This opens up a final perspective: as Logos, God is "over all" and "in all" at the same time. He is not a foreign exterior for things but, rather, their inmost interior: what we found earlier in the idea of conscience becomes even deeper here. God is no strange law imposed from without but, rather, the inmost center of all entities. Their "idea", as the

Greeks used to say. But precisely in this most profound in-being [*In-sein*], his infinite transcendence [*Über-sein*] remains. In Jesus of Nazareth I encounter the most authentic features of my self, and therefore I can speak with him, therefore I can understand him, therefore I can become one body, that is, one single existence with him and those who are his. Therefore, however, I also remain ever on the way to him, because he is always infinitely more.

FOURTH THESIS

God should be proclaimed in Jesus Christ

In the Logos predicate, the belief in the Creator passes over into belief in Jesus Christ. In him we see the Father (Jn 14:9). We learn who God is especially and most often by looking to Jesus Christ. The Son allows us at the same time to recognize the Father's features. For this reason, the Jesus of the Gospels first and foremost belongs in Christian discourse about God: there is no other "historical Jesus". The one who comes from the Father's bosom (Jn 1:18) has told us who God is. The decisive elements for the image of God, accordingly, are first of all the central phases in the story of Jesus: Incarnation—Cross—Resurrection—Ascension—Sending of the Spirit.

The Incarnation: God is such that he can become man. He is such that he wills to become man. What do these two things tell us? First, how close the creature man is to God, since God can be man, since he speaks, thinks, and loves as man. But also how far God is, since even at this proximity the creature cannot recognize his God.

The Cross: this is where we have to learn what omnipotence means. Omnipotence that joins with love without giving up truth. For truth remains indestructible, and it cannot and will not be snuffed out by God; this is the sole reason why there is no compromise, no agreement with what everybody wants. Only because truth abides does love become lethal. Truth without love does not have to die, but only judge; love without truth likewise does not have to die, but only yield. But where the two are together, the Cross comes to pass. Christian history has filled these statements with the living experience of faith and prayer. The history of the image of the Cross and of devotion to the Cross is a commentary on the Good Friday mystery for which no erudition can substitute: an exegesis of God in terms of the experience of the Crucified, which speaks to us also if we enter into it.

The Resurrection of Jesus Christ as the unveiling of God himself: God is a God of life, of the living—that is probably the first insight that is sparked here. He gives a future. He is our future. And once again: he is power. Certainly, the Creator proves his power, not in childish miracles, but rather in the ongoing marvel of an intelligibly constructed world. But the intelligible order of this world is not closed off from him; rather, it is so constructed that it perpetually remains in his hands, while he in his way opens it up above and beyond its momentary aspect. Its present regimen is death. But this barrier does not oblige God. He can act; he can overcome death, and he has acted. The Resurrection is not a random miracle but, rather, the beginning of the definitive future of the world. As such, it is God's deepest incision in the world and, thus, the most dramatic testimony to the fact that God is, that he really is God. It is a theo-logical phenomenon: it shows Him, and for that very reason it is our hope.

To affirm God in Jesus Christ means, finally, to affirm him as freedom. He is free to act in time. He is free to do something that cannot be attributed to eternal necessity. He is so free that it is a scandal for philosophy and natural science. And yet this freedom is the opposite of arbitrariness: it is strictly related to truth and to love in that unity without which neither one would be itself. The measure of this freedom is not necessity but, rather, truth and love. Man's freedom, again contradicting our calculations about the universe in other respects, points to the free God. It gives us an inkling of him. It is the core of our being-in-God's-image. But it is a freedom that points to God only if it finds its place within the triune framework of truth, love, and freedom.

Another element of Christology is faith in the Second Coming of Christ. For our discussion this means: Who God is, is manifested irrevocably but not completely in Jesus. He still is walking along with us. The space for the togetherness of man and God has still not been paced off and suffered through. At the deepest and most authentic level, nothing more can be changed. Someone who enters into union with Jesus Christ has stepped into the center of God's reality. But in the unfolding of the creature "man" that is yet to come, another thing will be unfolded also: what God did when he assumed this puzzling human nature: he remains the same for all time, and yet he still has to be discovered ever anew until the end of days.

God should be preached as he is reflected in the Law and the Gospel

Who and what God is becomes visible also in and through what he is for us, what he demands of us, and what he gives us. He becomes visible in the mirror of "salvation history". Its stages remain, in one way or another, stages along that path which leads to God. The Old Testament is not simply extinct, merely an era from the past that we preserve out of a simply antiquarian interest. It is still the present—inserted, of course, into the larger whole that came about through Jesus Christ. The Pauline struggle for freedom from the Law has in many sectors of the Christian tradition (contrary to its original significance) overly distorted our view of the unity of the Testaments. The Law is not (as it occasionally seems in Luther, for example) the expression of a God who contradicts himself and appears as his own enemy. Instead, the two together, the Law and the Gospel, reveal the one God.

Even in purely historical terms, one must say that the Gospel includes the Law within itself. It holds fast to the assurance that man is called and challenged by God, that he has a task and a responsibility. That is not set aside but, rather, intensified. The Sermon on the Mount is not just a mirror of human inadequacy; it is intended as a guide for man. Conversely, the Law has evangelical features; for the man of the Old Testament, it is not simply a crushing demand; rather, it is the way, for which he thanks God; the light that is provided for his feet, which helps him to find salvation.

This means: Discourse about God, whether we like it or not, has also to do with moral obligation. Anyone who reduces religion to morality loses something decisive. But someone who erases the moral demand from the Christian image of God has decisively misunderstood precisely *this* God. There may be religions without morality, and there certainly are amoral deities. The hallmark of Israel's God and of the God of Jesus Christ is precisely the fact that he is a moral entity, indeed, the fullness of moral values in person. When the God of Israel is called "Holy", this increasingly signifies in the Bible, as history marches on, not just the characterization of God's particular sphere of power, but, rather, his moral quality as the defender of justice and as the embodiment of moral values. This is not a blindly willful God who unaccountably does what he pleases; the standard that he set for man in the Ten Commandments is at the same time the expression of his own immovable nature. The Decalogue is not just a demand made on man; it is also a revelation of what God is. Moral values are one of the most intense reflections of God: from them one can ascertain who the God of the Bible is. This means, once more, that the Christian faith in God is universal and that its significance for mankind extends beyond the Church: the values-related demands in which he expresses himself apply to all mankind and are comprehensible for all mankind. They have become a decisive educational factor for mankind and depend, now as always, on his form, on his reality. The God whose holiness is morality affects and concerns all men; the universality of the God who is understood in this way manifests itself not least importantly in the fact that he perpetually becomes the destiny of his own people, in which he must, as it were, reveal himself and does so when his people contradict the moral standard. He never sides with this people; he sides with 'the truth itself.

The Gospel does not abolish this revelation of God—the Cross corroborates it with God's fatal commitment to his own Word, and of course it also goes beyond mere demands. God can forgive without destroying the claim of truth and of values because he himself has suffered for them. God can forgive. That does not mean that he has become some grandfatherly figure: how often he has been misinterpreted in that way and literally devalued.[4] Nor does it mean, therefore, that everything has now become a matter of indifference. God does not forgive man contrary to man's impenitence. Only where a longing for forgiveness is alive can there be a response. And the longing for forgiveness has a very real form: one's own readiness to forgive—love.

The fact that in the history of God with man the Law appears first and then the Gospel indicates perhaps that there are still today, again

---

[4] See the passages from Heinrich Heine and Friedrich Nietzsche in Henri de Lubac, *The Drama of Atheist Humanism*, trans. Edith M. Riley, Anne Englund Nash, and Mark Sebanc (San Francisco: Ignatius Press, 1995), 21 and 168, which satirize the metamorphosis of the image of God from the OT to Christianity.

and again, stages in the proclamation of Christianity that are unalterable. Grace cannot be preached to a man whose conscience is silent and who no longer knows the most common moral values. In order for grace to be able to work at all, he must first know that he is a sinner. The first conversion is and remains the conversion to the "Law". And because we stand again and again at the beginning, we need this conversion again and again. Then, to be sure, there is the moment when a second conversion must take place, as we find in the history of the saints from Paul to [John Henry] Newman. The self-satisfied moralist, just like the self-destructive scrupulous person, must learn that there is forgiveness. Scrupulosity, too, is an expression of self-righteousness, especially so: it no longer waits on the Lord, it refuses to believe that I am capable of forgiveness. And thereby it denies in truth the God who suffered for sinners and thereby revealed himself no less than in the thunder and lightning on Sinai.

SIXTH THESIS

The proclamation of God finds guidance in biblical discourse about God, especially in the parables of Jesus, in the experiences of the saints, and in the faith-reflection upon these experiences

Someone might object to all the foregoing theses by asking: Well and good, but in what language can we speak about God? The answer to that today generally runs as follows: "Only in our language, naturally. Our language, though, is that of a worldly world; it is a worldly language. Therefore one can speak about God now only in a worldly fashion." There are many problems involved with such a statement, which cannot be discussed in this article, for instance the question of what "worldly discourse" actually is and, related to this, the observation that language is bound up with a language community and that a language that is available to everyone just does not exist.[5]

But we will leave that. The demand for a worldly discourse about God seems justified, after all, first by the mere fact that we can show

---

[5] This idea is developed in more detail in my article on short formulas of the faith ["Kurzformeln des Glaubens"] in *Internationale katholische Zeitschrift Communio* (1973).

that even the Bible speaks "in a worldly fashion" about God. Recall the parables of the prophets. Isaiah produces for the people a popular song about a bad vineyard (Is 5:1–7). A worldly thing. And that is the way he speaks about God. Yet if we are to avoid stating a half-truth, we must now ask also: *How* does the worldly discourse become a proclamation of God? The popular song becomes a riddle, and this is devised in such a way that it is basically no riddle at all, but, rather, at the conclusion, a cry of indignation, the indictment of a people that enjoyed all of God's benevolence and was a distinct disappointment for him. Nevertheless: a profane story, in which the word "God" does not appear at first, makes visible to men who they are and who God is—the story bursts its framework and points beyond itself. And thereby the framework of this world is exploded, so to speak, and its references beyond itself become an appeal to the listeners.

In Mark 12:1–12, Jesus returns to the core of the vineyard story from Isaiah and relates it in a new way: as a story of the tenants who promote themselves to owners, reject all of their master's attempts at reconciliation, and finally kill his son. And thus in the renovated parable, his own mystery becomes visible, his Passion, which had been hinted at only remotely in the parable of Isaiah. To me it seems important to say that with this passage Jesus enters into the tradition of prophetic discourse about God and then certainly actualizes it anew. Although he is the Son, he does not start from zero; rather, he speaks within the framework of tradition, which he creatively continues and brings to its destination.

With that, it seems to me, two things become clear. The biblical parable tradition points first to the limit of all discourse about God: in every case, speech can only remain a likeness that slowly leads up to the reality from outside, taking man along on the way to this reality, without ever quite being able to reach it. This parable tradition is connected with Israel's historical experience and relevant to it. On the one hand, it takes up the simple human experiences of Israel so as to make them an instrument of discourse about God; on the other hand, however, it refers back again and again to the religious experiences that have already occurred and deepens them.[6]

For us this means that preaching must enlist the whole breadth of

---

[6] The parables of Jesus pose problems for the philosophy of language and systematic theology; on these issues, see E. Biser, *Die Gleichnisse Jesu* (Munich, 1965); Biser, *Theologische Sprachtheorie und Hermeneutik* (Munich, 1970).

reality so as to make it transparent, a window through which to look at God. The continual task of preaching is to spell with the alphabet of the world so that it becomes discourse about God. When one speaks about God in this "worldly" way, it cannot mean simply stopping at the world but, rather, must begin an approach to transcending the world, which cannot be self-contained. It has to mean that the faith classifies the whole of reality under the comprehensive dominion of God.

In this process of recasting worldly discourse into discourse about God, preaching is guided by the discourse that has already been uttered about God. We noted that Jesus himself did not start from zero when he constructed his proclamation but, rather, developed it in a continuation of the prophetic tradition. Analogously, one can say that whereas the New Testament establishes no definitive images, it does present authoritative images, which must be returned to again and again for interpretation and reflection. The real scribe, the one who is truly "learned in Scripture", is distinguished by the fact that he brings forth both new and old (Mt 13:52), that he renews the language and, in so doing, keeps it a coherent language that has not just now been created by him. In this work of refurbishing the old and going on to new possibilities of language, however, it is always a matter of accepting the guidance of biblical imagery and holding fast to the intrinsic range of the biblical image of God, which extends from lion to lamb, from lord to slave. In all this, the preacher today is not alone; he does not stand before a two-thousand-year gulf between him and the Bible—the living interpretation in the experience of the saints is the inner connection that supports him, and without it intimate acquaintance with the Bible degenerates into mere historicism.

SEVENTH THESIS

The proclamation of God must lead to prayer and come from prayer

Any statement about a person one does not know is just theory, second-hand testimony. Only someone who knows God can speak intelligibly about him, and everyone can know him, can become a first-hand witness and herald, for in the togetherness of prayer he gives himself to each one of us to experience.

When I sketched the first outline of these reflections, I happened upon the second reading for the twenty-fifth Sunday in Ordinary Time in Year B of the liturgical readings: James 3:16—4:3. In this passage, James energetically addresses the crisis in the Jewish-Christian Church; we encounter a reflection of the same crisis discernible as the background for Matthew 23 as well. Matthew 23, as is well known, contains a very harsh attack against the class of "teachers" who appear here under various titles: rabbi, *kathegetes* [guide], scribe, and the Pharisees are also addressed. When Matthew sets forth here the words of the Lord so extensively and pointedly (and further develops them), one may see this at the same time as an attack against the spread of a Jewish-Christian rabbinate that plainly considered itself independent and was drifting away from its pastoral responsibility, claiming special privileges and tending to be merely theoretical. Related to this is the admonition in James 3:1: "Let not many of you become teachers"; do not think that theory and doctrine are the main tasks of a Christian. The monumental indictment by James of faith as theory and his appeal for works could also be based precisely on this concrete situation of his congregation.

Interesting also now is the more detailed description given by James of the crisis in the congregation. He contrasts an empty, sterile, and destructive erudition with true wisdom, which is manifested in a person's way of life, work, and goodness. But the cleverness of those whom he is addressing leads, not to these attitudes, but rather to disorder (3:13ff.). James portrays this disorder and conflict very dramatically: Among you there are those who are destroying themselves; among you jealousy prevails; among you wars are being waged. This does not mean to say that they have been killing each other but, rather, that they have "been the death of" each other, as we would say today, ridiculed the other and tried to dismiss him. The same is meant by "wars". They are fighting; one tries to push the other aside and to silence him.

But now James asks: Why is that so? He finds two main reasons. The one is: You are slaves of your "passions" (4:1). You are subject to the dictatorship of your impulses, your covetousness, your self-seeking. Each one wants only himself. Besides that there is the second reason: This is so because you do not pray (4:2b). Certainly prayers are said among them, too; James admits it in the very next verse (4:3). But this prayer is such that it cannot really be described as praying. This

mention of the usual prayers there does not invalidate the first statement but rather corroborates it. In effect, to tell the truth: you do not
pray. According to James, everything would look different if, instead
of speaking with and against each other in a cold war, the congregation
would speak together to God.[7]

That, however, is a decisive statement. Discourse about God loses
its unifying power and becomes divisive, empty theory when it no
longer proceeds from the experiential context of living conversation
with God. Without prayer, preaching dries up by itself.

[7] On this whole subject, see the penetrating interpretation of the text in F. Mußner, *Der Jakobusbrief* (Freiburg, 1964), 157–80.

7. Praying in Our Time

Preliminary Reflection: World View and Prayer

It is difficult for us to pray. Prayer does not fit into our theory of life and our understanding of reality. We have come to question its meaningfulness and its intrinsic validity. After all, is it not part of a magical and animistic understanding of nature that we simply can no longer share? This seems to be the case most conspicuously with those prayers that refer directly to worldly realities: the procession through the meadows in a rural parish, the blessing of the weather that implores protection from storms and asks for sunshine, rain, and fruitfulness. That seems to make sense only if one imagines that the world is guided by animated causes that dole out wind and storm, rain and sun, and hence can be won over by talking to them, or become angry when neglected. But once the direct mechanical causal connection is recognized, we attack the problem with rational methods: with all that science has to offer so as to make life safe. And so for today's way of thinking, prayer seems not only unproductive and ineffective, but a virtual flight from reality: it replaces world-changing action with a passive waiting on otherworldly powers. In this connection, critics often point to the symbolic scene in Bertolt Brecht's *Mother Courage*, in which the peasants helplessly invoke a silent God with their prayers, while the mute girl Kattrin rescues the town of Halle by awakening the watchmen with her drumming.[1] Indeed, this appears to be a snapshot of the present-day attitude toward prayer: it is not praying for otherworldly help that seems appropriate for man but, rather, caring for the needs of this world. Consequently, only humanitarian and humanizing activity is thought to be real worship; only man's service to his fellowman is true religion. At best, prayer could be allowed to continue in modified

---

Translated by Michael J. Miller.

[1] Bertolt Brecht, *Mother Courage and Her Children*, trans. John Willett (London: Methuen, 1980).

form as recollection and preparation for action. In the background, at the same time, there is a deliberate concentration of thought and deed on this world which is at our disposal, whereas God's world, the "eschaton", is rejected as something foreign to reality and alienating.

Now one could immediately start asking all sorts of questions here: What is authentically human, and when is a man humane, when is the world humanized? When have you succeeded in making someone happy, in freeing him from misery, and so on? But let us return to our point of departure, and then automatically we will be led finally to these questions as well. The real starting point of the line of thinking developed above is, after all, the notion that prayer is meaningless in our world view because it has become ineffective, and it has become ineffective because we know how the world works: it is not animistic but mechanical. But now we must ask a heretical question: Was animism (that is, the doctrine that the world is guided by animated causes) really *entirely* false? Or have we perhaps gone now to the opposite extreme by thinking *only* in mechanical terms? Is man, for example, nothing? As an organic whole, as a living, thinking, feeling, perceiving nature, does he not add a new factor to the world by which something novel happens in it? Even more concretely: Can what is specifically human be dismissed as inconsequential? Are trust and mistrust, then, fear and hope, egotism and love not powers that change the world? Can love really do nothing, or is it a power that builds up the world, because it creates intuition, looking, and listening and thus releases forces that transform the world? But if it is true that there is a spiritual causality, that love is a reality and therefore effective, why should the dialogue with love that holds the world together not be able to change man and the world with him? Through such reflections, however, it becomes evident that in saying Yes or No to prayer, one in fact decides on a theory of life and does not merely perform or omit an incidental individual act. In the question of prayer to which these reflections are devoted, the question of God and, thus, of our basic understanding of reality as a whole is always and necessarily dealt with as well. Consequently, the decision to pray has a very comprehensive character: praying means recognizing that there is a creative love by which everyone lives and which is accessible to everyone. A creative love from which the world comes and which is contemporary to every individual because it is eternal.

In this regard, the talk about the "other world", as we often call

God's world, conceals the heart of the matter instead of revealing it. For this all too easily leads to the notion of a second spatial world to which the Christian relates, to the detriment of concrete reality. The real alternative is different, as the reflections thus far may already have shown: it lies in the choice between a strictly mechanistic and a personal world view. If the world is just a system of mechanical processes, one can be active and reactive within it only by strike and counterstrike, by thrust and counterthrust. If, on the other hand, the foundation of the world is spirit (that is, looking and loving, hearing and loving), then man as a spirit (that is, as a being that likewise looks, hears, and loves) is related to this prior foundation, and the real axis of the world passes through the dialogue between the two. Prayer, then, is not a sport that one can take or leave but, rather, the center of human self-realization: the recognition, and indeed the realization of the recognition of the fact that man is not alone but, rather, exists only while being watched and loved and that he must actively accept this being-watched, this inability of his existence to be concealed or isolated, if he is to avoid running aground in self-contradiction, cut off from his own roots. This essential inability to be alone on the part of man, this radical and total openness and exposure of his existence, simultaneously becomes his real foundation, which is why he must live with unlocked and unblocked doors, so to speak, and with reference to others. Now at the same time this already indicates the initial standards for correct, Christian, Christ-like prayer, from which basic statements about the eschatological existence of the Christian must follow as well. But let us remain for the moment at the concrete level by simply and pragmatically asking: What actually happens in prayer?

The Prayer of Petition as the Starting Point for the Movement of Prayer

If we ask this, we run into a second barrier, which in many respects explains the first. Our crisis in prayer is fundamental, yes, but it is also simply practical: we do not quite know how it is done, and perhaps all the great fundamental difficulties are after all just an ideological super-structure that is supposed to justify this practical inability of ours to cope with prayer. Because we are unable to do it, we invent a theory that tells us that we could not have been able to do it in the first place, because it no longer works at all and makes no sense any more. At whichever end we start, we run into difficulties: the prayer of petition, now, seems to be really just a misunderstanding of our self and God —ultimately God is not our servant, the alibi for our egotism and our laziness, and in the final analysis we should do our own work ourselves. But we are much less successful at the prayer of praise and adoration, and it basically seems to us a bit silly: What can it possibly matter in God's sight when we stammer some praise of him that is probably more like a caricature; would we not praise him better by trying to be such that something of the "image of God" becomes recognizable in us? And with that we have arrived again at the starting point.

How should we begin, then, to find a doorway? Now man is a disappointing, failing being, who again and again finds that he is helpless, and the most characteristic thing about him is precisely the cry of distress, the SOS call for help. And so the history of prayer begins, not just in the Old Testament, with the cry, "O LORD . . . we beg you!" (Ps 118:25, cf. Num 12:13, and 2 Sam 15:31), with this protest against affliction, with lament and struggle for God; yet the prayer that Jesus gave as the model for all prayer when he was asked, "Lord, teach us to pray" is a prayer of petition, also. And again: the Mass begins with the *Kyrie eleison*, the cry of the blind man on the road leading from Jericho to Jerusalem, who hears that Jesus of Nazareth is passing by (Mk 10:47). By no means should we imagine that we are too good to place our existence before God as it is; its fundamental situation is just that of needing help, the necessity of having a chance to express ourselves, to entrust ourselves, to beg. "Man is a beggar before God", says Augustine, and it is still true today. Why, then, do we lock ourselves up so defiantly in a self-sufficiency that does not even exist? Why do we hide behind the gloomy mask of self-mastery and thereby cramp and repress the essential thing, precisely this fundamental dependence of man upon being able to call, to speak, to beg: it is the most fundamental repression of our decade and the core of so many neuroses: the repressed center. Although Freud described religion as the universal neurosis, as a physician, C. G. Jung was obliged to make the diagnosis that the repression of God was the core of all neuroses and that the cure could come about only through the release of that tension.[2]

---

[2] C. G. Jung, "Psychoanalysis and the Cure of Souls", *The Collected Works of C. G. Jung*, vol. 11 (Princeton, Princeton University Press, 1968).

Really, then, why not start off with *Kyrie eleison*—the blind beggar at the side of the road on which we hear that Jesus will pass by? Why not really lay our lives before him, including our inability to believe and to pray? Even in doing precisely that, worship is immediately rendered: if we really say *Kyrie eleison*, if we really cry to God out of the depths of our misery, this is a recognition of what we are and what he is; it is worshipping his glory. For in doing that we say, honestly, "Look at me, God, I am nothing, but You are everything; I am full of misery, but You are rich enough to heal all the misery in the world; I am sinful and wicked, but You are full of extravagant love. You do not love as men do, who love only those who are sympathetic to them; You also love the beggar in rags, the prodigal son. You do not love because *we* are good but, rather, because *You* are good. . . ."

To petition God really means nothing other than to place ourselves entirely in God's hands. To petition God means humbly to acknowledge God's surpassing glory and to let him have that glory without wanting to copy it. A beggar who behaves as though he were a rich man who is defiant and proud is a stupid, ridiculous figure. A man who acts as though he does not need God's gifts, is no less so: all the knowledge in the world about causality in nature cannot change this fundamental fact one bit. Nature does not run as it must; rather, it runs as God wills. A man who is no longer capable of petitioning God cannot truly live: he becomes a caricature of himself, a beggar who disguises himself in vain as a millionaire.

And so, I think, this daily entrusting of ourselves to God should be the very simple and human starting point of our prayer. If we do that, then this effort automatically leads beyond itself and takes a step forward. Again, perhaps we can illustrate the process involved in the liturgy of the Mass: it begins with the threefold *Kyrie*, the remnant of petitions that were supposed to and should reflect the need of the day, the need of everyone. It then gathers the whole thing into the *Oremus* ["let us pray"] of the priest and in the "collects" [proper prayers of petition], which touch upon the contingent features of the day, the contingent features of the individual—prayers that, as it were, sift through the multiplicity of private petitions and begging and sort out the good fish from the bad fish in that great net and thus shape the common prayer of the congregation: the things about which, indeed, everyone can pray and whereby they are at the same time directed toward what is authentic, above and beyond their contingent and momentary concerns.

The Purification of Petition

This suggests a fundamental state of affairs: speaking with God must also be a process taking place in us and for us—a process in the literal sense, so that in it we go forward, advance toward God, and walk away from ourselves. By taking what oppresses us, what entangles us in anxiety, diminishes our freedom, and makes us unhappy . . . , by neither simply putting our wishes, desires, intentions, and longings into action nor merely carrying them around inside of us, but, rather, by turning it all into prayer and expressing and discussing it in the presence of God, it is held up to a standard that scrutinizes, rectifies, and purifies it. A standard that forces us to bid farewell to some things or at least to let go of them. There is an ancient, well-known story in which the senselessness of the prayer of petition was supposed to be proved even within the context of pagan antiquity. The mother of two daughters first visits one of them, who asks her to pray to Zeus for rain so that her flowers will grow. Then she calls on the other daughter, who implores her to pray for sunshine because she is planning a journey. Now what is the unfortunate mother supposed to say to Zeus? After all, he cannot grant both things at the same time. . . . Anyone who comes before God with such a request must in fact learn at the same time interiorly to place his wish, his will on a par with that of the other, because looking to God means looking to the Father of all, in whom all requests are united. Someone who prays in this way perhaps does not necessarily have to give up *this* wish, but he must *let go* of it and, thereby, let *himself* go so as to allow himself to be changed in the process. In this way, of course, prayer is not just a psychotherapeutical process, the transformation of the subject, but precisely because it is not only that, it is that also: striving for God, when it is done in earnest and with the "divine God" in mind, can always be at the same time a struggle with ourselves, striving to let our "self" go and to turn to God.

The transformation of our desire and, thus, of our self through this metamorphosis in prayer becomes even clearer when praying is done quite consciously as praying with Christ, in Christ's name, as Christian prayer. Here a look at Jesus' farewell discourse can help our progress. Prayer offered in the name of Jesus has an unconditional promise of being heard. Anything is granted to this prayer (Jn 16:23f.; cf. Lk 11:9, 13). Yet part of this promise is the fact that it is made while facing the Cross and, therefore, at the moment when, humanly speaking, everything is lost. Prayer in Jesus' name is a prayer that faces and presupposes the Cross. The promise that anything will be granted paradoxically goes together with total refusal: the cup does *not* pass. But what is this "anything" that seems at the same time to be a complete nothing? Both John and Luke have given the contents of it a precise name: in Luke (11:13) it is the Holy Spirit: the Gift of God is God himself. Anyone who asks God for less is asking him for too little. He, his Holy Spirit, is the divine Gift, the bread that he gives as his "all" and in which everything is given. In John, the all-encompassing gift is called "joy". Only the man who has left "everything", namely, himself, can find everything, namely, the fullness of indestructible joy. Only the person who begins to leave aside the apparent "everything" of his private wishes can learn at all what "everything" really is for a man.

But let us go back again, for we had boldly anticipated an end of a process that we all know only in terms of its beginning. At this point, that is, at the place where prayer becomes recognizable as transformation and purification of our will from desire into love, from egotism into a willingness to serve, the meaning of set prayers becomes manifest also. They are intended, not just as an aid to the weakness of our imagination, to the inability of our speech and thought—although they are that, too—but rather, by involving us in the prayer of another person, they serve that process of expropriation which true prayer must be by nature. By making us enter into the prayer of another, they make our praying objective, they draw us away from ourselves and, at the same time, set standards, for these petitions to God are demands on ourselves: to take up these petitions, to enter into them, to accept them as our true petitions. The petitions of the Our Father are signposts: unless there is a transformation of our "self", they cannot become *our* petitions. Probably this comes to mind most immediately, again and again, in the fifth petition: Forgive as we have forgiven. How often we should fall silent and blush at this petition! But actually the same thing is no less true of the other petitions. For whom is the petition about God's name, that defiled and disfigured name, a personal concern? And one could continue in this way down to the last two petitions. The next-to-last ("lead us not into temptation") always reminds me of Augustine's admission in the *Confessions* that even in his stormy, stressful years, he certainly did pray for chastity, but always with the thought in the back of his mind: "Please do not give it to me right away." And then the last petition: Deliver us from evil, from *malum*. What is actually bad, "evil" for us? And what is the salutary need that must remain? Perhaps the truth in this regard is often exactly the opposite of what we wish for. What is pleasant to us can be from the Evil One, and what causes us pain can be for our salvation. But other prayers, too, can become standards here, train us, force us to examine our conscience, and purify us. I will mention only the prayer of Saint Nicholas von Flüe, which is so great in its simplicity: "My Lord and my God, take from me everything that distances me from you. . . . Give me everything that brings me closer to you" [CCC 226]. Yet even repeating this prayer honestly presupposes quite a purification of our wishes!

The Transition to Adoration and the Eschatological Character of Prayer

To the extent in which we give ourselves over to this process of expropriation which praying logically demands, we become free: free from our "self" and, thus, truly available to be used by God for others. To that extent, our prayer will also become adoration, and adoration will become comprehensible to us and be something other than the silly parroting of praises that cannot in fact give God glory. Let us look once again at the liturgy of the Mass. Between the cry for help in the *Kyrie* and the expropriating gathering thereof into the common *Oremus* stands the *Gloria* with this peculiar sentence: "We give you thanks for your great glory." At first glance this seems to be a meaningless exaggeration: thanking God, not for what he is for us and for what he has given us, but rather for what he himself is. Giving thanks for the fact that he is and for the way he is. And yet such a statement expresses the real essence of love and its true clear-sightedness: If love is the movement of human existence arriving at its goal, then the glance that love creates is also true insight. But love arrives at its goal only when

I love someone, no longer for the sake of something, but for his own sake. When I am happy, no longer about what I get from someone, but rather about what that person is and when I can even sense this independently of my own receiving of this, his "existing": when I am simply happy that the other is there, regardless of what I get from it. "It is good that you exist"—only when one can say this is one loving.[3]

Francis Xavier magnificently formulated this type of discovering God in prayer in his well-known prayer[4] (which is astonishingly similar to Indian bhakti devotion): "O God, I love you, not because you can give me heaven or condemn me to hell, but simply because you are my God. I love you, not for your heaven's sake, but because you are you. That is enough." In my opinion, we can grasp here what the saying from the farewell discourse means: "In that day you will ask nothing of me" (Jn 16:23). Bultmann comments that this depicts "the eschatological existence". That is right. But how pale and unreal remains our notion of what that is. It occurs in prayer that remains faithful to its direction: existence without asking, which has forgotten itself for the Thou of God. Which no longer asks about itself. And thus is really free "to love the other as myself". . . . In this respect, these three ways— prayer, love of God, and love of neighbor—prove at their destination to be completely identical. Adoration is freedom sprung from the root of true freedom: the freedom from oneself. And therein it is "salvation", "happiness", or, as John calls it, "joy", the absolute answer to prayer. And in just that way it is total availability, letting go so as to serve however God may use me.

No doubt, that is an end that no one ever possesses completely, for then one would really be in the "eschaton". Indeed, what the "eschaton" is and what it is like must be defined precisely in terms of this and only in terms of this. But, on the other hand, neither is it just an end that is floating about somewhere like a distant *fata morgana*; rather, it is an end that constantly extends into the way itself and toward which we are constantly reaching out. Thus prayer is ultimately training for the eschaton and, at the same time, its anticipation, the way in which

---

[3] See Josef Pieper, *About Love* (Chicago: Franciscan Herald Press, 1974), esp. 57ff.

[4] On this subject, see F. Rauhut, "Gebet der vollkommenen Gottesliebe", in *GuL* 25 (1952): 344–64. On the related Indian prayers, see Theodor Ohm, *Die Liebe zu Gott in den nichtchristlichen Religionen* (Freiburg, 1950), 218–35.

it is supposed to become the decisive force of our present day: promise as reality here and now. It is an approach to the attitude that the Letter to the Hebrews describes when it says that upon his entrance into the cosmos Christ spoke the words, "Sacrifices and offerings you have not desired, but a body have you prepared for me. . . . Behold, I have come to do your will, O God" (Heb 10:5, 7). Christ's Incarnation is described here as a prayerful process of handing over his own will to the universal will of God. And this act of comprehensive willingness to serve is becoming-flesh, the preparation of a body as the instrument of service. And conversely, this becoming-flesh, that is, the fact that his whole existence is at God's disposal, is henceforth the sacrifice to God par excellence and the comprehensive locus of all prayer. Christian prayer occurs at this place, which is indicated by the words, "a body have you prepared for me." It is entering into this act of Incarnation, placing the "body", that is, earthly existence, at the disposal of the universal will of God in him who is the expression of this will. In this movement, and in the measure in which it perfects this movement, it is prayer in Jesus' name: participation in the Incarnation and, thus, participation in the "eschaton". For the eschaton is ultimately no one and nothing other than the glorified Christ as the abode of a new humanity: He is the true "land" of the future, to which all promises lead.

Concluding Remark: The Prayer of the Mute

But let us return again to very concrete statements. In concluding these reflections, I would like to tell a story that leads right back again to our situation of questioning, speechlessness, and problems and yet perhaps can suggest once more its openness and its possibilities. Edmond Michelet, in his book *Freedom Road*, which describes the first weeks after his arrest as a member of the French Resistance during World War II, narrates the following incident. In the transit camp where they were stationed for a time on the way to Dachau, two young Jewish secondary school students had also been interned, one of whom declared himself proudly to be a freethinker. A few days later during drill practice, the two young Jews were mistreated by the guard in such a way that when it was over they were thought dead and carried back into the camp. The mood in the room that night was gloomy; the prisoners tried to cheer each other up by taking turns reciting a poem by memory.

> We were already sleepy, when in the middle of the night, out of the darkness, we heard a voice say, "But I have a poem to recite, too." Suddenly we no longer wanted to sleep; we were speechless. It was the voice of our young freethinker-Jew from the previous night, whom we all thought dead.
> "So," he continued, "'The Virgin Mary at Noon', by Paul Claudel." And he began slowly, emphasizing each verse:

> > It is noon. I see the church open and am drawn in.
> > O Mother of Jesus Christ, I do not come to pray,
> > I have nothing to offer you and nothing to ask of you.
> > I come, O Mother, only to look at you,
> > to see you, to weep for joy, knowing
> > that I am your child and that you are there!

Michelet continues:

> One ought not to be presumptuous. I cannot say, therefore, whether I will get to heaven someday, but I have the feeling that, if this greatest of all graces is granted to me, I will surely find my little blue-eyed freethinker-Jew from Camp Neue Breem there, who fell asleep with the words of Paul Claudel on his lips. . . .[5]

The speechlessness of a human being who is able to say nothing more to God can become a prayer, if this very speechlessness is brought before the God who listens. It can amount to more than all-too-garrulous and facile formulas that are empty and carry within them nothing of the Exodus of true praying. There is no human situation that cannot become prayer, that would not be immediately present to God. We must only open the door and grasp the hand that is always offered to us. In some way or another, we all share more or less in the speechlessness of our generation when facing God. And that is a good thing, because precisely in this way, through us and through our efforts, this

---

[5] Edmond Michelet, *Die Freiheitsstraße* (Stuttgart, n. d.; original French edition, 1955), 44 ff. The full text of the hymn can be found in Paul Claudel, *Oeuvre Poétique* (Paris: Gallimard, 1967), 539–41.

speechlessness can come to share in the praying of all centuries, can become a part of it. If we are capable of nothing but being silent before God, let us do it, then, and we will see that this silence changes and that it changes us and changes the times. By having time for God, by making our time God's time and thus opening up his time—the "eschaton"—in doing so, we serve mankind: precisely in this way. We should not allow ourselves to be led astray by those who have no time, who use all time only as their time: this is the task that is set before us Christians in this hour of history and that we should calmly and patiently venture to undertake.

CHRIST

8. Theses for Christology

1. The starting point for Christology in the New Testament is the fact of the Resurrection of Jesus Christ from the dead: The Resurrection is God's way of publicly taking the side of Jesus in the proceedings that Jews and Gentiles had organized against him. God's defense of him confirms:

   a. his interpretation of the Old Testament in opposition to political messianism and to apocalyptic thinking pure and simple; and

   b. the claim to divinity on account of which he had been condemned to death.

2. The Resurrection thus makes it possible to interpret the crucifixion of Jesus in terms of the Old Testament concept of the suffering just man that finds its climactic expressions in Psalm 22 (21) and Isaiah 53. This in turn brings in the idea of representation and, as the words of Jesus at the Last Supper indicate, a continuity with the sacrificial tradition of Israel, a tradition that is here linked to Isaiah 53 and reinterpreted in terms of martyrdom: Jesus is the true lamb of sacrifice, the covenant sacrifice in which the deepest meaning of all Old Testament liturgies is fulfilled. Thus the way is cleared for the concept of redemption and for the essential significance of the Christian liturgy.

3. The Resurrection of Jesus is the basis of his abiding lordship. This assertion has two consequences:

   a. The Resurrection of Jesus confirms the belief in a general resurrection that had not yet become a clear part of Israel's creed, and thus

---

Translated by Matthew J. O'Connell.

it provides the basis for the specifically Christian eschatological hope.

b. God's defense of Jesus against the official interpretation of the Old Testament as given by the competent Jewish authorities makes possible in principle that freedom from the letter of the Law that will lead to the Church of the Gentiles.

4. The claim to divinity that the Resurrection of Jesus confirms finds expression in the image of Jesus sitting at the Father's right hand. As a result of the claim, application is made to Jesus of the Old Testament messianic promises that take pointed form in such texts as Psalm 2:7: "You are my son, today I have begotten you." The initially numerous and varied ways of expressing the divinity of Jesus evidently yield priority, as time goes on, to the concepts "Christ" (Messiah) and "Son". These were the ones that corresponded best to the Old Testament promises and to the claim of the historical Jesus as remembered by the community.

5. Constitutive for the faith of the growing Church was the consciousness that in this interpretation of the person of Jesus it was not posthumously bestowing a theological transfiguration upon a teacher in Israel but was, rather, interpreting the words and work of Jesus in an objectively correct way. Consequently, the remembrance and retention of the words of Jesus and of the course of his life, especially his Passion, were from the beginning an essential factor in the formation of Christian tradition and in the norms applied to it. The identity of the earthly with the risen Jesus is fundamental to the faith of the community and rules out any later separation of the historical from the kerygmatic Jesus.

6. The primary function of the formula "You are my son, today I have begotten you" is to interpret the event of the Resurrection; it says, that is, that the Resurrection is the elevation of Jesus to his throne, the proclamation of his kingship and sonship. But since the Resurrection was at the same time seen to be essentially a confirmation of Jesus' claim to divinity, a claim for which he had to undergo death on the Cross (Thesis 1b), it became evident that the title of Son must in principle be applicable to him even before the Resurrection and that it is a valid description of what Jesus was.

7. The implications of all this are brought out with full clarity in the Gospel of John. Here Jesus does not simply proclaim the Word of God; he is himself God's Word in the whole of his existence. In him God acts as a human being. Consequently, it now becomes fully clear that in Jesus two lines of Old Testament promise and expectation converge: the promise of a Savior who is of David's lineage and a directly theological promise that sees God himself as the ultimate salvation of Israel. At the same time, Jesus' claim to divinity, as handed down in the Synoptic Gospels, here acquires its full context; the words and actions of Jesus in which he in fact presents himself as God become intelligible.

8. Given the increasing reflection on the presuppositions of the Easter event in the person of the earthly Jesus, it is understandable that the traditions regarding the birth and childhood of Jesus should become part of the official tradition of the Church. The great prophets were called by God "from their mother's womb", but Jesus, who is superior to the prophets, was actually conceived by the power of that Spirit who had called the prophets. This already makes it clear that his consciousness of divine status is based, not on a subsequent call, but on what he is from the very beginning.

9. While the Gospel tradition reports the normative words and actions of Jesus, the professions of faith elaborated by the growing Church endeavor to single out the central reference points of the tradition. The process of developing christological creeds begins with the confessions of faith associated with the first Easter; it reaches a certain completion at the Council of Chalcedon. Two main assertions of this Council are to be emphasized:

   a. Out of all the christological titles expressing dignity and rank, which were used from the beginning in the effort to verbalize the mystery of Christ, the Council chooses as the most normative and comprehensive the designation "Son of God". This title by now has behind it the whole weight of belief in the Trinity; it fits in, too, with the central place of John's Gospel in thinking on Christology.

   b. In speaking of two natures and one person, the Council is attempting to bring out the paradoxical character of the title "Son". Jesus is a man and possesses human nature in the fullest sense. At the same time, he is one with God, not simply by reason of his conscious dedication to the Lord, but by reason of his very being. As Son of God, he is just as truly God as he is truly man.

10. The concept of redemption thus acquires its ultimate theological depth. The being of man is incorporated into the being of God. But this ontological assertion has meaning only if there is presupposed the concrete, real, loving human reality of Jesus in whose death the being of man is concretely opened to God and given over into the possession of God.

9. What Does Jesus Christ Mean to Me?

To begin with, I might give this question an answer that is more theoretical in kind: I believe that Jesus Christ enables me to have some idea of what God is and what man is. God is not simply the bottomless abyss or infinite height that sustains all things but never itself enters the sphere of the finite. God is not simply infinite distance; he is also infinite nearness. One can confide in him and speak to him: he hears and sees and loves. Although he is not within time, he has time: even for me. He expresses himself in the man Jesus, although not exhaustively, since Jesus, though one with him, nevertheless addresses him as "Father". God remains the One who is infinitely more than all visible things. Only in the lonely prayer of Jesus, only in Jesus' addressing him as "Father", is he to be known. At the same time, however, he draws very close to us in this utterance of the name "Father".

What about the insight into man? Man is such that he cannot stand the person who is wholly good, truly upright, truly loving, the person who does evil to no one. It seems that in this world only momentarily is trust met with trust, justice with justice, love with love. The person who exemplifies all these virtues quickly becomes insupportable to others. People will crucify anyone who is really and fully human. Such is man. And such am I—*that* is the terrifying insight that comes to me from the crucified Christ. Along with this insight, however, goes another: Man is the creature who is capable of being an expression of God himself. Man is so made that God can enter into union with him. Man, who seems at first sight to be a kind of unfortunate monster produced by evolution, at the same time represents the highest possibility the created order can attain. And this possibility becomes a reality, even if it be amid the saddest kind of failure on the part of the human race.

I interrupt here to note that these statements of principle have a

---

Translated by Matthew J. O'Connell.

real-life basis, namely, the way that Jesus Christ entered into my life. I encountered him initially, not in literature or philosophy, but in the faith of the Church. This means that from the beginning I knew him, not as a great figure of the past (like Plato or Thomas Aquinas), but as someone who is alive and at work today, someone whom people can encounter today. It means, above all, that I have come to know him within the history of the faith that has its origin in him and according to the vision of faith that received its most enduring formulation at the Council of Chalcedon. In my view, Chalcedon represents the boldest and most sublime simplification of the complex and many-layered data of tradition to a single central fact that is the basis of everything else: Son of God, possessed of the same nature as God *and* of the same nature as we have. In contrast to the many other approaches that have been attempted in the course of history, Chalcedon interpreted Jesus theologically. I regard this as the only interpretation that can do justice to the whole range of tradition and sustain the full impact of the phenomenon itself. All other interpretations become too narrow at some point; every other conception embraces only one part of the reality and excludes another. Here and here alone does the whole of the reality disclose itself.

In the last analysis, everything else follows from this principle. First of all, the fact that for me Jesus and the Church are not separable, any more than they are to be simply identified with each other. Jesus is always infinitely more than the Church. It did not take the recent Council to tell us that as Lord of the Church Jesus also remains her standard. I have always experienced this truth as both a consolation and a challenge. It is a consolation because we have always known that the scrupulosity of the rubricist and the legalist finds no echo in him and in the limitless magnanimity of spirit that blows like a vigorous breeze from the words of the Gospels and brings all excessive reverence for the letter of the law down like a house of cards. We have always known that intimacy with him is as independent of the ecclesiastical rank a person has as it is of knowledge about juridical and historical niceties. This has made it possible for me to approach externals in a corresponding spirit of tranquility. In this respect, I have always experienced the person of Jesus as liberating and a source of optimism. On the other hand, I have never been able to forget that in many respects he requires much more than the Church dares to require and that his radical words call for radical decisions of the kind Anthony, the Desert Father, or Francis of Assisi made when they took the Gospel in a fully literal way. If we do not accept the Gospel in this manner, then we have already taken refuge in casuistry, and we remain afflicted by a gnawing feeling of uneasiness, by the knowledge that like the rich young man we have turned away when we should have taken the Gospel seriously.

I have said that the acceptance of Jesus Christ within the Church in no way neutralizes the personal impact that repeatedly rouses us and summons us to go beyond inherited ecclesial forms. Now, as I reflect further, I become conscious of another, very similar point. Like the first, it may seem a paradox, but in fact both follow a profound internal logic. The fact that I have learned to know and see Jesus Christ by means of Chalcedon's interpretation of him does not mean that I must now eliminate part of the tradition on the grounds that it seems insufficiently divine and therefore cannot be harmonized with what the dogma asserts. The opposite is the case: ecclesiastical tradition, in which the historical movement founded by Jesus has remained vitally alive down to our own day, gives me at the same time a trust in biblical tradition. I credit biblical tradition with greater truthfulness than I do the attempts to reconstruct a chemically pure historical Jesus from the test tube of historical reason. I trust the tradition in its entirety. And the more reconstructions I see come and go, the more I feel confirmed in my trust. It becomes increasingly clear to me that the interpretation given by Chalcedon is the only one that does not have to interpret anything away but is able to include everything. Any other interpretation must eliminate larger or smaller parts of the historical data in the name of its supposedly superior rational insights. But the authority that compels such deletions is only the authority of a particular way of thinking whose historical limitations can often be clearly shown. In the face of such partial authorities, the vital power of the tradition carries incomparably greater weight with me. For this reason, I do not regard the dispute about the *ipsissima vox*, or the actual words Jesus spoke, as very important. I know that the Jesus of the Gospels is the real Jesus and that I can entrust myself to him with far greater security than I can to the most learned reconstructions; he will outlast them all. The Gospel tradition, with its great breadth and its range of tone, tells me who Jesus was and is. In it he is always present to be heard and seen anew.

In conclusion, I must add that the person who believes with the Church encounters Jesus directly in prayer and in the sacraments—especially in the Eucharist. But anyone who starts talking about prayer and the sacraments quickly realizes that the early Church's "discipline of the secret" was far more than a temporary application of a custom taken over from pagan religions. In its essence, that discipline points to a realm that can find meaningful expression only in the experience that faith makes possible.

10. Following Christ

The most famous devotional book in Christendom and, next to the Bible, the one with the widest readership bears the name *The Imitation of Christ*, or, to use a more scriptural turn of phrase, *The Following of Christ*. By now other best sellers have crowded this one into the background, and even the Christian who reads it today must admit that it reflects the spirit of a bygone age that was deeply fearful of the world, so much so that it cannot give a complete picture of the Christian mission, even though the spirit of inwardness, simplicity, and silence that breathes through it appeals to us in this stressful, turbulent century.

In any case, whatever may be the judgment passed on this famous but controversial book that comes to us from the twilight years of the Middle Ages, it suggests a question that remains valid and needs to be asked anew: What does "the following of Christ" really mean? Is this following a real possibility at all for contemporary man? Or is it perhaps *the only* way of being and becoming man, so that the Christian not only could maintain, with a little effort, that it is still possible today to live a meaningful life as a Christian, but would in fact also be able to offer *the* decisive possibility of being human, in which the real nature of the enigma that is man comes to light in the first place.

I.

Let us go back to our first question: What does "the following of Christ" mean? Originally, the phrase had a very simple and nontheoretical meaning. In plain terms, it meant that individuals decided to abandon their profession or trade, their mundane affairs, and the everyday life they had lived until then and, instead, to walk with Jesus. In other words, it meant a new calling, that of the disciple, whose life

Translated by Matthew J. O'Connell.

now consisted in walking with the Master and completely trusting in his guidance.

"Following", in this sense, is something quite external but at the same time something very interior as well. Something external: an actual walking behind Jesus in his travels through Palestine. Something interior: a new direction for one's life, which no longer has business, the earning of a livelihood, and one's own wishes and ideas as its central points of reference but is surrendered to the will of another, so that being with him and being at his disposal are now the really important content of a human existence.

A little scene involving Jesus and Peter makes very clear the renunciation of one's own concerns, the turning from self that this following entails. Shortly after the multiplication of the loaves, which seems to be a decisive turning point in his public ministry, Jesus makes known to his disciples for the first time the dark mystery of his coming Passion. He is not to be the brilliant Messiah they must have hoped for when they saw the multiplication of the loaves, wherein he seemed at last to be revealing himself as the new Moses who had power to repeat the miracle of the manna. No, he would instead be covered by the dark shadows of the Cross; he would suffer much and finally be killed. "And Peter took him, and began to rebuke him", says the Gospel. "But turning and seeing his disciples, he rebuked Peter, and said, 'Get behind me, Satan! For you are not on the side of God, but of men'" (Mk 8:32–33).

Peter had attempted, as it were, to stop following and to take the lead, determining for himself which way to walk. But he is uncompromisingly put back in his place: Get behind me! To follow really means to go behind, to move in the direction prescribed, even if this direction is completely contrary to one's own wishes. Precisely because the word "follow" is meant so literally, it affects the innermost depths of man.

In this light, we can already understand to some extent what is meant when the calling of the disciples and, thus, the essence of discipleship are depicted in the Gospels in a few stereotyped words of Jesus: "Follow me!" These words contain, first of all, a summons to give up a previous occupation. At a deeper level, however, they are a summons to give up one's very self in order to live entirely for him who, for his part, willed to live entirely for the word of God: so much so that later reflection could acknowledge him as the incarnate Word of God himself.

In the course of Jesus' life, the meaning of "following" becomes more specific and concrete. His message, in which he set forth for his listeners the full magnitude of God's claim but also the full breadth of the divine mercy, had brought him into conflict with Israelite official-dom. He was excommunicated from the synagogue, and his execution was a foregone conclusion. In this situation, "walking with Jesus" ac-quires a new tonality that found expression in the saying: "If any man would come after me, let him deny himself and take up his cross and follow me" (Mk 8:34).

This saying, too, has originally a very realistic meaning: Anyone who joins Jesus enters the company of an outcast and must be prepared to be condemned as Jesus was and to end up on the Cross. This is why early Christians understood martyrdom as a way of following Christ and even regarded the martyr as the one who completely fulfilled the meaning of "following", that is, who gave up his very self in witness to the Word.

II.

Perhaps these reflections on the sources seem at first glance more likely to discourage us than to provide us with real guidance. In any case, the message of the following of Christ seems further removed from us now than it was when we began! After all, it is no longer possible for us to walk after Jesus the man, and we no longer think of martyrdom as the normal crown of Christian existence, so that the idea of preparing ourselves for martyrdom seems rather theoretical, apart from the many other questions that suggest themselves in this context.

If we look more closely, however, it soon becomes clear that the out-ward historical forms that the following of Jesus assumed at first are not the decisive thing. The decisive thing is rather the interior existen-tial transformation for which any outward circumstances and activities are only a preparation. This transformation, which is the real content of the following of Christ, tells us that this following is possible in every age.

We have already seen how even the earliest accounts point to this interior dimension of following. The Gospel of Saint John and the Letters of Saint Paul the Apostle tell us what the "transformation" entails in the situation of the Church after the Lord's departure and, therefore, in *our* situation as well. Thus the term "follow" crops up again in the parable of the Good Shepherd, where we read: "When he [the shepherd] has brought out all his own, he goes before them, and the sheep follow him, for they know his voice" (Jn 10:4). In this passage, to follow means to recognize Jesus' voice and to follow that voice through the confusion of voices with which the world surrounds us.

To put it even more clearly: "to follow" means to entrust oneself to the Word of God, to rate it higher than the laws of money and bread and to live by it. In short, to follow means to believe, but to "believe" in the sense of making a radical decision between the two and, in the last analysis, the only two possibilities for human life: bread and the word. Man does not live on bread alone but also and primarily on the word, the spirit, meaning. It is always this same radical decision that confronts disciples when they hear the call, "Follow me!": the radical decision to stake one's life either on profit and gain or on truth and love; the radical decision to live only for oneself or to surrender one's self.

Now we can also see what the real point of cross and martyrdom is. All we need do in order to understand them is to read what follows in Mark after the saying about carrying the cross: "For whoever would save his life will lose it; and whoever loses his life for my sake and the gospel's will save it" (Mk 8:35). The Gospel of John clarifies this saying with the marvelous parable of the grain of wheat that cannot bear fruit unless it falls into the earth and dies (Jn 12:24–25). Only in losing himself can man find himself; only by giving himself away does he come to himself. The real and decisive martyrdom of genuine self-renunciation is and remains the basic condition for following Christ, even in the comfortable times when a Christianity that is protected by a benevolent State might be inclined to forget the shadow of the Cross. Need we add that the following of Christ, understood in this way, expresses the basic law, not only of the incarnation [*Menschwerdung*] of God but also of man's authentic humanization [*Menschwerdung*]?

This brings us to a final remark. We can now see the point at which faith and love, so often in conflict in the course of history, coincide. In Saint Paul's Letter to the Ephesians there are these profound words: "Be imitators of God . . . and walk in love, as Christ loved us and gave himself up for us" (Eph 5:1). To follow Christ means to accept the *inner* essence of the Cross, namely, the radical love expressed therein, and thus to imitate God himself. For on the Cross God revealed himself as the One who pours himself out; who surrenders his glory in order to be present for us; who desires to rule the world, not by power, but by love and, in the weakness of the Cross, reveals *his* power, which operates so differently from the power of this world's mighty rulers.

To follow Christ, then, means to enter into the self-surrender that is the real heart of love. To follow Christ means to become one who loves as God has loved. That is why Paul can make the astounding statement that to follow Christ is to imitate God and to enter into the basic movement that characterizes God himself. God has become man so that men might become like God. In the last analysis, following Christ is nothing other than man's becoming man by integration into the humanity of God.

11. Belief in Creation and the Theory of Evolution

In the mid-nineteenth century, when Charles Darwin developed the idea of the evolution of all living things and thus radically called into question the traditional notion of the invariability of the species created by God, he inaugurated a revolution in our world view that was no less thoroughgoing than the one we associate with the name Copernicus. Despite the Copernican revolution, which dethroned the earth and increasingly expanded the dimensions of the universe toward the infinite, as a whole the firmly established framework of the old world view continued to exist and to insist, without modification, on the temporal boundary of the six thousand years that had been calculated from the biblical chronologies. A few examples may illustrate for us the tenacity (almost unimaginable today) with which people used to take for granted the narrow temporal parameters of the biblical world view.

In 1848, when Jacob Grimm published his *History of the German Language,* he regarded the age of mankind—six thousand years—as an undisputed postulate that needed no further reflection. W. Wachsmuth declared the same thing as a matter of course in his widely acclaimed *General History of Culture,* which appeared in 1850 and in this respect was no different from the general history of the world and of peoples that Christian Daniel Beck had published in its second edition in 1813. The examples could easily be multiplied.[1] Let these suffice to indicate the narrow horizon within which our view of history and of the world still ranged a hundred years ago and to show how unshakable was the

---

Translated by Michael J. Miller.

[1] This material is taken from J. Dörmann, "War Johann Jakob Bachofen Evolutionist?" *Anthropos* 60 (1965): 1–48, specifically 23ff.

Bible-based tradition of thought taken entirely from Judeo-Christian salvation history; what a revolution it must have been, after the immeasurable expansion of space that had preceded it, for a similar abolition of boundaries to take control now of time and history! In many respects the consequences of such a process are even more dramatic than those of the Copernican revolution could ever be. For the dimension of time touches the creature man incomparably more deeply than that of space; indeed, now the notion of space, too, is once again relativized and changed, inasmuch as space loses its firm, definable form and is itself subjected to history, to temporality. Man appears as the being that came to be in and through endless changes; the great constants of the biblical world view, the original condition and the final condition, become unfathomably remote—the basic understanding of reality changes: becoming replaces being, evolution replaces creation, and ascent replaces the Fall.

Within the context of these reflections, we cannot thoroughly investigate the host of questions that are posed thereby; we merely wish to state the problem of whether the fundamental world views of creation and evolution can (contrary to first impressions) coexist without forcing the theologian to make a dishonest compromise and for tactical reasons to declare the terrain that has become untenable as superfluous anyway, after having not long ago insistently made it out to be an indispensable part of the faith.

The problem has various levels, which we must distinguish from each other and evaluate separately. First, there is a relatively superficial aspect of the whole matter, which is really not entirely theological: the pre-Darwinian idea of the invariability of the species had been justified in terms of the idea of creation; it regarded every individual species as a fact of creation that had existed since the beginning of the world through God's creative work as something unique and different alongside the other species. It is clear that this form of belief in creation contradicts the idea of evolution and that this expression of the faith has become untenable today. But with this correction (and we will return again later to examine its significance and problematic character), we have not exhausted the entire scope of the concept of creation. When one rules out all individual creations and replaces them with the idea of evolution, then the real difference between the two concepts first emerges; it becomes clear that each one is based on a different way of thinking, a different intellectual approach, and a different way of framing the question. The extension of the concept of creation into the individual structures of reality was of course able for a long time to conceal this deeper difference and, thus, the real problem. Belief in creation inquires into the fact that there is being as such; its question is why anything exists at all instead of nothing. In contrast, the idea of evolution asks why precisely these things exist and not others, whence they acquired their particularity, and how they are connected with other formations.[2] Philosophically, then, one would say that the idea of evolution is situated on the phenomenological level and deals with the actually occurring individual forms in the world, whereas the belief in creation moves on the ontological level, inquires into what is behind individual things, marvels at the miracle of being itself, and tries to give an account of the puzzling "is" that we commonly predicate of all existing realities. One could also put it this way: Belief in creation concerns the difference between nothing and something, while the idea of evolution examines the difference between something and something else. Creation characterizes being as a whole as being from somewhere else. Evolution, in contrast, describes the inner structure of being and inquires into the specific "from where" of individual existing realities. Perhaps for the natural scientist, the problem as framed by belief in creation appears to be an illegitimate question that man cannot answer. The transition to the evolutionary way of looking at the world is in fact the step toward that positivistic form of science that deliberately restricts itself to what is given, tangible, and empirically observable by man, thereby rejecting from the realm of science as unproductive any reflection about the real foundations of reality. In this regard, belief in creation and the idea of evolution designate, not only two different areas of inquiry, but also two different thought forms. That is probably the cause of the problematic relation that one senses between the two even after their fundamental compatibility has become evident.

But this leads us already to a second level of the question. We have learned to distinguish two aspects of belief in creation: its concrete expression in the notion of the creation of all the individual species by God and its real intellectual starting point. We have established that

---

[2] Cf. H. Volk, *Schöpfungsglaube und Entwicklung* (Münster, 1955).

the first aspect, that is, the concrete form that the idea of creation had taken in practice, has been abolished by the idea of evolution; here the believer must allow himself to be taught by science that the way in which he had imagined creation was part of a prescientific world view that has become untenable. But as far as the actual intellectual approach is concerned, the inquiry into the transition from nothingness to being, we have managed for the time being to note only the difference between the two thought forms; the theory of evolution and belief in creation belong, with respect to their ultimate fundamental orientation, to entirely different intellectual worlds and have nothing at all directly in common. But what are we to think of this apparent neutrality that we have thus stumbled upon? That is the second level of the inquiry, which we must now pursue farther. Here it is not very easy to make progress, because there is always something very delicate about comparing thought forms and about the problem of whether they can be related to each other. In doing so, one must try to position oneself *above* both thought forms and thus easily ends up in an intellectual no-man's-land, in which one appears suspicious to both sides and soon gets the feeling of straddling the fence. Nevertheless, we must make the attempt to grope our way farther. As an initial observation, we can state that the inquiry of evolutionary thought is narrower than that of belief in creation. By no means, therefore, can evolutionary doctrine incorporate belief in creation. In this sense, it can rightly describe the idea of creation as something of no use to it: by its very methodology, it is founded upon the compilation of positivistic material, and such a belief has no place within its scope. At the same time, of course, it must leave open the question of whether the further inquiry proposed by faith is per se justified and possible. In any case, it may regard this, in terms of a particular concept of science, as extra-scientific, but it cannot rule out the question as a matter of principle or say that man should not address the question of being as such. On the contrary: such ultimate questions will always be indispensable for man, who confronts the ultimate in his very existence and cannot be reduced to what is scientifically demonstrable. But this still leaves us with the problem of whether the idea of creation, being the broader subject, can for its part accept the idea of evolution within its parameters or whether that contradicts its fundamental approach.

Reasons of various sorts seem at first glance to favor the latter argu-

ment; after all, the natural scientists and theologians of the first generation who said so were neither foolish nor malicious: on either side,
they certainly had their reasons, which we must take into account if we
do not want to arrive at hasty syntheses that will not withstand challenges or that are simply dishonest. The objections that come to mind
are of quite different sorts. One can say first, for instance, that belief in
creation has been expressed for centuries as faith in the creation of the
individual species and in the notion of a static world view; now that
this has become untenable, the belief cannot abruptly toss this ballast
aside; rather, it has become entirely inapplicable. This objection, which
today no longer seems very serious to us, becomes more acute when
one reflects that even today faith still necessarily regards the creation
of one particular creature as indispensable: the creation of man. For
if man is only the product of evolution, then spirit, too, is a random
formation. But if spirit evolved, then matter is the primary thing and
the sufficient cause of all the rest. And if that is so, then God vanishes
and, with him, Creator and creation automatically. But how is man
—one among many beings, however excellent and great he may be—
to be kept out of the chain of evolutionary developments? Now this
shows that the creation of individual creatures and the idea of creation
itself cannot be separated quite so readily as it may have appeared at
first. For it appears to be a matter of principle here. Either all individual
things are the product of evolution, including man. Or else they are
not. The second hypothesis is ruled out, and so the first remains, and
this appears now, as we have just realized, to call the whole idea of
creation into question, because it abolishes the primacy and superiority of spirit, which in some form are to be regarded as a fundamental
prerequisite for belief in creation.

Now some have tried to get around this problem by saying that the
human body may be a product of evolution, but the soul is not by any
means: God himself created it, since spirit cannot emerge from matter.
This answer seems to have in its favor the fact that spirit cannot be
examined by the same scientific method with which one studies the
history of organisms, but only at first glance is this a satisfactory answer. We have to continue the line of questioning: Can we divide man
up man in this way between theologians and scientists—the soul for
the former, the body for the latter? Is that not intolerable for both? The
natural scientist believes that he can see the man as a whole gradually

taking shape; he also finds an area of psychological transition in which human behavior slowly arises out of animal activity, without being able to draw a clear boundary. (Of course, he lacks the material with which to do so—something that often is not admitted with sufficient clarity.) Conversely, if the theologian is convinced that the soul gives form to the body as well, characterizing it through and through as a human body, so that a human being is spirit only as body and is body only as and in the spirit, then this division of man loses all meaning for him, too.

Indeed, in that case the spirit has created for itself a brand-new body and thereby cancelled out all of evolution. Thus, from both perspectives, the theme of creation and evolution seems to lead in man's case to a strict either-or that allows for no intermediate positions. Yet according to the present state of our knowledge, that would probably mean the end of belief in creation.

With that, the beautiful harmony that seemed to stand out clearly on the first level of the inquiry has completely dissolved again, and we are back where we started. How are we to make any progress? Well, a little while ago we had touched upon a middle level that at first seemed unimportant but now could prove to be the center of the inquiry and the starting point for a defendable answer. To what extent is faith bound up with the notion that God created the individual fundamental realities of the world? This way of framing the question may seem at first somewhat superficial, but it follows logically from a general problem that could very well represent the middle stratum of our whole question: Can the notion of a world of becoming be reconciled with the fundamental biblical idea of the creation of the world through the Word, with the derivation of being from creative meaning? Can the idea of being that is expressed therein coexist intellectually with the idea of becoming as outlined in the theory of evolution? Concealed within these questions is another quite fundamental question about the relation between world view and faith in general. This will be a good place to start. For in trying to think at the same time as a believer in creation and as a scientist (that is, according to the theory of evolution), obviously one will attribute to faith a different world view from the one that previously was accepted as the authentic world view of faith. In this process, actually, we even find the heart of the whole matter around which our reflections have been circling:

the faith is robbed of its world view, which seemed however to be the faith itself, and is connected with another. Can one do this without dissolving its identity?—that precisely is our problem.

Here it may be somewhat surprising and at the same time liberating to learn that this question was not asked for the first time in our generation. Rather, the theologians in the early Church were confronted in principle with the same task. For the biblical world view, as expressed in the creation accounts of the Old Testament, was by no means their world view; basically it appeared to them just as unscientific as it does to us. Although people often speak simply of "the ancient world view", it is a considerable mistake to do so. Viewed from outside, it may appear unified to us; for those who lived in it, however, the distinctions that seem insignificant to us were decisive. The early creation accounts express the world view of the ancient Near East, especially of Babylon; the Church Fathers lived in the Hellenistic age, to which that world view seemed mythical, pre-scientific, and in every respect intolerable. One consideration that helped them, and ought to help us, is that the Bible is really literature that spans a whole millennium. That literary tradition extends from the world view of the Babylonians to the Hellenist world view that shaped the creation passages of the Wisdom literature, which give a picture of the world and of the creation event completely unlike that of the familiar creation accounts in Genesis, which of course are not uniform themselves. The first and the second chapters of this book present largely contrasting images of the course of creation. But this means that, even within the Bible itself, faith and world view are not identical: the faith *makes use* of a world view but does not coincide with it. Over the course of biblical development, this difference was clearly not a theme for reflection but, rather, was taken for granted: that is the only way to explain the fact that people changed the forms of cosmological speculation in which they portrayed the idea of creation, not only in the various periods of Israel's history, but also within one and the same period of time, without seeing that as a threat to what was actually meant.

The sense of this internal breadth of faith began to disappear when so-called literal exegesis started to gain wide acceptance and many people lost sight of the transcendence of the Word of God with respect to all of the individual forms in which it is expressed. However, at the same time—from around the thirteenth century—the world view also became fixed in a way hitherto unknown, although in its basic form it was by no means a product of biblical thinking but, on the contrary, could only with some effort be reconciled with the fundamental data of biblical faith. It would not be difficult to uncover the pagan roots of that world view, which later on was thought to be the only Christian world view, and to point out the seam by which we can tell even today that the faith made use of it although it could not become identical to it. But we cannot go into that subject here; we must limit ourselves to the positive question of whether belief in creation, which has outlasted so many different world views and at the same time has influenced and leavened them by its critique and thus furthered the development, can continue to exist as a meaningful statement in light of the evolutionary understanding of the world. At the same time, it is clear that the faith, which was not identical to any one of the previous world views but, rather, answered a question that leads back behind the world views and then of course becomes entrenched in them, cannot and should not be identified with our world view, either. It would be foolish and untrue to try to pass off evolutionary theory as a product of the faith, even though the latter can be said to have contributed to forming that intellectual world in which the theory of evolution could come about. It would be even more foolish to regard the faith as a sort of illustration and corroboration of the theory of evolution. The level of its questioning and answering is completely different, as we determined earlier; all we can try to do is to determine whether the fundamental human question with which faith is associated can still be legitimately answered, even in present-day intellectual circumstances, as it is by belief in creation, and, thus in what form the evolutionary world view, too, may be understood as an expression of creation.

In order to move forward, we must examine more closely both the creation account and also the idea of evolution; both of these things, unfortunately, are possible here only in outline form. Let us ask first, then, starting with the latter topic: How does one actually understand the world when it is viewed in evolutionary terms? An essential component, of course, is the notion that being and time enter into a fixed relation: being *is* time, it does not merely *have* time. Only in becoming does it exist and unfold into itself. Accordingly, being is understood dynamically, as being-in-movement, and it is understood as something directed: it does not always revolve around the same state of affairs but, rather, advances. Admittedly, there is a debate over whether the concept of progress can be applied to the evolutionary chain, especially since there is no neutral standard available that would allow us to say specifically what should be regarded as better or less good and, consequently, when we could seriously speak of an advance.

Nevertheless, the special relation that man assumes with respect to all the rest of reality entitles him to regard himself as the point of reference, at least for the question about himself: insofar as he is at issue, he is no doubt justified in doing so. And when he measures in this way, the direction of evolution and its progressive character are ultimately indisputable, even if one takes into account the fact that there are dead ends in evolution and that its path by no means runs in a straight line. Detours, too, are a path, and by way of detours, too, one arrives at the goal, as evolution itself demonstrates. Of course the question remains open whether being, understood in such a way as a path—that is, evolution as a whole—has a meaning, and it cannot be decided within the theory of evolution itself; for that theory this is a methodologically foreign question, although of course for a live human being it is the fundamental question on which the whole thing depends. Science rightly acknowledges its limits in this regard and declares that this question, which is indispensable for man, cannot be answered within science, but only within the framework of a "faith system". We need not be concerned here with the opinion of many people that the Christian "faith system" is unsuited to answering this question and that a new one must be found, because they thereby make a statement within their own faith-decision and outside the parameters of their science.[3]

With that, however, we are now in a position to say precisely what the belief in creation means with regard to the evolutionary understanding of the world. Confronted with the fundamental question, which cannot be answered by evolutionary theory itself, of whether meaninglessness or meaning [*Sinn*] prevails, this belief expresses the conviction that the world as a whole, as the Bible says, comes from the Logos, that is, from creative mind [*Sinn*] and represents the temporal form of its self-actuation. From the perspective of our understanding of the world, creation is not a distant beginning or a beginning divided up

---

[3] Cf. W. Bröker, *Der Sinn von Evolution: Ein naturwissenschaftlich-theologischer Diskussionsbeitrag* (Düsseldorf, 1967), esp. 50–58.

into several stages, but, rather, it concerns being as something temporal and becoming: temporal being as a whole is encompassed by the one creative act of God, which gives to divided being its unity, in which at the same time its meaning consists, a meaning that is unfathomable to us because we do not see the whole but are ourselves only parts of it. Belief in creation does not tell us what the meaning of the world is but only that there is one: the whole back and forth of being-in-becoming is the free and, therefore, inherently risky actuation of the primordial creative thought from which it has its being. And so today, perhaps, we can understand better what the Christian dogma of creation was always saying but could hardly bring to bear because of the influence of the model from antiquity: creation should be thought of, not according to the model of the craftsman who makes all sorts of objects, but rather in the manner in which thought is creative. And at the same time, it becomes evident that being-in-movement as a whole (and not just the beginning) is creation and that, likewise, the whole (and not merely what comes later) is, properly speaking, reality and its proper movement. To summarize all this, we can say: To believe in creation means to understand, in faith, the world of becoming revealed by science as a meaningful world that comes from a creative mind.

But this already clearly delineates also the answer to the question about the creation of man, because now the foundational decision about the place of spirit and meaning in the world has been made: the recognition of the world of becoming as the self-actuation of a creative thought includes also its derivation from the creativity of the spirit, from the *Creator Spiritus*. In the writings of Teilhard de Chardin, we find the following ingenious comment on this question: "What distinguishes a materialist from a spiritualist is no longer, by any means (as in philosophy, which establishes fixed concepts), the fact that he admits a transition between the physical infrastructure and the psychic superstructure of things, but *only* the fact that he incorrectly sets the *definitive* point of equilibrium in the cosmic movement on the side of the infrastructure, that is, on the side of disintegration."[4] Certainly one can debate the details in this formulation; yet the decisive point seems to me to be grasped quite accurately: the alternative: materialism or a

---

[4] Cited from Claude Tresmontant, *Einführung in das Denken Teilhard de Chardins* (Freiburg and Munich, 1961), 45.

spiritually defined world view, chance or meaning, is presented to us today in the form of the question of whether one regards spirit and life in its ascending forms as an incidental mold on the surface of the material world (that is, of the category of existing things that do not understand themselves), or whether one regards spirit as the goal of the process and, conversely, matter as the prehistory of the spirit. If one chooses the second alternative, it is clear that spirit is not a random product of material developments but, rather, that matter signifies a moment in the history of spirit. This, however, is just another way of saying that spirit is created and not the mere product of development, even though it comes to light by way of development.

With that we have reached the point at which we can answer the question of how in fact the theological statement about the special creation of man can coexist with an evolutionary world view or what form it must assume within an evolutionary world view. To discuss this in detail would naturally go beyond the parameters of this essay; a few notes must suffice. We should recall first that, with respect to the creation of man, too, "creation" does not designate a remote beginning but, rather, has each of us in view along with Adam: every man *is* directly in relation to God. The faith declares no more about the first man than it does about each one of us, and, conversely, it declares no less about us than it does about the first man.

Every man is more than the product of inherited traits and environment; no one results exclusively from calculable this-worldly factors; the mystery of creation looms over every one of us. This would then lead to the insight that spirit does not enter the picture as something foreign, as a second substance in addition to matter; the appearance of spirit, according to the previous discussion, means rather that an advancing movement arrives at the goal that has been set for it. Finally, it would have to be noted that, if anything, the creation of spirit is least of all to be imagined as an artisan activity of God, who suddenly began tinkering with the world.

If creation means dependence of being, then special creation is nothing other than special dependence of being.[5] The statement that man is created in a more specific, more direct way by God than other things in nature, when expressed somewhat less metaphorically, means simply

---

[5] P. Smulders, *Theologie und Evolution: Versuch über Teilhard de Chardin* (Essen, 1963), 96.

this: that man is willed by God in a specific way, not merely as a being that "is there", but as a being that knows him; not only as a construct that he thought up, but as an existence that can think about him in return. We call the fact that man is specifically willed and known by God his special creation.

From this vantage point, one can immediately make a diagnosis about the form of anthropogenesis: The clay became man at that moment in which a being for the first time was capable of forming, however dimly, the thought "God". The first Thou that—however stammeringly— was said by human lips to God marks the moment in which spirit arose in the world. Here the Rubicon of anthropogenesis was crossed. For it is not the use of weapons or fire, not new methods of cruelty or of useful activity that constitute man, but, rather, his ability to be imme- diately in relation to God. This holds fast to the doctrine of the special creation of man; herein lies the center of belief in creation in the first place. Herein also lies the reason why the moment of anthropogenesis cannot possibly be determined by paleontology: anthropogenesis is the rise of the spirit, which cannot be excavated with a shovel. The theory of evolution does not invalidate the faith, nor does it corroborate it. But it does challenge the faith to understand itself more profoundly and, thus, to help man to understand himself and to become increas- ingly what he is: the being who is supposed to say Thou to God in eternity.

12. *Gratia Praesupponit Naturam*
Grace Presupposes Nature

Reflections on the Meaning and Limits of a Scholastic Axiom

The following lines were written around ten years ago for the *Festschrift* in honor of Gottlieb Söhngen's seventieth birthday as a token of thanks to the theology teacher whose inspiration was behind this paper. I would like to add a short prefatory remark from our present perspective: In reaction to an undifferentiated optimism about nature that was fond of citing Thomas Aquinas and his positive concept of nature, Söhngen emphatically called attention to Karl Barth's critique of this harmonizing theology and, thus, at the same time brought the Reformation critique of Catholic nature-theology to bear on the latter's claim. Söhngen's own essays on the analogy of being and of faith were marked by an effort to hold fast to the biblically based seriousness of this critique without giving up the claim of belief in creation, which Catholic theology expresses in its Yes to the ontological dimension.

The following reflection adopts this basic approach. In contrast to a truncated Thomism that rightly became an object of polemical attack by Reformation thought, it attempts to call to mind again that other side of Scholasticism which is perhaps best characterized by the name Bonaventure. Of course it also tries to defend the right of "nature" in faith against Barth's one-sidedness. Today, at some remove from the battle lines that were drawn then, I would emphasize this aspect even more clearly: Since Thomas can no longer be presupposed, he should now be discussed especially as a contrast to Bonaventure.[1] There is nothing

---

Translated by Michael J. Miller.

[1] In this connection I would like to refer the reader to the recently completed dissertation by my student Michael Marmann, *Gratia praesupponit naturam*, a penetrating study, by means of a contrast between Augustine and Thomas, of the indispensable contribution of Saint Thomas to this question.

about the general tenor of the essay that I want to change, however; that may justify its inclusion in this volume just as much as the continuing relevance of the question, even though no one speaks about Scholastic axioms any more. The two aspects of the problem that we will examine here represent at the same time the two essential aspects of the crisis by which Christendom is being shaken today. On the one hand, the theological denial of nature has been easy to combine with eschatological Marxism, which knows no "nature" but only facts that must be changed in order to bring a disastrous world to salvation. As a third member of this alliance, we should mention Sartre's existentialist nihilism: man has no essence, only existence; each individual creates his essence anew for himself. What he is, is decided only by what he makes. Against this denial of nature, the Creator and his creation must be defended—not just when the unvarnished arbitrariness of an essence-free pragmatism is experienced by the individual up close, but because of the inmost claim of the faith, which believes that grace does not need the destruction of creation—of nature—in order to be great. On the other side stands a naturalism that regards the distinction between nature and grace as the building up of a totally meaningless supernatural world that must be dismantled as an "ideology" in favor of what alone is real: Christianity is only allowed to interpret what life is, nothing more. Here, conversely, under the pretext of dispensing with ideologies, man is left uncritically to himself and to the powers that be, which can suggest to him that they are reality and life. In the end, the naturalism that melts grace down into nature leads to the same result as the supranaturalism that disputes the existence of nature and, by denying creation, makes grace meaningless as well. The fanaticism of those homilists who mock nature, presumably for the sake of grace, is always frighteningly close to the cynicism of the atheists who mock God for the sake of his creation. The following reflections address this complicated problem.

1. The Problem

The axiom "Gratia praesupponit naturam" [Grace presupposes nature] (or "Gratia non destruit, sed supponit and perficit naturam"[2] [Grace does not destroy but supposes and perfects nature]) had become almost a sort of slogan during the [early twentieth-century German] Youth Movement. A central point of the religious sentiment of that time was corroborated by this axiom in a really exciting and felicitous way. A new ethos of truthfulness had made a breakthrough, a desire for undisguised naturalness that challenged all convention, all "bourgeois" formality; the fresh vitality of the youth, with their unspent optimism, their love for life, for the world and everything beautiful that it brings forth, rebelled against the limitations and precautions of the adults, whose sensible world had nevertheless revealed the real depths of its misery in the First World War. No, they no longer wanted to continue living in the stifling atmosphere of the old conventions; they wanted out; they were looking for freedom, for nature, with its pure nobility and its intact dignity. No doubt a good dose of Nietzsche's thinking was concealed in this ethos, the fierce scorn that he poured out on the virtue of the virtuous (which, unfortunately, was often enough really counterfeit), the relentless candor with which he uncovered the vacuity behind the anxiously guarded formulas, the passion with which he stood up for man—all that had now really caught fire and left its mark on the vitality of those young people. Who would not have been moved by words like these:

> Oh, just look at those tabernacles which those priests have built for themselves! Churches, they call their sweet-smelling caves! . . .
> Who created for themselves such caves and [penitential staircases]?

[2] On the history of the axiom and its individual formulations, see J. Beumer, "Gratia supponit naturam: Zur Geschichte eines theologischen Prinzips", *Gregorianum* 20 (1939): 381–406, 535–52. A brief overview can be found also in Michael Schmaus, *Katholisch Dogmatik*, 3rd and 4th eds., vol. 2 (Munich: Hueber, 1949), 188–91. On the importance of the subject, see E. Przywara, "Der Grundsatz 'Gratia non destruit, sed supponit et perficit naturam': Eine ideengeschichtliche Interpretation", *Scholastik* 17 (1942): 178–86; J. Alfaro in *Lexikon für Theologie und Kirche*, 2nd ed. (Freiburg, 1960), 1169ff., with further bibliography.

Was it not those who sought to conceal themselves, and were ashamed under the clear sky?

And only when the clear sky looks again through ruined roofs down upon grass and red poppies on ruined walls—will I again turn my heart to the [dwelling places] of this God.

They called God that which opposed and afflicted them: and surely, there was much hero-spirit in their worship!

And they knew not how to love their God otherwise than by nailing [man] to the Cross![3]

In this situation, in which Christianity likewise seemed to have fallen to this general dismantling of all conventions, people rediscovered the axiom "Gratia praesupponit naturam" as a saving power. It opened up a brand new possibility of Christian consciousness: being a Christian does not mean breaking with nature at all; rather, it means heightening and perfecting it, as the great, fulfilling affirmation. The Catholicism that had brought forth this axiom appeared as the religion of Both-And: spirit *and* body, God *and* man, grace *and* nature—as the great universal harmony. All you needed was to rediscover this true Catholicism (as opposed to the short-winded asceticism of the nineteenth century) in order to recognize that here this Yes to the beautiful purity of nature had always been alive, this joyful affirmation that was just starting again to make headway against a supernaturalism that supposed it was honoring God by crucifying man. The theology of the previous era was being read with new eyes: people again recalled the doctrine of the Greek Church Fathers about the consecration of the world in the flesh of Christ, the great idea of Saint Irenaeus about the recapitulation of the whole world in Christ, about bringing the world back to its real home in the Body of the Lord. People reflected once more on the sacred mystery of the Incarnation, on this unfathomable fact that God became "flesh" and thus "world" and that from then on the flesh, the world, desires to be the expression and the dwelling place of the divine, that therefore the orientation of religious living can no longer be a flight into the spirit but, rather, leads straight into corporeal matters, in which God still wants to become flesh once more. All this, however,

[3] *Thus Spake Zarathustra*, trans. Thomas Common (Amherst, N.Y.: Prometheus Books, 1993), "The Priests", 113f.

was focused as though by a magnifying lens into the axiom "Gratia praesupponit naturam", in which this theology of the *analogia entis*, of the great "catholic" harmony, found its central expression. Indeed, the very word "catholic" seemed to express this basic thought: the idea of the all-embracing, of the great, universal Yes of the analogy of being.[4]

As the paradoxical march of history would have it, at the same time such ideas were blazing a trail in Catholicism, a renewal was taking place in Protestantism with diametrically opposite premises. In the vanguard, Karl Barth—who in his own way was also affected by Nietzsche's revolutionary pathos—gave expression to a completely different experience of man and God. Now Barth, too, acknowledged a nature in which the grace of Christ "is internal and not external, natural and not foreign" to us; indeed, grace could even be called our "law of nature". But man as he really lives in history, man in his autonomy vis-à-vis God and in his reflection on himself, does not live in his true nature; instead, an unnatural state has become his nature.[5] To continue and perfect that state would mean to accomplish the self-destructive conclusion of man, to canonize his misery instead of leading him into salvation. For this sort of man, grace cannot be continuation or perfection but only disruption, paradox, thwarting. This explains, then, Barth's famous judgment on the *analogia entis* in the foreword to his *Church Dogmatics*: "I regard the *analogia entis* as the invention of the Antichrist, and I believe that because of it it is impossible ever to become a Roman Catholic, all other reasons for not doing so being to my mind short-sighted and trivial."[6]

This idea is difficult to comprehend within the context of Catholic

---

[4] See the basic presentations by O. Köhler, "Jugendbewegung", *LThK*, 2nd ed., vol. 5 (Freiburg, 1958), 1181f., and F. Messerschmid, "Katholische Jugendbewegung", *RGG*, 3rd ed., 3:1020ff. The idea of the analogy of being has been explored most thoroughly by E. Przywara; of his works, see especially "Natur und Übernatur", in *Ringen der Gegenwart* (Augsburg, 1929), 1:419–42; *Religionsphilosophie katholischer Theologie* (Munich, 1926); *Analogia entis* (Munich, 1932); "Analogia entis", *LThK*, vol. 1 (Freiburg, 1957), 468–72.

[5] Citations (from the first edition of the *Commentary on the Letter to the Romans*) can be found in Hans Urs von Balthasar, *The Theology of Karl Barth*, trans. Edward T. Oakes, S.J. (San Francisco: Ignatius Press, Communio Books, 1992), 66. Still fundamental to the debate on the problem of the *analogia entis* and the *analogia fidei* [analogy of faith] are the various works by Söhngen on this topic; see esp. "Analogia fidei I & II", *Catholica* 3 (1934): 113–36; 176–208; *Die Einheit in der Theologie* (Munich, 1952), 235–64.

[6] *Kirchliche Dogmatik*, vol. 1, pt. 1, p. xiii.

theology; in order to get a clearer view of it and, thus, of the matter in question, the reader might allow us to interpolate another consideration, which attempts to shed a little more light on the whole subject in terms of the contrast between the Catholic and the Reformation concepts of sin, as van de Pol has admirably presented it.[7] One can say that the Catholic understands sin in general to be an action that goes against God's will: an act, therefore, that can be circumscribed and defined—so much so that he can count his sins and confess them, one after the other, stating the approximate number of times for each, in the sacrament of penance. The Reformed Christian, in contrast, is of the opinion that this understanding of sin is too pointillistic and too moralistic. He believes that you are completely mistaken about man's true situation if you single out from his life certain sinful points and try to eradicate them, so to speak, and then act as though man is otherwise in order. The Protestant thinks, instead, that the individual acts of trespass are only symptoms of an underlying general condition. In every instance, these transgressions express the *real* sin that precedes them. Van de Pol quotes in this connection a characteristic statement from the "Foundations and Perspectives of the Faith" of the Dutch Reformed Church: "Sin is not this or that bad deed but, rather, the broken relationship to God; it is disbelief. Consequently, we seek our happiness in ourselves and in other earthly powers."[8]

If we try to follow this line of thought farther in its own objective meaning, we might formulate it more generally and basically: Man's sin consists of the fact that in the end he seeks himself in everything, that selfishness is the secret driving force of all his activity. This does not exclude a morality that is quite orderly, but it does mean that even the best moral attitudes and actions of man are somewhere and somehow corroded by the fundamental attitude of selfishness, self-assertion, which man can never entirely get rid of. And to press the point further, one could reflect that the Pharisees, for instance, from a purely moral perspective, certainly stood upon a considerable height. But precisely their case shows that *mere* morality is not enough, because it is obviously incapable of overcoming this insidious secret of selfishness, which

[7] W. H. van de Pol, *Das reformatorische Christentum* (Einsiedeln, 1956), 313ff.

[8] *Fundamenten en Perspektieven von Belijden* ('s-Gravenhage, 1949), art. 2, p. 19, quoted in van de Pol, *Das reformatorische Christentum*, 316f.

theological tradition somewhat misleadingly calls "concupiscence". But now Reformation spirituality says that just this fundamental attitude of selfishness underlying one's individual acts is "*the* sin" of man, of which the individual sins are only secondary outgrowths. And it adds: This attitude of selfishness, of self-assertion, is man's "natural" stance —it came to be so through original sin. It is his "nature" to be selfish. This means that he is by nature a sinner. And does not Saint Paul say, in fact, that "we were by nature children of wrath" (Eph 2:3)? And do not the existential analyses of contemporary philosophy and psychology corroborate this disillusioned view of man, who lives in the state of being "unauthentic" and of having "fallen" into "anonymity", in a state of arbitrariness and fear, out of which only a repeatedly renewed decision to surrender himself can save him?[9]

2. *The Individual Elements of an Answer*

All this raises a question that is not just theological bickering but concerns the very heart of Christian existence in this world: the very concrete question of the kind of stance that the Christian should take in this world and toward this world. Now by way of an answer, one could first very simply point out that "nature" means something quite different in these two cases—in the world-friendly theology of the analogy of being and in the stern dialectic of the early Barth. In the first case, it is the opposite of artificial and man-made things and, thus, what is original and in keeping with creation; in the second case, it is the historically determined condition of man, which includes the features of his unholy history from Adam onward. But is anything really gained by this elucidation? Or would not Barth just have to say to the theologians of the analogy that this is precisely their error, that they believe in a pure nature without artifice and as it was at creation, which does not exist, because in this era of the world all human "nature" has become artifice, that is, distorted beyond recognition by its history? In order to get an answer, we must dig a bit deeper and ask, on the one hand,

---

[9] Cf. the references in R. Bultmann, "Neues Testament und Mythologie", in *Kerygma und Mythologie* (Hamburg, 1954), 33ff.

what Scholasticism really meant to say originally with this axiom and, on the other hand, where Sacred Scripture stands with regard to our talk about "nature" and "natural".

a. The Original Understanding of the Scholastic Axiom

When our axiom first appears, it initially has a very simple ontological meaning. It means to say that grace is not a self-subsistent, independent creature but, rather, an act of God *upon* a creature that already exists; that it is therefore not a substance in itself but an event that "presupposes" (= *praesupponit*!) a bearer, a point of reference for the event. The saying, therefore, initially implies no value judgment about nature but, rather, is a statement about the ontological status of grace.

As Bonaventure formulates it, "Gratia praesupponit naturam sicut accidens praesupponit subjectum" [Grace presupposes nature as an accident presupposes a subject]. This more precise version of our axiom takes us a step farther.[10] Nature is regarded here purely in terms of its status as a subject, in its fundamentally formal capacity to become the bearer of qualities and the goal of actions. It is not viewed in terms of its material characteristics, whether of a superior or of a lesser sort, as though it would determine the particular "color" or modality of grace. Bonaventure explicitly denies that when he says: "Ubi melior est natura, frequenter minor est gratia et qui hodie minor est in merito, cras fortassis erit major"[11] [Where nature is better, there is often less grace, and someone who is less meritorious today will perhaps be the greater tomorrow]. He and his contemporaries were still very much aware of the paradox of divine activity, whereby the first can become the last, and the last first (Mk 10:31). They still realized that God can bestow the miracle of his magnificent, recreating grace even upon a man who has only very weak and limited "natural" talents at his disposal and that, conversely, someone who is richly endowed in

[10] II Sent., d. 9, a. un q. 9 ad 2 (ed. Quaracchi 2:257b). For particulars about the Scholastic interpretation, see the study by Beumer, "Gratia supponit naturam".

[11] Ibid., corpus (p. 257 a). Compare ad 2: ". . . gratia nostra conformis est gratiae angelorum, quamvis natura nostra non sit eiusdem speciei cum eorum natura" [Our grace is similar to the grace of the angels, although our nature is not of the same species as their nature]. It is expressly stated that grace among men in the next world will constitute a degree of order that does not result from nature.

"natural" gifts can fail in God's sight, that his natural strength can also become for him an obstacle that bars the way to the humility of faith. And how could they have forgotten this, when they looked at that woman who said about herself, "He has regarded the low estate of his handmaiden. . . . He has scattered the proud in the imagination of their hearts, he has put down the mighty from their thrones, and exalted those of low degree" (Lk 1:48, 51–52)—or when they thought about the words of Saint Paul: "Not many of you were wise according to the flesh, not many were powerful, not many were of noble birth; but God chose what is foolish in the world to shame the wise" (1 Cor 1:26f.)?

Therefore, we can declare that "nature" in the Scholastic axiom means the formal definiteness of what is human or, still better, of the particular man in his humanness as such, which is to be the point of reference for the grace event. In any case, it originally says nothing about the question of how the concrete man in view is constituted with regard to grace. But no doubt the Scholastic theologians devoted much thought to that as well, and we cannot retrace their speculations in detail here. It will suffice to pick out one influential example: Saint Bonaventure's ideas about the "nature" of man. First, an observation at the perimeter of the problem. Bonaventure distinguishes repeatedly between the "natural course" of worldly things and a "miraculous course" with which God interrupts the "course of nature". Thus "nature" with its normal laws and God's freedom are contrasted. Upon closer inspection of the passages, the reader soon notices that this distinction is an abbreviation. When Bonaventure wants to be exact, he recognizes, not two, but three "courses":

cursus naturalis	*cursus voluntarius*	*cursus mirabilis*
[natural course]	[voluntary course]	[miraculous course]

This means that human will is presented as a separate middle order between mere nature and God's own freedom. This, in turn, corresponds to the fact that when speaking concisely, Bonaventure distinguishes between *natura* and *supernaturalia*, *natura* and *gratia* within man himself, but when he speaks at greater length, he again sets up three relations:

a natura	*a libero arbitrio*	*a Deo*
[by nature]	[by free will]	[by God]
|	|	|
habitus innatus	*acquisitus*	*infusus*[12]
[innate habit]	[acquired habit]	[infused habit]

Between the general realm of nature and the specifically divine realm, he interpolates the realm of what is distinctively human. Each of these districts has its own area of topics and its own form of knowledge, so that finally we have the following overall scheme:

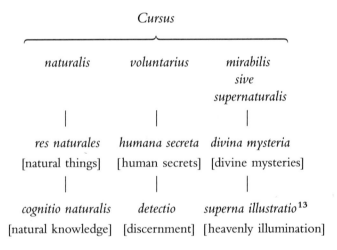

Cursus

naturalis	*voluntarius*	*mirabilis* *sive* *supernaturalis*
|	|	|
res naturales	*humana secreta*	*divina mysteria*
[natural things]	[human secrets]	[divine mysteries]
|	|	|
cognitio naturalis	*detectio*	*superna illustratio*[13]
[natural knowledge]	[discernment]	[heavenly illumination]

In this subdivision, "nature" is distinguished from the free-will activity of the person: man's personhood is not included in the general concept of nature but, rather, represents a separate order between God's revelatory actions and what is merely "natural". The opinion about nature and spirit that is connected with this becomes clearly evident in the answer to the question of whether the human will could have lifted itself out of guilt without divine grace. It is clear that the answer to this

---

[12] IV Sent., d. 4, p. 2, a. 2, q. 2c (IV 114 b). Extensive references to what is said here about Bonaventure's concept of nature can be found in my paper "Der Wortgebrauch von natura und die beginnende Verselbständigung der Metaphysik bei Bonaventura", in P. Wilpert, ed., *Die Metaphysik im Mittelalter*, Miscellanea Mediaevalia, vol. 2 (Berlin, 1963), 483–98.

[13] II, d. 23, a. 2, q. 1c (2:538).

is negative. It is instructive, though, how Bonaventure argues in favor of this No against the objection that the body can overcome sickness by itself, and so the spirit, which after all belongs to a higher order than the body, should also be able to overcome by itself its sickness, sin. The saint replies that the comparison falls short, or, rather: there is no real comparison at all. For the principle of bodily healing is nature, while the principle of spiritual healing is something "above nature" (supra naturam): grace. Nature is still preserved in a case of bodily sickness and, therefore, can bring about a recovery, whereas grace is lost through sin, so that a fresh infusion of divine love is needed in order to restore the original life of the soul.[14] The importance of such a statement is difficult to overestimate. For it means that in Bonaventure's view, the human soul is entirely beyond the realm of mere nature. A merely natural soul is inconceivable; an essential feature of the soul is that it cannot subsist in itself alone. It must be preserved by something that is greater than itself, by something "supernatural". This "supernatural" thing does not thereby cease to be a freely given grace (that is to be feared only from the standpoint of a naturalism that fails to see that the category of spirit is precisely freedom); it does not cease to be "supernatural" and, thus, something that cannot be derived from mere nature. But just as real at the same time is the unique structure of the soul: the immediacy of its relation to God is so intimately essential to it that it cannot exist properly except in being preserved immediately by God: at every moment, spirit surpasses pure nature. In contrast to all attempts in past or more recent times to naturalize spirit, this makes perfectly clear the unique structure of the soul, which can exist only in the manner of dialogue and freedom.

Although the nature of man cannot be defined while disregarding the freedom of the spirit, this implies also that it must not be defined while disregarding its history. And so there is no ahistorical naturalness of man. We could demonstrate by means of a whole series of examples the fact that Bonaventure is conscious of the imprint of history upon "nature". It will suffice to mention the two most important passages here. Whereas post-Tridentine theology usually knows of only two do-mains of norms, which are both unhistorical—the natural law as the domain of *natura* alongside *supernatura* with its supranatural system of

---

[14] II, d. 28, a. 1, q. 1 ad 2 (2:676b).

laws—Bonaventure, following tradition, speaks of a triad that is thoroughly historical in character:

| *tempus legis naturae* | *legis scriptae* | *legis gratiae.*[15] |
| [era of the natural law] | [of the written law] | [of the law of grace] |

The mere conformity to natural law is a historical stage of mankind, its lowest, which does continue to be in effect as the basis for the rest but is surmounted in principle by a stepwise ascent. After God spoke with the patriarchs, it was surpassed by the entirely new level of direct dialogue with God, as this occurs preeminently in grace.

The other example is provided by the doctrine of original sin, when Bonaventure—again drawing upon tradition, especially on Augustine and Anselm—calls original sin a "culpa non personalis sed naturalis" [a guilt that is not personal but natural] and logically speaks then about man's "natura corrupta",[16] which of course does not prevent him from distinguishing in his Christology between the "nature" of man that Christ was able to assume and the sin that he did not assume.[17] Again it becomes evident that the nature of man is marked by its history, even though simultaneously an inmost core of an imperishable order of creation still gleams, which makes it possible for this nature to become a space in which grace can work, indeed, the locus of the Incarnation of the Son of God.

One more thing must be added if the picture is to be in some measure complete. Besides all the observations about nature "from below", Bonaventure is acquainted also with the view from above. But if we observe nature from its true point of reference, from God's perspective, it becomes evident that in the end all nature is "grace"—"hoc totum quod fecit, fuit gratia"[18] [all this that he made was grace]—and that the *cursus naturalis* is at bottom a *cursus voluntarius*. All of nature is in its inmost depths the outpouring of a will, is voluntaristically structured in terms of the primordial creative will, to which alone it owes its existence.

[15] IV, d. 8, p. 1, a. 1, q. 2c (4:182a–b); *De mysterio trinitatis* q. 1, a. 2, opp. 10 (5:53b–54a); *De perfectione evangelica*, q. 2, a. 1c (5:129a) and *passim*.

[16] Brev., p. 3, c. 6 and 7 (5:235f.); II, d. 31, a. 2, q. 2c (2:752b).

[17] III, d. 2, a. 2, q. 1 ad 2 (3:45b).

[18] I, d. 44, a. 1, q. 1 ad 4 (1:783b). Extensive citations can be found in my treatise "Wortgebrauch von natura". Cf. J. Auer, *Die Entwicklung der Gnadenlehre in der Hochscholastik*, vol. 1 (Freiburg, 1942), 348–53.

The decisive thing remains the fact that nature, in man, is encompassed by a twofold freedom: by God's freedom and man's own freedom. And it is marked by the dual-single history that results from the partnership of man with God: by the vocation from God that calls man to surpass himself and, thus, to come into his true authenticity as well as by the refusal of man who wants to be only a man, who is afraid to set out beyond himself and, thus, fails to achieve himself. Let us leave the question there, at a place where a very clear answer to the question about the meaning of our axiom begins to emerge, so as to listen, before anything else, to the voice of Sacred Scripture.

b. The Answer of Scripture

Since all the essential New Testament passages in which the word φύσις appears in a sense pertinent to our discussion are concentrated in the writings of Saint Paul,[19] it should suffice to analyze in the following pages his use of this word. A closer look at the usage of the Apostle allows us to identify three different albeit overlapping semantic fields for the word *physis*.

1. First, we find a biological or (with regard to man) a racial concept of nature corresponding to the Jewish roots of Paul's thought. Indeed, for the Jew, race, namely, the lineage of those who were descended from Abraham, was at the same time a theological category: salvation is fundamentally bound up with the children of Abraham. For all others, "race" then likewise becomes theologically significant, but in a negative way: since they are not descended from Abraham, they do not belong to the covenant people and do not come under God's promises. We find this concept of nature in the following passages:

Romans 2:27: ἡ ἐκφύσεως ἀκροβυστία = "those who are by nature uncircumcised" = those who by reason of their birth do not belong to the race of the circumcision = non-Jews. The equation is clear: Φύσις = race, descent by birth.

Romans 11:21: τῶν κατὰ φύσιν κλάδων οὐκ ἐφείσατο = "God did not spare the natural branches." The whole passage about the olive tree makes this racial understanding of nature very evident: there are those who, by nature, according to their racial descent and bloodline, belong to the olive tree, Israel, and there are branches that were grafted

---

[19] The passages are compiled and briefly analyzed by O. Kuß, *Der Römerbrief* (Regensburg, 1957), 72ff.

on later, that did not grow "naturally" from the tree but originated elsewhere.

Galatians 2:15: ἡμεῖς φύσει Ἰουδαῖοι καὶ οὐκ ἐξ ἐθνῶν = "we ourselves, who are Jews by birth and not Gentile . . ." (the same meaning is found, *mutatis mutandis*, in Galatians 4:8: τοῖς φύσει μὴ οὖσιν θεοῖς = "to beings that by nature are no gods").

2. There is also, however, a passage in which Paul uses a concept of nature that he is obviously borrowing from the popular Stoic philosophy: nature, not in the sense of a bloodline or a biological category, but rather in the sense of an essential structure that is rationally understood. Now the Stoic picture is not drawn exactly and thoroughly; rather, it is presented only in a very attenuated, popular-science sense; nonetheless, it is there. The Greek roots in the thinking of Saint Paul make their presence known.

The text of Romans 2:14 reads: ὅταν γὰρ ἔθνη τὰ μὴ νόμον ἔχοντα φύσει τὰ τοῦ νόμου ποιῶσιν. [= "When Gentiles who have not the law do by nature what the law requires"]. *Physis* suggests the law to the Gentiles. Those who according to their biological *"physis"* are non-Jews and hence do not have the law by that title, are nevertheless inspired by *physis*, metaphysically understood, to follow the law. Nature is for them a law.

We find this concept of norm applied concretely in Romans 1:26, which speaks about φυσικὴ χρῆσις and παρὰ φύσιν χρῆσις, about "natural" and "unnatural" sexual relations, meaning here the normal sexual intercourse between a man and a woman as opposed to homosexual behavior. It is clear that here the "nature" of man and the behavior prescribed by it is understood as genuine guidance for man. Finally, this concept is found in a much weaker and very generalized form in 1 Corinthians 11:14 also, where again a "natural" matter—the difference between a man's head of hair and a woman's—is taken as guidance concerning right ("natural") behavior.

It is striking that in these two specific instances, Romans 1:26 and 1 Corinthians 11:14, the biological relevance to the metaphysical concept is very strong: a concrete biological fact offers guidance. In this regard there is clearly semantic unity with the first usage of the word.

3. With the coming of Christianity arose a new situation in which, on the one hand, the biological concept of nature becomes a theological concept in a new sense: nature is understood, not in terms of

biology or rational metaphysics, but rather in terms of the concrete history that has taken and is taking place between God and man. We find Christianity distinguishing itself, the development of a typically Christian way of thinking that as yet has no categories of its own but is already beginning to develop them as it addresses issues, even in a concept that is at first peripheral.

In Ephesians 2:3, Paul speaks with his compatriots, the Jews, and points out to them that they, too—or from his perspective "we"— have sinned καὶ ἤμεθα τέκνα φύσει ὀργῆς ὡς καὶ οἱ λοιποί = "We were by nature children of wrath, like the rest of mankind." For the Jews, this was an unheard-of and positively nonsensical statement (linguistically nonsensical as well). "By nature", on account of their birth, the others, the non-Jews, are children of wrath. The Jews, however, are not, precisely because of their nature. We see that *physis* per se here belongs to the biological usage and again means something like "on account of our birth, according to our natural origins". But it acquires a completely new meaning, inasmuch as Paul now declares to the race of the redeemed: Not only the others are by nature children of wrath, but we are, too. All are. The universality of this statement objectively abolishes the racism that is still present linguistically and replaces it with a completely new universality. Paul, the Christian, no longer takes a natural, racial event as his point of departure; instead, salvation comes from the spiritual event of believing; merely natural existence, in and of itself, is in any case without salvation. As the "People of God" concept is divested of its racial and biological connotation, so necessarily is the concept of nature along with it. By birth, according to one's natural origins alone, no one is saved [*im Heil*], but, rather, everything is in ruins [*im Unheil*]. This means that concrete nature, as it is in fact bestowed on man in his birth, is not a salvific order. Not only is it not "God", as the Stoics taught, but it is also not a direct expression of the divine intentions, because it does not fall to man's lot, so to speak, directly from God; rather, it is warped and disfigured by a long human prehistory that burdens it. It is marked not only by him who once created it, but it likewise and even more clearly bears the traces of man, who has abused it.

If we try to summarize the Pauline data, we find that Paul no doubt attributes to nature a certain guiding character, but it by no means assumes the status of an unambiguous and absolute norm. Man receives true enlightenment about his being, not from "nature", but rather from his encounter with Christ in faith. Nature can very well be the sign of the Creator, but it is not so with perfect clarity, because it is also the expression of man's highhandedness. Once again we find, as in Bonaventure's writings, the nature of man in tension between two freedoms: God's and man's. But Paul's letters reveal even more momentously the resulting conflict, the peculiar tension of the human being, which announces itself in a nature that is just as much the expression of God's call (Rom 2:14) as it is that of his wrath (Eph 2:3).

3. Attempt at a Synthesis

"Gratia praesupponit naturam." According to all that we have meditated upon, this axiom is correct and fully biblical in saying that grace, the encounter of man with the God who calls him, does not destroy what is truly human in man but, rather, salvages and fulfills it. This genuine humanity of man, the created order "man", is completely extinguished in no man; it lies at the basis of every single human person and in many different ways continuously has its effects on man's concrete existence, summoning and guiding him. But of course in no man is it present without warping or falsification; instead, in every individual it is caked with the layer of filth that Pascal once aptly called the "second nature" of man. Man has obtained for himself a second nature, the core of which is the susceptibility to egoism—concupiscence. This is also why in both ancient and modern languages the word "man" has a peculiarly ambiguous set of connotations, in which high and low, noble and base things are strangely intertwined. This ambiguity is significantly reflected in Goethe's half-ironic, half-serious self-portrait:

> As a boy, reserved and defiant,
> As a youth, perplexed and arrogant,
> As a man, ready for action,
> As an old man, reckless and cranky—
> Upon your tombstone folks will read:
> That was a man indeed!

The same thing is evident even more profoundly in a quotation by Cardinal Saliège that I once read on a calendar page:

With the phrase "that's only human" people excuse everything nowadays. People get divorced: that's only human. People drink: that's only human. Someone cheats on an examination or in a competition: that's only human. Someone squanders his youth on vice: that's only human. People work sluggishly: that's only human. People embezzle: that's only human. There is no vice that people do not excuse with this formula. In this way people designate with the word "human" the weakest and basest features of a man. Often it is even used as a synonym for beastly. What a peculiar language! After all, humanity is precisely what distinguishes us from the animals. What is only human? The intellect, the heart, the will, the conscience, holiness. Those things are human.

And is not this ambivalence of the word "man" epitomized in a truly moving way in "the" man who is the standard, goal, and perfection of all humanity, who called himself the "Son of man" and in this expression united exaltation and lowliness in a span that reaches from the glory of God down to the abyss of utter rejection?[20]

It is clear: the way that grace travels to reach man has to pass through the "second nature", breaking open the hard shell of vainglory that covers the divine glory within him. And that means that there is no grace without the cross. De Lubac once expressed it strikingly:

> The whole mystery of Christ is a mystery of resurrection, but it is also a mystery of death. One is bound up with the other, and the same word, Pasch, conveys both ideas. Pasch means passing over. It is a transmutation of the whole being, a complete separation from oneself which no one can hope to evade. It is a denial of all natural values in their natural existence and a renunciation even of all that had previously raised the individual above himself.[21]

Only the humanity of the Second Adam is the true humanity, only the humanity that endured the Cross brings the true man to light. The

---

[20] On the concept of the Son of Man in the Synoptic Gospels, see J. Schmid, *RNT*, 4th ed., 2:160ff.; a thorough discussion can be found in O. Cullmann, *Die Christologie des Neuen Testaments* (Tübingen, 1957), 138–98. Concerning the more recent debate about the meaning of the title, see J. M. Robinson, *A New Quest of the Historical Jesus* (Naperville, Ill.: A. R. Allenson, 1959), 100–104.

[21] H. de Lubac, *Catholicism: Christ and the Common Destiny of Man*, trans. Lancelot C. Sheppard and Sr. Elizabeth Englund, O.C.D. (San Francisco: Ignatius Press, 1988), 367.

humanism based merely on what is noble about man eventually leads to man's self-assertion and self-idolization and the refusal of God's new reality. Let us listen once more to de Lubac:

> Christian humanism must be a *converted humanism*. There is no smooth transition from a natural to a supernatural love. To find himself, man must lose himself, in a spiritual dialectic as imperative in all its severity for humanity as for the individual, that is, imperative for my love of man and of mankind as well as for my love of myself. *Exodus* and *ecstasy* are governed by the same law.[22]

Meanwhile, of course, one must not lose sight of the other side of the whole thing. Although the created order of true humanity is no longer the concrete order of man, it is not a mere abstraction, either, not just a name. Despite everything, it intrudes again and again into reality as well. This has to be a permanent warning against an eccentric spirituality. In contrast to that, there is in fact something like common sense, a sound human understanding in which the consciousness of the abiding order of creation makes itself known; man should allow himself to be corrected again and again by this awareness and to be called back to the ground of reality. This knowledge about the abiding power of the created order ought to give to the Christian's ethos of the Cross a salutary sobriety that safeguards him against all fanaticism, eccentricity, or extravagance; indeed, a holy optimism will illuminate Christian life from that source and guard the Paschal way, which often enough is hard, against all false melancholy and impress on it the victorious gladness that befits the Christian as someone who hopes.

Perhaps we can go yet another step farther here. Earlier we acknowledged that it is the "nature" of the spirit to be beyond all "nature" and to be constantly surpassing itself. It is essential to the spirit not to be self-satisfied, to bear within itself the arrow pointing beyond itself. Contemporary philosophy recognizes with increasing clarity this "being related beyond oneself" as the essence of spirit, in which it is constituted as spirit in the first place.[23] But if that is the case, then the "exi"

[22] Ibid., 368. Cf. van de Pol, *Das reformatorische Christentum*, 324, citing similar statements of K. Barth. The law of the "Exodus" is impressively expounded also by E. Przywara, *Alter und Neuer Bund* (Vienna, 1956), for instance at p. 119.

[23] See, for example, H. Conrad-Martius, *Das Sein* (Munich, 1957), 118–41, esp. 133. See also the fundamental approach of Karl Rahner's philosophy in *Hörer des Worts* (Munich, 1940).

[Latin: "go forth"] that begins the revelation to Abraham is this perpetual fundamental law of exodus, which is perfected in the Christian mystery of the Pasch and is confirmed as the definitive fundamental law of revelation and, at the same time, also as the fundamental law of the spirit, the genuine fulfillment of the yearning cry that arises out of its nature. Then the Cross is not the "crucifixion of man" at all, as Nietzsche thought, but rather his true healing, which saves him from the deceptive self-sufficiency in which he can only lose himself and miss out on the endless promise that lies within him for the sake of the bourgeois mush of his supposed naturalness. Then the Paschal way of the Cross, this breaking down of all earthly assurances and their false satisfactions, is man's true homecoming, the true cosmic harmony in which God will be "everything to everyone" (1 Cor 15:28), in which the whole world is a song of praise to God and to the Paschal Lamb who was slain (Rev 5).[24]

In fact, the Cross is not the destruction of man, but, rather, the foundation of true humanity, about which the New Testament says the unfathomably beautiful words: "The goodness and loving kindness of God our Savior appeared" (Tit 3:4). The humanity of God— this is indeed the true humanity of man, the grace that fulfills nature.[25]

---

[24] E. Przywara has examined in depth the fulfillment of the *analogia entis* in the Cross in his underappreciated late work *Alter und Neuer Bund* (Vienna, 1956); cf. my review in *Wort und Wahrheit* 13 (1958): 220f.

[25] See the literature mentioned in n. 21, and also G. Söhngen, *Humanität und Christentum* (Essen, 1946).

13. The Christian and the Modern World

Reflections on the Pastoral Constitution
of the Second Vatican Council

Rarely has a word affected the people of our time so much as the word *aggiornamento*, which John XXIII coined in connection with his plan for a council. Admittedly, it can be translated only with difficulty into German, because the term "adaptation", which we might be inclined to reach for first, shifts the center of gravity in such a way as to express too much and at the same time too little. Too much, because it gives the impression that the Church wants to take what is up to date as the standard for her being and her message, whereas it can only be a matter of giving new thought and new expression to the one indissoluble truth and reality that has been placed for the Church in good hands by her Lord, so that she, in her earnestness and greatness, in her joy and her inexorable claim, can finally have a full hearing again and penetrate into our hearts. But the word says too little if it gives the impression that this "adaptation" is only an external tactical or educational measure based on an ownership that is per se completely secured, as though the Church did not also have to enter internally into the process of translating the message of yesterday into today, without which the message cannot truly be lived and cannot truly be proclaimed. In this translating or carrying-across the stream of the ages, another "transition" occurs, in which the essence of the Church that lives on the Paschal Mystery—the Easter Passover—is necessarily fulfilled.

The enthusiasm that the word and idea of *aggiornamento*, the "updating" of Christianity (as we could perhaps translate it), met with on all sides may have many different causes and probably also to a great extent some that were based on a misunderstanding. Nevertheless, it

Translated by Michael J. Miller.

shows that this was a response to a real need, that men, even believers, found it difficult in a world that had become so completely different to understand the old word of the Christian message as the perpetually new word of the forever "new" covenant of God with mankind, so that they often thought they were positively forced to live simultaneously in two worlds: in the past, to which the faith referred them, and in the present, in which their occupations put them. The scandal of the faith seemed as though doubled: whereas it is already difficult enough for a man to allow himself to be lifted above earthly things into God's world, now, in addition, it seemed that he could do that only by adopting a certain anachronistic way of thinking about and looking at earthly history and its realities. The real hope that arose so movingly from the word *aggiornamento* and touched hearts was that this anachronism would disappear, along with the doubling of the scandal of faith that was based upon it.

In keeping with this initial idea, the Council wanted to help get rid of the secondary scandal. It did this by its attempt to give the liturgy a more transparent and intelligible form; by its efforts to distinguish what is essential about the Church from what is inessential and, accordingly, to make sure that these insights were translated into the Church's constitution; finally, it tried in the Pastoral Constitution on the Church in the Modern World to take up the specific problems of contemporary man and to relate the Christian mission as well as Christian hope to his situation. In this work, the concept "world" noticeably moved to the center of the deliberations. Even before the Council, the idea had become widespread that the modern Christian must be "open to the world". Whereas this demand had at first been presented as a moral attitude, it soon acquired an ontological depth: Christian faith is based on God's turning toward the world; in the Incarnation, he stepped out of his glory and became man, and thereby he himself became "world". The modern secularization of the world, according to this theory, is not only factually a product of the Christian faith in creation and the Incarnation, but it fundamentally corresponds also to its essential orientation: The Christian must want the world to be worldly (and not sacral, numinous, or divinized) in order to remain true to God's mission, for he created the world as world and in Christ burst the sacral bonds by substituting his life and suffering for the temple worship and replacing the temple priests with servants of the Word and servants of joy.[1]

The idea of "world" became connected with the notion of historicity: world exists only as a temporal world; hence the time in which one happens to live is the authentic sign of God. Therefore, anyone who wants to read God's signs must get involved with today; temporality as an open entity is, to this way of thinking, simultaneously the expression for the fact we find the world, not as something already existing, but rather only as an entity to be created, and this is just what defines man: the fact that he is called into time and thus into creativity. Starting from impulses like these, "the modern world" became the main theme of this, the most voluminous conciliar document, which tried to define anew the place of Christianity. The dilemma that it faced consisted not only in the fact that today's world is an extraordinarily multilayered entity that defies summary description—it shared this difficulty with everyone today who tries as a sociologist, psychologist, or futurist to make statements about the general direction of the world of today and tomorrow. The document, however, had to go a step farther and relate this immense assemblage to the constants of Christian tradition and, on the basis of that, help man to find his way, to arrive at decisions that will really shape the future. As it did so, the optimism of secularization theology collided with the words of Scripture, which speak much, much differently about the world; although many were willing to condemn the stance of previous Christian history as an erroneous attitude or at least as merely the product of an earlier time, this raised a question that could not simply be ignored by anyone who wanted to hold fast to the faith of the apostles.[2]

In the midst of this struggle, the following reflections were written

---

[1] Cf. A. Auer, *Weltoffener Christ*, 3rd ed. (Düsseldorf, 1963); J. B. Metz, *Christliche Anthropozentrik* (Munich, 1962); *Zur Theologie der Welt* (Mainz, 1968); groundbreaking studies along these lines have been written by F. Gogarten, esp. *Verhängnis und Hoffnung der Neuzeit*, 2nd ed. (Stuttgart, 1958), and also by A. V. Bauer, *Freiheit zur Welt* (Paderborn, 1967). For the debate about the priesthood that is mentioned briefly in the text, I refer the reader here to just one "Document of the German Bishops on the Priestly Ministry": *Schreiben der deutschen Bischöfe über das priesterliche Amt* (Trier, 1969).

[2] I present in depth the issues in this debate, which became decisive for the problem of postconciliar Catholicism, in my little book *Die letzte Sitzungsperiode des Konzils* (Cologne, 1966), 25–44 [published in English as part four of *Theological Highlights of Vatican II* (New York: Paulist Press, 1966)].

down; they were and are intended to help bring about, first, a clarification of terminology and, then, subsequently to contribute also to a clarification of thought, faith, and action.

1. What Does "World" Mean?

If we want to arrive at an answer that is not subject from the outset to all sorts of uncertainty and does not uncritically place itself at the service of fashionable "concerns" instead of contributing to a critical refinement of those concerns, it will be necessary first of all to look for clear terminology. Therefore we must first ask: What does the word "world" actually mean? The uncertainty hidden behind it is no doubt one of the chief sources of the multiple misunderstandings that encumber our inquiry. Closer inspection shows that the term "world" (in connection with the question about "the Christian and the world") includes several levels that are quite different. We can distinguish four stages in which it appears.

1. "World" can mean, first, simply the existing cosmos; it then designates the extrahuman reality that was not made by man but, rather, is presented to him as a given. If we take this meaning as our basis, then the question about the Christian attitude toward the world is clearly decided. For the Christian understands the existing cosmos as God's good creation and, thus, as a thought of God that has taken shape, as God's outwardly directed fullness in which we encounter our Creator. As a result of this belief in creation, he will at the same time see this reality as a task: for in the biblical creation account, the creation of man is connected with the commission to subdue the earth (Gen 1:28). The created world is not just a place of wonder for man; rather, he is also assigned to shape it. That which comes from the consciousness and thought of God is to be permeated, so to speak, by the consciousness and thought of man and is thus to be brought to its fulfillment in its God-given spiritual meaning.

Of course, one could pause already at this point and ask whether Christendom really has put into practice this world-ethos that is set before it in the creation doctrine of both Testaments, which in contrast to the Greek world-ethos had something utterly revolutionary about it. For the Greek, despite all his joy in the cosmos, the world is by no means determined on the whole by thought; instead, even though it is formed by the "idea", nevertheless the cosmos as matter, according to its material consistency, is essentially non-rational, indeed unintelligible, the real adversary of the intellect. That is why Greek thought knows no creator-god, either, but only a subordinate god, the demiurge, who shapes matter and imparts the forms to it. God himself, so to speak, does not dirty his hands with the world. This corresponds to the negative appraisal of work that is characteristic of antiquity: as with the gods, so too for men, work can only be a matter for the lower social strata. For the free man, in contrast, as for the highest divinity, it is fitting to devote himself solely to speculative contemplation of eternal truth. The full extent of the Christian revolution becomes clear, in contrast, when Christ in the Gospel of John defends his "working" on the Sabbath by referring to the Father, the Creator God, who "is working still, and I am working" (Jn 5:17). The backdrop for this—a scandal that was ultimately incomprehensible in antiquity—is the fact that Christ, whom faith acknowledges to be the Son of God, lived in the world as the son of a laborer (*tekton*), indeed, as a laborer (Mk 6:3; cf. Mt 13:55), and on that account was despised by his own people.

But—we must continue now—how long was it until Christendom grasped the reappraisal of values that came to pass here? That required an external impetus, one that admittedly owed its existence ultimately to the new realities that proceeded from the faith: the impetus given by the scientific and working world of the nineteenth and twentieth centuries. Incidentally, it should also be mentioned in this connection that the scientific dealings with the world that were developed by the natural sciences had to conquer their territory through a conflict with the historical form of the faith, but at the same time they would have been unthinkable without the transformation of man's understanding of the world brought about by faith. For only a world that is no longer full of gods but is per se, as something created, merely "world"; only a world in which sun and moon are no longer divine rulers of the cosmos but merely lamps hung by the Creator (Gen 1:14-18); only a world that comes as entirely from the Logos and therefore is thoroughly "logical" could be the point of departure for an objective, scientific exploration of the world, which not accidentally developed precisely in distinctively Christian lands.[3] But even there, how far Christendom was left behind in return!

2. If we look somewhat more carefully at man's actual dealings with the "world" that we encountered in what was just said, we will very quickly realize that the simple understanding of the "world" as creation is based on a certain abstraction and that going beyond it leads us to a second level of the concept of world. For "world" can also mean the reality confronting man that man has already shaped. And here the matter first becomes really concrete, since a man living in history does not get to deal at all with the created world pure and simple. The world that he encounters and to which he relates his behavior is never merely God's creation; instead, it is always a world that has already been shaped and stamped by human effort.

If one tries, however, to arrive at an evaluation of the "world" (under this more realistic aspect) that will support an ethos, then the question becomes much more differentiated than before. Since the question will recur in another line of argument, let us be content for the moment with a thought that results from a glance at the Bible. Sacred Scripture identifies as the founder of the first city on earth the fratricide Cain or his son (it is not unambiguously clear from the text). In this context, the city stands as the epitome of the man-made world, as the summary of civilizing realities as a whole. Along these same lines, Scripture includes the first inventor in Cain's genealogy. This inclusion is no accident; it is a stylistic device by which the biblical author expresses a judgment on technical realities. He regards these things as being marked by man's willfulness, by the hubris of someone who wants to manage without God. The story of the Tower of Babel (Gen 11:1–9) repeats this judgment once again in an impressive way.

Yet one cannot call the overall attitude of the Bible hostile to culture by any means. Sacred Scripture concludes with the image of the holy city descending from heaven and, thus, sees the perfection of the world in the image of the city. The stamp of human culture thus appears at the same time as the abundance of fulfillment at which the world is

---

[3] Cf. G. Söhngen, "Entgötterung der Welt", *MThZ* 6 (1955): 16–20; J. Frings, *Das Konzil und die modern Gedankenwelt* (Cologne, 1961); W. Goez, *Naturwissenschaft und Evangelium* (Heidelberg, 1954); especially important for the nuanced character of his statements is G. von Rad, *Das erste Buch Mose*, 7th ed., ATD 2/4 (Göttingen, 1964), 34–53.

supposed to arrive, as the prefiguration of the definitive security of a
world that is forever formed by the Spirit.[4] In this respect, the judgment on what we might call technology, culture, and civilization remains ambivalent. These realities are promises and dangers at the same
time. In any case, however, Sacred Scripture offers grounds for neither
a one-sided demonization nor a one-sided glorification of technology
and civilization.

3. The whole thing becomes more lucid if we take a third step by
realizing that even the civilized world exists, not in and of itself, but
only in union with the men who form and sustain it. That means that
the second aspect, too, still involved a certain abstraction when we
observed the man-made world in itself, whereas it does not exist in
itself at all, but only in union with man, who continuously shapes it.
"World" necessarily includes man in it; it is not something that one
could separate neatly from man and set in opposition to him. Rather, it
implies a certain complex of human behaviors insofar as they are related
to the extrahuman reality that is ordered to man. So then we could
define "world" precisely as the totality of those human behaviors in
which man is related to the shaping of his earthly forms of existence.
One might very well say that we usually have this state of affairs in
mind when we say "world": the world that exists among men and in
their world-related behavior. This is an important realization; for if the
"world" cannot be divided from man, then this means that it cannot
be neatly separated from and set in opposition to the Church and to
Christians, either. Indeed, the world exists in them, too: they themselves are a part of what we call world, and thus the dialogue with the
world is always to some extent dialogue of Christians with themselves.
The term "world" simply describes one pole of their own existence;
the question of "the Christian and the world" accordingly implies, at
bottom, the question of the inner polarization of Christian existence
itself, that is, the question of how the two poles that are involved in
shaping the parameters for earthly existence and in centering on the
eternal should be coordinated in the life of the Christian.

This realization seems to me to be of great importance also because

---

[4] See in this volume the essay "Resurrection and Life Everlasting" as well as my article
"Schöpfung" in the *Lexikon für Theologie und Kirche* 9:460–466.

it makes evident at the same time the fact that what is Christian never exists in an entirely worldless way. Because it consists of men whose behavior is "world", it will itself always make its appearance concretely in worldly connections. This interweaving of what is Christian with the world can easily lead to the situation of an apparent conflict between faith and the world, while in reality what is Christian is not being defended against the world but, rather, just one particular historical form of Christian involvement in the world against another; for example, faith may appear to be opposed to the world, but in reality it is only an opposition between the thirteenth and the twentieth century, because the thirteenth-century polarization of Christian existence is equated with the faith as such. In the conflicts between faith and world that arise again and again, it will be necessary in any case to keep a watchful eye on these sorts of dangers.

4. Although the term "world" in our reflections thus far has acquired more and more anthropological and, thus, ethical content, we must now note that one last refinement of the concept of world is possible that frames it still more narrowly. One can narrow down the concept of world in such a way that one does not understand it generally (as we have just done) to mean man's behaviors in relation to earthly existence but, rather, exclusively that behavior through which man makes a decision *in favor* of this world alone and *against* what is godly and eternal. This is the usage of the term "world" that we usually encounter in the Gospel of John and in the First Letter of John. The world about which he speaks here could be defined as the total complex of man's behaviors that are contrary to the faith. John means this reality, which in its own way constitutes "world", when he speaks emphatically about "this world"; Paul means it, too, when he talks about the present age or even about Satan as the god of this earthly era (2 Cor 4:4).[5]

Although the world, understood in this way, is intrinsically and authentically the opposite of what the Church tries and ought to be by her nature, this world does not constitute a self-contained realm, either, alongside the Church and strictly separate from her. Rather,

---

[5] The Johannine expression "the ruler/prince of this world" has the same sense: John 12:31, 14:30, 16:11. This touches on the problem of the "authorities and powers", about which see H. Schlier, *Mächte und Gewalten im Neuen Testament* (Freiburg, 1958).

inasmuch and insofar as willfulness—the tendency to separate oneself from God, to pass him by and to cast him aside—exists in us, too, the world exists in us, in the midst of believers and in the midst of the Church. And conversely, inasmuch as the simplicity of obedience, the patience of bearing with one another, the truthfulness that does not seek its own advantage, and the simplicity of true love do exist among non-Christians, it is not the world that is present there but, rather, the essence of what the Church ultimately should be. These insights lead to several conclusions that are important for the elucidation of our question.

a. If the world is understood in the sense just described as the totality of behaviors contrary to the faith and thus as the essential contradiction of the faith, then it goes without saying that it is a negative concept that calls our attention to the necessity of the crucifixion, to the law of the grain of wheat that must fall to the earth and die in order to bear fruit.

b. However, the world, understood in this way, is not a self-contained alternative to the Church, which simply stands outside of her and thus should be opposed; rather, it is the willfulness that asserts itself over and over again within us, which tries to drive us away from God and, hence, subjects *each* of us to the law of the Cross. The fact that this anti-God tendency is called "world" indicates its universality, which means that it cannot be contrasted to the Church but, rather, must be assessed as a part of the situation of every person, and of the Christian as well.

c. Hence the Christian ethos with regard to earthly realities cannot be derived simply from this negative concept of world, because the point of departure and the breadth of the concept are aimed at something completely different. I think that this insight is of great importance and accounts for a whole series of confusions that not infrequently bog down the discussion of our question. All too easily one inadvertently shifts from the second and third connotations introduced here to the last level of meaning and thus encounters hopeless contradictions that lead either to the trivialization of the world's profound hostility to the faith or to inordinate pessimism or to strange mixtures of these two positions.

2. *Characteristics of the Modern World*

Whereas what we have said clarifies somewhat the concept "world" as it is presented in the tradition of biblical faith, the second, more difficult part of our task remains: the question about the characteristics of the "modern" world. To say anything even remotely exhaustive about it is impossible. What we can do is attempt to gain some insight into the historical peculiarity of the era starting in the nineteenth century in comparison with earlier stages of history. Without trying to be in any way comprehensive, one can still clearly note two distinctive features that characterize the modern era's relation to the world: the experience of the unity and essential worldliness of the world and the experience of the "malleability of the world".[6] Let us try now to consider more closely the meaning of these two formulas.

a. The Experience of the World's Unity

The discovery of America at the beginning of the modern era led, as it were, to the "demythologization" of the earth and the ocean. The earth was discovered as earth, as the one world of the one human race. A brief note on intellectual history might illuminate what is meant by this. In Canto 26 of the *Inferno*, Dante depicts his meeting with Ulysses (Odysseus), who tells him about his final adventures, a subject on which *The Odyssey* by Homer is silent. According to his account, after returning home the hero could not stand being in the house for very long, and he set out once again on a much more daring journey: He sailed through the Straits of Gibraltar; he crossed the boundary set for men that even the demigod Hercules had respected, and traveled out onto the ocean at the world's limits. The "mad voyage" (as Dante calls it) ended when Odysseus ran his ship aground on Mount Purgatory—he did not cross with impunity the limits that are set for man.[7] The real "Ulysses", Columbus, who sailed across the ocean one and a half centuries after Dante, was not shipwrecked on Mount Purgatory but, rather, discovered—America.

[6] See H. Freyer, *Theorie des gegenwärtigen Zeitalters* (Stuttgart, 1958), esp. 15–31.
[7] On the transformation of the figure of Ulysses in Dante, see the excellent analysis by A. Rüegg, *Die Jenseitsvorstellungen vor Dante* (Einsiedeln-Cologne, 1945), 2:108–17.

There is more to this contrast than an entertaining bit of intellectual history. It is the expression of an intellectual upheaval that still has by no means been overcome internally. Once it was taken for granted that the world passed into the metaphysical and eternal at its edges; now, in the discoveries of the modern era, it is discovered to be pure world on all sides. It is everywhere nothing but just that—world. The de-mythologization of the world inaugurated by Columbus is followed by the discovery of Copernicus and its consequences: the demythologiza-tion of the heavens. The measurements of astronomy inconsiderately reveal that the "heavens", too, which we see above our heads, are not "Heaven" but, again, just "world". The heavens are not—as Dante portrays them, in keeping with the theology of his time—an ascending cosmos of ever more exalted metaphysical consistency leading up to the "empyrean", the firmament in which God dwells; they, too, are a world of the same sort as the one that we inhabit.[8]

From the nineteenth century on, this spatial demythologization of man's world view was increasingly accompanied by another tempo-ral one. The world is recognized as a world of becoming, a world in which there is no longer room for divisions into "prelapsarian" and "after the Fall", pre-redemption and post-redemption. The structure of the world and the behavior of living beings exhibit no differences before and after the appearance of man, says the scientist; the structure of history and the behavior of man remain the same throughout all of the historical era, says the historian. Both deny the divisions that form the coordinate system of the theological view of history: theological elements have vanished from the measurable temporal record of the world just as they did from spatial geography. Here, too, the world has become one and the same "world". Neither discovery invalidates the faith, but they fundamentally change the presuppositions according to which it must be developed and explained. In both instances, the faith would dangerously misunderstand itself if it tried to deny the new data; it must instead accept them as presuppositions of its own message if it is not to degenerate into an anachronism. And in this regard, of course, it still has a lot to do.

[8] I tried to indicate some features of the late Scholastic theological geography of heaven, on which Dante's world view is based, in my essay: "Der Mensch und die Zeit im Denken des hlg. Bonaventura", in *L'Homme et son destin d'après les penseurs du moyen âge* (Louvain and Paris, 1960), 473–83. A thorough background is provided by P. Duhem, *Le Système du monde*, 5 vols. (Paris, 1913–1917).

b. The Experience of the World's Malleability

The experience of the worldliness of the world leads automatically to the recognition of its malleability, which as of the early nineteenth century introduces the second phase of the modern era, the era of the technological shaping of the world. The changes that have occurred through the latter in man's overall relation to reality as well as in the general orientation of his existence have been described often enough and do not need to be repeated here. In fact it is self-evident that man's situation has become different, when he no longer finds the in-itself character of nature anywhere but rather encounters only himself on all sides, when he no longer deals immediately with the *ars Dei* [handiwork of God] but only with man's technology, which has become for him the space that he inhabits.[9] Let us assume that this is well known and turn right away to the consequences for man's fundamental intellectual stance. They are extraordinarily far-reaching.

1. Our relation to work and to our earthly duties has changed. Whereas antiquity mused about the real ideal of complete liberation from earthly care so as to have "leisure for the truth", and whereas being occupied with worldly matters seemed to the ancients to be a burden and a distraction from what is essential, modern man regards service to the world almost with a sort of religious fervor. He has no tolerance for flight from the world and little for leisure; he sees man's positive potential as the ability to change the world, to exhaust its possibilities, and to enhance its inhabitability.

2. Our relation to culture and science has changed. While Tertullian's proud saying, "What does Jerusalem have to do with Athens?"[10]

---

[9] See the works cited in nn. 1 and 3; also R. Guardini, *Das Ende der Neuzeit* (Basel, 1950); H. U. von Balthasar, *Die Gottesfrage des heutigen Menschen* (Vienna, 1956); J. Ratzinger, "Neuheidentum", *LThK* 7:907–9. The fact that the modern natural sciences increasingly confront man only with himself is demonstrated within the parameters of scientific thought by W. Heisenberg, *Das Naturbild der heutigen Physik* (Hamburg, 1955), 7–23.

[10] "Quid ergo Athenis et Hierosolymis? Quid Academiae et ecclesiae? Quid haereticis et christianis? Nostra institutio de porticu Solomonis est qui et ipse tradiderat Dominum in simplicitate cordis esse quaerendum. Viderint qui Stoicum et Platonicum et dialecticum christianismum protulerunt. Nobis curiositate opus non est post Christum Iesum nec inquisitione post evangelium" [What indeed does Athens have to do with Jerusalem? What agreement is there between the Academy and the Church? What do heretics have in common with Christians? Our instruction comes from "the porch of Solomon", who had himself taught that the Lord should be sought in simplicity of heart. Those who have produced a Christianity composed of Stoic, Platonic, and dialectic elements shall one day see (how durable their doctrine proves to be)! We have no need of curious disputation after

certainly expresses a particularly extreme standpoint, it is nevertheless characteristic of a basic intellectual disposition. The great Doctor of the Western Church, Augustine, allows science in his program for education only to the extent that it helps students to understand Scripture and to build up their faith.[11] Looming over the entire medieval period was the word *curiositas*, which it used to describe that thirst for knowledge which ultimately can only lead man away from what is really important, which is not science, but wisdom. And seeing his colleagues in the philosophy faculty at the University of Paris pushing for the autonomy of the sciences, Bonaventure said that it profits a man nothing if he learns how to measure the world but forgets how to measure himself.[12] At the end of the Middle Ages, the little book on *The Imitation of Christ* emphatically said No once again to a scientific mentality that ignores salvation—which, however, has become one of the characteristic components of the modern era and of its understanding of existence. As you see, the difficulty that the Christian has in orienting himself to modern science has roots that run very deep. It would be an oversimplification to speak here about long-standing dysfunctional developments, as a glance at the First Letter to the Corinthians shows: the folly of the Cross and the wisdom of the world cannot be united in a facile synthesis. In this regard, the question we have encountered has existed to a certain extent from the beginning: in a world that has been rendered "scientific", its scope is simply far more comprehensive.

3. Finally, our attitude toward human community has also changed. Antiquity and the Middle Ages tried to cope with the question of the other person's need by means of *caritas*, through a momentary alleviation of need that nevertheless changes nothing about the overall situation as such, which was considered irreparable anyway in a world that was bound for destruction.[13] Today, in contrast, we find an almost fanatical insistence on justice, on the establishment of conditions and

---

knowing Christ Jesus, nor of subtle inquiries after hearing the Gospel!], *De praescr. haer.* 8:9–12, *CChr* 1:193.

[11] *De doctrina christiana*, lib. II. Cf. F. X. Eggersdorfer, *Der heilige Augustinus als Pädagoge* (Freiburg, 1907), 107–30.

[12] *Coll in Hex* I, 24 (ed. Quaracchi, 5:333a). Concerning the disputes forming the background of the text, see J. Ratzinger, *The Theology of History in St. Bonaventure*, trans. Zachary Hayes, O.F.M., 2nd ed. (Chicago: Franciscan Herald Press, 1989), 134–63.

[13] Such a claim misconstrues the actual situation in the Middle Ages; see G. Ratzinger, *Geschichte der kirchlichen Armenpflege* (Freiburg, 1884).

ordinances that guarantee to each what is his due, so that he no longer needs "alms". Accordingly, to the modern observer the charity of yore appears in a rather dubious light; he actually sees it as an attempt to do without justice, which is the prerequisite for real charity.

Meanwhile, something like a critique of these trends can be noted in the fact that technological development is slowly reaching a saturation point that could lead to its self-destruction if it does not allow itself to be stimulated and limited by ideas about values that are considered obsolete. We could easily demonstrate this with regard to each of the three points we have just mentioned as an example of the new outlook. What enhances the inhabitability of the world? Now that technological conveniences have reached their ultimate stage of development, a longing arises for the simplicity of the way in which things were done originally; the self-made world that surrounds man on every side becomes a prison that elicits a cry for freedom, for something completely different. It is becoming evident that free time is no substitute for leisure, that leisure needs to be learned anew if work is to retain its meaning. Man, who is exhausting the world's resources for himself, ends by destroying the world and, thus, his own living space—this is no longer the Cassandra cry of technophobic romantics but, rather, the account that technology gives of itself. Thus, "values-free" science becomes a nightmare and the real defendant in this whole development: ideology trumps everything unless a sober desire reawakens for wisdom and contemplation and the inner freedom they impart. And finally: it is still clear that a love that is supposed to replace justice is no love at all, but it is becoming even clearer that a justice that tries to make love superfluous is a satanic illusion—especially when one looks at societies that try to cure man through the system alone and thereby turn morality into a fanaticism about the future while destroying man from within.

In this conflict of experiences and findings, the dilemma of modern Christianity becomes clear. On the one hand, the modern era is running away from it in the name of the ideals of freedom, the humanization of the world through the power of human reason, and justice, and this creates the impression that the driving forces for this exodus from the Church are drawn from the core of the Christian message; one gets the impression that the most essential tenets of Christianity are put into practice precisely in this classical movement of the modern era and that the Christian, therefore, must set out as quickly as possible so as to enter into this movement and to help drive it along, so as to become a true Christian precisely through an unconditional solidarity with the spirit of the modern age. On the other hand, the question remains whether the Christian ought to take up the task of being a corrective influence and, thus, protect man against himself. That is why the path of Christianity in the modern era zigzags curiously: during the Enlightenment, it decisively boarded the train of modernity; then, after the upheavals of the French Revolution and the wars that that started, it made a rather terrified retreat into specifically ecclesial activities; then, after gaining new strength, it increasingly disparaged the alleged ecclesiastical ghetto of that period (while overlooking the great initiatives that were going into effect at the time in the fields of education and social services through the founding of new religious communities and lay movements) and professed a new, more radical solidarity with the spirit of the present age; and, finally, the dilemma of division in the world at large and within the Church. The tragic one-sidedness of the final conciliar debates was due to the fact that they were dominated by the traumatic sense of being behind the times and an eagerness to catch up with modernity, which was blind to the inner ambiguity of the modern world and could not be brought to confront the difficulty of the real situation by the excessively doctrinaire, scholastically rigid reaction of the conciliar opposition. What was not settled in the conciliar debates must therefore be worked through laboriously in the postconciliar Church; but perhaps putting up with the situation together is the only way to gain the knowledge that leads forward.

3. The Christian and the Modern World

If we are to find an answer, it seems to me important to start by distinguishing between the situation of the individual Christian and the task of the Church as Church. The two aspects are complementary but not identical and therefore must be examined separately.

1. The kind of relationship that man has with earthly reality today can be described as an ethos of work, science, and striving for a just order. In this regard, it is the same "world" with which the Christian has to deal. The question about the relation of the Christian to "the modern world" is therefore precisely a question about his relation to

these realities or to the ensemble of relations that this expression designates. Clearly, elements of human willfulness and the rejection of God—in other words, of the world in the Johannine sense of "this world"—*can* at any time operate within this new relationship and in fact *do* operate in a considerable measure. To that extent, "the modern world" calls for vigilance and a critical sense on the believer's part. Meanwhile, it seems to me no less clear that that ensemble of relations which we have recognized as the objective content of "the modern world" does in fact contain elements that come from the center of Christianity. What Christian charity actually desires and must desire —to create equal opportunities for every man, the same ones that we ourselves have; to lighten the burden of every man's existence; to enable every man to bring to perfection his God-given gifts; to lead men out of their divisions into unity—that is certainly not the only motive of the modern scientific and working world, in which Marxist criticism and other ideologies can present disagreeable interests under nice-looking masks; yet this motive is included in it, and a concrete, creative Christian critique of "the modern world" ought to purify the "interests" toward that end.

Today we are confronted with the paradox of having to realize precisely that *curiositas* of science and of the scientific world is capable in many respects of carrying out the impulse of Christian charity more radically than the individual charity of ancient and medieval Christianity. Why should the Church hesitate to admit this and to be grateful that something of her own returns to her from outside in a new and challenging form? It should be the Christian's task, not to stand aloof from the modern world as a nay-sayer, but rather to purify today's scientific and working world from within, to exorcise it, and thus to free it for the purposes of Christian charity. By living this charity in the midst of the world, and only by doing so, can the Christian help to discern critically what elements of the powers "of this world" (in the negative sense) are in fact at work in it at any given time. Although in view of the undeniable presence of this factor *also*, the Christian's Yes to "the modern world" must be a critical affirmation, this of course cannot mean that he should make a half-hearted commitment—because there is no alternative. It cannot mean that he should participate by just being drawn along instead of pulling some of the weight himself. A half-hearted effort is useless. The Christian's response to today's problems cannot be to believe half of the time and the rest of the time to be swept along by a world from which he cannot get off. His response must be, rather, to believe totally and out of the totality of the faith to encounter the totality of the modern world—in other words, to act within functioning technological structures out of the responsibility of love. Such whole-hearted service in the task facing the modern world, then, really does not mean infidelity to the folly of the Cross for the benefit of a naïve optimism about progress. The very objectivity of the service undertaken in this way—if the whole thing is to be understood now in terms of the heart of Christian charity—requires a willingness to practice daily self-abandonment, without which there is no self-discovery. Christian asceticism does not become superfluous, even though its forms change. And it is clear that the service of personal love does not become superfluous, either, however much the face of the world may change. Without that service, the fundamental impetus of Christian charity about which we spoke would lose its credibility.

And finally: one consequence of critical affirmation, which does not exclude but rather demands whole-heartedness, will be that the Christian will perfect the working world in such a way that he makes it a means to greater freedom. That is its own goal, too, but freedom remains empty as long as it assumes the shrunken form of "free time", a technological change of pace, and thus amounts to little more than a disguised lack of freedom. Freedom is full only when it becomes room for the eternal; to unburden man physically and temporally by technology in this sense can become a real "liberation" of man, freeing him anew for what is eternal, but this hope is as yet unfulfilled. For that very reason it is an imperative of the first order for the Christian.

2. As for the task of the Church, modern theology has traveled a remarkable path over the last ten years. It began with the idea, developed in the [early twentieth-century German] Youth Movement, of "bringing home" the world and its values. But these values, once they were "brought back home", proved to be stronger than the house in which they had been lodged, and so the homecoming world turned into the idea of the worldly world: the notion that Christianity calls for the worldliness of the world, not its Christianization; truly Christianizing the world, according to this theory, means secularizing and de-sacralizing it, freeing it from taboos so that it can come into its own. The next step brings about the complete reversal of the original

movement: now the world is no longer brought into the Church; the Church herself has to be drawn instead into the movement of secularization. Her task, supposedly, is to critique society, to be the official critic of its primary institutions. Finally, this criticism acquires its own systematic dogma, and Church is viewed as a political entity, as part of the political liberation movements of this world.

This sketch of a decade of theological development displays the whole miserable state of theology, which is centered on our topic. A well-grounded confrontation with it is among the most urgent tasks facing the Church today. It cannot be accomplished here, in a reflection on the conciliar debate about the Church and the world.[14] Instead, I will just offer one little completely unguarded remark to indicate the general direction in which the discussion, in my opinion, must lead. It is not difficult to ascertain from the Gospel that the task of the Church as Church cannot be to take root in earthly things, by virtue of which she would try to construct something like a special Catholic world under her own direction, so to speak. Rather, there is only one world for all people; the task of the Christian (and thus of the Catholic) cannot be to create his own world for himself. His task is, rather, to permeate the one world of all men with the spirit of Jesus Christ. What the Church has to offer the world is not a private model world, which in truth would very quickly become a very typically human world again, as all attempts of this sort in history have amply demonstrated. What she has to offer the world is, rather, that which she alone can give: the Word of God, by which man lives no less than by the bread of this earth. Man is and remains a being in which not only the stomach hungers but also the mind and the heart; a being which endures hunger not only for food but also for meaning, for love, for infinity, and which cannot live without these truly human, no: godly gifts. In the technological world, too, and especially in it, this human hunger continues, and the Church owes it to mankind not to keep it in suspense by supposedly building a better earthly world (which she cannot accomplish) but, rather, to respond to its hunger and to uncover this hunger where it may have been forgotten. She should select only as many institutions —entities rooted in the flesh of the earth—as are really necessary for

---

[14] On this subject, see H. Peukert, ed., *Diskussion zur "politischen Theologie"* (Mainz and Munich, 1969); H. Maier, *Kritik der politischen Theologie* (Einsiedeln, 1970); Maier, *Kirche und Gemeinschaft* (Munich, 1972); H. Kuhn, *Der Staat* (Munich, 1967).

this service to the Word. The measure of concrete institutionalization and of earthly involvement lies in this: in the requirements of the Word of God, and nowhere else.

Note that this brings us back to our point of departure: to the tasks confronting a council that tried to compose a document about the Church in the modern world. The difficulty of this task has been demonstrated more clearly perhaps by the stammering attempts at an answer at the conclusion of this essay than by the elaboration of the questions that preceded them. And nevertheless: in this regard, too, we must not forget that it cannot be the task of the Church (as portrayed in the Council) to create here something like an official, intellectual model world—a scientifically elaborated synthesis of all the existential questions of modern man, which would necessarily be greeted by everyone with enthusiasm and without hesitation. In retrospect, one will probably have to accuse the Council of forgetting the modesty of earlier councils and of over-exerting itself along those lines and, so, of attempting too much. Thus many statements of a document that is well-intentioned per se and also to a great extent really useful will more or less rapidly become outmoded. The decisive thing is the attempt to arouse the conscience and to summon it to responsibility before God, who has shown himself in Jesus Christ as Word and Love, which on the Cross became both the crisis and the hope of the world.

14. On the Understanding of "Person" in Theology

The term "person" along with the idea behind this term is a product of Christian theology; in other words: it first sprang from the confrontation between human thought and the realities of the Christian faith in general and in this way entered into intellectual history. As Gilson put it, in the concept of person we encounter one of those contributions that the Christian faith made to human thought and made possible in the first place, that developed not simply from man's own philosophizing but, rather, from the dialogue between philosophy and the premises of the faith, in particular Sacred Scripture. More precisely, the term "person" arose out of two questions that Christian thought was forced to face from the beginning as centrally important: the questions "What is God?" (the God whom we meet in the Bible) and "Who is Christ?" In order to answer these two basic questions, which came up as soon as Christians started thinking about their faith, this speculation applied the Greek word *prosopon* = in Latin *persona*, which previously had had no philosophical significance or usage at all, and thus gave it a new meaning and opened up a new dimension of human thought. Although over the centuries this line of thought has ranged far from its origin and developed beyond it, it is still secretly but vitally dependent on that origin. Therefore, in my opinion, we cannot understand at all what "person" really means without going back again and again to probe those origins.

For this reason, the reader will excuse me if I, when asked as a systematic theologian about the dogmatic term "person", do not expound on the latest notions of modern theologians but, rather, try to lead the way back to the origin, to the wellsprings from which the

---

Translated by Michael J. Miller.

Lecture given at a conference on the understanding of "person" in education and related academic fields. The lecture form has been retained with slight modifications; this provenance may justify the sketchy, provisional nature of the text.

idea of person was born, and without which it could not continue to exist. The subdivision of our topic proceeds automatically from what we have just said. We will simply examine somewhat more closely the two sources of the term "person", the source in the question about God and the source in the question about Christ.

1. The Term "Person" in the Doctrine about God

a. The Source of the Term "Person"

The first figure that we run into is that of Tertullian, the great Western theologian. Tertullian shaped Latin into a theological language and with an ingenious, almost incredible assurance was able to set down in writing a theological terminology that later centuries could not surpass, because at the first attempt it coined permanently valid formulas for Christian thought. So it was Tertullian who also established for the West its formula for presenting the Christian idea of the Divinity: God is "una substantia—tres personae", one Being in three Persons.[1] At this point the word "person" enters intellectual history for the first time with its full import.

Several centuries passed before this statement could be intellectually assimilated and mastered, so that it was no longer merely a statement but really became an insight into the mystery, which it taught Christians to apprehend somehow, if not fully to comprehend. When we say that Tertullian was able to coin the expression but that the intellectual assimilation took place in a second phase, the question arises: How did he manage to find this word with such almost somnambulistic assurance?

Until recently, that was a riddle. Carl Andresen, a dogmatic historian from Göttingen, succeeded not long ago in illuminating the matter to a great extent, so that the source of the term "person", its real wellspring, is more or less clear to us today.[2] The answer to the question "How

---

[1] The definitive formula of the West reads: *una essentia—tres personae*; Tertullian had said *una substantia—tres personae*, and Augustine: *una essentia—tres substantiae*.

[2] C. Andresen, "Zur Entstehung und Geschichte des trinitarischen Personbegriffs", *ZNW* 52 (1961): 1–38. The patristic passages that I cite in the following paragraphs are taken from Andresen's essay.

did the term *person* come about?" is this: The origin lies in so-called prosopographic exegesis. What does that mean? In the background is the word *prosopon*, which is the Greek equivalent of *persona*. Prosopographic exegesis is a form of interpretation that had already developed in ancient literary criticism. It observed that, in order to enliven the story line dramatically, the great poets of antiquity did not simply relate events but had persons appear and make speeches or placed words in the mouths of the gods that moved the action forward. In other words: as a literary device, the poet creates roles through which he can depict the action in dialogue. The literary critic uncovers this artistic device; he shows that the persons have been created as "roles" in order to dramatize the action (originally the word *prosopon*, and the later form *persona*, simply meant "role", the actor's mask). Consequently, prosopographic exegesis is an interpretation that brings this artistic device to light by making it clear that the author has created dramatic roles, characters in a dialogue, in order to enliven his poem or narrative.

Now Christian writers came upon something quite similar as they were reading Sacred Scripture. They found that here, too, the action moves forward in dialogue. Most importantly, they found the striking fact that God himself speaks in the plural or converses with himself (think of passages such as, "Let *us* make man in our image and likeness", or of God's remark in Genesis 3:22: Adam "has become like one of us", or of Psalm 110: "The LORD says to my lord . . .", which, according to the interpretation of the Church Fathers, is God's dialogue with his Son). This fact, that God himself is presented in the plural and as speaking with himself, was now treated by the Church Fathers in artistic terms by means of prosopographic exegesis, which thereby acquired a new meaning. Justin (d. 165), writing in the first half of the second century, says that the sacred author introduces various *prosopa* here, various "roles". But actually this word no longer means "roles" at all here, because the term acquires a completely new reality from faith in the Word of God; the roles that the sacred author introduces are realities, are dialogical realities. And so here the word *prosopon* = role is about to make the transition to giving birth to the idea of "person". I will cite here only one passage from Saint Justin to illustrate this process: "When you hear that the prophets speak sentences as though a person is speaking (ὡς ἀπὸ προσώπου), then do not suppose that they are being spoken by those Spirit-filled men (= the prophets) them-selves, but rather by the Logos who moves them."³ Justin is saying, therefore, that the speaking roles in dialogues that are introduced by the prophets are not mere literary devices. The "role" really exists; it is the *prosopon*, the face, the person of the Logos, which here is really speak-ing in dialogue *along with* the prophet. This demonstrates quite clearly how the premises of the Christian faith reshape and renew a system of interpreting texts that already existed in antiquity. The literary device of having dramatic roles appear that enliven the presentation with their dialogue reveals to the theologian the One who is performing the real role here, the Logos, the *prosopon*, the Person of the Word, which is no longer merely a role but a person.

Tertullian, in composing his writings not quite fifty years later, was already able to draw upon a copious tradition of such Christian proso-pographic exegesis, in which the word *prosopon* = *persona* had already gained its full reference to reality. I will make do with two examples. In *Against Praxeas*, Tertullian writes:

> [H]ow it is possible for a Being who is merely and absolutely One and Singular to speak in plural phrase, saying, "Let us make man in our own image, and after our own likeness;" whereas He ought to have said, "Let *me* make man in my own image, and after my own likeness," as being a unique and singular Being? In the following passage, however, "Behold the man is become as one of us," He is either deceiving or amusing us in speaking plurally, if He is One only and singular. . . . Nay, it was because He had already His Son close at His side, as a second Person, His own Word, and a third Person also, the Spirit in the Word, that He purposely adopted the plural phrase, "Let *us* make;" and, "in *our* image;" and, "become as one *of us*".⁴

We see here how the phenomenon of *intra*-trinitarian dialogue brings out the idea of the person who is a person in the authentic sense. Ter-tullian speaks in a similar way in his interpretation of Psalm 110, verse 1, "The LORD says to my lord . . .".

---

³ Justin Martyr, *First Apology*, chap. 36.

⁴ *Against Praxeas* 12, 1–3, in *Ante-Nicene Fathers*, ed. Alexander Roberts and James Don-aldson, vol. 3 (Peabody, Mass.: Hendrickson, 1995), 607; *C Chr* 2:1172f., Andresen, "Zur Entstehung", 10–11.

Observe also the Spirit speaking of the Father and the Son, in the character of a third Person: "The Lord said unto my Lord, Sit Thou on my right hand, until I make Thine enemies Thy footstool." Likewise in the words of Isaiah: "Thus saith the Lord to the Lord mine Anointed [Christ]." . . . [I]n these few quotations the distinction of *Persons in* the Trinity is clearly set forth. For there is the Spirit Himself who speaks, and the Father to whom He speaks, and the Son of whom He speaks.[5]

Now I do not intend to go into the historical details of these passages but simply to summarize briefly the implications for our topic of the idea of person. It seems to me that we can draw two conclusions. First, the term "person" developed out of acquaintance with Scripture, as a requirement for interpreting it. It is a product of familiarity with the Bible. And, second, it developed out of the idea of dialogue, in other words, as an explanation of the phenomenon of the God who speaks dialogically. To put it yet another way: the Bible with its phenomenon of the speaking God, with its phenomenon of the God who is *in* dialogue, called forth the concept of person. Now the individual exegeses that the Fathers offer are of course random and as such outdated, but the overall exegetical direction they follow did in fact capture the intellectual orientation of the Bible, inasmuch as the basic phenomenon that we encounter in the Bible is that of God who speaks and man who is spoken to—the phenomenon of partnership with man who is called by God in the Word to Love. But this brings to light the core of what person can mean in truth. Summarizing the previous discussion, we can say: the term "person", because of its origin, expresses the idea of dialogue and of God as the dialogical Being. It means God as the Being that lives in the Word and subsists as I and Thou and We. Based on

---

[5] *Against Praxeas* 11, 7–10 and 13, in Roberts and Donaldson, *Ante-Nicene Fathers* 3:606; C *Chr* 2:1172. In my opinion it would be important to investigate the preliminary rabbinical stages of this prosopographic exegesis that led up to the concept of person. The reader may find interesting material for this purpose in E. Sjöberg, "Geist im Judentum", in *ThWNT* 6:385ff. Sjöberg shows here that in the rabbinical texts the Holy Spirit is often portrayed in personal terms: He speaks, cries out, admonishes, mourns, weeps, rejoices, comforts, and so on. He is also presented as speaking to God. Sjöberg comments "that the stylistic device of personification and dramatization is typical of rabbinical literature" and "that the personal reaction of the Spirit is always connected with the words of Sacred Scripture" (386). Perhaps a closer examination could bring to light the fact that the patristic development of the concept of person had this rabbinical exegesis rather than ancient literary criticism as its point of departure.

this knowledge of God, man's own nature has become clear to him in a new way.

b. Person as Relation

With that we have described the first stage of the struggle to express the Christian concept of God. I would like to add briefly another perspective on the second major stage, in which the concept of person reached its full maturity.[6] Around two hundred years later, at the turn of the fifth century A.D., Christian theology had come so far as to be able to state clearly in well-defined concepts what is meant by the thesis: God is one Being in three Persons. It was now determined that in this formula "person" is to be understood as *relation*: There are three Persons *in* God, and they are by their very nature—according to Augustine and late patristic theology—relations. Therefore, they are not substances alongside one another; rather, they are nothing other than actual, real relations. I think that this idea from the theology of the late patristic era is very important. In God, person means relation. Relation, relatedness, is not something added on to the Person but, rather, *is* the Person himself; here the Person exists by his very nature only *as* relation. To put it even more concretely: the first Person begets, not as though the act of begetting a Son was something added on to the complete Person, but rather he *is* the act of begetting, of surrendering himself, of pouring himself out. The Person is identical with this act of self-giving. Therefore, one could define the first Person as self-giving in fruitful knowledge and love—not the self-giving one in whom there is an act of self-giving, but rather self-giving itself, pure act. An idea that reappeared only in this [twentieth] century in modern physics is anticipated here: that there is such a thing as pure actuality. We know that in our century scientists have attempted to reduce matter to waves, to the pure actuality of flowing. What may be a dubious idea in that context was declared by theology in the fourth and fifth centuries to be true about the Persons in God: that they are nothing other than the act of relating to one another. "Person" in God is the pure relativity of being turned toward each other; it is situated, not on the level of substance —the substance is *one*—but rather on the level of dialogue, of being related to one another. In this way, Augustine could then try to make

[6] For the historical background of this description, see A. Grillmeier, "Person II", in *LThK* 8:290–292 with additional bibliography.

the interplay of Trinity and Unity at least intuitively comprehensible, when he says, for instance: "In Deo nihil secundum accidens dicitur, sed secundum substantiam aut secundum relationem" (In God there is nothing accidental but, rather, only substance and relation). Here relation is acknowledged as a third characteristic fundamental category between substance and accident, the two great categorical forms of ancient thought, and we are again confronted emphatically and clearly with the Christian novelty of the personalist idea. Here, as it seems to me, the contribution of faith to human thought becomes quite exceptionally vivid and obvious: the Christian faith gave birth to this idea of pure actuality, of pure relativity, which does *not* lie on the level of substance and does not affect or divide the substance per se, and thus brought the personal phenomenon plainly into view.

We are standing here at a place where the speculative probing of Sacred Scripture, the assimilation of the faith through man's own thinking, seems to have reached its absolute summit, and we will be able to note with amazement that precisely here the way immediately opens back into Sacred Scripture, which clearly expounded this very phenomenon of pure relativity as the nature of person, especially in Johannine theology. In it we find, for instance, the formula: "The Son can do nothing of his own accord" (5:19). But the same Christ who declares this also says: "I and the Father are one" (10:30). This means: they are one precisely because he has nothing of his own, because he does not set himself up alongside the Father as a separate substance but, rather, is oriented toward him in total relativity and represents nothing but relativity toward him, a relatedness that singles out and reserves for itself nothing of its own. And this is applied in turn to the disciples (and here we find now the implications for anthropology) when Christ says: "Apart from me you can do nothing" (15:5). At the same time, though, he prays "that they may be one, even as we are one" (17:11). Thus it is part of the nature of discipleship also that man does not reserve what is merely his own, does not strive to develop the substance of his self-enclosed ego, but rather enters into pure relativity directed toward the other and toward God and precisely in this way truly comes to himself and comes into the fullness of what is his own, because he enters into union with that to which he is related.

I think that this leads to a profound and thoroughgoing illumination of both God and man, the decisive elucidation of what person must mean based on Scripture: *not* a self-enclosed substance, but rather the phenomenon of total relatedness, which of course can ultimately enter into its fullness only with the one who is God, yet which is a signpost pointing the way for all personal being. Thus at the same time we have reached the point at which the doctrine about God passes into Christology and anthropology—as we will see farther on.

One could pursue this line of thought about relation and relativity in John much farther and demonstrate that it is one of the main themes or even *the* predominant theme of his theology, at any rate of his Christology. I would like to mention just two more examples. John adopts the synoptic and late-Jewish theology of mission, which had already expressed the idea that the one sent has no meaning of his own, insofar as he is sent, but rather stands for the sender and is one with the sender. John further elaborates this idea of mission from late Judaism (which initially is merely functional) by portraying Christ as *the* one who is sent, who is wholly and by his very nature "the One Sent". The late Jewish proverb "The one whom a man sends is like the man himself" now acquires an entirely new and deeper meaning, because, apart from his being-sent, Jesus has nothing else at all; he is by his very nature "the One Sent". He is like the sender himself precisely inasmuch as he is oriented in the sheer relativity of his existence toward the sender; the content of the Johannine concept "the One Sent" could be described in these terms: here the complete absorption of being into "Being from and for someone" is declared. The content of Jesus' existence is "Being from someone and for someone", the sheer openness of his existence without any reservation of what is merely his own. And once again an expansion of the concept into Christian life follows, about which Scripture says: "As the Father has sent me, even so I send you" (20:21).

The second example is the Logos concept, the concept of the WORD, which Jesus is described as being. John takes up again here a paradigm of theological thought that is extremely widespread in both the Greek and the Jewish intellectual world and naturally adopts a series of connotations that are already developed within it, so as to apply them to Christ. Perhaps one could maintain, however, that the new element that he imparted to the Logos concept lies significantly in the fact that what was decisive to him was not the idea of an eternal rationality— as the Greeks supposed—or whatever other speculations there might have been previously, but rather the relativity of the existence that is inherent in the concept of Logos.

For, once again, it is true that word is essentially from someone else and for someone else; word is existence that is entirely way and openness. Many other passages modify this idea still further and clarify it, for instance when Christ says in one place: "*My* teaching is *not* mine" (7:16). Augustine wrote a marvelous commentary on this verse by asking: Is that not a contradiction? Either it is my teaching or it is not my teaching. He finds the solution in the statement: Christ's teaching is Christ himself, and he himself is not his own, because his "I" exists entirely in terms of the Thou. His commentary then continues verbatim as follows: "Quid tam tuum quam tu, quid tam non tuum quam tu?": What belongs to you so much as your self, and what belongs to you so little as your self? Your self is, on the one hand, what is most peculiarly yours and, at the same, time that which you own the least in and of yourself, that which is most truly not your own, which can be "I" at all only in terms of a "Thou".

Let us sum up: In God there are three Persons, which means, according to theology's interpretation: persons are relations, pure relatedness. Now initially this is only a statement about the Trinity, yet, at the same time, it is the fundamental statement about what matters in the concept of person in general, the inauguration of the concept of person in the life of the human mind and the origin that supports it.

One more concluding remark: Augustine—as we have already indicated—expressly set out to carry this theological statement over into anthropology by describing man as the image of the Trinity and trying to understand him in terms of this concept of God. In doing so, however, he unfortunately took a fateful shortcut, to which we will have to return later, inasmuch as he reads the Divine Persons into man's interior as corresponding to faculties within the soul and sets up a correspondence between man as a whole and the Divine Substance, so that the trinitarian concept of person is not applied immediately and with its full import to the human condition. But for the moment, this is meant only as a suggestion that will be clarified later on.

2. The Term "Person" in Christology

In Christology we find the second source from which theology once again used the word *persona* to help it out of a dilemma and, thus, presented a new task for the human mind. The riddle "Who and what is this Christ?'' was answered by theology with the formula: He has two natures and one person, a divine and a human nature, but only a Divine Person. And so the word *persona* appears again here. It must be said, of course, that this statement has been the object of terrible misunderstandings by the Western mentality and that these must first be dispelled in order to arrive at the actual meaning of the christological concept of person. An initial misunderstanding, which has in fact occurred again and again and still does, is to understand the statement "Christ has only one, namely, a Divine Person" as a diminution of the wholeness of Jesus' humanity. It is all too easy to think as follows: Personhood is the highest, most characteristic summit of humanity; it is lacking in Jesus; therefore humanity is not present in him in its entirety. The notion that there is a deficit of humanity in his case has become the point of departure for a great variety of falsifications, and, thus also of many aberrations, for instance in the theology of the saints and of the Mother of God. In reality, this formula does *not* mean that something is lacking in the humanity of the man Jesus. This factual finding, that absolutely *nothing* is subtracted here from what is human in him, has been achieved bit by bit through debates in the history of dogma, for there were always new attempts to show that something was cut off somewhere. First Arianism and Apollinarism maintained that Christ had no human *soul*; Monophysitism denied that he had a human *nature*. After these two fundamental errors had been refuted, weakened forms of them appeared. Monotheletism says that Christ did have everything except a human will (which is the core of the personality). After this, too, had been refuted, Monenergism appeared, claiming that Christ did have a human will but not the exercise of that will, which was accomplished by God. All of these are attempts to situate the concept of person somewhere in the inventory of the mind. One error after the other has been refuted, in order to determine that the statement is not meant in that way; there is absolutely nothing missing; there can be and there was no subtraction from his humanity. I think that when we trace the course of this struggle, in which Jesus' humanity had to be, so to speak, stocked up and formally declared bit by bit, we see what a tremendous effort and intellectual transformation there was behind the elaboration of this concept of person, which in its approach is quite foreign to the Greek and Latin mind: it is not understood substantially but existentially, as we will see in a moment.

From this vantage point, Boethius' concept of person, for instance, which in fact went on to be generally accepted in Western philosophy, can be criticized as entirely inadequate. Boethius, remaining on the level of Greek thought, defined person as "naturae rationalis individua substantia", as the individual substance of a rational nature. Clearly this concept of person stands completely on the level of substance; that cannot explain anything concerning either the Trinity or Christology; it is a statement that stubbornly remains on the level of the substantialist thinking of the Greek mind. Richard of Saint Victor, in contrast, at the beginning of the medieval period, found a concept of person taken from Christian thought; he defines person as "spiritualis naturae incommunicabilis existentia", a distinct and incommunicable existence of a spiritual nature. This formula rightly notes that "person" in the theological sense lies, not on the level of essence, but rather on the level of existence, and Richard thereby helped to stimulate a philosophy of existence, which as such had not been made the subject of philosophy at all in antiquity. Philosophy then had been limited exclusively to the level of essences. Based on this contribution of the Christian faith to man's intellectual apparatus, Scholastic theology developed categories of existence; its limitation consisted only of the fact that it restricted them to Christology and the doctrine of the Trinity and did not apply them productively to the full spectrum of intellectual life. This seems to me to be the limitation of Saint Thomas in this matter as well, that he proceeds in theology on the existential level with Richard of Saint Victor but treats the whole matter as if it were a theological exception, whereas in his philosophy he remains to a great extent faithful to the other approach of pre-Christian philosophy with Boethius' concept of person. The contribution of the Christian faith to the totality of human thought is not fully realized; it remains divorced from it as a theological exception, although the *sense* of this novelty is precisely to call the *totality* of human thought into question and to set it on new paths.

That brings me to the second misunderstanding that prevented Christology from having its full effect. The second great misunderstanding lies in the notion that Christ is the absolutely unique ontological exception, which must be treated as such and as such offers an object for very interesting speculations but must remain strictly sequestered as an exception to the rule and must not be mingled with the rest of human thought. I think that it is helpful to recall here a methodological insight that Teilhard de Chardin developed in an entirely different area. In considering the question about the essence of life—is it just an accident on a tiny planet within a great cosmos, or is it symptomatic of the direction of all reality?—he cites as an example the discovery of radium and writes, "How should we interpret the new element? As an anomaly, an exceptional form of matter? . . . As a curiosity or as the beginning of a new physics that is yet to be founded?" Modern physics, Teilhard goes on to say, "would not have developed if physicists had stubbornly regarded radioactivity as an anomaly".[7] This highlights a decisive point that is methodologically and quite generally true of all scientific reflection: the apparent exception is in reality very often the symptom that impels man to recognize the inadequacy of his previous patterns, that helps him to break open that pattern and to conquer a new realm of reality. The exception indicates to him that he has designed his boxes too narrowly, so to speak, that he must explode them and go beyond them in order to see the whole. Christology was originally meant in this way: in Christ, whom the faith certainly does present as unique, is revealed to be not only a speculative exception; rather, in him is manifested for the first time the truth about what is meant by the riddle named "man". Scripture expresses this by calling Christ the last Adam or "the second man". Thus it characterizes him as the genuine fulfillment of the idea "man", in which the orientation of the creature "man" first becomes fully evident. But if that is how matters stand—in other words, if Christ is not the ontological exception but, rather, based on his exceptional position, is the revelation of the entire creature "man"—then the christological concept of person is also for the theologian the index for how "person" must be understood in the first place. In fact, this concept of person (or, more exactly, the new dimension that has become evident here) has served again and again as fuel in intellectual history and has moved development forward even long after it had come to a halt in theology.

After these two fundamental misunderstandings have been rejected, the question remains as to the positive meaning of the formula, "Christ has two natures in one Person." I must confess, first, that here the theo-

---

[7] Quoted in Claude Tresmontant, *Einführung in das Denken Teilhard de Chardins* (Munich, 1961), 41f.

logical answer is not yet completely mature. Although theologians have worked hard in the great battles of the first six centuries to determine what "person" is not, they have not explained with equal clarity what the word designates positively. That is why I can only attempt to give something like a suggestion that might show the lines along which further thought would have to be given to the matter.[8]

I think that two things can be asserted: a. The essence of mind or spirit in general is being-in-relation, the capability of seeing oneself and the other. Hedwig Conrad-Martius speaks about the "retroscendence" of the spirit, the fact that the spirit is not only there but, as it were, investigates itself and knows about itself, presenting a double existence that not only *is* but also *understands* itself and *possesses* itself. Accordingly, the difference between matter and spirit would consist of the fact that matter is what is "thrown upon itself", while spirit is what "designs itself", that it is not just there but is what it is in surpassing itself, in looking out to something else, and in looking back to itself.[9] Whatever the details of that may be—we do not have to examine it more closely here—openness, relatedness to the whole, is an essential element of spirit. And it comes to itself precisely by the fact that it not only *is* but also reaches beyond itself. In going beyond itself, it *possesses* itself; only by being with the other does it become itself and come into its own. Or, to put it yet another way: Being with another is its form of being with itself. This recalls a basic theological axiom, which is applicable here in a peculiar way: Christ's saying "only he who loses himself can find himself" (cf. Mt 10:39). By the very nature of the thing, the fundamental rule of human existence that is expressed there with reference to salvation characterizes the essence of the spirit, which comes to itself and achieves its own fullness only by going away from itself, by going to something or someone other than itself.

We must go another step farther. The spirit is that entity which is able to think not only about itself and existence in general, but also

---

[8] Compare the following discussion with the instructive essay by B. Welte, "Homoousios hemin", in A. Grillmeier and H. Bacht, *Das Konzil von Chalkedon III* (Würzburg, 1954), 51–80; also H. Conrad-Martius, *Das Sein* (Munich, 1957). As for the patristic period, note especially Maximus the Confessor, who went the farthest in explaining positively the (christological) concept of person; cf. Hans Urs von Balthasar, *Cosmic Liturgy: The Universe according to Maximus the Confessor*, trans. Brian E. Daley, S.J. (San Francisco: Ignatius Press, and Communio Books, 2003), 235–55.

[9] H. Conrad-Martius, *Das Sein* (Munich, 1957), 133.

about the wholly other, transcendence, God. Perhaps that is even the real distinction between the human mind and other forms of consciousness found in animals: the fact that the human mind can think about the wholly other, the concept of God. Then we can say: the other, through which the mind comes to itself, is ultimately that wholly Other which we, in our stammering way, call God. If that is the case, then we can further clarify now what has been said previously within the parameters of faith and can say: If man is more at home with himself and is more himself, the more he is capable of reaching beyond himself, the more he is with the other, then man is more himself, the more he is with the wholly Other, with God.

In other words: mind or spirit comes to itself by way of the other; it becomes fully itself the more it is with the wholly Other, with God. And to formulate it yet another way (because to me this thought seems important): relatedness to the other constitutes man. Man is the creature of relatedness. He is the more himself, the more totally and deliberately his relatedness reaches out toward its final goal, toward transcendence.

b. From here we can try a second approach and add that in Christ, according to the testimony of the faith, there are two natures and one Person, that of the Logos. But this means that being-with-the-other is radically present in him. Relatedness toward the wholly Other is already there at every moment as the foundation of his consciousness and the basis of his existence. But such being-totally-with-the-other as we find in him does not abolish his being-with-himself but, rather, brings it to fulfillment. Naturally one will admit that the terminology that was selected, "una persona—duae naturae", remains contingent and is not entirely unproblematic. But the decisive result for the concept of person and for our understanding of man is, it appears to me, completely clear nonetheless: In Christ, the man who is entirely with God, humanity is not abolished but, rather, arrives at its highest potential, which consists of self-surpassing that leads into the absolute and of having one's own relatedness caught up into the absolute character of divine love.

In terms of Christ, the new Adam, however, this results at the same time in a dynamic definition of man. Christ is like a signpost indicating where humanity is tending (since as long as history is under way, humanity never completely catches up with itself). At the same time, it becomes evident that such a definition of humanity shows man and the person in their historicity. If person is relatedness toward the eternal, then the being-on-the-way of human history is implied at the same time along with the relatedness.

c. Finally, in conclusion, a third thought. Christology, it seems to me, has still further significance for our understanding of the concept of person in the theological sense. It adds to the idea of I and Thou the idea of We. For Christ, whom Scripture calls the last Adam and, thus, the ultimate man, appears in the testimonies of the faith as the comprehensive space in which the We of men is gathered in to the Father. He is not only a model to be followed, but he is also the inclusive space in which the We of mankind is gathered into the Thou of God. Here, now, something that has not been sufficiently examined in modern philosophy, even Christian philosophy, comes to light clearly: in Christianity there is not simply a dialogical principle in the modern sense of a purely I-Thou relationship—neither from the perspective of man, who is stationed in the historical continuity of the People of God, in the comprehensive historical We that supports him; nor from the perspective of God, who for his part is not a simple I but once again the We of Father, Son, and Spirit. On *both* sides there is neither the pure I nor the pure Thou; rather, on both sides the I is nestled in the larger We. Precisely this last point—that God, too, is not a pure, simple I toward which man is tending—is a fundamental idea of the theological concept of person, which expressly denies the divine monarchy in the sense of ancient philosophy and has explicitly refused to define God as pure *monarchia* and unity;[10] as a matter of principle, the Christian concept of God has given to multiplicity the same dignity as unity. Whereas for the ancient world, multiplicity appears only as the disintegration of unity, for Christian faith that believes in the Trinity, multiplicity belongs together with unity from the start.[11]

With this trinitarian We, with the fact that God, too, exists as a We, the space of the human We is already and simultaneously prepared. The Christian's relation to God does not simply mean, as Ferdinand Ebner has depicted it rather one-sidedly, I and Thou; it means, rather, as the

[10] Cf. E. Peterson, "Der Monotheismus als politisches Problem", in *Theologische Traktate* (Munich, 1951), 45–147.

[11] Cf. J. Ratzinger, *Introduction to Christianity*, trans. J. R. Foster, rev. ed. (San Francisco: Ignatius Press, 2004), 92, 139ff.

prayers of the liturgy teach us daily, "per Christum in Spiritu Sancto ad Patrem". The one Christ is therefore the We into which Love, namely, the Spirit, gathers us, who thus signifies the bond uniting us at the same time with one another and to the common Thou of the one Father. This We-reality of God comes to light in the three-step formula "through Christ in the Holy Spirit to the Father" and inserts us into the We of God and, thus, into the We of our fellowmen; the exclusion of this We-reality of God from Christian piety came about as a result of the previously mentioned anthropological decision within Augustine's doctrine on the Trinity and was one of the most momentous developments of the Western Church, which fundamentally influenced both the concept of Church and also the understanding of the person, which now was squeezed into the individualistically narrowed I-Thou relationship, which in this narrowness ultimately loses the Thou as well. As a consequence of Augustine's doctrine on the Trinity, in fact, the Divine Persons were entirely enclosed within God's interior and to the outside God became a pure I; thus the entire We-dimension lost its place in theology,[12] and the individualized I-Thou relationship became increasingly narrow, until finally, in transcendental philosophy (for example, Kant's), the Thou can no longer be found, either. Precisely this leveling of the I and Thou into a single transcendental consciousness probably opened the way in Feuerbach (that is, in a place where you would have least expected it!) to an escape toward the personal and, thus, gave impetus to go back to the origin of our own being, as our faith knows it to be revealed once and for all in the Word of Jesus, the Christ.

---

[12] For Augustine's trinitarian theology until 391, see O. du Roy, *L'Intelligence de la foi en la Trinité selon St. Augustin* (Paris, 1966); for the subsequent development, see M. Schmaus, *Die psychologische Trinitätslehre des hlg. Augustinus*, 2nd ed. (Münster, 1967). Today, of course, I would no longer judge so harshly as I did in this paper, because for Augustine the "psychological doctrine of the Trinity" remains an attempt at understanding that is kept in balance by factors in tradition. More radical was the development that Thomas brought about by treating separately the philosophical doctrine of one God and the theological doctrine of the Trinity: it led Thomas to regard as legitimate the formula "God is *una persona*", which in the early Church was considered heretical (*Summa Theologiae* III, q. 3, a. 3 ad 1). On the topic of "We", see H. Mühlen, *Der Heilige Geist als Person*, 2nd ed. (Münster, 1967).

15. Farewell to the Devil?

The Gospel for the First Sunday of Lent, which relates the temptation of Jesus by "Satan", provides year after year an opportunity to reflect on that mysterious power hidden behind the name "Satan". Additional impetus to consider this question came not long ago from Tübingen; in 1969, the Old Testament scholar Herbert Haag had published a booklet with the significant title *Abschied vom Teufel* [Farewell to the devil], which culminates in the statement: "By now we have understood that the term 'devil' in the New Testament simply stands for the term 'sin' " (p. 52). Recently, when the Pope emphasized the real existence of Satan and objected to the attempt to dissolve him into an abstraction, Haag accused him of relapsing into an early Jewish world view: Paul VI, he said, is mistaking a world view in Sacred Scripture for an article of the faith.

What is to be said about that? First of all, a methodological observation is important here. Even Haag cannot deny that Satan and the demons play an important role in the New Testament. Even he cannot dispute the fact that in the New Testament the word "devil" is by no means an equivalent for "sin" but, rather, signifies an existing power to which man is exposed and from which Christ frees him, because only Christ, the "stronger one", can bind "the strong man" (Lk 11:21–22; cf. Mk 3:27). The claim that we have understood that "devil" can be replaced by "sin" appears in Haag's booklet by way of persuasion without any real justification; the "justification" is concealed in a formulation that again by its self-evident character tries to forestall closer inspection. "In keeping with the Jewish notions at that time, the devil appears in the New Testament as the exponent of evil. Jesus and the apostles moved within this world of ideas just as their compatriots did" (p. 47). On the one hand—and this is undeniable from the passage

---

Translated by Michael J. Miller.

itself—it is admitted that Jesus and the apostles were convinced of the existence of demonic powers, but at the same time it is assumed to be quite clear that they were the victims of "the Jewish notions at that time". From this it is not difficult to draw the next conclusion, that is, that "this notion is no longer compatible with our world view" (p. 27). This means that the reasoning for the "farewell to the devil" is based, not on the testimony of the Bible, which presents the opposite theme, but rather on our world view, with which this theme is "incompatible". In other words: Haag bids the devil farewell, not in his capacity as exegete or interpreter of Scripture, but rather as a contemporary, who considers the existence of a devil untenable. The authority by which he hands down his judgment is therefore that of his contemporary world view, not that of a biblical exegete.

Now one might think that that settles the question, for it has become clear that Haag judges *contrary* to the biblical text, on the basis of *his* notions, what is supposed to be "compatible" with modern thinking. But things are not quite that simple, for in the Bible there are in fact statements that cannot be included in its faith testimony but must be described as the framing world view within which the actual thought is expressed. This is true, for example, of the geocentric world view, which was at first defended as biblical doctrine against Copernicus and Galileo, until it was recognized that the Bible is not competent in matters of astronomy. This is true for the question of how the world came about, which in some eras Christians tried to see described literally in the first chapters of Genesis, until commentators found their way back again to the recognition of the early Church that we are dealing here with statements about God's might and man's task, but not about natural science. It must be noted also that by no means is it always obvious how far the doctrinal message of the Bible extends and what may be only the temporally contingent vehicle for its real theme. Thus, during the Middle Ages the idea of the earth as the center of the universe had fused so thoroughly with the belief in the Incarnation of God, with the hope of a new heaven and a new earth, that the heliocentric world view appeared to be an attack on the very core of the faith: Is God, then, supposed to have become man on a planet that, viewed astronomically, was insignificant in the midst of a gigantic universe? Had not the decisive act of salvation thereby become placeless? Only through a difficult struggle did what is and is not necessary for a profession of faith in God's "descent" dawn on Christian thinkers. Consequently, one strike against Haag is the facile way in which he determines what is compatible with the modern world view and what is not; another strike against him is his false claim to make a decision as an exegete, even though he is speaking as a philosopher and his only philosophy is obviously an uncritical modernity. Still, perhaps we are really dealing here only with a world view that determines a certain perspective on the matter, in which we must separate the content from the form— and that problem has not yet been resolved unambiguously.

With that the question arises: How can we clarify the matter? How can we avoid a repetition of wrong-headed, harmful feuds like the Galileo controversy; conversely, how can we keep the faith from being truncated for the sake of modernity? The fact that this, too, has happened, from Reimarus down to the German Christians of the Third Reich, is usually not mentioned in warnings about new Galileo affairs, even though the consequences of such alternative, conformist Christianities were probably far more disastrous than the trial of Galileo, which, after all, was not just the product of ecclesiastical inflexibility but the struggle of a whole society, which had to cope with the crumbling of the intellectual foundations of previous history and had to learn again, with the changing of the times, how to distinguish between "fixed stars" and "planets", between permanent orientation and transient movement. There are no standards that one can apply immediately and unhesitatingly in every case that occurs; drawing boundaries remains a task that again and again requires intellectual effort as well, and so people will appreciate a struggle to determine a boundary of the faith, as long as the willingness to make corrections, on the one hand, is supported by well-founded knowledge and, on the other hand, one does not forget the insight that the faith can be put into practice only by believing with the Church and that it is not subject to private decisions about what is or is not be regarded as defensible.

Therefore, although there is no standard that automatically indicates in all particular cases where faith ends and where world view begins, there is still a series of aids to judgment that show the way as we look for clarifications. An initial standard results from the relationship between the two Testaments. Indeed, the Bible does not exist uniformly but, rather, in the harmony of Old and New Testaments, which interpret each other in the contrast between them and in their unity. Above all, it should be said that the Old Testament is valid only in union with the New, under its auspices, by its scale, just as the New Testament admittedly discloses its contents only through constant references to the Old. This state of affairs is generally recognized with regard to one point: the legal precepts of the Old Testament are not valid according to the letter of the Law, but, rather, they are valid insofar as they are part of the history leading up to Christ, in whom they are taken up and thus set aside. But the same basic pattern that Paul clearly developed for the question of the Law determines the relation between the Testaments in general. If commentators during the past century had kept this as clearly in view as the Church Fathers did, then the whole debate about the creation account would not have taken place. For the creation account in Genesis, accordingly, as an Old Testament passage, is not directly true, in its bare literal meaning, but rather insofar as it has been taken up into the New Testament perspective, within the scope of Christology. If we apply this standard, it becomes clear that John 1:1 is the New Testament assimilation of the Genesis passage and condenses its colorful depictions into the one statement: In the beginning was the Word. Thus everything else is relegated to the world of imagery. What remains is the origin of creation from the Word, which is reflected in the Old Testament in many words.

What does this standard signify for our question? Anyone who applies it comes upon an amazing result. Whereas just now, in the question about creation and in the question about the Law, we found that the New Testament, as compared to the Old, contracts the matter into a simple central truth, exactly the opposite happens here, in a movement of expansion. The notion of demonic powers enters only hesitantly into the Old Testament, whereas in the life of Jesus it acquires unprecedented weight, which is undiminished in Paul's letters and continues into the latest New Testament writings, the captivity letters and the Gospel of John. This process of amplification from the Old Testament into the New, along with the extreme crystallization of the demonic precisely in contrast to the figure of Jesus and the persistence of the theme throughout the New Testament witness, is telling. It allows us to say that in the early history of the Old Testament faith, discourse about demonic powers had to be set aside, because at first any ambiguity about faith in the one and only God had to be firmly opposed. In an environment saturated with idols, where the boundaries between good and bad gods were blurred, any mention of Satan would have detracted from the clarity of the decisive profession of faith. Only after the belief in the one God, with all its consequences, had become the unshakable possession of Israel could the view be widened to include powers that overrun the world of man, without letting them challenge God's uniqueness. This historical process is still important, inasmuch as it gives us information that is binding even today about the hierarchy among the articles of faith. First and foremost is God's divinity, his uniqueness. The Christian faith goes to God and sees the world from his perspective; the Christian, as Gregory of Nyssa says in connection with the Book of Qoheleth (Eccles 2:14), "has eyes in his head", meaning that they are directed upward, not downward. He knows that someone who fears God has nothing and no one to fear and that the fear of the Lord is faith, something quite different from servile fear or dread of demons. But fear of the Lord is also something quite different from a boastful recklessness that is unwilling to see the seriousness of reality. Part of true bravery is not concealing the extent of the danger but, rather, being able to perceive the reality in its totality. And, conversely, this now makes the phenomenon of "amplification" clear: the more man stands on God's side, the more realistic he becomes; the clearer the contours of reality are manifested, the clearer the opposite of the Holy One becomes as well: the beautiful masks of the devil no longer deceive someone who sees from God's perspective.

This leads right to a second standard. One must ask in each case what relation there is between a statement and the interior act of faith and of faithful living. Statements that remain merely theoretical forms of contemplation but do not enter into the authentic living out of the faith cannot normally be reckoned as part of the core of Christianity. On the other hand, a tenet that does not appear merely as a theoretical form of contemplation but is stationed within the experience of the faith and appears in the life of faith as a datum of experience has a very different rank. Thus the idea of the rising and the setting of the sun and of the central position of the earth could be a self-evident and in many respects profitable form in which to contemplate the faith, but it did not belong to the specific experience of the faith. Mysticism, with its unitive way, tended instead to relativize all paradigms based on a world view. In this regard, it seems to me extraordinarily important that the struggle with the power of demons is part of the authentic religious way of Jesus himself. The Bible tells of his temptations (Lk 22:28), not just about the one that is depicted at length; it goes so far as to say that Jesus came into the world in order to destroy the works of the devil (1 Jn 3:8). This formula summarizes what Jesus himself says in the series of sayings about the stronger man and the strong man, about the power of demons, whose kingdom he brings to ruin in the power of the Holy Spirit (Mk 3:20–30). It is striking that he, who did not want to let himself be made into a miracle worker, reckoned the battle against demons as a central part of his mission (cf., for example, Mk 1:35–39) and that this authority consequently is a central part of the authority that he confers upon his disciples: they are sent "to preach and have authority to cast out demons" (Mk 3:14f.). The spiritual battle against the enslaving powers, the exorcism pronounced over a world blinded by demons, is an inseparable part of Jesus' spiritual way that belongs to the heart of his own mission and of the mission of his disciples. The figure of Jesus, his spiritual physiognomy, does not change whether the sun revolves around the earth or the earth moves around the sun, whether or not the world came to be through evolution; but it is critically altered if you cut out the experiential struggle with the power of the demonic kingdom.

Closely connected with this is the third standard. The Bible without the Church would be only a collection of literature. Hence whenever one goes beyond the necessary scholarly research into its strictly historical component and examines the Bible as a book of faith and looks for the difference between belief and unbelief, this correlation must play a part. As we have already said, faith can be put into practice only by believing together with the whole faith community; it dissolves when it is left to the whim of the individual. And so as a further standard, we should ask to what extent statements have been accepted as part of the Church's faith. Now the faith of the Church is not something that can be delineated with complete clarity; otherwise things would be simple. Therefore, we must take a closer look and try to find out how far something has entered into the authentic interior act of faith, into the fundamental form of prayer and life, above and beyond the variations of tradition. Thus, for instance, the battle over the divine Sonship of Jesus, over the divinity of the Holy Spirit, and over the Trinity of Persons in God was waged in view of the consequences for the baptismal liturgy, for the eucharistic liturgy, and, hence, for the significance of

Christian conversion that is announced in baptism. Basil, for example, who settled the last debate over the divinity of the Holy Spirit, argued this question quite strictly in terms of the intrinsic demand of baptism and its liturgical form. The truth for him was that baptism is not a liturgical game but, rather, the solemn ecclesial form of the existential decision implied in being a Christian. One must be able to take baptism at its word, especially in its central action. It indicates what takes place in becoming a Christian and what does not. But now, to return to our question, exorcism and the renunciation of Satan are part of the central action of baptism; the latter constitutes, together with the pledge to Jesus Christ, the indispensable door through which one enters into the sacrament. Thus, baptism leads man into the existential model of Jesus Christ so as to be with him in his battle and in his freedom. It is based on his spiritual experience and transfers it to someone who decides to follow Christ. When man steps into the light of Jesus Christ, the devil is convicted and thus can be conquered. Again, it is true that one would change baptism and, thus, the conduct of Christian life if one tried to obliterate the reality of demonic power. Moreover, here, in connection with the question about the Church, the experience of the saints, those exemplary believers, should be included—I am saying: their experience, not all of their ideas. This experience corresponds to Jesus' experience: the more visible and powerful holiness becomes, the less the devil can conceal himself. In this respect, one could even say that the disappearance of demons that supposedly leaves the world without danger goes hand and hand with the disappearance of holiness.

Finally, as one last standard, we must mention the question of "world view", that is, of compatibility with scientific knowledge. Of course the faith again and again becomes a critique of what is considered in any age to be modern or is unquestioningly accepted as certain, but it cannot contradict certified scientific knowledge, which in this way has to set negative check points that must be considered. Now it would be nice to know on what basis Haag decided "that this notion is no longer compatible with our world view". Clearly it is contrary to the average taste; the fact that it finds no foothold in a world that is seen from a functionalistic perspective is equally obvious. But there is no room in pure functionalism for God, either, and no room for man as man, but only for man as a function; this means, therefore, the collapse of a lot more than just the idea of the "devil". In the name of what philosophy does Haag pronounce his verdict? That remains difficult to discern; apparently his point of departure is a highly oversimplified personalist plan. The more profound forms of personalism, however, have certainly recognized that one cannot possibly explain all of reality with the categories of I and Thou—that precisely the "in between" that connects the two poles with each other is a reality of its own, having its own force. Ideas from Asian thought throw this connection into even bolder relief today. Psychological illness, they say, for instance, is not simply a situation of the "I", but is based precisely on a disturbance of the "in between"; the "in between" is disordered, frustrated, dysfunctional, perverted, and that is why the "I" is out of joint, too. The "in between" is a fateful power, which our "I" can by no means completely control; to think that it can is an almost foolhardy sort of rationalism. Here, it seems to me, modern thought places at our disposal a category that can help us to understand again more exactly the power of demons, whose existence is of course independent of such categories. They are a power of the "in between", which man encounters at every turn without being able to apprehend it. This is just what Paul means when he speaks about "the world rulers of this present darkness"; when he says that our contest is against them, the spiritual hosts of wickedness in the heavenly places, and not against flesh and blood (Eph 6:12). It is directed against that firmly established "in between" which, so to speak, chains men to each other and cuts them off from one another, which does them violence by mimicking freedom. Here a very specific characteristic of the demonic becomes clear: its facelessness, its anonymity. If someone asks whether the devil is a person, we would probably have to answer more accurately that he is the Un-person, the disintegration and collapse of personhood, and that is why he characteristically appears without a face and why his being unrecognizable is his real strength. In any case, the fact remains that this "in between" is a real power, or, more precisely, a collection of powers and not just the sum of human selves. The category of the "in between", which thus helps us to understand in a new way the nature of the devil, performs yet another, parallel service: it enables us to explain better the real contrary power that has likewise become ever more foreign to Western theology: the Holy Spirit. From this perspective, we could say: He is that "In between" in which the Father and the Son are one as the one God; in the power of this "In between", the Christian confronts that demonic "in between" which "interferes" everywhere and obstructs unity.

Such an "enlightened" theologian as Harvey Cox recently opined that the mass media, in the patterns of behavior they glorify, invoked "the unexorcised demons"; "a clear word of exorcism" is therefore very much needed (*The Secular City*, 1966, p. 167). Perhaps he means that only allegorically; I do not know. But any Christian who peers into the abyss of modern life and sees at work there the power of the seven demons that have returned to the freshly swept house to carry on their mischief, knows that the exorcizing task of the believer is beginning to acquire again today that urgency which it had at the dawn of Christianity. He knows that he owes the world a service and that he is shirking his duty if he helps the demons to cloak themselves in that anonymity which is their favorite element.

CHURCH

16. On the Spirit of Brotherhood

Just as in the commercial world there is an insidious devaluation of currency when the coins in circulation are no longer backed by a corresponding weight of objective assets and production, so too the currency of the mind—the word—is in danger of being emptied out by a kind of inflation when the force of convictions and views is no longer able to keep the scale from tipping toward the surplus verbal coins that are issued so carelessly. Many of the greatest words of the human mind—heart, love, and happiness, for example—have succumbed to devaluation in this way; the profound Christian word "brotherhood" seems today about to suffer the same fate. We said before that words are the currency of the mind because in them the mind of one person imparts itself to another; someone who values the word for the sake of the mind will do two things when inflation threatens to consume the word: he will use the great coin of the word sparingly and not take it upon his lips when it is doomed to meaninglessness; on the other hand, he will try to strengthen those convictions which lend life and strength to words.

What is the intellectual backing behind the word "Christian brotherhood"? The central point on which this word lives, in which its force is rooted, is nothing other than the central point of Christian reality in general: the table fellowship of the faithful with the risen Lord. People have always experienced sharing a meal as the most effective way of creating fellowship; here, though, when they eat the one divine bread that the Lord himself desired to become for us, this is raised to the highest power: it is in the final analysis nothing other than incorporation into

---

Translated by Michael J. Miller.

the Lord's Body, into the realm of the risen Christ; the process that takes place here is meant to be quite concrete, as we can understand from the bold saying of Saint Paul, who declares outright: "You are all one in Christ Jesus" (Gal 3:28). The unity around the table of the Lord is at the same time an expression of the hospitality of Christians, since anyone who shares in the Lord's table is also challenged to share and live in community; he is, moreover, the fellow lodger of the other in the fullest sense. Here, of course, one might immediately ask: Who still really feels that way today? Or even: Who still puts that into practice? But let us just leave such thoughts to one side in the hopes that the matter we are talking about is itself urgent enough to make such importunate questions superfluous. Yet one more thing should be said about the Eucharist—again from our vantage point: Just as a human meal, if it is to be human, consists not only of food but also of the spoken word, so too at the Lord's Supper, along with the heavenly food, the Word of the Lord is presented as nourishment and illumination for the spirit. Thereby, however, the radius of the brotherhood established by the eucharistic celebration is significantly extended, for the bread— the Body of the Lord—includes and unites only those who are present; the Word of the Lord, however, also expresses an obligation precisely for those who are outside. In this part of the liturgy, a Christian hears words such as these: "And if you salute only your brethren, what more are you doing than others? Do not even the Gentiles do the same?" (Mt 5:47). "Truly, I say to you, as you did it to one of the least of these my brethren, you did it to me" (Mt 25:40). He hears the account of the creation of the world, which tells him that all men are just "one Adam", one single mankind; that all men—whether high- or low-born, whether Christian or pagan—are the likeness of God (Gen 1:26f., 5:1). He hears that God wills the salvation of all men (1 Tim 2:4). He prays the Our Father and thus joins together with all God's children into a single "We". He hears that the Lord accomplished the ministry of his life "for many" (Mk 10:45; 14:24), that is, for mankind. Thus he recognizes that the family of God that gathers in the Church does not have a self-contained existence but, rather, is there in order to keep our eyes and hearts open for all the children of God.

One more thing becomes clear from this perspective, which at the same time leads us back again to our point of departure. Phrases like "We are all brothers" have become part and parcel of the word inflation that we are experiencing these days. It is considered good manners to play the highest currency right away. In early Christianity people used such important words more sparingly. Not as though there was a lack of universalism, but they were obviously of the opinion that such hasty declarations might express a self-deception rather than a reality. They knew that humanity is not simply a static reality that is bestowed ready-made on the individual but, rather, that it includes the constantly repeated imperative to *become* a man; they knew also that brotherhood is a task that still awaits its achievement. Man, who at first regards the other, the stranger, the person of lower degree by no means as a brother but, rather, as a stranger and acts accordingly, is called to discover his forgotten brother and, thus, to make a mere possibility a reality. And at the same time he is called to witness to others who likewise do not know about their secret affinity and to open their eyes by his brotherliness and thus to replenish the brotherhood; and by the creative power of love he is called to found a sibling relationship that initially consists only of a divine call but not yet as an interpersonal fact. Human realities do not exist without the human being, without the free engagement of his mind and heart. Being human is always in both the indicative and the imperative at once. Brotherhood, just like love, is a profound human fact, part of that "goodness and loving kindness [Vulgate *humanitas*] of God" (Tit 3:4) which has appeared in Christ, so as to make us into true human beings—into children of God.

17. The Anthropological Basis
of Brotherly Love[1]

Christian consciousness is going through a crisis today that does not stop even at its most fundamental decisions. Questions with which it has long been acquainted as objections from outside are now tormenting it from within as well. At the same time that Christians are discovering a new enthusiasm for hope, which for many centuries was the forgotten virtue, they are, remarkably, distancing themselves from faith and charity, which are suddenly perceived as dubious in comparison with the compelling motivation of hope. Christian charity addresses itself to the individual, and it does so here and now. But, people ask, does not such charity in the here and now mean simultaneously the reinforcement of that Now, a pious excuse for dispensing with the overall change that is required? Does not such action conform with the status quo and thus cloud our view of how horrible the system itself is, and should it not therefore be considered dangerous in the long run and harmful to people, because it strengthens power that deserves to be shattered? Furthermore, such charitable action benefits the individual, but it thereby remains isolated and bypasses the collective responsibility for the whole of society. Is not charity to an individual an escape from justice for all?

These objections become even more insistent when we talk about *Schutz* [literally "protection": a general category of social services including "shelter", "financial support", and "advocacy"], "mission" and the like: that is supposedly adopting a paternalistic attitude, whereby the secure and the righteous confront those who are insecure and at risk and act patronizingly from a position of superiority that does not call itself into question.

Translated by Michael J. Miller.

[1] Lecture presented at the celebration of seventy-five years of service by the Catholic *Mädchenschutzvereine* [associations for the protection of young women] in Bavaria (now called the Verband für Mädchensozialarbeit, e.V., the League for Social Services to Young Women, a registered association) on April 25, 1970, in Munich.

In such a situation it is sensible, indeed, absolutely necessary to rethink the basis of one's own activity and to examine anew the direction in which it leads. How did Catholic *Mädchenschutzvereine* [associations for the protection of young women] come about? What is their purpose, and what do they actually accomplish? How does this relate to the fundamental events of the Christian faith? And how does it relate to the questions by which this faith finds itself called into question in today's crisis situation?

1. *The Sociological and Ecclesiological Context of the Catholic "Mädchenschutzvereine"*

a. The Sociological Point of Departure

Let us try to proceed in chronological order. What actually happened in 1895 when, at the suggestion of Father Cyprian Fröhlich and in parallel with the already existing Lutheran-Evangelical Verein der Freundinnen junger Mädchen [League of Benefactresses of Young Women], the Marianischer Mädchenschutzverein [Marian Association for the Protection of Young Women] was founded in Munich but had to be constituted as an independent association because the German National Committee of the aforementioned Lutheran organization rejected any affiliation with it due to its denominational character? It was a response to the exploitation and endangerment to which young people were exposed, especially in foreign countries, in particular through the activity of ruthless employment agents. The task of the association was to protect young women from such abuses and also to provide them with positive assistance in coping with their new situations: soon it not only made boarding houses and employment counseling available but increasingly initiated educational facilities of various sorts as well.[2]

The Bahnhofsmission [train station mission] was the most conspicuous way of taking on these duties, and therefore it may illustrate most readily the historical context of this foundation. This was an attempt to respond, at the beginning of the twentieth century, to the new situation, which was symbolized, at first notoriously, by the train station.[3]

[2] *1895–1955 Katholischer Mädchenschutz*, Festschrift, 16f.
[3] See Karl Rahner, "Bahnhofsmission", a lecture on the sixtieth anniversary of the association, in *Sendung und Gnade* (Innsbruck, 1959), 427.

The train station, after all, is the spot where, on the one hand, worlds meet, where proximity and distance mesh; it is the place of encounter, the transition point between here and there. But of course at the same time it is also the place of unfamiliarity, anonymity, mobility, which cuts one off from old roots. All of this can be seen today in many of our West German cities when the train station becomes the meeting place for "guest workers". The train station is for them, in their foreign surroundings, the point that connects them with their fatherland; it is like a window overlooking home from abroad, the promise of the journey that leads back. In this way it represents a bit of home, yet as such it is also the most profound expression of the unresolved homesickness that remains and thus simultaneously the symbol of their status as uprooted foreigners.

Now the spiritual experience that we encounter here clarifies the general crisis situation at the beginning of the twentieth century, to which the founding of the association sought to respond: the old agrarian civilization was coming to an end, and even the city that had been informed by the humanistic culture was entering into a phase of fundamental transformation. The age of the technopolis was drawing near, as Harvey Cox labels this new form of city and, thus, also the new forms of civilization and of human community that were developing then and becoming with ever-increasing rapidity the fate and problem of us all. The characteristics of the rising technopolis are, according to Vidich and Bensman, whom Cox cites, mobility, economic concentration, and mass communication. Of course we would have to add with Cox that mass communication is accompanied by individual anonymity and impersonality.[4] The basic form in which mankind and man experiences himself and fulfills himself is essentially transformed with the increasing influence of the technological phenomenon. Man is confronted with a new phase of his history, in which new possibilities spring up along with brand new risks. All of this began to affect the individual strata of society with varying speed; the new danger to man that arose here and cried out for protection—man's protection from himself and for his sake—naturally became noticeable first and most urgently among the socially marginalized and the weak: among those who went directly from the fixed agrarian social order to the cities and were thrown into the mobility and anonymity of the modern age,

---

[4] Harvey Cox, *The Secular City* (New York: Macmillan, 1966), 4.

because that was the only place where they could hope to make a living; this was even more true of a woman than of a man because of the weaker position that was assigned to women in any case at that moment in Western society.

The foundation by Father Fröhlich and Countess Preysing, which followed the example of its Lutheran counterpart, was at its core simply a response to this new basic situation of man at the place where it assumed its neediest form. It was concerned with giving to the woman in the midst of mobility the home she needs and with offering to the man who passes from the agrarian to the technologically defined world financial assistance in coping with that transition. Such activity, however, corresponds not only to the specific demand of the historical hour, which made itself heard in the widespread need that Father Cyprian discussed at the meeting when the Association was founded; it corresponds also to the nature of the Church and signifies the application of her commission to the given historical situation. What was being done here, after all? It was an attempt to set up, in the midst of mobility, a context that would support and shelter man; a context that would protect him from the modern highwaymen who waylaid and misused people in many ways as the objects of their own business dealings. Furthermore, it was an attempt, in the midst of anonymity, to offer personal communication, which is the fundamental medium of self-discovery and self-realization. That means, however, that the Church at any given locality had to recognize that she is the Church for all people and to make herself available to them. In late antiquity, the Church came into being as a community of people who for the most part must have felt that they were "strangers and sojourners", in a sort of train-station situation, if you will: not a closed society that lived its corporate life and was unwilling to be bothered with others, but, rather, the open space of those who, scattered throughout the inhabited world, professed the name of Jesus Christ and all remained open to one another and to everyone who was seeking the truth about human life.

b. The Model of the Open Church as a Response to the New Situation

But this means that the Church in all places is still only the one Church. We are experiencing today a rediscovery of the principle of the local Church. There is a new awareness of the fact that Church is formed at a particular place and that she has her most immediate and fullest realization there. At the same time, the middle levels of ecclesial realization—bishops' conferences and the ecclesiastical regions associated with them—are being discovered and experienced anew, especially in terms of the noticeably increasing use of vernacular languages in the liturgy. This, too, has its significance as a rejuvenation of ecclesiastical structures and as an opportunity to include the manifold specific possibilities of individual peoples in the Church as a whole. But both movements can turn into negative developments, namely, when a community becomes self-contained and self-satisfied or, likewise, when individual national regions autonomously go their own way and forget that they are Church only thanks to the universal Church and for the sake of the whole. Whereas ten years ago we had to remind people that the parish is not just an administrative district but is itself Church, now we need to be reminded that the universal Church is not merely an organizational umbrella but, rather, truly represents the Church herself and that the parish continues to be Church only if it is part of the whole. For no one can have for himself alone the Incarnate Christ, who is the authentic life of the Church and dwells wholly among us in every church gathering, this Christ who desires to make every gathering that occurs in his name wholly his Church. He is wholly in the individual, and in the whole he is only One. Hence no one can have him without the whole and certainly not in opposition to the whole. And, hence, being part of the whole is the foundational criterion for whether a congregation gathers in *his* name and, consequently, is Church. Its foundational criterion is its not being self-contained, its non-autonomy, its openness to the whole of the Church. Its criterion is that it does not want to be something special but, rather, embodies at this place the one Church, which is the same everywhere and only in that way is herself.

What does all this mean for our topic? Well, it means that the founders of the Association for the Protection of Young Women and all who have continued its work since then have put into practice in their own way this model of the open Church. In the simplicity and realism of a faith that does not ask a lot of questions but lives that much more[5] and lays hold of the reality that much more surely, they made

---

[5] Cf. Cyprian, *De bono patientiae* 3: ". . . non loquimur magna, sed vivimus" (we do

it plain—through deeds, not through theories—that the early Church
model, with its combination of local community and universal openness, offers a direct response to today's society, which is characterized
by mobility and concentration, if only we dare to live this old model
in a new way today and to accept it with all its consequences. In the
bewildering debate about the Church of the future, about the Church
in the age of the technopolis, one preliminary decision has been made
in this regard that is exemplary and of which we have not yet become
sufficiently aware precisely in its current relevance. This seems to me to
be true in two senses. First, the foundation of this association means
that the Church at a given place does not enclose herself in a local
church or in a particular congregational existence that is organized in
some other way; instead, she knows that, rather like the Church at the
train station (but also in all the other areas in which the association
works), she is an open Church of those nonintegrated people and lives
accordingly. In the midst of the anonymity that results from mobility,
she understands herself as the one Church that encompasses all spaces
of human mobility and offers herself everywhere as the one Church
that is home in every foreign land. This readiness to understand herself
continually as the open Church—which is not divided into languages
and population groups but, rather, is at the disposal of the whole as
the presence of the whole at this place—seems to me to be fundamental, and it even reveals a very specific contribution that the Church
makes in addressing the problems of our time: mobility alone creates
no unity, just as concentration alone brings about no communication.
Being a Christian, however, properly understood, always includes a
certain transcending of one's own situation, ethnicity, language, and
social status (and not the sacral sclerosis thereof): it posits a reality
that can be fulfilled only by convergence with the whole. The mobile,
concentrated, and anonymous society of today needs precisely such an
element of convergence if it is to live. And such convergence cannot
become a reality as a theoretical ideal, but only in the sober patience of
those who actually station themselves at those places of mobility and
anonymity, who have in practice devoted themselves to the accomplishment of this convergence.

---

not discuss much, but we live—nowadays we would probably have to put it the other way
around: "We do discuss a lot, but we scarcely live at all"), CSEL III, 1, p. 398, 21.

c. A Model for the
Responsibility and Freedom of the Layman

The other thing that seems important to me in this connection is that what has been going on here has been essentially a lay initiative that simply takes note of the inner necessity of the faith and freely puts it into practice as a necessity. I fear that today we are rather far removed from such spontaneous implementations of what faith demands and that we have become wrapped up to the same degree in an almost hopeless theorizing that speaks quite emphatically about the necessity of praxis. In light of such an important and exemplary lay movement as this one, it seems to me that there is no avoiding the observation that the so-called discovery of the laity in the Church, as it is being pursued today, is obviously headed in the wrong direction. Catholics today increasingly understand the theology of the *laity* as a new form of ecclesial *ministry*, which is of course a self-contradiction. For a layman either is a layman or he is not. A theology of the laity that is promulgated as a fight for proportionate representation in Church government is a caricature and remains one even when this misunderstanding is hidden beneath the concept of synodal Church governance. And, unfortunately, this is not just a theoretical blunder; it is also mismanagement of personnel in the Church and a failure to fulfill her mission: when theology becomes a theory of Church politics and a battle for a share in Church governance, all the impetus is directed inward. As a result, the Church is concerned only with herself and wears herself out in the process. She uses up the strength that is actually given to her in order to serve, in order to be there for others, on the debate about power and just to keep herself going. But Church, correctly understood and living correctly, does not look to herself; rather, she goes out from herself and works for others.[6]

But that is precisely what happens here. The layman demonstrates his freedom and his indispensability by doing what the Church *must* do, what is a necessity for her and what can happen within her only when it is done freely, by a free initiative. But this is precisely what we need again today, very urgently: to turn away from ecclesiastical self-concern and to turn toward the people who are waiting for us. Continuing such initiatives boldly and fearlessly, even when current

---

[6] Cf. J. Ratzinger and H. Maier, *Demokratie in der Kirche* (Limburg, 1970).

trends have nothing to do with them and they do not receive very much support from the clergy—that is the true freedom and the true necessity of the non-ordained Christian who lives by faith, even today. For then and only then does the Church prove to be the force of the future, which is not overtaken by society as it advances toward the technopolis but, rather, is needed by society in an entirely new way.

In this connection we might mention yet a third feature of the whole movement. In the chronicle from the year 1902, we read that the newly founded association in Regensburg had instituted evening courses in stenography, bookkeeping, business correspondence, commercial mathematics, French, and soon even typing. . . . "It encouraged many associations, . . . but always stepped back as soon as an association had become independent."[7] The Church herself and as such is not a social services institution or a school for adult education. But in appropriate situations, she can assist in the task of developing necessary initiatives to help people cope with and make their way in modern society, and she will immediately set such initiatives free as soon as her assistance has achieved its purpose. She cannot exchange her message for social service, but the power of this message will again and again bring forth new social initiatives, just as she surpasses the scope of these initiatives and leads to that greater good which will continue to be a requirement for man even in a technological society.

To summarize the previous reflections, we can say that the work of the Mädchenschutzverein applies the universality and identity of the one Church to a concrete place in human history and human life in a practical way and tries to translate it into the reality of daily life.

2. The Anthropological Background

a. Brotherhood Derived from Our Brother, Jesus Christ

But this suggests the next step, which leads us to the intrinsic reason for the Church's universality and identity and, thus, by touching upon the heart of the matter—the question about man himself—brings us right back to the problems with which we started. For now the question is: From where does the Church acquire her identity? How can

---

[7] *Festschrift* 1955 (see n. 2), 26f.

she dare to be the same in all times and at all places and to help man discover his identity in mobility? Only in complete dependence on her center, based on her faith in Jesus Christ, the Son of God, who is at the same time the "last man", that is, the definitive design of man and the union of all human designs into their Omega. From Christ she knows that there is only one Father of all men. From him she knows about the inviolable identity of humanity and, thus, the human dignity in all men. In terms of the one Father, she recognizes that all men are brothers and sisters—something that unfortunately is not a fact in historical reality but that thus becomes an all the more urgent imperative for the believer, who cannot rest content with a general ontological brotherhood (important as that is). As a disciple of God, who himself created facts and has himself entered into the factuality of human life and suffering, she must instead struggle for the factuality of what is fundamental: revealing to men their brotherhood and living her own life in terms of this discovery. The believer should be driven by the restlessness of a discoverer who must make his epochal finding known, win acceptance for it, and develop a practical application.

And that is the fascinating thing about the great figures from the history of the association: Father Cyprian Fröhlich, Countess Christiana von Preysing, Luise Fogt, Baroness Marie von Hohenhausen, Ellen Ammann—the fact that one senses in them this passion of the discoverer that did not allow them to rest, for which they spent themselves; the fact that one can see again in them that Christ is a revelation for man, no, *the* revelation of man for man. In comparison, how petty it all seems, what we are witnessing today: the debate about competencies and the offended exaggeration of every grievance, as though it were heroic to dwell on grievances and to enumerate over and over again the injuries that one has suffered over the course of time from the Church or for the Church.

b. The Individual and the Whole

The Church and this association, which derives its vitality from the fundamental impetus of the Church's faith and attempts to bring it to bear on a particular place, are concerned about universal brotherhood, nothing more and nothing less. But, one might ask now what is actually being accomplished? Who is actually being reached? In this connection, a passage from the Chronicle seems to me to be important. In the year

1903, we read: "A sort of pimp asked a lady of the train-station mission about the 'purpose of the association' and, after listening to her reply, said, 'That's ridiculous; you get one woman, while I can have ten or more every day.' Having said that he disappeared. . . . And this *one*—honored ladies! Do you still find it ridiculous to wait for this one at the train station—to wait, even if it takes a hundred hours a month, so that you seem to wait in vain for ninety-nine of them: What is that *one*? The entire price of the Precious Blood of Jesus Christ! And for you . . . what is that one for you? Saint Chrysostom gives you the answer: 'Nothing in the world equals the value of a single soul. . . .' "[8]

This language may sound rather lofty, but it expresses something decisive and lasting that can easily escape our view today, given the mass misery that confronts us and given the impact of the social problem upon us. I had already mentioned at the start that nowadays people object to the service of Christian brotherly love by questioning whether it bypasses necessary changes to the situation, whether it helps the individual but overlooks the collective problem. The Church, so the saying goes, distributes umbrellas, whereas it is a question of changing the overall weather conditions. Now, although this very same comparison is apt to recall the limitations of such efforts, there is certainly no disputing that the concern is justified in principle. No doubt there must be a decisive effort to build the technopolis as a city of man and to employ on such a future-oriented collective task all the resources that it deserves.

But man is not just raw material for the future; he himself is the ultimate purpose. And he is never exhaustively defined by circumstances; rather, he always remains a new question extending into infinity that demands a personal answer that can never be planned completely in advance. That is why there will never be circumstances that make personal, caring, and loving action on man's behalf superfluous. That is why concern about the future can never become an excuse for wear and tear on the present and why the fight for the collectivity can never replace dealing with the individual. Hence, besides planning and perhaps militant efforts also for the future of society as a whole, there must be a struggle on behalf of man here and now as well, in the circumstances and possibilities of today, for the individual who is in

[8] Ibid., 27.

need and at risk today. Planning for the future, when it is done in a positive way, is love of those who are most distant. It does not replace love of neighbor, of those who are closest. Perhaps planning for the future and the practical service of love of neighbor here and now will fructify one another more in the future than they have in the past. But the real heart of Christianity is and remains love of neighbor. Indeed, every individual is loved infinitely by God and has infinite worth. As Pascal profoundly comprehended it, Christ says to every man, "In my agony I thought of you. I shed this drop of blood for you."[9] If a person has been able to give meaning to an individual, to just one person, through his love, then his life has been infinitely worthwhile. And it will always be the case that men thrive when they encounter the sort of love that gives meaning—that will be true in all circumstances; no reform and no revolution will be able to make this gift superfluous. And conversely: in all circumstances it has been redemptive when, in the midst of a world of hostility and alienation, someone has appeared who emerged from the collectivity and has been a brother. These redemptive encounters, which are recorded in no history book, are the true, the inner Church history, which we forget today more than ever on account of the history of institutions. For only by helping to redeem others are we ourselves redeemed; only by protecting others do we receive protection; only by caring for others are we cared for as well. Once we recognize that there are two sides to the process, we will be careful about accusing others of paternalism: anyone who seriously begins to care about the protection of others will soon find that by doing so he himself receives protection, that the others rescue him as he rescues them. And perhaps today we engage in so much backbiting and are so helpless in our Christian identity because we try too much to help only ourselves. . . .

Conclusion: A Jewish Story and Its Christian Meaning

Allow me to conclude with one of the Hasidic stories by Martin Buber, which poses very pointedly the question about that love which is based on biblical faith and is addressed to the individual here and now. The story relates that Rabbi Levi Yitschak of Berditshev agreed one

---

[9] Cf. Étienne Gilson, *Die Philosophie des hl. Bonaventura*, 2nd ed. (Darmstadt, 1960), 282.

day with the leaders of the congregation that they should invite him
to their meetings "only when they were thinking of introducing a new
custom or a new regulation". The story continues:

> Once he was invited to a meeting. Immediately after greeting them,
> he asked, "What is the new custom that you wish to introduce?"
> They replied, "From now on we want the poor to stop begging at
> the threshold of the house; instead, a box will be set up, and all the
> well-to-do will put money into it, each according to his ability, and
> the proceeds will be used to care for the needy."
>
> When the Rabbi heard this, he said: "My brothers, did I not tell
> you not to take me away from teaching and invite me to your meet-
> ing on account of an old custom or an old rule?" The astonished
> leaders objected, "But, Master, this is a new arrangement that we are
> discussing today!"
>
> "You are wrong", he exclaimed. "It is an ancient one, an ancient
> custom that comes from Sodom and Gomorrah. Recall what is re-
> lated about the girl in Sodom who offered a piece of bread to a beg-
> gar: how they seized the girl and undressed her and left her as food
> for the bees because of the great outrage that she had committed.
> Who knows, perhaps they too had a congregational box in which
> the well-to-do put their alms, so as not to look their poor brethren
> in the eye!"[10]

Are we not also in danger of reviving this ancient custom under the
pretext of adopting the latest methods? Is not that fanatical reaching
for the utopia of the perfect future, in which improved conditions are
supposed to banish forever all misery and all need for protection and
care, an escape from the present, from the individual whom the present
threatens to destroy and in whose eyes we could also read the indictment against us, who share in the responsibility for this time and yet
have forgotten him? For our sake, God became an individual, and in
the crucified Christ he looks each of us in the eye. This glance of the
God-man concerns us personally; it is the real theological and anthropological point of departure for the abiding necessity of the service of
Christian brotherly love in all its forms.

---

[10] Martin Buber, *Werke* (Munich and Heidelberg, 1963), 3:345f.

18. Church as the Locus of Service to the Faith

The word "Church" does not have a good reputation today. We are in almost the same position as the people in the last century of the Middle Ages, whose impression of the Church was summed up in the call for a reform of the Church in her head and members. Every day we hear about new shortcomings of her officials: one minute we are disturbed by the obstinacy of those who defend tradition, and the next minute we nevertheless have to shake our heads again over the high-handedness of others who on account of their personal problems think they have to raise the alarm in public. To us the institutions of the Church seem antiquated, often petty; a modern consciousness of human rights and insights into the social consequences of the Christian message are making headway only with effort. We often get the impression that some demands of the Church that are (or could quite easily become) outmoded are being defended with an undiscerning stubbornness that lays burdens on people instead of helping them to be free; Jesus' judgments on the scribes and Pharisees then come to mind, and we have the impression that they apply to those who serve the Church no less than to those who served the synagogue. Conversely, we also observe once more a peculiar opportunism of the Church with regard to the trends of the times; she is suddenly inclined to accommodate where she ought to put up resistance, and again and again we get the impression that she is all too much in thrall to the mentality of certain groups that prevent her from being a force for unification and reconciliation, which of course should be her task. Add to all that the fact that the scandals of Church history are ceaselessly laid at our door. Slogans like Inquisition, witch trials, persecution of the Jews, and so on, are household words today for every last one of our contemporaries, noticeably creating the general impression that the Church of

---

Translated by Michael J. Miller.

the past was in any case a failure and that if the Church is worth any commitment at all, one must write off everything to date and start over from the beginning.

But can we actually put any trust in such novel promises? Who is vouching, then, for the quality of the Church of the future? And based on what? One might argue: If no lasting good could come from the work of Jesus and the apostles, then who are the prophets to whom we can entrust ourselves now? Thus a commitment to a Church that is now finally becoming quite different inevitably seems like an unsecured bill of exchange, with no convincing arguments to encourage us to sign it. And for all these reasons, the courage to devote one's whole life to the service of the Church is fading away more and more.

What are we supposed to say about it? Perhaps it is good to look first at what our faith itself has formulated from within as an answer to such questions. This answer says that the Church is "strength in weakness", a combination of human failure and divine mercy. Next, it is part of the Church's nature that she is divine and human, rich and poor, light and dark all at once. God became a beggar and entered so much into solidarity with the prodigal son that he appears virtually identical to him, that he himself is the other, precisely that lost and prodigal son upon whom all the vices of history are laid. According to the proclamation of the faith, the Church, precisely as a sinful society, is the expression of the Divine Mercy, of God's solidarity with sinners. That in turn means that she is, on the one hand, debased by all human failure, yet at the same time something from God is preserved within her and remains effective, giving man hope and salvation. According to this account, then, the Church is by nature "paradoxical", dimorphic, a mixture of failings and blessings.

The urgent question arises: Is that so? I believe that one certainly can recognize the truth of these statements by examining the situation with a modicum of patience and objectivity. For besides the Church history of scandals that is drummed into us so relentlessly nowadays, there is also the other Church history, which is a story of hope, a path of light starting from Jesus and becoming now wider, now narrower, but never completely disappearing as it goes through the centuries. Let us remember just a few details so as to snatch this other Church history back from oblivion. We can hardly imagine today what it meant in 217 for a slave in Rome to become pope. According to the law of the ancient world, a slave was regarded, not as a person, but as a thing. In the Church, however, he was a brother and, as brother, equal. This peculiar feature of the Church was so strong, in comparison with the old pagan society, that it could have far-reaching consequences in events that were, indeed, only a symptom of the power of the Christian revolution that achieved its effects, not by terror, but by an interior transformation. A few centuries later, when the ancient world collapsed under the Germanic onslaughts, the Christian faith again proved to be the decisive force for reconciliation, which managed to bring together the new world of the conquerors and the old world of a great but weary culture, so that the conquerors and the vanquished, the barbarians and the heirs of the wealth of ancient culture, saw one another in turn as brothers and became capable of building a new world together. Through the message of the faith, both sides came to see that they belonged to one single God and not to different hostile deities, that they were equally loved by their one brother Jesus Christ, and that he had suffered for the one people as well as for the other. Augustine, who saw the Vandal attack upon Africa coming and died during the siege of his diocesan city, had pointed out more than once that the peace of Christ extends farther than the power of the Roman Empire to keep the peace and that the faith could and must embrace barbarians and Romans equally.

Then in the High Middle Ages, from within a Church that had become wealthy and identified with society, the sterling character of Saint Francis emerged, who was a magnificent example of a Christian critique of society: voluntary solidarity with the poor, which distinguished the faith from the ruling powers, is one side of his program, while the idea of peace is the other—both inner peace, as opposed to the disorder of the power struggles among the various strata of medieval society, and also external peace: mission as opposed to Crusade, striving for unity in the world based on God's unity. Naturally these initiatives had only very fragmentary consequences politically, but they were there; they were lively forces that appeared on the scene again and again by virtue of the Church's living faith.

These statements are true even for the darkest hours of Church history: amid the horrible incidents of the Spanish colonization of America, men like the Dominican priest Las Casas rose up, who relentlessly fought for the human rights of the oppressed. It must be said, to the credit of the Spanish crown, that they listened seriously to such voices and tried again and again, with various approaches, to create a colonial law based on respect for men, even though they lacked the power to ensure that that law, which was Christian in its inspiration, would be accepted in the other hemisphere. Out of this struggle, and long before the Enlightenment, Spanish Scholasticism developed the concept of international law by which we still live today. The faith of the Church was, admittedly, misused again and again as a pretext for the pursuit of personal and national claims to power, but at the same time this faith always remained, nevertheless, the prophetic salt that rankled and disturbed the mighty. The cry for liberty, equality, and fraternity that became increasingly intense in the modern era is incomprehensible without the faith that was preserved in the Church.

The Church's faith was expressed, however, in still another way that is more difficult for us to see and yet no less decisive. Man does not live on bread alone—we really ought to know that very well today, in a time when people have enjoyed their prosperity *ad nauseam*, so that they now revolt, not against poverty, but against prosperity. Someone who is as well-fed as can be and can afford everything he wants starts to notice that that is still much too little. If someday everybody has everything he wants, he will still be far from happy. On the contrary, the Western world of today proves that then he is just beginning to be completely unhappy, that that is when his problems really start. In this respect, man cannot be redeemed by bread and money. He hungers for more. The escape into drugs, which is now becoming a mass phenomenon, demonstrates that all too clearly. The Church through all those centuries gave people an awareness of their intrinsic dignity that no one could take from them: along with the gift of hope, she gave them the meaning of the faith, which makes them rich and free. It is quite obvious how foolish it is to describe all that as "the opiate of the people", now that people do in fact take opium precisely because they have the prosperity that is supposed to make the opiate superfluous.

And furthermore: figures like Vincent de Paul or Mary Ward, or whatever the names of the many modern founders of religious orders may be, show that the Christian faith not only negatively provoked protests that are critical of society but also positively gave individuals the strength to serve, without which a society is doomed to decline. Today, when we Germans have to recruit nuns from Yugoslavia, Spain, or even from India and Korea to staff our hospitals and nursing homes (although Asia itself could urgently use its personnel), this points up a shortage in our society that very soon will probably have weightier consequences than the much debated "education shortage", which tends to mistake schooling for education and forgets man for the achievements. With money you can buy a lot, but not the spirit of selfless service; you can perhaps borrow that for a time from other nations, but if it is permanently lacking in the social organism of a people, its accomplishments stand on clay feet, and its collapse is unavoidable in the long term. Here we can see that a people cannot live on its production alone (as the naïve materialism of our public opinion supposes) but, rather, needs intellectual and spiritual forces in order to continue. People today smile or even laugh at the fact that the Church throughout the centuries has elicited the strength to serve and has been able to impart meaning to that service. Thus "undemocratic" virtues such as humility, patience, the voluntary restriction of one's own freedom for the sake of another's freedom, in the view of our progressive contemporaries, at best prove how reactionary those who practice them are or even prompt the critics to label them "the fashioning of idols", as though these virtues benefited only the ruling powers. "They are beneficial to the suffering", one ought to reply—but probably the laughter and the smiles in this regard will soon pass anyway.

Let us return to our starting point. Perhaps the observations that we have tried to make about the "other Church history" may sound rather apologetic. Nevertheless, it is simply necessary now and then to recall facts that are ignored or repressed; the suspicion about "apologetics" is not infrequently just one part of the repression that resists remembering. There is the approach in which anything dark is repressed—that is supposedly "apologetics"; there is also, however, the opposite approach, in which one is willing to see only what is dark so as to be entirely liberated from the past, but in that way, too, man falls into self-deception and loses his way. If we are trying to be realistic, we must acknowledge both: in the Church there is the constant darkness of serious human failure, but in her also abides a hope that man needs in order to be able to live. One might say: she is like fertile farmland on which the best wheat grows if it is tended; if it is neglected, however, it can also become a collection of all sorts of weeds. Or to use another image: she is like a people with great talents; such a people can become a blessing if it uses its gifts correctly; it can also become a curse if it misunderstands them.

This is the basis of our responsibility for the Church. She is God's planting, as faith tells us, but to a very large extent she is also left in our hands, so that the weeds can overrun the wheat, the olive tree can put forth leaves and remain fruitless—to use images from the Bible. However, the question of what is to become of the Church is not as unimportant as the fate of some pigeon breeders' association, the formation or disappearance of which we note without any particular emotion. For preserved in the Church are the sources of spiritual power for human life, without which this life becomes empty and society disintegrates. In the explosive situation in which we find ourselves today, mankind no doubt needs an abundant supply of technological know-how in order to make coexistence and survival possible. But by technological know-how alone it cannot be saved, for it makes new possibilities for production and new possibilities for destruction available simultaneously; indeed, the possibilities for production are often just as easily possibilities for destruction. If along with the increase in technological know-how the spiritual reservoirs of mankind dry up, then it is doomed to self-destruction. Mankind needs a framework of meaning that imparts the strength to serve, which creates an interior freedom from the world and thereby gives individuals the ability to live and work unselfishly, because a man's hope is more deeply rooted than his external career aspirations. Yet all that cannot last without the mighty force of a living faith that is in itself disinterested. In this regard, service to the faith is an existential need for man, even today and especially today. The technician who strives to find new possibilities of material survival and the believer who is at the service of the faith and seeks new ways of spiritual survival are working at two different sides of one and the same common task. They should not allow themselves to be played off against each other but, rather, should extend to each other a helping hand with the one project to which they are committed.

From all that has been said it should probably be obvious by now that no service is rendered to anyone by a Church that we make for ourselves, one that is cut off from her spiritual foundations. Conversely, it should be no less clear that Church needs our commitment in the struggle to bring forth good fruit on her land and that this is a task for mankind as a whole.

19. Bishop and Church

The tenth anniversary of the appointment of our bishop provides an opportunity to call to mind again those years—so rich and full and momentous for the life of the Church—in which our Chief Shepherd has performed his ministry as "servant of Christ and steward of the mysteries of God" (cf. 1 Cor 4:1); above all, it invites us also to reflect anew on the nature of his ministry at a time when the dream of a merely "charismatic", "brotherly" Church calls into question that ministry and the institution in general.

The English word "bishop" is derived from the Greek work *episkopos*, which goes back to the New Testament. What does it mean? The oldest passage in which it appears gives no explanation: Saint Paul's Letter to the Philippians (written around 55/56) begins with a general greeting from Paul and Timothy to all the faithful in Philippi together "with the bishops and deacons". In terms of Greek etymology, bishop means the same as "overseer". The word was used in the Greek world for a variety of occupations that in some way had to do with supervision; it had not acquired a neat or precise definition. We can determine what meaning it took on in its fusion with the language of the Christian faith only from the next two instances of the word in the New Testament: in the First Letter of Peter, Jesus Christ himself is described as "Shepherd and Bishop of our souls" (2:25, Douay Rheims; the RSVC reads "Shepherd and Guardian"); in the qualifications for priesthood with which Peter concludes his Letter, this idea crops up again, when the Apostle exhorts the presbyters to tend God's flock, "watching over them" [*episkopountes*, in the Vulgate *providentes*], not for personal gain, but willingly, not lording it over their charges, but as supportive examples (5:2). Both passages show that Peter heard

Translated by Michael J. Miller.

This essay was written in 1972 for the tenth anniversary of the episcopal consecration of the Bishop of Regensburg, which coincided with the Wolfgang Year (millennium of Wolfgang, who was made Bishop of Regensburg in 972).

in the Greek word "overseer" the connotations of the biblical word "shepherd" and understood it in this sense. In the Acts of the Apostles, which were written at around the same time, we find the same process of linguistic and doctrinal history: Paul exhorts the priests of Ephesus in his farewell discourse [20:28] to care for the whole flock, in which the Holy Spirit has made them "guardians" ("bishops"). So we can say that the word "bishop" continues the tradition of the biblical shepherd; it challenges a man who performs this ministry to follow in the footsteps of the "Good Shepherd", Jesus Christ, and gives him this Shepherd as a model. This means care, watchfulness, keeping the whole group together so as to heed the voice of the Lord; it means responsibility for unity and for making sure that it is the unity that comes from Christ; finally, it means a contrast to the hireling, who is just looking for a livelihood, whereas the true shepherd has the welfare of the flock, of the Church, in mind. And that always means also in some way a willingness to share in Christ's Passion, because this work of keeping the flock together can please neither the wolves nor all of the sheep all of the time.

With that, the main orientation of the episcopal ministry is clear; its specific duties can be explained in terms of another passage from the Acts of the Apostles, which does not speak directly about "bishops" yet had a decisive influence on the subsequent image of the bishop. Chapter 8 relates that Philip converted the people of Samaria to faith in Christ and baptized them. Upon hearing about this conversion, the apostles sent Peter and John to that district. Through prayer and the imposition of hands, they called down the Holy Spirit upon the new Christians, for he had not yet fallen on any of them; only in this way were they fully incorporated into the Church of Jesus Christ (see Acts 8:5–17). Luke is not concerned here about sacramental or canonical rules, that a deacon can only baptize and the bishop alone can confirm, but rather about something much deeper which at the same time forms the basis for the later subdivision in the administration of the sacraments. He means to say that part of the process by which the Samaritans become Christians is their insertion into the whole apostolic Church, their connection with the whole and especially with the apostolic origin as well as with the authorized guarantors of that origin. This means that just as no man can be a Christian by himself but only together with others, with the living community of believers, so too no congregation, no region, can be Church by itself. It can do so only by opening itself up to the whole and by being aligned with the apostolic tradition, of which the apostles and their successors are the guarantors. Expressed in the classic words of the Creed, this means: both catholicity and apostolicity are necessary elements of the Church, the living unity with the whole, which is represented and realized by the unity of the officeholders. Church is not just here, but throughout the earth; Church is not just today, but also yesterday and tomorrow. Only when both are accepted—unity with others, with the whole, and unity with those who went before us in faith, unity with the Church of all times—is Church truly present.

The expression and guarantee of this connection is the ministry of the bishops. They embody, with the successor to Peter at the head, the unity of all the individual local Churches with one another and with the apostolic beginning. The difference between bishops and priests expresses precisely the fact that in the Church, not only are there many congregations alongside one another, but they all belong to each other. With that we return once again to the event in the Acts of the Apostles. The Church in the West as a rule has reserved confirmation, the completion of baptism, to the bishops, so as to make it clear that becoming a Christian means incorporation into the universal Church, into the Church of the apostles. That is why it is administered, not by the pastor of the locality in question, but rather by the representative of the whole, by the visible witness to the unity and continuity of the universal Church. The same could be said even more aptly about priestly ordination: the threefold commission of the priest—preaching, guidance, sacramental ministry—can come again and again only from the authority of the universal Church. Moreover, this has important consequences for the Catholic understanding of the priest. A man never becomes a priest alone (just as no one becomes a Christian alone); rather, priestly ordination means acceptance into the *presbyterium* of a bishop. Normally priestly ministry exists only in the communion of priests led by the bishop—every one of them relies on the communion as a whole; the whole is supposed to support him, just as he supports the whole. That is also why no one needs to do everything or to know how to do everything; that is why even the most isolated work, if it is a meaningful part of the whole, derives from that whole its full priestly significance.

But this sheds light also on the task of each individual Christian. For the catholicity embodied by the bishop applies in some way to each individual and can acquire practical significance only when it is supported by the individuals, too. It requires us in our faith always to remain open to others everywhere. The Church brings this catholicity to bear at the heart of the eucharistic liturgy when she has every congregation that celebrates the Eucharist commemorate the local bishop and the successor to Peter, the pope, and at the same time combines with this a remembrance of all the faithful before us and around us. This means that the Eucharist is never the private celebration of a locality or a social circle but, rather, always bears the fundamental mark of universality, of the universal Church. It means, furthermore, that a particular Church may not set up her own theology, her own idea about ecclesiastical ministry and ecclesial piety, as an absolute but, rather, is perpetually responsible to the whole Church and for the whole Church. This obligatory connection back to the whole is salutary, as is evident especially in times of political or intellectual crises. Only the connection with the catholicity of the universal Church preserved the Catholic Church in Germany during the Third Reich from upheavals of the sort that Lutheran-Evangelical Christianity had to endure and kept her in unity with the apostolic tradition; the Church in Holland after the Council would have been spared many incidents if she had lived more by the principle that no part can become its own self-sufficient standard.

There is another observation that we should add. Together with Church tradition, we call the bishops successors to the apostles. The complicated and rich content of this formula cannot be explained in detail here. Two remarks may suffice. This formula points first to the collegial character of the episcopal ministry: just as the Twelve were called together by the Lord, so too a bishop does not stand alone but, rather, shares fundamentally in the apostolic heritage by the fact that he stays with the whole. Then there is another point: "apostle" means "one who is sent", and the Latin translation of "apostle" is "missionary". During the lifetime of the apostles, the "bishops", it appears, were the ones responsible for pastoral care in a given locality, while the apostles carried on the work of the missions. If the bishops became the successors of the apostles after the end of their "apostolate", then this means that now they, too, assumed a missionary responsibility. The Church can never stop at the circle she has gathered. She must always proclaim the Word of God anew to those who have not yet heard it, because this Word is a light that shines for all men and that all men need. Thus, within the episcopal ministry there is always a dynamic feature as well, a concern that the Church should expand her growth into mankind and into the future. This means, in turn, that every Church headed by a bishop must look beyond herself and become fruitful, so that the Word of God can advance into new places. The best way that she has of preserving herself is to become fruitful for others.

When we say that, what immediately comes to mind is the memory of our great Bishop Wolfgang of Regensburg and of the missionary responsibility that urged him to spend his best years in Hungary and that was again demonstrated in his founding of the Diocese of Prague. But above all, we look to the present: to the struggle for catholicity and apostolicity, to the debate with sheep and wolves today. That God may continue to give our Bishop the strength and the grace to carry on is our wish in this year of commemorations.

20. On the Meaning of Church Architecture

In his important book *Der Kirchenbau des 20. Jahrhunderts in Deutschland* [Twentieth-century Church architecture in Germany], Hugo Schnell showed that we live in a century that includes one of the greatest blossomings of church architecture and, in addition, contributed something entirely new: an orientation that looked, not to the cloister or cathedral church, but rather to the parish church.[1] So it is all the more worrisome that this flowering suddenly stopped, and today the question arises with increasing sharpness, within the Church and in a theological context: Should we be building churches at all? The boundary between the sacred and the secular, so the argument goes, has been breached by the crucified Christ, and sequestering the sacred would be a throwback to pre-Christian religiosity. The pragmatic and the theologically correct seem to join forces here: The multi-purpose space, which is used in the morning to celebrate Mass, during the day for lectures, and in the evening for socials, seems to be not only the more economical but also the objectively more appropriate solution.

In the context of such reflections I was strangely moved when I came upon the chapter entitled "Civic Temples" while reading Solzhenitsyn's novel *The First Circle*. The author tells about the old Communist Rubin, who even in Stalin's prison has lost nothing of his unconditional Marxist faith and in his mind works ceaselessly to perfect Marxist theory and the Marxist society. In this connection, he carries a remarkable project in his pocket, which is likewise entitled "Civic Temples". Rubin recognizes that in his atheistic society moral coherence is shattered, the Party has taken the place that was once reserved for God, and man is threatened with self-destruction. "Maybe at present it was more important for the Soviet Union to improve public morality than to build

---

Translated by Michael J. Miller.

[1] H. Schnell, *Der Kirchenbau des 20. Jahrhunderts in Deutschland* (Munich and Zürich, 1973), esp. 222–27.

the Volga-Don Canal or the Angarastroi [Angara Dam]." He tries to respond to this dilemma by suggesting the building of civic temples, in which critical occasions of human life are to be celebrated in solemn ceremonies with collective participation. "Indeed the whole architectural ensemble of the temple must breathe majesty and eternity." In addition, there would have to be "temple attendants", "who enjoyed the love and trust of the people because of their own irreproachable, unselfish and worthy lives".[2]

Solzhenitsyn—a former Marxist who has become pensive after many sufferings and is groping to find a new path to God—attributes this idea to one of his characters; my sense is that much more about the questions of contemporary man is revealed in this idea than in the overly insistent talk about "desacralization". Such slogans are used by men who break the fetters of a churchliness that is becoming too narrow for them and are just moving forward into the modern perception of the world. In Rubin's idea, on the other hand, we hear a man who has made his way through today's world and is raising the questions of tomorrow. Anyone who looks at the stone wilderness of the growing major cities and senses the abandonment to anonymity and management that half-suffocates the people in it, physically and psychologically, will probably say: If such a thing did not yet exist—the idea of the cathedral, a space for retreat, immersion, and silence, a finger pointing to the mysterious and the eternal—then it would have to be invented, because we need it. In the words of Josef Pieper:

> The more the absolute claim of the merely utilitarian threatens to coat all of existence with a film, the more man needs every once in a while, for the sake of a truly human life, this chance to be able to emerge from the frenzy of sights and sounds (buy this, drink that, eat this, amuse yourself here, demonstrate for or against) that incessantly cries out to him and to step into a space in which silence reigns and thus true listening becomes possible, listening to *the* reality on which our existence is based and by which it is constantly nourished and renewed.[3]

[2] Alexander Solzhenitsyn, *The First Circle*, trans. Thomas P. Whitney (New York and Evanston: Harper & Row, 1968), chap. 67, pages 416–20.

[3] Cf. J. Pieper, *Problems of Modern Faith: Essays and Addresses*, trans. Jan van Heurck containing the essays "The Sacred and 'Desacralization'", 13–46; "What Is a Church? Preliminary Reflections on the Theme of the 'Sacred Building'", 87–115.

In all that we have said thus far we have of course argued only in terms of today, of what man is and needs today—which of course is not unimportant or irrelevant from the Christian perspective. Nevertheless, we must now pose the genuinely theological question: What does it look like from the perspective of the Bible, of the sources of Christianity?

From this viewpoint, is an ecclesiastical space thinkable? And if so, what function should be assigned to it? In this connection, it is correctly pointed out over and over today that the Cross of Jesus Christ, in the faith of the New Testament, means the end of the old Temple; its subsequent destruction by the Romans merely accomplished in fact what had already occurred in principle when Jesus cried out just before he died. The Evangelists suggest this idea when they report that at the moment of Jesus' death the curtain of the Temple was torn in two. As the Evangelists understood it, this can mean, on the one hand, that the curtain that until then had veiled the Holy of Holies was taken away, so that now God's grace, no longer concealed, was accessible to all mankind. He, the Crucified One himself, is now the Holy of Holies, which is now set up for the general public worldwide; his outstretched arms are the open gesture of divine favor, which desires to "draw all men to himself" (cf. Jn 12:32). We can also understand it symbolically as a sign of the destruction of the Temple. After Israel had driven out "the Son", the Temple became a "den of thieves", empty inside—God is no longer in it but, rather, in him who was crucified outside the city walls.[4]

Both interpretations lead to the same answer to our question, so we can allow them both to stand here on an equal footing. We could summarize this finding in the formula: Jesus, the Crucified and Risen One, has replaced the Temple. Or, in a way that more clearly applies to our question: What the Temple was for the Old Testament is supplied for the Church, not by any building, but rather by a man—the God-man Jesus Christ. This already clarifies in principle what is right about the theories of "desacralization" and what is wrong. After the death of Jesus, the directly sacral character that belonged to the Temple for Israel, in keeping with the Deuteronomic Law, could no longer be

---

[4] I have developed and documented this idea extensively in my essay "Auferbaut aus lebendigen Steinen", in *Kirche aus lebendigen Steinen*, ed. W. Seidel (Mainz, 1975), 30–48.

attributed to any building in the world. Neither Saint Peter's Basilica in Rome nor any other church in Christendom can ever signify for believers in Jesus Christ something analogously central and irreplaceable, as the Temple was for the people of the Old Covenant. Every church building ultimately points to Him, the true center of the Church.

But that does not also mean, conversely, that now sheer profanity has taken the place of the previous sacrality. Certainly, the crucified Christ is the expression of a love that goes "to the end" (cf. Jn 13:1); his outstretched arms were seen even in the early Church as a symbol of what is called today "the horizontal dimension of Christianity". They are a gesture of worship (the primordial Christian posture of prayer), but at the same time they are a gesture of embrace directed to all mankind, and the two are inseparably intertwined: by his openness to mankind, Jesus glorifies the Father. Perhaps we should learn again to understand the priestly prayer posture of outstretched arms more in terms of this ancient theology; incidentally, it is mentioned explicitly in the new Second Eucharistic Prayer, which deliberately refers to the outstretched hands of the Lord, on the basis of this historical background. But now the radical love of Jesus is the new Temple after all, *for this reason*: because in him God's love is revealed at the same time, because in him the divine nature enters into human nature and joins with it even down into the abyss of death. That means, however, that the love of Jesus Christ cannot be replaced by any human fellowship whatsoever but, rather, is absolutely unique and, of course, in precisely that way calls us to participate in it.

This means, however, that the reduced emphasis on cult and the spiritualization brought about by the Christian faith is not a transition to a general spirituality, to a general rationality, but rather the appropriation of the spirit of history to the flesh of Jesus Christ. What happens is spiritualization, liberation from the constraint of the letter and of its externality, but the spirit that is the terminus of the spiritualizing process is the one about whom Paul says: "The Lord is the Spirit." The letter is set free into his hands. Spirit and truth, which according to John 4 are the space of Christian worship instead of the old Temple, are not the expression of a philosophical program along the lines of the allegorical reinterpretation of outmoded religions that philosophy attempted in late antiquity; instead, they refer, on the lips of the Johannine Christ, to the one who says about himself, "I am the

Truth." Christian spiritualization is at the same time incarnation. The Platonizing theology of the Church Fathers, for instance Augustine, was not always able to maintain this paradox in all its keenness; this is evident in Augustine's theories of art, when he tried to relegate images and music to the Old Testament, because they belonged to the earthly people of God and not to God's spiritual people. He did not experience the Second Council of Nicaea, which amounted to a decisive victory over the Platonic misunderstanding of Christianity—a victory that has received too little attention in the West—by maintaining the paradox of a spiritualization that is incarnation. The Council, which in its affirmation of the image sees the inner consistency of the Incarnation and which in the East is still celebrated on the Feast of Orthodoxy as the watershed between pre-Christian and Christian Hellenism— this Council is the ready-made answer to the problem of desacralization, which arose in the West in the sixteenth century and by now in the twentieth has assumed its most acute form. Iconoclasm is not the breakthrough from the Old Testament into the New but, rather, the destruction of the Incarnation and thus a relapse into the Law, which could permit no images because the Image had not yet appeared.[5]

Let us return to our subject. The new worship of God is rooted in the love of the Son. It is vitally dependent on it. This means, in turn, that the faith community of Jesus is vitally dependent on gathering around him, the crucified and risen Lord. This gathering, which we call Eucharist, is the heartbeat of its life. In it, the faith community remembers that central event of the Cross and Resurrection and, in remembering, receives the Presence. And for that purpose we build churches. As Christians we need a house for gathering, which by the way cannot exist without interior recollection. In order for Christians to "collect themselves", that is, gather, they must first be able to recollect themselves from all distraction and enter into that silence which does not separate but unites. For nowhere is man so alienated from himself and from others as in the noisy shouting of a demonstration; nowhere is he so close to himself and to others as in shared silence that then opens itself to the meaningful word. When we calmly investigate this approach, it becomes evident also how easily this theologically

---

[5] On this subject, see Christoph Schönborn, O.P., *God's Human Face: The Christ-Icon*, trans. Lothar Krauth (San Francisco: Ignatius Press, 1994).

central fact joins forces with the primordial human urges that in every age have led to "sacred buildings" and that even in an atheistic world necessarily awaken the idea of "civic temples" or secular cathedrals. The church space is built for gathering and recollection into the Lord, who is present in the eucharistic celebration. As a building, therefore, it must express the ideas of "gathering" and "recollection" and must express the fact that inside there is God's presence, an incursion of the eternal into time. The building itself with its walls is not the presence of God, as was probably often assumed about the Temple in the pre-Christian era. But it does point to the gathering that this place is, alludes to it symbolically, and makes it possible. And in this respect, it indirectly bears in itself some of the features of that gathering. And in a new, that is, Christian way that makes it "sacral", worthy of reverence and love.

Let us pause a moment before we draw further consequences, for urgent questions are arising. Is a house not enough for the eucharistic gathering, for the Lord's Supper? Indeed, is it not more appropriate to celebrate it in an everyday house rather than in a space specifically designated for that purpose? This question seems to have a point, since in fact the celebration of the Eucharist took place at first in the houses of Christians, and church buildings became common on a large scale only after the time of Constantine—the notion that this very fact is a sign of the Constantinian Romanization and imperialization of the Church is almost unavoidable. Now first, of course, we should warn the reader here against an archeologism that, remarkably, is akin to many types of progressivism: the conviction that only what is old is authentically Christian and that everything that came afterward must be regarded as arbitrary, if not as almost degenerate. This standard, which sees nothing at all between the Bible and us and mistakes antiquity for truth, is based . . . well, squarely on a mistake. Christianity has its original and guiding message in the Bible, but the claim expressed in the Bible matures fully over the course of history, and thus things that are biblically essential in a Christian way can appear in all eras. Even though it appeared late, it can still be the discovery of something authentic, a product of the real inner history of the faith. That is why the Council Fathers of Trent, in their debates about the concept of tradition, already distinguished between that which is only old (even though it may have been in the Bible, such as the veiling of women) and what is original in the sense of authentic. Paul started by preaching in the synagogue; merely pointing out that he had to celebrate the Eucharist in houses does not prove that this was for Christianity an intrinsically necessary or even a more suitable form. On the contrary, we find in Paul's writings, upon closer examination, a decisive boundary that he draws between house and church: the nourishing meal that used to precede the Eucharist had degenerated. He says: I hear that there are divisions, when you gather *"in ecclesia"*—this could be translated "in church", although it cannot mean that (1 Cor 11:18). But then he adds: "Do you not have houses to eat and drink in? Or do you despise the church of God . . . ?" (verse 22). He throws the *agape* feast out of the "churches" and relegates them to the houses. Now he is making, not yet a spatial distinction, but rather a spiritual one: the gathering that is supposed to represent the Church must be completely imbued with the memory of the Lord; it must be "sacral", one could say. However, the separation of meal and Eucharist that Paul is attempting here had radical consequences above all for liturgical history. The Christian form of the liturgy, what is distinctive about Christian liturgy, becomes detached from its native Jewish soil, in which Jesus handed it down. Since then, as J. A. Jungmann has demonstrated, no one called the Eucharist the Lord's Supper again until the sixteenth century; it was simply named the Eucharist. Paul further underscored this intervention of his by firmly and decisively opposing all table conviviality with the saying: "For as often as you eat this bread and drink this cup, you proclaim the Lord's death until he comes" (v. 26). He points to the reality that is represented in the Eucharist, to the crucified Lord. The Cross is lifted up wherever the words of this Thanksgiving are spoken. And this produces a space of reverence (which automatically assumes a spatial form, too), as well as the external conditions for it.

There is a further point. Although the Eucharist is celebrated in a house, it is not a domestic circle. According to the conviction of Christians from the very beginning, those who meet for the Eucharist do not form a social group or a circle of friends but, rather, the public entity of the People of God, which is comparable, in the status that it claims, not to any cultic associations, but solely to the political entity of the Roman Empire and its citizenry. This paradox—that the numerically quite insignificant group of Christians understood themselves, not on the level of private worship associations, as one might easily have supposed, but rather as having the magnitude of the *Imperium Romanum* —was so important to the Christians that they risked martyrdom, although they could easily have spared themselves much trouble if they had come together as friends, as families. There is no getting around this state of affairs, which has been set forth impressively by Erik Peterson. In this regard, there was an intrinsic reason that led the Christian assemblies to gather in the imperial building called the basilica, when public law allowed this public self-expression of their claim. Hence the cathedral is a form that sprang up from within Christianity and not a political adaptation or a political aberration.[6]

Of course the basilica had to change step by step as Christian church architecture developed out of its ancient form. It adopted some of the functions of the old synagogue: the dwelling place of the Word. It acquired the principal function of being the place of the eucharistic thanksgiving. Beyond that, we must ask also what things, in terms of the intrinsic facts of Christianity, are important for a building that represents the Christian *ecclesia* and serves it. Let us repeat first once again: Such a building must be designed in such a way that gathering and recollection at the Eucharist is possible there. It must be such that the proclamation of the Word and common prayer can take place there. But soon additional elements appear: the gathering of the People of God is achieved first and foremost in baptism, and therefore the church building must also be a space that is suitable for the common celebration of baptism and is capable of reminding the faithful of it. And again one could add: Wherever the memory of baptism becomes concrete, it must again and again in this world mean "penance"—that is quite essential. Therefore church must be a place for that also. And finally: gathering means silence, it means recollection, and it means prayer. Thus a church building must also be a space that invites Christians, beyond the common worship of God, to stay awhile, to pray, to be silent before the Lord, whose eucharistic closeness remains beyond the common celebration.

No doubt this function did not come into existence in church architecture until very late; nevertheless, contrary to all archeologism, I consider it to be one of its most essential tasks. It was prepared for early

---

[6] Cf. E. Peterson, *Theologische Traktate* (Munich, 1951). See also my essay "Auferbaut aus lebendigen Steinen".

on. First by the fact that Paul inexorably relegates feasts to the profane realm. This process acquired for Augustine an exemplary significance; in a lifelong battle he tried to gain acceptance for the apostolic decision in his African homeland and thereby, in my opinion, created one of the basic prerequisites for the oratories of the Middle Ages and the Catholic modern era. Christians had grown accustomed to having feasts in honor of the dead over the tombs of the saints, which means even in the basilicas; these regularly ended in inebriation, so that drunken squalling had become the regular music of the houses of God. In Italy, Augustine learned that this was a particularly African custom; so he opposed it, initially out of his sense of catholicity, but also because of the Pauline directive and, finally, while citing again and again the cleansing of the Temple by Jesus, which certainly, as a prophetic anticipation of the New Covenant in the house of the Old, is inimitable; but its goal, to make the outer courtyard of the Gentiles, which Israel had occupied with its own cultic needs, once again into a place of prayer for all peoples—this goal does indeed require the place of prayer that Augustine was rightly unwilling to see misused as a place of drunkenness. In order for this place of prayer to assume its definitive form, many other things still had to happen; above all, there had to be a consciousness of the abiding presence of Christ in the Eucharist.[7]

Thus slowly, through various incentives, this new Christian thing developed: churches that are church all day long. Churches in which the Church is always alive, because praying people always encounter there the mystery of the Lord, of his death and Resurrection. After all, someone who prays in church does not pray to God in general but, rather, to the God who through Jesus constantly places on our lips the Word of the Eucharist and the word of prayer that is sure of an answer. Someone who prays *in* church always prays *with* the Church, not alone. Praying churches are the new gift that the Church and her faith have given to mankind. This is something that could never exist in the old temples, the *cellae* of the gods. Only with this development is Christianity perfectly distinct—only now is the Christian form found; really, even humanly speaking, I consider these praying churches to be one of the most precious things that the Christian spirit has produced.

---

[7] On this subject, see J. Ratzinger, *Volk und Haus Gottes in Augustins Lehre von der Kirche* (Munich, 1954); J. van der Meer, *Augustinus der Seelsorger* (Cologne, 1952).

Recently Lutheran-Evangelical friends have repeatedly come up to me and said that it makes them sad to find the Catholic churches empty all day, too, without people praying in them, people who for a little while or a longer time recollect themselves and, in so doing, embody the living Church throughout the day in the church space and maintain that space as Church, keeping it open as the shared house of the Father by going in and out as a matter of course. (They even keep it open in a very literal sense: when there is no longer any quiet praying by the faithful, churches have to be locked, because they become too unsafe.) Many of these friends told me that they felt this as a loss for them, too: the open churches had been ultimately something owned by all of Christendom, the breath of the Eternal in the midst of our busy world, which benefited the whole in incalculable ways. A church that only "functions", that is merely "functional", no longer accomplishes its special purpose: to be the space in which we step out of the world of agendas and into the freedom of God. Building such spaces is, especially today, a worthwhile task, which becomes even more relevant the more isolated modern man becomes in the residential towers of our cities.

ESCHATOLOGY

21. On the Theology of Death[1]

The physician and the pastor both care for the life of men. Each one, on his own level and in his own way, tries to ensure that the life of man becomes richer, fuller, more secure, that it becomes freer and happier, in a word: that it becomes to a greater extent "living". The saying in which the Lord clothed the meaning of his mission is also the expression of their commission, whose authority they acknowledge: "I came that they may have life, and have it abundantly" (Jn 10:10). But this very care for life necessarily includes an encounter with the phenomenon of death. Working for human life automatically means also coming into conflict with the reality of death. For human life is centrally marked by death. At every moment it already bears its contradiction within itself. That is why in every age man's consciousness of life has been at the same time a consciousness of death also, or at least of mortality. This can be substantiated by the words of that early Father of the Church Gregory the Great: "In comparison to eternal life, temporal life should be called death rather than life. For what else is this daily exhaustion and decline than a long, drawn-out dying?" just as it can be substantiated by the medieval saying "In the midst of life we are surrounded by death"

Translated by Michael J. Miller.

[1] This short meditation—originally a lecture given to the Ärztegesellschaft Sankt Lukas [St. Luke Society of Catholic Physicians] in Munich—adopts several fundamental points from the "eschatology textbook" by a systematic theologian at the University of Erlangen, Paul Althaus, *Die letzten Dinge*, 6th ed. (Gütersloh, 1956). It tries to extend his ideas from the perspective of Catholic theology. I hope to be able to deal with the whole subject soon with even greater precision in the section on eschatology [*Eschatology: Death and Eternal Life*, trans. Michael Waldstein (Washington, D.C.: Catholic Univ. of America Press, 1988)] in the series *Kleine katholische Dogmatik*, edited by J. Auer and myself, taking recent literature into account.

or by Heidegger's observation about man, who is cast into nothingness and must attempt to travel upon the roaring sea of nothingness armed with joy. Most impressive perhaps is the wonderfully terse formula by Claude Bernard: "La vie, c'est la mort" (Life is death). This also expresses the fundamental insight that death does not simply punctuate the conclusion of a life, which for its part would then be *only* life while death would remain, as it were, outside of that life and touch upon it only from outside; rather, "living" itself is "dying": dying is inherent to life, the *processus* of living is per se also the *processus* of dying into that life, so that that whole life is imbued, as it were, by death and in its movement is both a movement of living and a movement of dying. Hence, understanding human life means understanding a process of dying.

The question about death is therefore raised peremptorily by life itself. It is posed inescapably to anyone who really cares about life. And if he does not just want to care for and preserve this life externally but also tries to fill it with meaning and thus give it its true greatness and potential, then he will not be able to avoid the question about the meaning and senselessness of death. In this meditation, I would like to try to show briefly how this question about the meaning of death is answered from a Christian faith perspective. Of course in doing so we cannot forget that questions like those about life and death can in the final analysis never be answered simply with a formula but, rather, find their true answer only in the lived appropriation of the formula. In this regard, everything that is merely *said* here is evidently provisional in character.

1. Non-Christian Interpretations of Death

a. Idealistic Interpretation of Death

What is "death"? In order to understand (with the qualifications just mentioned) the Christian answer to this question in its austere clarity, it is necessary to distinguish it from another answer with which it is all too easily and all too often confused. By this I mean the explanation that can be described as the idealist interpretation and is generally—although not with complete accuracy—attributed to Plato.[2] For the idealist understanding of existence along the lines of the "Platonism"

---

[2] For a critique of the interpretation of Plato that has become conventional among theologians, see J. Pieper, "Tod und Unsterblichkeit", *Catholica* 13 (1959): 81–100.

of late antiquity, the entire world of material being is "phenomenal" or apparent being, a lower degree of being, a mere shadow of being. Naturally this brings about an enormous devaluation of all visible becoming and transience. This, however, affects above all one's explanation of human living and dying; indeed, in man something unique takes place: material and spiritual being are united in one single nature. According to the "Platonic" hierarchy of being, the material component, the body, as a matter of principle can be only a de-authentication of what is truly human, that is, of the spiritual component. Dying, then, is simply being set free for what is authentic; it is liberation and redemption. Consequently, death is the "friend" who frees man from the imprisonment of the body and purchases his entrance into his authentic existence, the immortal, purely spiritual, and eternal being of the soul. (In this sort of idealism, therefore, there is "redemption": it is death!) Not infrequently over the course of history, this image of death as friend, the idealistic image of death, has been confused with the Christian image of death; of course we should not overlook either the fact that, despite all the weaknesses of the theory, a glance at the Cross has reaffirmed again and again the true center of Christian living and dying, which is unimaginable for any idealism.

But let us stay for the moment with our preface to the theological discussion. From the purely human perspective, there are important objections to the idealistic image of death: psychological and medical as well as philosophical objections.

The *philosopher* will ask: Is this understanding of being and world really justified? Admittedly, matter ranks below spirit. But does that mean that it is not God's good work, too? Although in terms of the Greek concept of the world it may be right to consider it inferior, can that be said by those who, after all, believe in the Creator who called what he created very good? And is man's body really a prison? Is man really composed of two layers, in the sense that the one just "stays" in the other as a guest, so to speak, and is happy when it can leave that much too inhospitable house? Or is it not instead a living union of spirit and body, embodied spirit and spiritually formed body, the two so unified that one without the other would no longer be a human being at all, who is one precisely *in* the other? Man is "authentic", is himself, precisely in the body; being human means "being in the body"; corporeality is the authenticity of man (cf. the identification of "σῶμα" and "self" in the language of the Bible and of early Hellenism).

Thus death is precisely an attack on the authenticity of man as well, which shatters the instrument of the spirit along with the body and suddenly interrupts this entity that has scarcely begun.

From the *psychological* perspective, one is tempted to object: This image of death as friend is "idealistic" but just not "realistic". In fact, death is experienced by man, not as friend, but as foe. Actually death prevails again and again simply in its sheer dreadfulness, beyond all other considerations: even the saints often could not master their fear of death. We might recall the remark by Saint Thérèse of Lisieux, "Never will I learn to die", or the impressive artistic rendering of the phenomenon of the saints' fear of death in Bernanos' *Dialogues of the Carmelites*. More profound than either of these, however, is the mystery of the agony of Jesus Christ himself, of which Scripture gives us a deeply moving account.

Naturally one could say: That is just the unavoidable discrepancy between ideal and reality. Even if we disregard for a moment the agony of our Lord, we must still at least admit that when the difference between ideal and reality is too great, the question unavoidably arises as to whether the ideal is set incorrectly and is itself in need of correction.

Medicine, too, will have misgivings about such an image of death. In this context, we must consider the following points: the physician's point of departure lies in the corporeal. So he is struck more forcefully by the immediate, concretely corporeal impression of death than is the philosopher, who judges the matter speculatively from his writing desk; he encounters the corporeal component of death with such overwhelming forcefulness that he is easily tempted to regard the corporeal aspect, not merely as one component, but as the only thing that is at stake here in the first place. Even the physician who does not go that far cannot possibly close his eyes to the fundamental role ordinarily played here by the bodily processes. Thus a Catholic physician writes: "Medicine sees in death a bodily failure. . . . One does not die because the soul leaves the body. One dies because the necessary conditions for bodily life are no longer present. The body leaves the soul and sets it free."[3] The soul does not leave the body behind as an empty shell; rather, the body fails in its service to the soul. It is not the soul's

---

[3] A. Faller, "Biologisches von Sterben und Tod", *Anima* 11 (1956): 260–68, citation at 266.

departure that makes it impossible for the body to work; rather, the failure of the body itself puts an end to life. On a broken instrument, the soul can no longer play.

b. Materialistic Interpretations

The inherent fragility of the idealistic interpretation of death is one decisive reason why in the modern era it has been increasingly displaced by the materialistic explanation of death, which has received considerable support from the exact findings of science. This explanation rules out the spiritual component and maintains that in death an organism ceases to be, just as it once began to be. This, of course, can then be combined with a wide variety of ethical interpretations: from Heidegger's challenge, in the face of nothingness, now in a final act of responsibility to fill this meaningless structure of life with the most sublime meaning by our own power, down to that other philistine existentialism that is formulated in terms that were already quoted in the Bible: "Let us eat and drink, for tomorrow we die!" (1 Cor 15:32; cf. Is 22:13).

Clearly, materialism is not Christian. But it seems to me important to emphasize that idealism, too, by no means coincides with Christianity. Rather, both are *human* attempts to cope with the problem of death; in this respect, both are part of the prologue to the Gospel and both can become an inquiry directed to the Gospel, a *praeparatio evangelica*. But neither one *is* simply the Gospel. The Old Testament—the divine *praeparatio evangelica*—adopts elements of the idealistic interpretation of death only in its later writings, but it gives both of them—the materialistic as well as the idealistic idea of death—a new meaning from the perspective of its faith in the one God.

2. The Christian Understanding of Death

a. The Old Testament

In Scripture, death is made out to be, not a friend, but rather "the last enemy" (1 Cor 15:26), who is swallowed up in Christ's victory (1 Cor 15:54f.), whose sting is sin (ibid.). With that Paul is simply continuing the Old Testament understanding of death. For the Old Testament, however, death is not the separation of body and soul and, thus, the liberation of the latter but, rather, the terrifying end of man, who is but a single whole.

> For there is hope for a tree,
>   if it be cut down, that it will sprout again,
>   and that its shoots will not cease. . . .
> But man dies, and is laid low;
>   man breathes his last, and where is he?
> As waters fall from a lake,
>   and a river wastes away and dries up,
> so man lies down and rises not again. (Job 14:7, 10–12)

Existence in Sheol (the underworld) is a mere shadow existence, the absolute emptiness of which is evident in the fact that Yahweh (who is a God of the living and not of the dead) does not care about Sheol, or rather, it has no relation to him. "For Sheol cannot thank you, death cannot praise you" (Is 38:18). "For in death there is no remembrance of you; in Sheol who can give you praise?" (Ps 6:5; similar expressions occur frequently in the Psalms). Thus, in contrast to idealism, the Old Testament (along with the New Testament) acknowledges the total human shock caused by the phenomenon of death, because it understands man realistically as a totality and, consequently, views death as the breakdown of human existence. It even intensifies this terror by understanding death as judgment; on the other hand, of course, a certain mitigation is also connected with that idea.

The Old Testament says of the matter that death is certainly first of all simply an organic event. An event from below. But it is not just that. Rather, the fact that this organic event exists is based on a decision by God. On a decision, moreover, that did not necessarily have to turn out that way. In man's nature there is another possibility as well: that of immortality. This does not necessarily mean that man still has that possibility in him as he exists here and now. But the idea of man allows for that possibility. We can even say that it would be the suitable possibility, the one actually destined for him. It is just that this possibility did not take effect. God has decreed that the fate of mankind, as it is, should be death. This occurs now as a simple biological necessity. But it is accordingly still not just an event from below but, rather, in principle, in terms of its inception, also an event from above. It comes not just from the laws of nature; it comes from God's hand. It is not the deterioration of something that has no permanence in the first place; rather, God breaks something that has to be broken. Certainly this undoes neither the seriousness nor the terror of death. Yet there still is a certain ray of hope, however insignificant it may be, or at least the start of such a ray of hope: death is not merely a natural fatality; rather, its existence depends on a spiritual decision of a free and sovereign will. Of course the Old Testament goes no farther. At its core it has nothing to say about any immortality of the soul, and it suggests the idea of resurrection only very late and in isolated passages. It leaves the situation open along the lines that we have just described.

b. New Testament

The New Testament links up with these open statements of the Old Testament. It allows the frightfulness, the sober seriousness of death to continue unabated. But it completes the message about judgment with the good news about grace. Therefore, it says first along with the Old Testament: Death is in itself a biological event. A sentence hanging over life. This event, which in itself is almost completely explained by that, is based on a spiritual decision, on a decision by God, which decrees an alteration of the original idea of man and of his potential. On God's decision, therefore, to break human existence, which ultimately is steeped in egotism and characterized over and over again by the spirit of false self-assertion. Thus far the New Testament agrees with the Old Testament. But now it adds: God made this first intervention in man's affairs, the decree of death. He added to it a second intervention, which does not cancel out the first but, rather, transforms it from within—he himself died, died so as to rise again and thus establish a new beginning. God breaks, not in order to break, but, rather, so as to form something new. The dying process as a whole is a process of breaking, but one is broken like a cocoon, from which the new form can emerge; the painful process of breaking is the way in which God shapes the new thing. God breaks the old Adam (collectively and individually) so as to form the new Adam out of him; bit by bit he breaks our willfulness and self-sufficiency so as to recast us for the freedom of his love. Death is the beginning of resurrection; the frightful aspects of death—the birth pangs of a new life.

Note well: The New Testament does not deny that death per se can be understood first as a bodily failure. But it adds that the existence of this bodily failure is based on a judgment by God. This is not immediately evident in the process itself; this is, rather, an understanding of the process that faith offers to us. And the New Testament goes on to add that this judgment by God has acquired a new significance in Christ and in terms of Christ, in such a way that out of the breaking-off of the old, the new proceeds, in such a way that precisely the necessity of dying, the constant breaking-off of the old that we must endure, is and can become the in-breaking of something new.

From this an ethical statement and a creedal statement develop. The ethical statement becomes evident when we reflect that death, after all, does not occur in an instant, not just at the conclusion of our existence; instead, the event of death takes place in all the breakdowns of our lives. All of these breakdowns, which together make up our *one* death, are, therefore, not just random annoyances and not just blind biological occurrences; rather, they are ultimately God's action upon us, through which he tears away from us our selfish, self-seeking, egotistical existence so as to reshape us according to his image. In practice this means: Death, as a movement that leaves its mark on human existence, must not be regarded by man himself as something merely biological or external but, rather, must be assimilated spiritually and humanly so as to come to the fruition that this event can and should have in us. This means, therefore, that for the human being everything depends on correctly grasping the dying movement in his life, starting from the little humiliation and onward to the major failures (of health, of physical or mental abilities: the death of loved ones is a part of a person's own death, and so on). What is at stake here has been described magnificently by Dietrich von Hildebrand under the headings "Readiness to Change" and "True Surrender of Self".[4] Man must therefore admit that death is not just something biological and translate that fact concretely into his own existence in such a way that he gives spiritual meaning to the dying process, which is present in any case; he must really accept it as a breaking-off of his self-assertiveness and as the development of a new freedom of spirit and of body and thereby transform its meaning or,

---

[4] In *Transformation in Christ* (Manchester, New Hamp.: Sophia Institute Press, 1990), 3–29, 481–500.

more precisely, make the already existing transformation of meaning fruitful in his life. In this way the dying movement, instead of being a blind fate, can become a very practical sort of training in true freedom and can become the process through which someone becomes a "new man"—which means precisely, a Christian.

Alongside this ethical statement and very closely connected with it there is a creedal statement. It says: The acceptance and spiritual re-working of the dying movement that we have just described is the ac-ceptance and spiritual assimilation of baptism. For what does baptism mean? Paul answers this question in the formula: "We were baptized into [Christ's] death" (Rom 6:3). Baptism means the union of our death with Christ's death. It means that we enter into the change in value that human death underwent through the death of Christ. That our death therefore acquires the value of a birthing process that we ourselves cannot give it. Baptism is participation in Christ's death and Resurrection, dying with Christ and thus gaining a share in the Res-urrection as the necessary fruit of death. As a sacramental dying with Christ, it is an anticipation of a real death: all of our dying, which marks and permeates our whole life as the constant *processus mortis in vitam* [advance of death into life], is now no longer merely our own dying but, rather, is because of baptism and for the sake of baptism an act of divine grace: the birth of the new Adam, the onset of resurrection. All of our dying is therefore a process of being graced: the metamorphosis of our existence into the new Adam. . . . Thus our definitive bodily death is ultimately nothing other than the conclusion of our baptism. The theology of death is the theology of baptism, and the theology of baptism is the theology of death. The whole process of dying is, if we accept it in faith, the realization of our being baptized, which comes to an end only on our deathbed: it is being overshadowed by the Cross of Christ and, thus, by the life of Christ. "The matter of baptism is as serious as death, and the matter of death is as joyful as baptism."[5]

c. Christianity and Idealism

Now one could ask whether at the end of the day this Christian an-swer to the problem of death is not identical in practice with the ide-alist answer. Naturally there are affinities. But we must not overlook

---

[5] P. Althaus, *Die letzten Dinge*, 86.

the fact that decisive differences remain. For us, too, a death, namely Christ's death, is "redemption", and our own death has a share in it—nevertheless, that does not mean the same thing as when idealism calls death redemption. For us, too, death is now surrounded by a gleam of grace, and yet it is not a "friend" in the idealist sense. Death is not "redemption" because the one good part of man is finally detached from the other, less valuable part: there is no such partitioning of human nature in Christianity. Rather, death is redemption, a blessing, because in it this entire unrefined existence, which is prone to sin and so ill disposed, is renovated and reworked into a new one. This means that death in itself remains for us a frightful negation of the whole man, but, in a marvelous reversal, this negation now becomes the prerequisite for a new, positive reality: out of the destruction is born the new thing. Thus Christianity, unlike idealism, does not simply deny the terror and frightfulness of death. Instead, that continues to exist, but it becomes, precisely as such, the instrument of grace and of salvation, in a reversal that could never be imagined from an earthly perspective but can only be decreed by God.

That means that the Old Testament view, or in general the "natural" aspect of death, which idealism denies, is by no means simply annulled in the New Testament (as it commonly happens in preaching that offers false consolation), nor is it declared invalid; it continues in full force, only it is set into a larger context. What we need to do here is to correct in general a false notion about the relation between the Testaments so as to see clearly in this particular matter as well. The Testaments should not be understood as a simple succession, a merely temporal juxtaposition and sequence, so that with the beginning of the New the Old would have only the value of a historical reminiscence. Rather, there is a genuine interpenetration, so that the Old Testament continues to live *in* the New Testament, and the latter is and can be only in this mutual dependence; the definitive abolition of the Old and its elevation into the merely New belong to the world to come, not to our "in-between" state. This can be illustrated by the relation between fear of the Lord and love of God. The New Testament does not simply abolish fear absolutely. But neither is it true that fear remains there as a separate act alongside of love, in such a way that their mutual proportions are shifted: for instance, fear is minimized, and love maximized. It is not a simple juxtaposition. Rather, the act of fear remains as such *in* the love and gives it its special meaning; more precisely: the act of love enters into the previous propaedeutic act of fear and transforms it without canceling it out; rather, it really retains it within itself as the "matter" that makes it possible. Specifically: God *in himself* continues to be for the sinful man a terrible majesty, but the very fact that he is per se the Terrible One, the one toward whom fear is always the initial fitting response on man's part, gives meaning to the other fact, that this inherently frightening God says: Fear not! This expression has its true significance only if God *in himself* is terrible; it is trivialized if one denies the terrible majesty of God, as idealism and a wrongly idealized Christianity do. Fear remains as the counterpoint of love; the latter acquires from this its real meaning and is enabled thereby; the two mutually define each other.

So it is also with death: the grace that makes us free has its special character in the very fact that death *in itself* is terrible and remains so. But precisely that which is terrifying per se becomes in Christ the instrument of grace and of life.

d. Practical Consequences

Christian preaching about death, accordingly, does not need to launch into misleading trivializations. It acknowledges the upsetting seriousness of death. Yet at the same time it can proclaim the new event that has taken place in Christ: that this same seriousness, in all its earnestness, is divine worship (seen from man's perspective) and blessing (from God's perspective), as Althaus says. Death as a whole, that is, that *processus mortis in vitam* which permeates our whole life, is as such our baptism, the gradual success of the new Adam. It is divine worship if we acknowledge therein our finitude and our unworthiness before God, our true insignificance, just as human worship of God ultimately must always be this acknowledgment of one's own lowliness and of the divine majesty. It is a grace-filled event, inasmuch as God snatches away from us our natural, self-willed, rebellious life at the tribunal of death so as to recreate us for the life of holiness and love. Basically everything is said with the observation that death (taken in each case as a whole) is the realization of our baptism. At the same time, it becomes evident how this theology of death is connected with the innermost intentions of Christian doctrine about morality and salvation. If its core precept is to love God and neighbor as oneself, then that means precisely the radical dethroning of self, becoming free from the ego, and, thus, the spiritual movement of death: the movement of death is identical to the movement into radical love. Thus, it becomes clear that I can just as well say "All that matters in Christianity is death and resurrection" as "All that matters in Christianity is love" or "All that matters in Christianity is the humility of faith." Viewed from within, Christianity is completely simple; it receives its wealth of content from the external multiplicity of human realities in which this one truth is proclaimed anew in each instance.

Another consequence of this Christian understanding of death, then, is the Christian attitude of the survivor. When Augustine at his mother's grave believed that he was not supposed to weep, that was not Christian but idealist thinking. From the idealist standpoint, mourning at the graveside (at least in the case of a "good" person) is in fact meaningless. Idealism means the negation of sadness. Not so Christianity: the attitude of the Christian is not the denial of sadness, and certainly not being disconsolate either (although the materialist has grounds for that), but rather consoled sadness. This means that sadness remains and has its rightful place, but it is actually at the same time consoled sadness, sadness that notwithstanding its seriousness can and should nevertheless be profoundly comforted and surpassed by consolation.

At the end of the day, this attempt at a theology of death produces a picture of the basic spiritual attitude that one might call the Christian man's realism. The Christian does not gloss over and deny the deep shadows that fall upon man's existence in this world. And yet these very shadows are also signs of hope for him, because he believes and, in believing, knows that they are shadows, which would not be there without the great light that casts them. And if the present belongs to the shadows, then the future is that much more in the possession of the light.

22. What Comes after Death?

The question of whether there is a future beyond death has always occupied men afresh and probably will never let go of them. In the case where life is experienced as suffering, the thought of a continuation of life after death can become a nightmare, as in Buddhism and many forms of Hinduism. This reflects the consciousness that man by his work deeply entangles himself in the dealings of this world, so that after his departure his roots, so to speak, remain stuck in it. The legacy of his actions has an ongoing effect; he remains wedged into the passion of this world, to which he himself supplied new fuel; as long as this legacy of his actions, his "karma", contributes to the suffering of this world, as long as he himself is not free, either, he continues to belong somehow in the tragedy of a life that consists of suffering. For such a world view, therefore, the goal must be to extinguish the karma, the still-smoldering flame of earthly being, and thus to sink into nirvana, the painless blessedness of the completely Other, which is so diametrically opposed to our "being as suffering" that in comparison it has to be called "nothingness".

Therefore, even in this desire to be extinguished into nothingness, there is very likely, albeit completely disguised, hope for what is authentic, for salvation from the being that is suffering. Although man's hope presents itself in this case as a yearning for nothingness, otherwise one much more frequently encounters feelings that run in the opposite direction: the man who has enjoyed the gift of being, of life, is terrified of the nothingness into which death seems to hurl him; he tries to flee from it. He yearns for life, for a future; indeed, man is so future-oriented that someone who no longer sees any future at all ahead can no longer endure the present, either—this is precisely why we are afraid, for example, to give an incurable patient unambiguous information about his condition. Of course, anyone who gives the matter

Translated by Michael J. Miller.

more careful thought will become quite aware that the sentiments of the Indian described earlier are by no means utterly foreign to him. No one can wish for himself that things will continue endlessly in this way; the endlessness of our everyday life is not a worthwhile goal, and therefore a medically induced immortality for man and mankind can only be a nightmare after all. Man is not psychologically equipped for the immortality of the body, and humanity would necessarily break into pieces from the internal tensions caused by the coexistence of generations that were speeding away from each other, not to mention the economic problems that would arise in such a world full of elderly people.

Thus man experiences tension, in that he wants infinity but necessarily fears endlessness; he needs a future, on the one hand, and, on the other hand, he cannot endure it. Therefore, he would have to die and live on at the same time—the complexity of his nature confronts him with this dilemma. What is authentically his would have to stay —the delicious gift of life, love, and joy; what is unauthentic would have to stop—the endless succession of care-filled days, in which he seldom touches what appears to him in truth to be "life", and then only from afar. But how is that supposed to come about? If the proper direction of the human yearning for the future compels us to distinguish between the tangible foreground of human routine and the authentic life that can be touched only occasionally and clandestinely, then with an intrinsic necessity the question about what is to come must lead beyond what is tangible and onto the trail of mystery. On the other hand, when it is a question of being or not being, man needs certainty more than anywhere else; if it is not given to him automatically, he tries to create it for himself.

The ways in which this has been tried are extremely diverse, yet when examined more closely they show an astonishing resemblance to one another. Anyone who walks through a cemetery today finds in the main the names of people who died in the last fifty years. The decorations on their graves show that living people remember them. Their children and their friends are still living; people still know about what they did, and their pictures are still in view—they remain present in the memory of those who loved them. In a sort of second life, they belong once again to this world. Some day the last ones who knew about them will die; their tombstone will be replaced by another; their names and pictures will disappear; and they will die, as it were, a second time, when people's memory, which gave them continued existence beyond physical death, is extinguished.

Thus in our modern world we can observe what amounts exactly to the explicit content of the belief in immortality in so-called primitive religions. Believers are convinced that there is no eternal afterlife but, rather, only a temporally limited life continuing after death, that the "spirit" of the deceased lives only as long as he is remembered— remembering gives him life; yet only a diminished life, as expressed in the notion of the dead as ghosts. The cult of the dead in ancient Egypt, viewed from this perspective, is a grandiose attempt to extort everlasting immortality by making one's memory ineradicable and building for oneself an abode on earth that will outlast all ages. Now, admittedly, these notions change and, with them, the external forms in which man tries to answer by deeds the question about his future beyond death; yet the fundamental idea that guides men therein remains amazingly constant as cultures come and go.

Let us try to put it somewhat more precisely; this will automatically bring us face to face with the Christian answer to our problem. Man's first experience is initially that of his mortality; he sees that in and of himself he has no permanence. While the art of medicine can extend the limits of his life, it cannot give him permanence, and even if it should someday raise the hope of discovering the herb of immortality after all, a living man cannot rely on such a vague promise. He has no permanence in himself; therefore he must look for it outside himself. He must, so to speak, entrust himself and his existence to what will still be after him, continuing long into the future. But how is that supposed to happen? The first way sought by the so-called primitive races above all, but then also by ancient Israel, was: a future through descendants. In one's children, one's own name and blood live on; in them the Israelite, for instance, hopes to obtain a share in the Messianic kingdom, in that age when there will finally be authentic life, that life which is worth continuing forever, because it brings the fulfillment and joy that we glimpse now but only momentarily. Hence, the worst thing for a man in Israel was to depart from this world childless and, thus, really to be excluded from the future, from life. If you look closely, there are two motives at work here: first, the notion of continuing one's memory along with one's name and, second, the attempt, by handing on the gift of life, to keep something of one's own substance alive as well. In contrast, ancient Rome staked more on the idea of fame: entrusting oneself to one's deeds and, thereby, continuing to live perpetually in mankind. Basically our present age [1969] with its Marxist emphasis is not all that far removed from such attempts to create a future. Now the future is the society that has done away with oppression and injustice; one belongs to the future, one has a future, by participating in the fight for that society. The common element of all these answers is that they seek man's future in a third thing that is not actually man himself; especially, however, the fact that they do not propose the solution in the form of a theoretical statement but, rather, through man's own activity in actively building a future for himself: they entrust the future, not to faith, but rather to action. For contemporary man, who accepts only verifiable, praxis-oriented knowledge, this seems to be the only way.

But is it really reliable? Will today's fight really bring about a just society tomorrow, and will this society in fact be a future for us also? Or is not that part of man which lives on, when he continues to exist in children, in his name, in his deeds, always just an unreal shadow that quickly disintegrates anyway? At precisely this point, the faith of the New Testament begins. It is in full agreement with man's conviction that he has no permanence on his own and hence can live on only if he lives in another. However, as this line of thought necessarily continues, such striving for life in another would make sense only if the other to whom we entrust ourselves does not in turn pass away as we do but rather really remains; furthermore, it would make sense only if this other could not only hold fast to a shadow of ourselves—our name, our inheritance—but could really keep *us* in existence. This can be the case, however, only if *God* remembers man: Only *he* remains; only *his* thought is reality. And this is precisely the hopeful certainty that biblical faith intends to offer: the Eternal One remembers man; man lives in God's remembering and, thus, lives truly as himself, for God's remembrance is not a shadow but reality.

Now, for us men of today, the questions really begin at this place where the outline of the Christian answer has become visible. I can elucidate only one of them in more detail within the framework of these reflections. We had previously observed that over the course of history, and today more than ever, man has tried to take the question of the future out of the realm of theory and faith and to make it a matter of human action. In this way, throughout all of history, death has become the most powerful stimulus of life; mankind has always lived far more in terms of its future than on its past, and from the sort of artifacts that the individual peoples have left behind we can gauge quite well the shape of their hope as well as their understanding of the question of death. But in this regard, what can we say about the Christian answer? Does it not send us back into the sheer passivity of mere expectation, which assigns no task to man and, thus, devalues his life? Is that perhaps why it has become so foreign to our active, praxis-oriented age? Now this answer involves a certain disempowerment of man in any case. His dream of giving himself immortality is in fact crushed. He is obliged to expect less of his own *power* and more of *love*, which he can now receive only as a gift. But with that we have already arrived at the second half of our answer: immortality, according to the Christian faith, fundamentally has to do with love. The only eternal thing is love; as *love*, God is eternity. And *his* love, in turn, is man's eternity; in being loved by eternal Love, he is lifted up imperishably. He is lifted up, because he himself can love. For him, too, love is the only thing that gives eternity; the measure and manner of his eternity depend on the measure and manner of his loving. But if his loving is his future, then the future for him is both doing and receiving —at the same time entirely his own and entirely what is given to him. The hope of man and of mankind is love—this is the answer of the Christian faith, which is thereby entirely realistic—oriented toward the sober praxis of everyday life—and entirely faith: open to the One who is not at anyone's disposal, who, far surpassing our accomplishments, bestows on us what no man is able to give: eternal life.

23. Resurrection and Life Everlasting

The apocalyptic age in which we live has turned the thoughts of Christendom more intensely again to the eschatological message of the New Testament, which after all derives its peculiar force and vitality from the tremendous anticipation of the end times. The New Testament is not primarily a report about the past but, rather, a book of hope, and the religion that proclaims it is a religion of hope that looks forward, to the future, to the end that is the true beginning.

Although such realizations in a certain sense cater to prevailing sentiment,[1] the attempt to overcome the individualistic reduction of the hope of salvation in Christian consciousness to "save your soul" and to replace it with a more universal perspective runs into considerable difficulties. Certainly, there is an increasingly widespread realization that history cannot merely be about the salvation of the individual or of many individuals as such, but is also (indeed, first and foremost) about the salvation of the world, of all history, into which all the godless ages must eventually flow in order to find in it their resolution and their salvific meaning. But to see this salvation of the world in the resurrection of the body and to look forward to it with a living hope is exceedingly difficult for contemporary man. There are many and various reasons for this, some of them typically modern, while some are the heritage of the early period in which Christianity became fused with Greek thought. The main modern obstacles are difficulties related to world view, because of which, according to Bultmann, "mythical eschatology", that is, the expectation of Christ's Second Coming and the general resurrection, is "finished".[2] Indeed, the belief in resurrec-

---

Translated by Michael J. Miller.

[1] Think for example of Gabriel Marcel's "philosophy of hope"; see especially his "Sketch of a Phenomenology and a Metaphysics of Hope" in *Homo Viator: Introduction to a Metaphysic of Hope*, trans. Emma Craufurd (New York: Harper Torchbook, 1962), 29–67.

[2] "Neues Testament und Mythologie", in *Kerygma und Mythos*, vol. 1, ed. H. W. Bartsch,

tion and the transformation of the world appears to be all too closely connected with a world view that is no longer ours. According to the insights of natural science today, movement is not something added secondarily to previously existing matter that is per se unmoved; rather, matter is moved "constitutionally", which is to say that movement is a part of its very nature.[3] Thus, movement and, therefore, constant change belong to the nature of things. The consequence of this, however, is that now the cosmos, which by its intrinsic nature is temporal and mobile, can scarcely be imagined any longer as the housing for the immutable life of the eternal today of resurrection glory, quite apart from the fact that the cosmos, understood in its purely physical materiality, is more difficult to bring into relationship with metaphysical realities than the cosmos of antiquity, which through and through was conceived of in metaphysical terms.[4] The same problems apply to the resurrected body itself, whereby there is an additional question about its identity with the earthly body—the possibility of which has always been perceived as a serious question, given the constant exchange of matter among things.[5] Besides these new encumbrances, there are the old difficulties: individualism and spiritualism—the great and dangerous heritage of the Greek mind—have from the start distracted our attention from the universal and the whole and concentrated it on the salvation of the individual soul, which is called for immediately. The resurrection of the flesh, that is, of mankind as a whole, restored to its corporeality, could appear in comparison to be only an afterthought, the importance of which would necessarily become still more questionable in light of the ascetical devaluation of the body. Thus, in matters concerning the resurrection of the dead, the mentalities of antiquity

---

3rd ed. (Hamburg, 1954), 16ff. See esp. 17: "Experiencing the world and subduing the world have developed to such an extent in science and technology that no one can seriously subscribe to the New Testament world view. . . . Thus the stories about Christ's descent into hell and ascension into heaven are finished, along with the expectation of the 'Son of man' coming amid the clouds of heaven and the rapture of believers into the air to meet him (1 Thessalonians 4:15ff.)." On the Resurrection in particular, see also p. 20.

[3] On this subject, see in particular the studies by A. Mitterer, especially "Konstitutionelle Bewegung", *Wissenschaft und Weltbild* 7 (1954): 241–50; a bibliography of Mitterer's works can be found in his volume *Die Entwicklungslehre Augustins* (Vienna, 1956), 21–26.

[4] I tried to show this in somewhat greater detail in an essay, "Gedanken zur Krise der Verkündigung", in *Klerusblatt* 38 (1958): 211f.

[5] See my article "Auferstehungsleib", in *LThK* I, 2nd ed., 1052f., and the literature listed there.

and of the modern era are opposed, each in its way, to the Word of God, which has burst in upon the world as a truly divine novelty. Again and again, however, the Word in the world meets with contradiction *before* it finds a connection; it must always search anew for its place—a "shelter"—within the structure of the human mind and is repeatedly perceived by man as a troublesome foreign body that tries to reduce his own well-designed edifice of thought to ruins.

Now one can try to free up some room for the Word by dismantling, bit by bit, the difficulties that are opposed to it and proving that they are insubstantial. That is certainly a very necessary path that must be traveled again and again, if only for honesty's sake in the sight of one's own intellectual conscience. But taken alone, it can never suffice, because ultimately it persists in a purely negative approach, whereas man has a positive nature that can and indeed must never be content with pure negation. So something else must be added: there must be an attempt to make the Word of God shine from within and, thus, to contrast its own positive power with the negations of the human mind and to expose them as negations. In the following paragraphs we will try to trace this path to the mystery of the resurrection.

Scripture is obviously very much aware of the impossibility of a direct, conceptually adequate representation of the realities in the end times. All human knowing is accomplished with reference to and within this world. Consequently, if human knowing is to make a statement about something that is not "world", it can do so only with the materials of this world; it cannot grasp that something in its proper being, as it is in itself, but only by means of approximations and similarities that exist within worldly being, therefore "analogously" in comparisons and images. Thus, we can speak about God only analogously, but the new world of the resurrection, too, which after all will no longer be "this world", can be expressed only in images that nevertheless have been taken from *this* world and, thus, do not directly depict the other thing that is to come in its ipseity, its selfhood. For this very reason these images do not need to be precisely defined and worked out to the last detail with logical consistency: the hovering, transitional quality that they often have expresses their own inadequacy and provisional character. From the variety of these images, a few fundamental, oft-recurring figures clearly emerge. The world of the resurrection is depicted under the image of the city, under the image of the festive meal, and occasionally at the same time under the image of the wedding as well: the city is the Bride, the wife of the Lamb (Rev 21:9), and the festive meal derives its splendor from the fact that it is a wedding feast (Mt 22:1–14). Let us try to examine these images in some depth and to understand what they reveal about the mysterious world of the resurrection, of the new life.

First, there is the image of the city. In the last book of Sacred Scripture, John has elaborated it with all the splendor of apocalyptic language. "And I saw the holy city, new Jerusalem, coming down out of heaven from God, prepared as a bride adorned for her husband" (Rev 21:2). It is a city of gold and precious stones, a city of perfect proportion and harmony, a city whose light and temple is God himself (21:9 —22:5). Upon closer inspection, one discovers that three levels of imagery intersect in this description of the city: the image of the heavenly canopy, the image of the garden of paradise, and the image of the city itself.[6] Included in the idea of the city are both the everlasting symbol of longing—the image of the starry sky with its shining beauty—and also the paradisiacal earth, an earth filled with fruitfulness, riches, and life: it is all this in one. The starry heavens and paradise, the two poignant figures of a restored, better world, are incorporated into the image of the eternal City of God, Jerusalem, which thus surpasses the other two figures. The mystery of the "heavens" and the mystery of the "garden", of the restored earth, are taken up into the mystery of the "city" and are preserved in it. This hope-filled prospect of the holy City of God, with which Sacred Scripture concludes, already runs like a leitmotif through the earlier books of the Old and New Testaments. In the Old Testament, all hopes for salvation gather in the image of the "renewed Jerusalem—religious hopes, but also ethnic and political expectations, as Jeremiah 3:17, Isaiah 60, Zechariah 2:9ff., and Haggai 2:7ff. show".[7] In the New Testament the image of the "beloved city" (Rev 20:9) is surrounded by reverence and an almost tender affection, for all the holy awe; besides the Book of Revelation, the Letters to the Galatians and the Hebrews evoke this image (Gal 4:25f.; Hebrews, chapters 11–13).[8]

---

[6] The image of Paradise is found in Revelation 22:1f. The features reminiscent of the ancient image of the heavenly canopy are enumerated by H. Strathmann, article "πόλις", *ThW* 6:532.

[7] Ibid., 524.

[8] Ibid., 530f. See esp. on p. 537, lines 37ff., the comment on the Letter to the Hebrews: "The fact that the author repeatedly returns to this notion and the solemn and reverent yet at the same time loving and grateful way that he dwells on this image of the heavenly Jerusalem show how important this line of thought is for him. . . ."

Certainly it would be a rewarding and pleasant task to make a historical analysis of the individual expressions of this idea and to trace its developments and transformations through all of Sacred Scripture and thus to bring out the spiritual content of the scriptural image of "the city".[9] But above and beyond that, one can pose the fundamental question: Why in fact does the Bible clothe the idea of the new world precisely in the image of the city? What is the nature of "city" in general that makes it an appropriate image for that future which the Bible tries to promise? Of course, it must be evident that the image of the city not only appears in the Sacred Scriptures of the Old and New Testaments but also plays a related role in non-Christian religious history: that of being the summary of human hope.[10] This shows that the experience of "city" was for men in every age an experience with deep religious significance. What is, therefore, this mysterious and great element in the reality "city" that preexists all individual statements about it and always resonates in them? Man in antiquity experienced the city as the overcoming of his original barbaric condition and as the cultural form of his existence, as the abolition of the insecurities and uncertainties that threatened natural man through the regularity of a secured order and, thus, as the symbol of the Messiah, of his existence.[11] It is the overcoming of loneliness and shelters man in the only place where he can be sheltered: in community with his fellowmen.[12] Thus the city, first of all, embodies the primordial experience of security and community. It is tragically ironic that during the last war man had to learn to see the cities, of all places, as the focal point of all insecurity and all danger. Thus, our generation had the painful experience of regaining once more an understanding of a scriptural message that had become vivid to its readers in the smoking ruins of Jerusalem, namely, the fact that "here we have no lasting city" (Heb 13:14). And yet the people, even among the ruins, could not stop loving their cities and venturing to rebuild them, often against all hope of succeeding, and today they

---

[9] The groundbreaking study of this idea is Strathmann's article, "πόλις", *ThW* 6:516–535. See also M. Schmaus, *Katholische Dogmatik*, 5th ed., vol. 4a (Munich, 1959), 277–99.

[10] See M. Eliade, *Die Religionen und das Heilige* (Salzburg, 1954), 424–29; G. van der Leeuw, *Phänomenologie der Religion*, 4th ed. (Tübingen, 1956), 453ff.; secondary literature on the Greek concept of *polis* in Strathmann, "πόλις", 516. See also J. Ratzinger, *Volk und Haus Gottes in Augustins Lehre von der Kirche* (Munich, 1954), 255–76.

[11] Strathmann, "πόλις", 520; cf. van der Leeuw, *Phänomenologie*.

[12] On the religious significance of solitude and community, see the very fine remarks by van der Leeuw, *Phänomenologie*, 270f.

shine again in a new way with the festive splendor of streaming life, the vital context of a manifold and rich existence. For that is part of the original experience of the city, that it embodies the wealth of existence, the fullness of its varicolored and bustling life. The experiences of security and community, of wealth and fullness, are thus the individual elements out of which the overall experience of "city" is built up. Of course, just as we can never again forget that cities became the focal points of all insecurity, so too there is now a contradiction, a question mark, after all the other statements. Although cities are places of festive human fellowship, they are nevertheless at the same time places of extreme loneliness. And the same walls that encircle wealth and fullness also harbor and conceal the most terrifying poverty and need without abolishing them. A profound ambiguity runs through the experience of "city", a discrepancy that makes us understand that the same Bible that ends with the prospect of the city as the image of perpetual salvation, describes the first murderer, Cain, as the founder of the first city on earth (Gen 4:17) and, thus, has the history of man's trouble begin with the founding of cities and interprets the city as a work of self-willed man who is rebelling against God.[13] Yet this very ambiguity is what teaches us to hope. The ideal nature of the city, which we find nowhere here below and of which we are nevertheless conscious in all cities of this world as a painful, insistent longing—someday that will exist in a fulfilled, perfected way. And also perfected then will be that profoundly comforting feeling of being "at home" which comes over man who knows that he is secure in the land and with the people that are his true "home". Who could deny that this image of the city, in which the imponderables outweigh all that can be said—that this image means infinitely more than the mere hope of an eternal happiness for the individual immortal soul?

Alongside the image of the City of God stands the image of the wedding, of the eternal wedding feast. Again, both of these images are of ancient origin. Beginning with the prophet Hosea, the image of God as the Bridegroom of his people runs through Sacred Scripture, together with the assurance of his loving care and his demand for reciprocal, bridal love. The banquet of the transformed world is foretold in Isaiah 25:6 as a "feast of fat things, a feast of choice wines—

---

[13] The story of the Tower of Babel is along the same lines. Cf. G. von Rad, *Theology of the Old Testament* I (Louisville: John Knox Press, 2001), 159f.; T. C. Vriezen, *Theologie des Alten Testaments in Grundzügen* (Neukirchen: Kr. Moers, [1957]), 42.

of fat things full of marrow, of choice wines well refined" that God will make "for all peoples" (cf. Is 34:6ff.; Jer 46:10; Zeph 1:7).[14] And finally, once already during Israel's years in the wilderness, God himself had set a table for his people directly, and he continued to sit down to table with his people in the sacrificial meals of the Temple worship; Christ had repeated the wilderness miracle of the manna in his miracle of multiplying the loaves and, thus, foreshadowed his new meal that was to be the anticipation and proclamation of the eternal feast and was to remain until the end of the ages. Again, it is true here also that both images extend far beyond the sphere of biblical faith into the general field of the history of religions, although with different forms and contents in each case.[15] For the wedding and the banquet are again primordial human experiences that reach down into religious depths. Thus the question is posed once more: What is that inner content of the banquet, of the wedding, that makes these things apt to be an expression of healing and life for all men? Here we can indicate initially that man's two most basic drives are behind both events: the instinct to feed and the sexual drive.[16] These are the events in which man tries to humanize these two drives and raises them from the level of merely animal instinct to the level of the spiritual and human. In a banquet, ingesting food is no longer a merely biological process but becomes a lively celebration of the fellowship of men with one another. Man experiences the delightful quality of things and experiences it fully in the company of those who rejoice with him; indeed, he senses the festivity of existence itself, which so often confronts him in a hostile or troubling fashion and yet, at the hour of the feast, stands there with open hands, as it were, in a gesture of extravagant giving, of joyful abandon. This generosity of existence, which is rich and gives of itself, also belongs to the experience of the meal. We see similar features in the

---

[14] See J. Behm, *ThW* 2:35; the passages illustrating the two images can be found in Behm, article "δεῖπνον", *ThW* 2:33ff.; E. Stauffer, article "γαμέω", *ThW* 1:646–55; J. Jeremias, article "νύμφη", *ThW* 4:1092–99.

[15] Concerning the image of the feast, we refer the reader especially to F. Bammel, *Das Heilige Mahl im Glauben der Völker* (Gütersloh, 1950). On the wedding feast, see van der Leeuw, *Phänomenologie*, passim, esp. 96ff. and 218ff.

[16] Van der Leeuw, *Phänomenologie*, 254; the sexual drive and the instinct to feed are at any rate the two major ladders upon which the will to power climbs and even soars into the sky and from which the awareness of helplessness then falls again. Food and drink, on the one hand, and sexual union, on the other, are therefore not just the two great symbols of communion with God; they are also the means by which human might is active.

wedding. The elevation of the biological process of sexual inclination into the fundamental spiritual act of eros, man's loving act of surpassing self, is crystallized, summed up, and confirmed in it. And again, man experiences here as well the gracious generosity of existence, which grants him the festive miracle of that love which he cannot just bring about by force but which, instead, approaches him, surprises and overwhelms him, and transforms his life, gives him a new interior center; indeed, in the most exalted moments, love, like an ecstasy, allows him to glimpse another life that is brighter and fuller than that of his ordinary, everyday routine. Thus, in many respects the experience that is behind the images of the banquet and the wedding is even more fundamental and powerful than the one that is expressed in the image of the city. It is defined first by the interpenetration of instinct and spirit, which includes the powerful basic forces of man's earthly component in the current of the spirit and thus establishes the unity of what is real, in which the two poles of reality—matter and spirit—fructify and productively permeate each other. Matter receives light and clarity from the brightness of the spirit, which permeates and illuminates its dullness; spirit receives depth, maternal warmth, and strength through the corporeal-earthly element that is wedded to it.[17] Then there is the experience of the gracious generosity of existence, which approaches man and bows to him. And so it is with the experience of festive joy that surpasses all limits and joins all creatures in fraternal fellowship. And at the innermost place, as though at the heart of the whole thing, stands the lived mystery of love.

Of course, here again, too, there is no mistaking the fact that in man's concrete reality all these experiences never exist intact. The festive beauty of the banquet cannot make us forget that for many of our fellowmen, the table of life is set all too sparingly, and, conversely, the meal itself all too easily degenerates into gluttony and dissipation, in which instinct gains the upper hand over the spirit instead of being united with it and ennobled by it. And, likewise, the festive beginning signified by a wedding can never cause us to forget that it is a beginning full of open questions and risks. But again, this ambiguity can teach us to hope for that pure essence of what is apparent here, for the true banquet without shadows and for the true wedding that is pure joy.

---

[17] On this subject, see the discussion by R. Guardini on the concept of "heart" in *Christliches Bewußtsein*, 2nd ed. (Munich, 1950), 185–96, esp. 187.

After all, they are just images, yet they are genuinely transparent to that ineffable experience that is the object of Christian hope. And so, here again, too, it is not difficult to see that such images announce a wholeness that is so great and expansive as to surpass by far the mere hope of immortality found in philosophy.

Perhaps we should simply leave this promise in the symbolic form in which we encounter it in Scripture. For in the final analysis, there is no way to elevate it to a concept, to the univocal, abstract status of purely objective, non-figurative statements, and only in an image does this promise have that immediate, heart-stirring character that is sensed by everyone who reads in the Book of Revelation the depiction of the new Jerusalem, who hears our Lord's parable about the wedding feast, who thinks of the virgins who are waiting with their lamps filled for the festive midnight hour when the Bridegroom will come. Yet man cannot completely renounce the attempt to penetrate it conceptually, a process whereby what his heart basically grasped long ago becomes clear to his intellect, also. Admittedly, what is gained in clarity by conceptual statements as opposed to the image is lost in terms of vividness and depth. As long as we keep that in mind, the conceptual analysis is not only justified and meaningful but is also a necessary task.

With this proviso, we can try to broach the question of what we learn objectively from the above-mentioned images about the world of the resurrection and what the central contents of the biblical and Christian hope of resurrection are in contrast to the philosophical doctrine of salvation. The first thing that comes to mind, no doubt, is the holistic character of Christian salvation. Wholeness is understood here in a double sense: it is the *whole* man who enters into salvation, and it is the *whole* world that shares in it. First, the whole man: Scripture attributes much less importance to the dualism of body and soul in man than Greek philosophy does. More decisive than this duality is another dyad found in the Bible: the one consisting of Creator and creature. The "dualism" of the Bible (if we can still use the word at all in that context) is differently situated from that of the Greeks; it is personalistic, not ontological. This means that for Scripture, the decisive line of separation runs, not through man, but rather between Creator and creature. The distinction of the levels within man himself loses all its importance in comparison to this great difference. The whole man is God's creature, and as such, precisely in this wholeness, he stands before his Creator and from his relationship to him receives either disaster or salvation. Salvation, therefore, does not simply result from the autonomous departure of an intellectual substance that is now detached from matter and continues to exist on its own and can have only a very incidental residual connection to the material parts that once clung to it; rather, it is the salvation of the *man*, of this particular creature of God, which despite its incontestable ontological stratification is nevertheless a genuine unity, a single work of the Divine Master. This completely different sort of opposition, Creator-creature (instead of soul-body), is at the root of the biblical doctrine of salvation and defines the holistic approach that seems so foreign to Greek philosophy: an approach that has created for itself a central form of expression in the idea of resurrection. From this holistic understanding of salvation follow a series of consequences with great logical consistency. Once we replace the idea of the *anima separata* [separated soul] with the notion of the one, ultimately indivisible creature "man", we have thereby stated also to a considerable extent what belongs inseparably to that man. "Man" is by nature always "fellowman" at the same time, and if man as man is to be brought into salvation, this must happen in community with his fellowmen, who together with him build up the full totality of humanity. Thus de Lubac is right when he says that the *anima separata* is subject to a twofold separation: from its own body and from the full communion of the Body of Christ.[18] And it goes without saying that the definitive fulfillment of this Body, which is accomplished at the end of the ages in the Last Judgment, does not merely signify an external addition to a blessedness that has long since been completed, but, rather, creates its real, final perfection for the first time. Another thing becomes clear from the approach just indicated: To man belongs not only his fellowman; to man belongs also the "world". Hence, if man as such and as a whole is to be brought into salvation, then the delightful mystery of things must also be preserved for him; all the instruments that God has created must join in, as it were, to the symphony of joy if there is to be full harmony. But this is precisely what we found suggested in all the figures of speech that we examined earlier. They were full of the mystery of communion and full of the beautiful splendor of things, of the "world", without which man cannot be completely human. These

---

[18] *Katholizismus als Gemeinschaft* (Einsiedeln, 1943), 116. Cf. *LThK* 1:1049.

images obviously intend to let us know precisely this: that even that element of the totality "man" which is made up of "things" and the "world" will be present in the definitive salvation; part of the definitive salvation will be a profound form of connection to the world as well, so that everything that was delightful and dear in God's beautiful world will return transformed.

A series of motifs from the figures of speech examined earlier have thus been translated into conceptual terms. One thing above all still remains that we found in the image of the banquet and especially in the image of the wedding feast: the idea of graciousness, of the gift that ultimately falls undeserved, "gratis", into our laps. This, too, can be understood from the previously discovered approach of the contrast between Creator and creature. Consequently, since the primary duality in Christianity is not "body-soul", man's eternal destiny cannot be thought of, either, in terms of the automatic, eternal continuance of the spiritual soul but, rather, is to be understood in light of this correspondence of Creator and creature. Instead of the monologue of the self-sufficient mind, we have the fateful dialogue of God with man; to break off that dialogue by guilt means the "second death", while its great potential is to become the eternal dialogue of love that is the real heart and center of all the blessings of "heaven".[19] Thus, all previous totalities that surpass the narrowness of the individual soul are built upon and excelled here by this last thing, which is simultaneously the first thing, by this dialogical orientation to God. In this respect, it is true that *all* salvation of man is based on an "awakening", an act of God's grace, and is never merely the logical conclusion of the account rendered of a human life, which follows with inner consistency from that life itself and in principle needs only to be ascertained. No, salvation is always based profoundly on graciousness, on the marvelous gift of God's gracious love.

When we look back on all the previous discussion, we might say that our examination of some fundamental eschatological images in Sacred Scripture has revealed a thoroughly religious core of the biblical belief

---

[19] The dialogical understanding of immortality in connection with Luther's view is expounded quite emphatically by P. Althaus, *Die letzten Dinge*, 6th ed. (Gütersloh, 1956), 110f., 114; the unacceptable exaggerations and one-sidedness apparent in this treatment are no reason to reject the idea as a whole. I attempt a systematic analysis in my essay "Jenseits des Todes", *Internationale katholische Zeitschrift* 1 (1972): 231–44.

in resurrection that, apart from all problems about world view, simply addresses man in his humanity and is meant to fill his life with the delightful mystery of hope. To believe in the resurrection, accordingly, means most deeply to believe in a dialogical salvation corresponding to God's free love; it means believing in a holistic salvation that affects man as man (not merely as a spiritual being) and, thus, affects him also in his relation to his fellowman and to the "world", thus in the true fullness of all his dimensions. Certainly with the acknowledgment of this core content the question about world view is not simply settled. But it does lose something of its urgent importance, which leaves us with a clearer view of the great future that has been promised to us and that we profess—with hearts that are unfortunately so lukewarm —whenever we say: "Et expecto resurrectionem mortuorum. Et vitam venturi saeculi" [And I look for the resurrection of the dead and the life of the world to come].

PART THREE

Meditations and Sermons

THE LITURGICAL YEAR

24. The Genealogy of Jesus

Saint Matthew the Evangelist begins his account of the Good News of Jesus Christ with the words: "The book of the genealogy of Jesus Christ, the son of David, the son of Abraham." He searches out the human ancestors of this man Jesus and attempts to locate him in relation to the history of the race. He shows the human origins of this life, which did not drop straight from heaven but grew on a tree with a long history and ultimately sprang from the two great roots named Abraham and David. Matthew is presenting Jesus the man, and for this reason his symbol as evangelist is the Son of Man.

The New Testament begins with man, just as the Old Testament had begun with the unfathomably profound soliloquy of the Creator: "Let us make man in our image, after our likeness." A man stands at the beginning of the New Testament and reminds us of the nocturnal vision in which Daniel sees four beasts coming up out of the sea: images, these, of the forces and powers of this world, the kingdoms that share dominion over this world and determine the course of history. Then, in a contrary motion to the beasts from the sea, he sees a man coming down from heaven: an image, this, of the holy people, of the holy power of the human amid the inhuman powers that rise from the deep.

The man Jesus stands at the beginning of the New Testament, but as one who comes from the history of mankind. In his genealogy, Matthew carefully plots the transition from the long and bewildering history set down in the Old Testament to the new reality that has begun with Jesus Christ. He sums up, as it were, this entire history in

Translated by Matthew J. O'Connell.

three sets of fourteen names and brings it down to him for whose sake alone, in the last analysis, it had existed. He shows that, as it traveled its many ways and byways, this history was, in a hidden manner, already bringing forth Christ; that during those centuries it was already, and at every point, one and the same God who was visiting his people and who now, in Jesus Christ, had become a brother to the human race. He brings out the inherent finality of history, which in the last analysis had no higher purpose than to produce this man Jesus.

We might apply a modern notion and make the same point in a different way. In the long ages preceding man's appearance on the earth, it was evidently nature's essential aim to be able some day to conceive and bring forth man, to be able in the course of time to develop an organism that would be capable of being transformed by the Creator into the new reality called man. Gropingly, advancing and retrogressing, in straight lines and by circuitous routes, nature felt its way, so to speak, until a context was created in which hominization could occur. At this point a new and higher task is set: mankind in its turn now exists in order to bring forth Christ. It exists in order to create the context in which the union of God and the world can take place. It lives its life with the purpose of becoming one with God. With a few short strokes of his brush, Matthew sketches the history of this lengthy journey. He describes the last stretch of the way to the definitive man, Jesus the Lord: the stretch from the call of Abraham onward.

We might ask: What kind of history must it have been that truly created at last the "space", the conditions, for the incarnation of God? What kind of men must they have been who traveled the final stretch of the journey? What integrity and maturity of spirit must have been attained at the point at which this supreme transformation of man and the world could take place? But if we approach the text with these kinds of expectations, we shall find ourselves disappointed. The history of which Jesus becomes a part is a very ordinary history, marked by all the scandals and infamies to be found among men, all the advances and good beginnings, but also all the sinfulness and vileness—an utterly human history.

The only four women named in the genealogy are all four of them witnesses to human sinfulness: among them is Rahab, the harlot who delivered Jericho into the hands of the migrating Israelites. Among them, too, is the wife of Uriah, the woman whom David got for him-

self through adultery and murder. Nor are the males in the genealogy
any different. Neither Abraham nor Isaac nor Jacob is an ideal human
figure; David certainly is not, nor is Solomon; and finally we meet such
abhorrent rulers as Ahaz and Manasseh, whose thrones are sticky with
the blood of innocent victims. This is a somber history that leads to
Jesus; it is not without its moments of light, its hopes and advances,
but on the whole, it is a history of shabbiness, sin, and failure.

We are tempted to ask: Is that the context into which the Son of
God could be born? And Scripture answers: Yes. But all this is a sign
for us. It tells us that the incarnation of God results, not from an ascent on the part of the human race, but from the descent of God. The
ascent of man, the attempt to bring forth God by his own efforts and
to attain the status of superman—this attempt failed wretchedly back
in Paradise. The person who tries to become God by his own efforts,
who highhandedly reaches for the stars, always ends up by destroying
himself. Thus the wretched course of Israelite history is a sign for us:
a sign that it is not through arrogance and self-exaltation that men are
delivered, but through humility, self-surrender, and service.

Consequently, too, it may be a very good thing that the greatest religious personalities have lived and live today outside the Old Testament
and even outside Christianity entirely. In Christianity, great religious
figures are not the main thing; Christianity represents rather the de-
thronement of religious figures. The thing that counts in Christianity
is obedience, humility in the face of God's Word. "An infant, or an
overdriven laborer, given faith, can take precedence before heroes of
asceticism",[1] because salvation comes, not from man's greatness, but
from God's gracious mercy. This passage of the Gospel should imprint
deep in our hearts once again this sign of God's descent, the saving
sign of his lowliness. It should once again convert us into persons who
do not shun a similar descent; persons who know that precisely in their
descent and in the little services life asks of them they are on the way
to Jesus Christ.

Matthew's genealogy begins with Abraham. It bears witness, therefore, to the fidelity of God, who carried out the promise he had once
made to Abraham: that Abraham would be the bearer of a blessing for

---

[1] Jean Daniélou, *The Lord of History: Reflections on the Inner Meaning of History*, trans. N.
Abercrombie (Chicago, 1958), 113.

the whole race. The entire genealogy, with all the disorders, all the ups and downs, that it represents, is a luminous testimony to the fidelity of God, who keeps his word despite all of man's failure and unworthiness.

Luke the Evangelist likewise gives a genealogy (Lk 3:23–38), but he has adopted a different viewpoint in constructing it. He traces the Lord's ancestry back, not simply to Abraham, but to Adam and the hands of God that formed man. He thus makes it clear that the community Jesus has established is not simply a new Israel, a people whom God gathers for himself in this world, but that the mission of Jesus embraces instead the whole of the human race. His mission is not aimed at salvation for one group, one set of people alone, but is directed to the whole race, the entire world. In Jesus Christ the creation of man first attains its true goal; in him the Creator's conception of man finds its full expression; in him the beast that lurks in all of us is overcome for the first time, and what is truly human is made present, for, as the second reading for the Dawn Mass of Christmas says: in Jesus "the kindness and generous love of God our Savior appeared" (Tit 3:4).

The face of Jesus Christ makes visible what God is, and it also shows us clearly what man is. God is the faithful and gracious One who pursues man into the thicket of his errors, seeks him out with everlasting pity, and takes human nature, like a lost sheep, on his own shoulders in order to bring it home to its origin. Man, though, is the one who ultimately, despite all his cleverness and greatness, could not find any better place for God than a stable or offer him anything but a history full of filth and inhumanity. In a profound sense, Jesus was indeed born in a stable and outside the city: outside the great achievements of the human race; outside its advances and accomplishments; amid wretchedness and poverty. This very fact should be a sign to us: all our greatness cannot save us; deliverance comes from the humble humanity of God, the loving kindness that shines in the face of Jesus Christ and calls us to the humanity of man, to the daily practice of loving kindness.

Finally, though, Matthew's genealogy is also Good News about Christ the King. The genealogy is made up of three series of fourteen names. Now if we write the number fourteen in Hebrew letters, we have the three consonants that make up the name David. Thus the number fourteen, which dominates the genealogy, is a symbol of kingship. It turns the genealogy into a royal genealogy in which not only the promise to Abraham is fulfilled but also the promise that accompanies the name of David. The meaning is that the One who is coming is the true King of the world. He is indeed the merciful God, but even in his mercy he remains the Lord God, the King to whose commands we are subject, the King who summons us and has a claim upon our obedience. Thus the genealogy at the beginning of the Gospel is at the same time a flourish of trumpets, as it were, for the King. It calls us into the presence of Jesus Christ. It calls us to a holy obedience to God's Word and to the service of the Lord Jesus: to serve him is to reign. Amen.

25. Lent

The expression *Fastenzeit*, "Season of Fasting", which we use in German to designate the period between Ash Wednesday and Easter, tells us but little about what the Church intends this season to be. Originally, this was the period when baptism was administered; the period, therefore, in which people became Christians. It was thought that this could be accomplished, not in one short moment of time, but only over the course of a journey of transformation or "conversion" that the individual had to travel step by step. Later on, when penitents and finally the entire Church were included in the journey, this reflected the awareness that we cannot travel this path all at once to its conclusion. No, it is a lifelong journey on which we must set out over and over again. The purpose of Lent, therefore, is to keep alive in our consciousness and our life the fact that *being* a Christian can only take the form of *becoming* a Christian ever anew; that it is not an event now over and done with but a process requiring constant practice.

Let us ask, then: What does it mean to become a Christian? How does this take place?

1. No One Becomes a Christian Alone

First of all, it seems important to me that the Church does not regard becoming a Christian as the result of a course of instruction or even of a training process. She regards it as a sacrament. This means that no one becomes a Christian by his own unaided power. No one can make himself a Christian. It is not man's business or within his competence to upgrade himself, as it were, into a great-souled person and finally into a Christian. On the contrary, the process of becoming a Christian begins only when a person sloughs off any illusion of autonomy and self-sufficiency; when he acknowledges that man does not create

Translated by Matthew J. O'Connell.

himself and cannot bring himself to fulfillment but must open himself and allow himself to be led to his own true self.

To be a Christian, then, means first and foremost that we acknowledge our own insufficiency and allow him—the Other who is God—to act upon us. Louis Evely once remarked quite correctly that the sin of Adam was really not his wanting to be like God; this, after all, is man's vocation, granted to him by the Creator himself. Instead, Adam's failure was that he chose the wrong way of seeking likeness to God and devised for himself a very shabby idea of God. Adam imagined that he would be like God if he could subsist solely by his own power and could be self-sufficient in giving life to himself as he saw fit. In reality, such misguided grasping at conceited divinization leads to self-destruction, for even God himself, as the Christian faith teaches us, does not exist in isolated self-sufficiency but is infinitely needing and receiving in his dialogue of love, giving himself and devoting himself, and only in this way is he fully divine. Man becomes like God only when he enters into this same movement; when he stops trying to create himself and, instead, allows God to create him. For it is still true today that man is not man's own creation but can be created for his own sake only by God.

This may strike us as a very old-fashioned way of thinking. Yet I am convinced that precisely in our day we would do well to discover anew the truth of this statement and to become aware that what I have been saying about individuals applies very much also to mankind as a whole. The human race is today setting itself up as the supreme reality; it is endeavoring to attain a fully human status but is unwilling to rely on any help except that which it can supply to itself. But in the process, the race is destroying its own humanity. Precisely by proclaiming a complete and pure humanness, it is undermining the humanity of man, as is evident on every side. Even mankind as a whole, then, is not autonomous but is dependent on something beyond itself.

Individuals do not become Christians, any more than they become human beings, on their own and by their own resources. Strange though it may sound to us today, we need to open ourselves in faith to the action of God.

No one becomes a Christian alone. This is to say that one can become a Christian only in a community of fellow believers and by the mutual help of shared faith and prayer. Certainly, part of being a Christian is—as we just heard in the Gospel—the practice of going to one's "quiet room", to the solitude of the struggling believer who exposes himself to the presence of God.

But there is more to it than that. Being a Christian also calls for fellowship. God comes to man only through other men. Even in the realm of the spirit, man is an unfinished being; even in the realm of the spirit, the fact remains that we can exist as men only by being from others and for others.

I think that the time has come for us to dispel the modern illusion that religion is the most intimate business, which we deal with by ourselves alone, and that these intimate matters should not be brought into the public arena. When we thus reduce faith to a spirituality that has no connection with reality, we first strip faith itself of its reality, but then we also rob human fellowship of its most precious dimension. The end result is the individual on one side and the pure collectivity on the other. Community, in which individuals remain themselves but at the same time encounter what is truly human in their fellows—this community is not built up when man keeps to himself what is deepest in him. Furthermore, man needs this kind of community if he is to be himself. That is why we have the duty of making public what is most intimately ours, of bringing it forth and allowing it to put its stamp on the world around us. It is up to us not to let the world be without God but, rather, to convey God into the midst of it through our faith.

2. A Season of Fasting

Alongside the commission to make our faith known to others, the call to make it something profoundly interior retains its full force. Here at last we come to the truth implied in the German word for Lent: "Season of Fasting". If individuals are to become Christians, they need the strength to overcome; they need the power to stand fast against the natural tendency to let themselves be carried along. Life in the most general sense was recently defined as "resistance to the pull of gravity". Only where such effort is expended is there life; where the effort ceases, life too ceases.

If this is true in the biological sphere, it is all the more true in the spiritual. Man is the creature who does not become himself on his own. Nor does he do so simply by letting himself be carried along and surrendering to the natural gravitational pull of living from day to day. He always becomes himself only by struggling against the tendency simply to live from one moment to the next and by dint of a discipline that is able to rise above the pressures of routine and to liberate the self from the compulsions of utilitarian goals and instincts. Our world is so full of what immediately impinges on our senses that we are in danger of seeing only the parts and losing sight of the whole. It takes self-control to see beyond what is right in front of us and to free ourselves from the tyranny of superficiality.

In the Church's [fourth] Preface for Lent, there is this noteworthy phrase: "Jejunio mentem elevas": You elevate our spirit through fasting. Twenty-five years ago [in 1945], when all of us [Germans] were set to fasting whether we liked it or not, we felt that these words were almost ironic. We felt that fasting prevented the spirit from freely being itself. But when we think back to that time and compare our present satiety with our hunger then, we do notice how true the phrase is. We realize that in many respects we used to have greater insight than we do now. We become aware that the satisfied person who no longer hungers becomes blind and deaf. He perceives only himself. Once we have realized this, perhaps we develop a new understanding for the images in Sacred Scripture that have been incorporated into the baptismal liturgy: the image of the person who is blind when it comes to God; the person who is deaf and mute, completely unable to perceive himself and the world. We become conscious that we need the discipline expressed in the word "fasting".

Now it is true that a good deal of fasting nowadays is done for medical, aesthetic, and other reasons. And this is good. But this sort of fasting alone is not enough for man. The goal of such fasting continues to be the self. It does not free the individual from the self but is practiced for the sake of the self. Yet people need a kind of fasting and renunciation that liberates them from themselves, liberates them for God, and thus liberates them for others as well. The summons that this season of fasting issues to us is certainly an uncomfortable one. But anyone who is at all awake to the situation of contemporary man —to his own situation!—also knows how much we need this call to a real fasting that is not turned in on the self.

Christian fasting should be a liberating departure from the self. The understanding has always been that the season of fasting should also be a season of fruitfulness in good works. "Good works": when we hear this expression today it is easy for us, according to our temperament, to laugh or scowl. But here again we must not be too easy on ourselves. We should turn our gaze to the starving peoples all over the world; then perhaps the smile or scowl will quickly vanish from our faces. For then we will realize that we cannot have a gracious God as long as we are full and those around us are starving.

3. A Church Journeying in the Wilderness

Allow me to conclude these reflections based on baptism by adding another perspective. In her liturgical language, the Church gives the name *Quadragesima*, "forty-day period", to the season we began on Ash Wednesday. In the season thus named, the Church uses the typological exegesis of Scripture in order to situate us in a certain spiritual context and continuity. Israel journeyed in the wilderness for forty years; Elijah walked for forty days to Horeb, the mountain of God; Jesus fasted in the desert for forty days. These forties point to a spiritual context and continuity that cannot be valid solely for the Bible but remain significant in post-biblical times as well. Consequently, during these days the Church of every age endeavors to situate herself within that continuity and to make it present for each of us.

Let us ask then: What is the point of this series of forties? In the later period of Israel's history, people looked back to the forty years of journeying in the wilderness as the time of first love between God and Israel, as the time of the great foundational revelation, as the time when God stood face to face with his people, spoke to them, and day by day gave them instruction for their journey. People saw that early period as the time when God still dwelled, as it were, in the midst of Israel, went before them in the forms of cloud and pillar of fire, fed them daily with manna from his own hand, and gave them water from the rock. The years in the wilderness thus appeared as a time of special predilection, special closeness, and directness in their relations with God.

Even from the purely secular viewpoint of the historian of religions, there is probably much that is correct in this later view. It seems that the nomads who lived in the wilderness were the first to discover monotheism. It seems that precisely this kind of world—where people have only the wilderness around them and the sky over them; where they have no secure refuge, no refuge into which to retreat, no habitation that they can divinize and worship, but are exposed every day to emptiness and the unknown—forced them to seek nothing but the God who holds the *whole* world in his hands and who can be everywhere present with men and knows them and is able to help them with his creative power, no matter where they are.

The time in the wilderness was, then, a time of special closeness to God. Admittedly, when we read the biblical account of Israel's journeying in the wilderness, we get quite a different picture. Here the time in the wilderness is described as one of extreme danger and great temptation; as a time when Israel murmured against its God, was dissatisfied with him, and wanted to return to paganism; as a time when it wandered about, traveled in circles, and could find no path to follow; as a time when it fashioned other gods for itself because the God who kept his distance could not satisfy it.

Surprisingly, we find the time in the wilderness to be an ambivalent one even for Jesus. After his baptism, in which he accepted the lot of the Servant of Yahweh, the lot of one who is dispossessed of himself and represents others, he goes into the wilderness and the immediate presence of the Father, so that in his union with the Father he may receive freedom from himself and for others. This process is one he repeats constantly throughout his life: Over and over again he goes into the desert, into solitude with the Father, in order to return then among men. But even for Jesus this period of special closeness to the Father is also a time of vulnerability in which temptation presses upon him: the temptation to reject the word, which is powerless, and love, which is defenseless, and, instead, to give people what they want, namely, bread and thrills and the triumph of political power that alone seems able to promise them salvation.

When we hear all this, we probably have to admit that the Scriptures are describing our own situation as well. In our day the Church in an entirely new way has been launched upon a forty-day period, a time in the wilderness. She has lost so many of her earthly habitations and securities. Not one of what seemed to be her sure supports holds firm any more. She sees only wilderness around her, forcing her to journey constantly onward; even God seems to be but a distant cloud that dissolves when we try to touch it. And the Church of our day, this Church in the wilderness, is pressed hard by the hallucinations and temptations of the wilderness. Now that the distant God has become so incomprehensible, she may think she should try what is closer at hand and interpret worldliness itself as Christianity and immersion in the world as the service of Jesus Christ—just as the golden calf was passed off as an image of Yahweh and as the true way, discovered at long last, of bringing the distant God near and worshipping him. The Church is being urged ever more loudly and insistently to exchange a distant and unreal redemption by the Word for a more robust redemption by bread and the sure path of politicization.

Our experience, then, is of a Church in the wilderness, a Church in her forty-day period. It is one of exposure to emptiness, to a world that seems, religiously speaking, to have become wordless, imageless, soundless; exposure to a world in which the heavens over us are dark and distant and incomprehensible.

And yet for us, too, and for the Church of our day this time in the wilderness can become a time of grace in which a new love grows out of the suffering in that faraway place. Although we often have the oppressive feeling that the manna of our faith will suffice only for the present day, God gives us that manna anew each day if we allow him to do so. Although we must live in a world in which it seems that God can be encountered only as One who is dead, he can strike living water even from dead stones.

Church in Lent, in her "forty days" in the wilderness. I think that during this season of fasting, we ought to take fresh courage to accept our situation in patience and faith and to follow fearlessly after our hidden God. If we journey on in patient faith, then for us, too, a new day can dawn out of the darkness. And God's bright world, the lost world of images and sounds, will be restored to us again; there will be a new morning in God's good creation. Amen.

26. Good Friday

I.

In the great *Passions* by Johann Sebastian Bach that stir us anew each year during Holy Week, the awful event of Good Friday is bathed in transfigured and transfiguring beauty. Admittedly, these *Passions* do not speak of the Resurrection—they end with the burial of Jesus—but their purity and nobility are derived from the certainty of Easter, the certainty of a hope that is not extinguished even in the night of death.

Nowadays, however, this confident and tranquil faith that does not need to speak of the Resurrection, because it lives and thinks in its light, has become strangely alien to us. In the *Passion* of the Polish composer Krzysztof Penderecki, the tranquility of a community of believers who live constantly in the light of Easter has disappeared. Instead, we hear the tortured cry of the persecuted at Auschwitz; the cynicism and brutal commando voices of the masters of that hell; the eager voices of the hangers-on as they join in the screeching, thus hoping to rescue themselves from the terror; the lashing whips of the anonymous, omnipresent power of darkness; the hopeless sighs of the dying.

This is the Good Friday of the twentieth century: the face of man is mocked, covered with spittle, beaten by man himself. From the gas chambers of Auschwitz; from the ruined villages and outraged children of Vietnam; from the slums of India, Africa, and Latin America; from the concentration camps of the Communist world that Solzhenitsyn has brought before our eyes with such passionate intensity: from every side the "bleeding head sore wounded, reviled, and put to scorn" gazes at us with a realism that makes a mockery of any aesthetic transfiguration. If Kant and Hegel had been right, the progress of the Enlightenment should have made man ever freer, more reasonable, and more upright.

Translated by Michael J. Miller.

Instead, the demons we had so eagerly declared dead rise ever more powerfully from the depths of man and teach him to feel a profound anxiety at his own power and powerlessness: his power to destroy, his powerlessness to find himself and master his own inhumanity.

The most terrible moment in the story of Jesus' Passion is doubtless the one in which he cries aloud in his extreme torment on the Cross: "My God, my God, why have you forsaken me?" The words are from a psalm in which Israel—suffering, oppressed, scorned because of its faith—cries out its need before the face of God. But this cry of supplication, uttered by a people whose election and communion with God seem to have turned into a curse, acquires its full dreadfulness on the lips of him who is himself the redemptive nearness of God in the midst of men. If *he* is conscious of being abandoned by God, then where is God still to be found? Does not this moment mark, in all truth, the darkening of the sun of history, the hour in which the light of the world is extinguished? Today, the echo of this cry, magnified a thousandfold, rings in our ears from the hell of the concentration camps, from the battlefields of the guerilla wars, from the slums of the starving and despairing: "Where are you, God, that you could create such a world, that you can look on while your most innocent creatures often suffer the most terribly, as sheep are led to the slaughter and cannot open their mouths?"

Job's ancient question has acquired an edge hardly ever matched in the past. Often, of course, the question is asked rather arrogantly, and behind it can be glimpsed a sense of malicious satisfaction, as when student newspapers repeat in overbearing tones what the students have had preached to them: that in a world forced to learn the names of Auschwitz and Vietnam no one can seriously talk any longer of a "good" God. But the insincerity that is all too often evident does not make the question any less valid. For in this our own hour of history, we all seem for practical purposes to be contemporaries of Jesus at the point when his Passion turned into a cry to the Father for help: "My God, my God, why have you forsaken me?"

What can we say in response to this cry? In the last analysis, the question Jesus asked is not to be answered with words and arguments, for it penetrates to a depth unfathomable to mere reason and the words that such reason produces. The failure of Job's friends is the inevitable lot of all who believe they can answer the question, positively or negatively, with clever thoughts and words. No, the question can only be endured, suffered through—with him and at the side of him who suffered it to the end for all of us and with all of us. An arrogant sense of having dealt adequately with it—whether in the spirit of the student newspaper or in the spirit of theological apologetics—can only miss the real point.

It is possible, nonetheless, to make a couple of suggestions. The first thing to be noted is that Jesus does not declare the absence of God but, rather, turns it into a prayer. If we want to unite the Good Friday of the twentieth century with the Good Friday of Jesus, we must integrate our century's cry of distress with Jesus' cry to the Father for help and transform it into a prayer to God who is nevertheless near to us. You may, of course, go a step farther and ask: "Is it possible to pray honestly as long as we have done nothing to wipe the blood from those who have been beaten and to dry their tears? Is not Veronica's gesture the least that must be made before there can be any talk of prayer? Can one pray at all with the lips alone, or does not that always require the whole person?"

But let us content ourselves with this first suggestion, which leads us to reflect on a second one: Jesus has truly entered into and shared the affliction of the condemned, while we—most of us, at least—have on the whole been only more or less involved onlookers at the horrors of the twentieth century. This fact is connected with an observation of some importance: Remarkably enough, the claim that there can no longer be any God, the claim, that is, that God has completely disappeared, is the urgent conclusion drawn by *onlookers* at the terror, the people who view the horrors from the cushioned armchair of their own prosperity and attempt to pay their tribute to it and ward it off from themselves by saying, "If such things can happen, there is no God!"

But among those who are themselves immersed in the terrible reality, the effect is not infrequently just the opposite: it is precisely then that they discover God. In this world of suffering, adoration has continued to rise up from the fiery furnaces of the crematories and not from the spectators of the horror. It is no accident that the people who in their history have been the most condemned to suffering, the people who have been the worst battered and the most wretched and who did not have to wait for 1940–1945 to be in "Auschwitz", also became the people of revelation, the people who have known God and made him visible to the world. And it is no accident that the man who has been the most afflicted and has suffered most—Jesus of Nazareth— was and is the revealer, nay, revelation itself. It is no accident that faith in God flows from a "head sore wounded", from a crucified man, and that atheism has Epicurus for father and originates in the world of the satisfied onlooker.

The awful and threatening gravity of a saying of Jesus that we usually set aside as inappropriate suddenly comes home to us here: A camel will sooner pass through the eye of a needle than a rich man enter the kingdom of heaven. Rich man? That means anyone who is well-off, saturated with prosperity, and knows suffering only from television. We should not be too ready to dismiss these words of Jesus, which are a warning to us, especially on Good Friday. Admittedly, we need not and, indeed, must not call down suffering and affliction on ourselves. Good Friday is something God imposes when and where he wishes. But we ought to learn even more fully—not only theoretically, but in our practical lives—that every good thing is a gift on loan from him and that we must account for it before him. We must also learn— again, not just theoretically, but in the way we think and act—that in addition to the Real Presence of Jesus in the Church and in the Blessed Sacrament, there is that other, second real presence of Jesus in the least of our brethren, in the downtrodden of this world, in the humblest; he wants us to find him in all of them. To accept this truth ever anew is the decisive challenge that Good Friday presents to us year after year.

II.

The image of the crucified Christ that stands at the center of the Good Friday liturgy reveals the full seriousness of human affliction, human forlornness, human sin. And yet down through the centuries of Church history, the crucifix has constantly been seen as an image of consolation and hope.

Matthias Grünewald's *Isenheimer Altar*, perhaps the most deeply moving painting of the crucifixion that Christendom possesses, stood in a monastery of the Antonian Hospitalers, where people were cared for who had fallen victim to the dreadful plagues that afflicted the West in the late Middle Ages. The crucified Jesus is depicted as one of these people, his whole body marred by the plague-boils, the most horrible torment of the age. In him the words of the prophet are fulfilled, that he would bear our griefs and carry our sorrows.

Before this image the monks prayed along with their sick, who found consolation in the knowledge that in Christ God suffered with them. This picture helped them realize that precisely by their illness they were identified with the crucified Christ, who in his affliction had become one with all the afflicted of history. In their cross they experienced the presence of the crucified Jesus and knew that in their distress they were being drawn into Christ and, thereby, into the abyss of everlasting mercy. They experienced his Cross as their redemption.[1]

In our day many have grown deeply mistrustful of this understanding of redemption. Following Karl Marx, they see the consolation of heaven in recompense for the earthly vale of tears as an empty promise that brings no improvement but only renders permanent the world's wretched state and, in the last analysis, benefits only those in whose interest it is to preserve the status quo. Instead of heavenly consolation, then, these people call for changes that will remove and, in this sense, redeem suffering. Not redemption through suffering, but redemption from suffering is their watchword: not expectation of help from God, but the humanization of man by man is the task for which they call.

Now of course one could immediately retort that this sets up a false dilemma. The Antonians quite obviously did not see in the Cross of Christ an excuse for not engaging in organized humanitarian aid addressed to special needs. By means of 369 hospitals throughout Europe, they built a network of charitable institutions in which the Cross of Christ was regarded as a very practical summons to seek him in those who suffer and to heal his wounded body; in other words, to change the world and put an end to suffering.[2]

We may ask, moreover, whether amid all the impressive talk about humaneness and humanization that we hear around us there is as real an impulse to serve and assist as there was in those days. One frequently has the impression that we want to buy our freedom from a task that has become too burdensome for us by at least talking grandly about it;

---

[1] See A. Zacharias, *Kleine Kunstgeschichte abendländischer Stile* (Munich, 1957), 132.

[2] See K. Hofmann, article "Antonianer" in *Lexikon für Theologie und Kirche*, 1:677.

in any case, we get along today in large measure by borrowing people for service roles from the poorer nations, because in our own country the impulse to serve has grown weak. But still we must ask how long a social organism can survive when one of its key organs is failing and can hardly be replaced over the long term by transplantation.

Admittedly, then, even—and especially—with regard to the activity required if we are to shape and transform the world, we must disregard the facile contrasts that are fashionable today and view the question differently. But by doing that, we have still not fully answered the questions we are discussing here. For in fact the Antonians followed the Christian creed in preaching and practicing not only redemption from the Cross but also redemption through the Cross. To do so is to bring out a dimension of human existence that increasingly eludes us today but nonetheless constitutes the very heart of Christianity; in its light alone are we to understand Christian activity for and in this world.

How can we come to see this heart of the matter? I will try to suggest a way by referring to the development of the image of the Cross in the work of a modern artist who, though not a Christian, was increasingly fascinated by the figure of the Crucified and was constantly trying to grasp the essence of it. I am referring to Marc Chagall.[3] He first depicts the crucified Jesus in a very early work that was painted in 1912. Here the entire composition forces us to think of him as a child; he represents the suffering of the innocent, the undeserved suffering in this world that by its very nature is a sign of hope. Then the crucified Jesus disappears completely from Chagall's work for twenty-five years; he reappears only in 1937, but he now conveys a new and more profound meaning.

This triptych on the crucifixion had a remarkable predecessor, another tripartite painting that Chagall later destroyed but of which an oil sketch in colors has survived. That earlier picture was entitled "Revolution". On the left, there is an excited crowd waving red flags and brandishing weapons; by this means the revolution as such is brought into the picture. The right side contains images of peace and joy: the sun, love, music; the idea is that the revolution will produce a transformed, redeemed, restored world. In the center, linking the two halves, is a

---

[3] For the following description, cf. H.-M. Rotermund, *Marc Chagall und die Bibel* (Lahr, 1970), 111–38.

man doing a handstand. Clearly there is a direct allusion to Lenin, the man who symbolizes the entire revolution that turns things upside down and transforms left into right; the kind of total change that leads to a new world is taking place.

The picture recalls a Gnostic text from the early Christian period in which it is said that Adam, that is, mankind, stands on his head and thus causes up and down, left and right, to be reversed; a complete conversion of values—a revolution—is needed if man and the world are to become what they should be. We might call this picture by Chagall a kind of altar to political theology. Just as he had expected the Russian Revolution of 1917 to produce salvation, so after this first disillusionment, he placed his hopes a second time in the French Popular Front that had come into power in 1937.

The fact that Chagall destroyed this picture shows that he buried his hopes a second time and probably for good. He painted a new triptych that has the same structure: on the right, a picture of the salvation that is coming, but purer and less ambivalent than before; on the left, the world in turmoil, but now marked more by suffering than by conflict and with the crucified Jesus hovering over it. The decisive change, and one that gives a new meaning to the two side panels, is to be found at the center: replacing the symbol of the revolution and its delusive hopes is the colossal image of the crucified Jesus. The rabbi, representing the Old Testament and Israel, who had previously sat at Lenin's side as if in confirmation of his work, is now at the foot of the Cross. The crucified Jesus, and not Lenin, is now the hope of Israel and the world.

We need not inquire to what extent Chagall in his own mind was intending to adopt the Christian interpretation of the Old Testament, of history, and of being human in general. Quite independently of the answer to this question, anyone who sees the two pictures side by side can derive an unambiguously Christian statement from them. The salvation of the world does not come, in the final analysis, from a transformation of the world or a political system that sets itself up as absolute and divine.

We must indeed go on working to transform the world, soberly, realistically, patiently, humanely. But mankind has a demand and a question that go beyond anything politics and economics can provide, that can be answered only by the crucified Christ, the man in whom our suffering touches the heart of God and his everlasting love. Indeed, man thirsts for this love; without it he remains an absurd experiment despite all the improvements that can and should be made.

The consolation that goes forth from him who bears the stripes meant for us is something we still need today, in fact today more than ever. In all truth, he is the only consolation that never degenerates into an empty promise. God grant that we may have eyes to see and a heart open to this consolation; that we may be able to live within it and pass it on to others; that during the Good Friday of history we may receive the Easter mystery that is at work in Christ's Good Friday and, thus, be redeemed.

27. The Mystery of the Easter Vigil

During this holy night, the Church endeavors to convey the meaning of the mystery celebrated in the Easter vigil, the mystery of the Lord's Resurrection. She does so in the language proper to her, which is the language of symbol. Three great symbols dominate the liturgy of this night of the Resurrection: light, water, and the "new song", that is, the Alleluia.

First, light. This is one of mankind's primal symbols. Whether in the North that thirsts for light or in the South that is intoxicated by light, for men everywhere it has become the image of the mysterious divine power that they know sustains them in existence. In fact, at one time light was much more than an image to people. Augustine himself was still so deeply moved by the resplendent beauty of light that he dared write: "Christ is not called 'light' in the same way that he is called 'cornerstone'. The latter name is applied to him by metaphor, whereas the former is meant in a literal sense" (*De Genesi ad litteram* IV, 28, 45). Earthly light is the most direct reflection of God's reality and gives us our best glimpse of him who dwells in unapproachable light (1 Tim 6:16).

During the two great holy nights of the Church year, Christmas and Easter, the symbolism of light fuses with the symbolism of night. On both occasions, the Church uses the interplay of night and light to show symbolically what the content of the feast in question is: the encounter of God and the world, the victorious entry of God into a world that refuses him room and yet in the end cannot prevent him from taking it.

This Christ-centered drama of light and darkness, of God and the world as they encounter each other, begins on Christmas, when God knocks on the door of a world that rejects him even though it belongs

Translated by Matthew J. O'Connell.

to him (Jn 1:5−11). But the world cannot prevent his coming. He himself becomes "world" in becoming a man. His coming seems a defeat of the light, which becomes darkness, but at the same time it is the first, hidden victory of the light, since the world has not been able to prevent God from coming, however carefully it may have barred the doors of its inns.

Now, on Easter, the drama reaches its central act and climax. The darkness has used its ultimate weapon, death. In orderly judicial fashion, it has declared Truth and Love to be the chief criminals of world history and has condemned the light-bringer. But the Resurrection effects the great reversal. Light has won the victory and now lives on invincibly. Most important of all, it has made a bit of the world its own and transformed it into itself.

Of course, with that the drama is not yet over. Its end is still to come; it will arrive with the Parousia of the Lord. It is still night, albeit a night in which a light has been lit. When the Lord comes again, the day will last forever.

This great drama of history, in which we live out our own lives, is the background for the liturgy of the Paschal candle with which the celebration of the Easter vigil begins. The church building, in the darkness of night, where you cannot see anything and people stumble and bump into one another—is this not in fact an image of our world? A world that, despite all our scientific knowledge and all our social achievements, is still in deep darkness. In fact, it often seems darker than ever. Despite all our specialized knowledge, the meaning of the whole has become increasingly incomprehensible, even for the believer who often enough is dismayed by the seeming absence of God, who cannot be found in worldly commotion. Who can fail to be deeply affected by the monstrous eclipse of God that we feel in Reinhold Schneider's *Winter in Vienna*? And who can deny that, amid all the everyday conveniences that cover all questions with a security blanket, he suddenly senses from time to time something of this eclipse of God that seems at a single stroke to call everything into question? Who is there who is not forced like Cardinal Newman to utter a plea into the night around him: "O God, you can bring light into the darkness! You alone can do it!" And who is unaware of how men come into conflict and are stumbling blocks to one another in this night that covers the world and so often conceals, not only the ultimate things, but even what is near at hand (our neighbor!)?

As we wait in the pitch-dark church for the Easter light, we should experience the consoling realization: God is aware of the night that surrounds us. In fact, he has already kindled his light at the heart of it. "Light of Christ!—Thanks be to God!" The night enables us to appreciate what the light is. It is brightness that enables us to see; that shows the way and gives direction; that helps us to know both others and ourselves. It is warmth that strengthens and quickens, that consoles and gladdens. Finally, it is life, and this tiny quivering flame is an image of the wonderful mystery that we call "life" and that is in fact profoundly dependent on light.

Soon the entire church is radiant with the bright light of the candles everyone is holding. Then it is no longer merely a celebration of the Resurrection; it is a foreshadowing of the Second Coming of the Lord, whom we are advancing to meet with lamps lit. It is a glimpse of the great eschatological feast of light, an anticipation of the wedding feast of God that is illumined by the gleam of countless candles. Something of the joy that marks a wedding should overwhelm us on this night so bright with candles.

And also, of course, the question: "Will I be one of those who sit at God's table? Will my lamp have enough oil for the everlasting wedding feast?" But perhaps it is even more Christian to ask ourselves the right questions about the present. The world is indeed dark, but even a single candle suffices to bring light into the deepest darkness. Did not God give us a candle at baptism and the means of lighting it? We must have the courage to light the candle of our patience, our trust, our love. Instead of bewailing the night, we must dare to light the little lamp that God has loaned us: "Light of Christ!—Thanks be to God!"

The second principal Easter symbol is water. Like the Paschal candle, the basin of water is set up in the middle of the celebrating community, adorned and celebrated with festive words, until the climactic moment when light and water are united in marriage, as it were, by the threefold dipping of the Paschal candle into the consecrated water. This rite may remind us of those precious moments when the sun is reflected in the clear, gleaming water of a mountain brook, and heaven and earth seem to become one in the mysterious union of water and light.

Water, like light, is a primal symbol for the human race. Historians of religion tell us that light is a "uranian", water a "tellurian" symbol. This means that light embodies the transcendent splendor of all that is heavenly, the magnificent but also dangerous life force that is beyond us, inasmuch as it is never at our disposal but gives or refuses itself freely. Water, on the other hand, embodies all that is precious on earth. Anyone who has ever been thirsty knows the truth of this. Anyone who has endured the grilling force of the sun for many hours on end and then suddenly stumbled on a fresh, sparkling spring of water knows that there is in fact nothing more precious than that bright, clear water. Thus, water awakens in us the memory of Paradise and fruitfulness. Finally, the opposite of all this is again what enables us to grasp fully what a wonderful thing water is. The dirt and burden of the day fall away as we wash ourselves in a bath, from which a person emerges as fresh as a newborn child.

On the basis of these experiences, the great river-countries of the ancient world—Egypt and Assyro-Babylonia—developed a kind of mystique in regard to rivers. For them the river is the mighty giver of life that goes its invincible way and has power to make the desert bloom. Even in Israel's hopes for salvation, the idea of the life-giving stream returns again and again, whether the writer is looking back to Paradise or forward to the spring in the Temple that gladdens the city of God with its streams of water (Ps 46:4; Ezek 47:1–12).

This whole mystery of water makes its presence felt in the Easter celebration; it is included in the latter but also raised to a higher level, without its original content being thereby diminished. For the Easter vigil tells us that a far more precious spring than any on earth has burst forth from the Lord's pierced side (Jn 4:10; 7:37; 19:34). The Cross of Christ is nothing else than his radical surrender of himself, his ultimate commitment in which he holds back nothing for himself but pours himself out totally for others. On the Cross, then, the truly precious wellspring of pure devotion, of extravagant self-giving love for God, was unsealed. All the priceless value of water is concentrated in it: the power to cleanse, fruitfulness, all that is refreshing and cheering and invigorating.

In baptism, this spring flows from Christ's Cross through the entire Church like a mighty stream and "make[s] glad the city of God" (Ps 46:4). We bathe in this stream and are reborn. It alone constantly transforms the wilderness of the world into fruitful land; for, where hatred and selfishness reign, there is a wilderness, and only where the spirit of loving service is at work will anything truly constructive be accomplished. We must never forget that the most precious spring in the world pours from the Cross and from death, or, rather, from radical self-surrender.

When the Paschal candle is then lowered into the basin of water, and heaven and earth are thus united in a symbolic marriage, the action has power to suggest still another thought to us. It may well say to us that the meager fruitfulness of the present earth is something to be appreciated and incorporated into the great mystery of life that is proper to God's reign. It gives us a fleeting glimpse of the miracle that will be the divinization of the earth: all that is noble and precious will not pass away but will be transformed and will share in the glory of what is eternal. In the waters of this world, which reflect the splendor of the sun, we already find something of the beauty of the new heavens and the new earth.

The third Easter symbol is the "new song", the Alleluia. Admittedly, we shall sing this new song in all its fullness only in the "new world", when God calls us by a "new name" (Rev 2:17) and everything has been made new. But we are permitted to anticipate something of all this in the great joy of the Easter vigil. For singing, and especially the singing of the new song, is in the final analysis simply the outward expression of joy. When we speak of the blessed in heaven singing, this is simply a metaphor for the joy that permeates their whole being.

Indeed, singing indicates that the person is passing beyond the boundaries of the merely rational and falling into a kind of ecstasy, for he can say what is merely rational (that is why overly rational people are seldom tempted to sing). This essential aspect of singing, in which the person passes beyond the limits of the rational and expresses his entire being, as it were, finds its climactic form in the Alleluia, the song in which the very essence of song achieves its purest embodiment.

The word "Alleluia" was originally a Hebrew expression meaning roughly: "Praise Yahweh!" But in the liturgy of the Easter vigil, there is only a distant allusion to this original meaning, for if the latter were the main point, the Hebrew word would have been translated. But actually we are dealing here with something that cannot be translated. The Alleluia is simply the nonverbal expression in song of a joy that requires no words because it transcends all words. In this it resembles certain kinds of exultation and jubilation that are found among all peoples, just as the miracle of joy, of being able and free to rejoice, manifests itself in every nation. Augustine heard this kind of wordless singing in the fields and vineyards of his native land and skillfully made it the theme of some delightful sermons. For example, he takes as a text the words of the Psalmist: "Bene cantate ei cum jubilatione": Sing well to him with jubilation (Ps 33:3, according to Augustine's Latin version of the Psalms), and comments:

> What does it mean to sing with "jubilation"? It means: to be unable to express in words, or to verbalize, the song that sings to you in your heart. As the harvesters in field or vineyard experience an increasingly jubilant sense of joy, they become incapable, it seems, of finding words to express this overflowing joy. They abandon syllables and words, and their singing turns into a *jubilus*, or cry of exultation. A *jubilus* is a shout that shows the heart is trying to express what it cannot possibly say. And to whom is such a *jubilus* more fittingly directed than to him who is himself ineffable? He is ineffable because your words cannot lay hold of him. But if you cannot express him in language and yet may not be silent about him, what other choice do you have but jubilation? What can you do but allow your heart to rejoice wordlessly and the immensity of your joy to overleap the boundary of syllables? "Sing to the Lord with a *jubilus*!" (*Enarratio* 2 in Ps 32, 1, 8)

Singing of this sort occurs in the Alleluia. It is the expression of a joy that overflows all barriers and washes them away.

Yet if the singing of the Alleluia is the third component in the dramatic symbolism of the Easter liturgy, then it is also a third component in the basic structure of man himself, who has this radical capacity to sing and jubilate. The Alleluia is like an initial revelation of what can and shall someday take place in us: our entire being shall turn into one immense joy. What a prospect! Should it not impel us, at least for this night, to forget all the trivial things that oppress and worry us and to let ourselves be swept up by this great expectation that is our future reality already present in us, though hidden, and thus truly to sing: Alleluia!

28. Resurrection as Mission

No other Easter account in the New Testament has such personal touches or so directly reflects how individuals experienced the risen Lord as do the Easter narratives in the Gospel of John. It begins with the puzzling reference to the race of the two disciples to the tomb—probably a foreshadowing of that tension between charism and office which is part of the Church's make-up and, at the same time, an indication of the only legitimate kind of competition that may exist between the two: vying to imitate Christ more faithfully, to believe more firmly, and to serve more willingly and lovingly.

The personal note is even more evident in the first appearance of the risen Lord as he meets Mary Magdalen. This grief-stricken, bewildered woman has ascertained that the tomb is now empty but has not been looted, since the cloths and bindings are lying neatly in their place and only the body has disappeared. She cannot imagine what has happened and therefore summons the disciples, who cannot understand it, either. Then she sees someone else: it must be the gardener, she thinks, and perhaps he can explain. "Sir, if you have carried him away, tell me where you have laid him, and I will take him away" (Jn 20:15). Only by the call of his voice does she recognize that it is the Lord himself.

This in itself is rather remarkable and is consistent with a phenomenon that occurs repeatedly in the Resurrection accounts. For example, the two disciples on the way to Emmaus likewise walk at the Lord's side without recognizing him. His interpretation of the Scriptures sets their hearts on fire, but only at the breaking of the bread are their eyes opened; then, just at the moment when they recognize him, he disappears.

Such details make it clear that Jesus is not simply a man who has returned from the dead like Lazarus or the young man of Naim; in

---

Translated by Matthew J. O'Connell.

that case there would be no question at all about recognizing him after two days. But Jesus does not simply take up where he left off on Good Friday with the intention of leading an earthly life for a short while longer. No, he now lives a new kind of life, and yet he is the same individual. But only when the heart becomes perceptive can the eyes likewise recognize him.

This very point is made quite clear, however, in the further conversation between Jesus and Magdalen. The fact that he calls her by name alerts her, and now she sees: forgetting about the Cross, she answers "My Teacher!" and expects everything to go on as it had before. But she is rebuffed: "Do not touch me", the risen Lord tells her, or, in a more accurate translation: "Do not [try to] hold me, for I have not yet ascended to the Father, but go to my brethren and say to them, I am ascending to my Father and your Father, to my God and your God" (Jn 20:17). What is that supposed to mean? Why should the fact that he has not yet ascended prevent her from touching him? Could he be touched if he had already ascended? Or is he in a hurry and unwilling to be detained at this earthly stage in his ascent?

The whole affair becomes at first sight even stranger when we look at the story of Thomas, in which the very opposite seems to take place: Jesus offers his hands and side for Thomas to probe, in order to assure the disciple that it is really he (20:27). How is it possible for Thomas to do what Magdalen is forbidden to do?

But on closer inspection, it is precisely the incident with Thomas that makes the earlier scene intelligible. After the happy reunion on Easter morning, Magdalen wants simply to return to the old intimacy and leave the Cross behind her like a bad dream. She wants to have "her Teacher" for herself as in the earlier days. But that is utterly incompatible with what has happened since then. No one can now have Jesus as "his rabbi" without reference to the Cross. For Jesus has now become the one who is exalted at the Father's side and accessible to everyone. Now he can be touched only as the One who is with the Father, as the One who has ascended. Paradoxical but true: here on earth, in a merely earthly kind of closeness, he is no longer touchable; but as the One who has ascended he can be touched!

It is possible now to touch Jesus by seeking him at the Father's side and allowing him to draw us after him on his journey. To touch now means to worship and implies a mission. That is why Thomas may touch him: the presentation of Jesus' wounds to Thomas is meant, not to make him forget the Cross, but rather to make it unforgettable. Jesus' action is a call to the mission of witnessing. And thus the touch becomes for Thomas himself an act of worship: "My Lord and my God!" (Jn 20:28). The entire Gospel has been leading up to this moment in which the touching of Jesus, the touching of the mortal wounds of him whom the powers of this world had crushed, becomes a recognition of God's glory.

In the light of this scene, the conversation with Magdalen becomes intelligible. There is no longer any private, merely human friendship with Jesus, any friendship limited to one's narrow circle. Now that he has passed through death, he belongs to all men. We can touch him only by entering upon his way, only by ascending with him and, in union with the Father and the Son, belonging to all. The attempt to hold on to him is replaced by a mission: "Go to my brethren" (Jn 20:17).

To know the risen Jesus, then, is to launch out on a journey that has him for its point of origin. Here, "horizontal" and "vertical" are not in opposition but demand each other: because he has ascended and because he is now with the Father, Jesus is now with all his brethren. When we "ascend" and adore, we too are released from the narrow confines of our own existence and we allow him to send us forth; we learn to share, in our own poor way, in his breadth. Faith, worship, service: all these are inseparably interconnected and manifest the dynamism of a life that is open to the world-transforming mission of the Lord who rose from the dead and ascended to the Father.

Finally, if we turn to the other example that we discussed, the disciples on the way to Emmaus, we find the same law at work: it is not simply walking alongside the Lord (we might say: not mere external membership in the Church) that produces recognition. No, listening to the Word is the beginning of recognition, and communion in the breaking of bread perfects it. The worship of God in Word and sacrament is the way in which we can encounter the risen Lord; the love that shares a meal with him opens our eyes. Then he whom we have recognized disappears, for he calls us to journey farther along the road.

Now at last it is clear in what respect our situation as Christians in the ongoing story differs from that of the first witnesses and in what respect it is the same. They alone had the privilege of seeing the risen

Lord and of being convinced directly by the corporeal reality of his life awakened from the dead; without the realism of this initial encounter, their mission would have come from a void. Yet for them it was true, as it is for all ages, that the risen Lord does not present himself as a spectacle merely to satisfy superficial curiosity; that we can "touch" him only when we allow him to draw us after him, that is, when we too "ascend"; that the touching must take the form of worship and mission; and that it is centered on the "breaking of the bread" and extends into everyday loving service. If we let him draw us after him, if we listen and love, then even today we can touch the risen Jesus— though certainly not in the same way as the first witnesses did. He is alive and goes before us. Those who follow know him.

29. Easter Today

"I do not know the room where exiled love lays down its victory
. . . nor where the smile of the child who was thrown as in play into
the playing flames is preserved, but I know that this is the food from
which earth with beating heart ignites the music of her stars!"[1] Thus
Nelly Sachs writes in one of her late poems. Beside it we may set
Bergengruen's fine poem, "Die heile Welt" [The world intact]: "In
the painful hours when the blood spurts from your heart, know this,
that no one can wound the world. Only its surface is scratched. Deep
in the innermost ring its core is safe and intact. And along with every
created thing you always share in it."

How strange such confidence has become for us! How ready we are
to admit that other, gloomy uncertainty: "I do not know the room
where exiled love lays down its victory." Does such a room exist at
all? Indeed, after Auschwitz, Algeria, Vietnam, Biafra, we can easily
grasp the reality of Good Friday: a crucified man who is humiliated
and treated like a worm and who finds himself abandoned by his God.
But the reality of Easter eludes us.

Theologians follow this same trend and only compound our bewilderment when they tell us that the resuscitation of a dead body
is a "miracle" with which man cannot do anything; even if it happened, they say, what difference would it make to us? Consequently
(they claim), we must be on the lookout for a different message, for instance, that despite the Cross, "the cause of Jesus continues." But has it
continued? Or are the other theologians right, the ones who tell us that
the cause of Jesus was promptly suppressed by his uncomprehending
disciples and turned into the very opposite of what it was meant to

---

Translated by Matthew J. O'Connell.

[1] Translated by Ruth and Matthew Read in Nelly Sachs, *O the Chimneys: Selected Poems*,
trans. M. Hamburger and others (New York, 1967), 233.

be: they made their Brother into a Master again and continued the enslavement of mankind under a new banner. Thus we may find this diluted and supposedly more accessible message of the Resurrection even
more dubious than the message that the faith of the Church proposes.
Has not the very *cause* of Jesus been slain and never brought back to
life?

Obviously, nothing is gained by expedients that aim at being accepted
by everyone and giving offense to no one. Let us admit the fact that
offense will be given, for nothing worthwhile is accomplished where
there is no opposition. On this assumption, let us then ask whether
there is still an Easter message that can be meaningful to us and for the
sake of which it is worth enduring opposition.

The question can be approached from quite different angles. Before
we turn to the person of Jesus, let us take as our point of departure
something closer at hand: the actual feast of Easter. This feast has a
very ancient past; it links the Christian faith with the history of Israel
and with the religious history of mankind in general. It seems to me
that what is specifically Christian can be understood here and in general only if one pays attention to how it is interwoven with the whole
human quest for God and for man's salvation and redemption. The
specifically Christian element does not represent a sudden, paradoxical
leap, as dialectical theology would persuade us. Rather, it is embedded
within the broad framework of human history, which it makes its own,
so that the old continues to exist, albeit transformed, and retains its
place in the larger whole of the new context.

The first level that is at work in the feast of Easter belongs to the
realm of what may be called "nature religion". Easter celebrates the
resurrection of the light, the resurrection of life. The lengthening of
daylight and the reawakening of nature give men the assurance that the
power of death and destruction does not have the last word. Easter,
then, celebrates the triumph of life. It celebrates resurrection and the
certainty that even the gloomy mystery of death serves the mystery of
life. It celebrates the fact that life comes out of death. "No one can
wound the world; only its surface is scratched." The grain of wheat
must die if it is to produce new life a hundredfold; death is a means of
life. Life lives on death. Through death it renews itself. Overcomes.
Advances, year after year.

Thus the mystery of death and resurrection becomes the central content of all religions. The knowledge of this mystery develops into a realization that the world stands upon death and continues to live precisely through death; that the world derives its existence from sacrifice; that sacrifice alone is truly creative.

This idea finds what is probably its most striking expression in the Purusha myth of the Rig-Veda: The gods offer Purusha as a sacrifice and immolate him; his members become the songs and chants of the Veda ("But I know that this is the food from which earth with beating heart ignites the music of her stars!"), the animals, the four castes of men, air, heaven, earth, the universe, and the gods. Only sacrifice is creative, and hence the cultus that makes the myth present and consummates the primal sacrifice here and now holds heaven and earth together. The continued existence of the world depends on it.

I think that it is not difficult to see that this stage in the history of religion and of mankind has by no means become simply meaningless or vanished entirely. Taking this as the point of departure, one could pursue two lines of thought. Easter can be understood as the feast, so to speak, of evolution, of life that ascends through all the catastrophes and also sustains us and gives us hope. And why should we not in good conscience allow this miracle to influence us (or maybe it is not a miracle at all . . .): the fact that life emerged from matter and that spirit arose from life and that despite all sidetracks and extinctions, the journey has continued and, amid all the devastation of our time, amid the larger Good Friday that we experience on every side, still gives us hope in an "Omega" whose outlines we believe we can already dimly perceive?

The other direction in which the recollection of that early stage of religion may lead us is the renewal of our consciousness that sacrifice was and still is the creative power at work in all new beginnings. Or are we incapable of grasping what the peoples of India—and not of India alone—have realized: that only self-surrender begets life; that only renunciation yields progress; that the world is founded on the reality of "sacrifice"?

In Israel, the ancient nature-based content of the feast of Easter was accompanied by a politico-historical content. Man receives life no longer directly from nature but, rather, within the context of a people and of that people's history. This historical perspective was superimposed on the earlier orientation with its focus on nature. Now Easter (Passover) became the commemoration of Israel's liberation from Egypt, a liberation that at the same time constituted Israel as a people. The ancient structure was still operative here, since Israel knew that it had become a people as a result of a sacrifice and that new life had come from death: specifically from the death of the Egyptian firstborn and from the blood of the lamb that had protected the doorposts of the Israelites from the onslaught of the destroying angel.

And so the Israelites celebrated Easter by repeating the death of the lamb and the sacrificial meal. Year after year, they again received the founding of their history, their existence as a people, from the foundational, sustaining sacrifice that had been offered at the beginning. Of course, many a catastrophe taught Israel with increasing clarity that a people cannot live solely on its past and that without a future there is no salvation for the present. And so Israel looked less and less to the past and more and more to a future deliverance. Remembrance turned into hope; remembrance of what had happened long ago became a cry to God that he would complete what he had begun, "redeem" Israel, and give it at last a "world intact".

Once again it is clear that this level of the Easter celebration, too, by no means belongs solely to a past stage of human history. For we, too, have our existence, our "salvation", concretely within a history and a political order; day after day we notice how much our "salvation" depends on the vicissitudes of this political order, which may bring us to catastrophe or, on the contrary, provide us with security. Anyone who stops at this level, of course, must end up either with a "theology of revolution", that is, an ideology that turns man's self-made future into a religion, or else with one version or another of a throne-and-altar theology, that is, a religious glorification of the status quo. In any case, merely mentioning these two possible outcomes shows how this stage of the history of religion is still a present reality and how relevant it is even when we do not advert to it.

And perhaps this should also stimulate the alert Christian to be critical of the religious claims of politics and to recall that man is the being who points beyond himself and destroys himself when he refuses this self-transcendence. A future that we make on our own, in which man alone sets for himself the standards of what is human, could only become an inhuman future. In this regard, it should be clear to us even today that only a future that we receive from God will be a "human" future. Thus we certainly might understand Easter as, among other things, a time for reflection on our own history and on the redemption and enslavement that history signifies for us. We may well celebrate Easter as a day of hope for the future. But the moment we ask what really can be hope for mankind, we cannot stop at man, since man is at least as much of a danger to himself as a hope.

But what does all this have to do with the Resurrection of Jesus, which is the specifically Christian content of the feast of Easter? As a matter of fact, the Resurrection of Jesus is closely connected with the two stages of the history of religion that we have just examined. The more man becomes conscious of his own depths, the more aware he will be that the triumph of life, which allows death to turn into a new beginning, is no triumph for man. For the fact that life goes on does not change the fact that when the individual has died, he remains dead. And so the awareness of death's power to yield life assumes a form that is melancholic, even tragic: Is not life, after all, only a game that voracious death plays in order to amuse itself? Is not death in reality the only powerful thing, while life is its servant? Indian myth once again expresses such thoughts very strikingly, for instance when it says: "And as soon as hunger had created time, he chose to eat it, but it was not enough to satisfy him. Then he created men, animals, and things and immediately consumed them." The process of becoming is a destructive power, blind and cruel; in the final analysis, it creates only in order to swallow up once again what it has brought into being.

When such experiences yawn like an abyss before us, political ideologies and the hopes that they hold out are no longer very helpful. For even the future promised by political movements is not a future for the person who lives and suffers now. However, the value of human life is too high, its claim too definitive, for it to be able to find satisfaction in planning conditions for a distant future while its own deepest desires are denied.

Faith in the Resurrection of Jesus means that there is a future for every man; the abiding cry for endlessness within him is answered. Through Jesus we know "the room where exiled love lays down its victory". He himself is this room, and he calls us to be this room with him and in dependence on him. He calls us to keep this room open within the world so that he, the exiled love, may come and settle perpetually in the world.

Certainly, the world is not "intact". "No one can wound the world; only its surface is scratched", says the poet, but that is contradicted by the image of the crucified Christ and our knowledge about the world, which was capable of inflicting deadly wounds even on its God. On the other hand, neither is the world the meaningless plaything of voracious death. It provides a room for exiled love, because through the mortal wounds of Jesus Christ, God has entered this world.

Or, to put it in the language of Teilhard de Chardin and his evolutionary vision of the world: The Omega Point offers us a hope because we can expect to be taken up into it; because the spirit and love are stronger than death; because there is something irrevocable about man, who will not be dissolved [*aufgelöst*] into nothingness but will be delivered [*erlöst*] from his isolation and incorporated into the unity of the definitive Man.

At this point, we really should start all over again and try to explain how this statement gives meaning to the notions found in nature religion and political religion; how these statements set us a task inasmuch as they oblige us to live even now as beings who are moving toward the Omega Point; how at the same time they set us free because they teach us that man's future is not something that he must build by his own unaided powers.

But we must conclude, so I will make one final observation. In his magnificent painting of the Resurrection, Matthias Grünewald depicts the risen Christ as a theophany, that is, as God's self-manifestation in this man who has passed through the sacrifice. In so doing, Grünewald has translated into artistic terms a basic aspect of the biblical and early Christian theology of the Resurrection and lent to the message a power beyond what words can attain. Indeed, he has put his finger on the heart of the matter: The Resurrection of Jesus gives us the certainty that God exists and that, as the Father of Jesus Christ, he is a God of men. The Resurrection of Jesus is the definitive theophany, the triumphant answer to the question of which really reigns: death or life.

God exists: that is the real message of Easter. And anyone who even begins to comprehend what this implies also knows what it means to be redeemed. He knows why in her prayers on this day the Church endlessly sings Alleluia, the wordless jubilation that is too intense to be articulated in everyday language because it embraces our whole life, with all that is effable and ineffable in it. To grasp something of this joy is to celebrate Easter.

30. The Ascension of Christ

Of all the major feasts of the liturgical year, none perhaps is more alien to the modern mind than the feast of Christ's Ascension. It seems too closely bound up with a mythical vision of the world that we have long since been unable to share. As a result, many Catholic Christians today find themselves asking the question Bultmann asked twenty-five years ago in his now famous essay, "The New Testament and Mythology": "What meaning . . . can we attach to such phrases in the creed as 'descended into hell' or 'ascended into heaven'? We no longer believe in the three-storied universe which the creeds take for granted."[1]

We may think the famous exegete has oversimplified matters somewhat when he continues, a little farther on: "No one who is old enough to think for himself supposes that God lives in a local heaven. There is no longer any heaven in the traditional sense of the word. The same applies to hell in the sense of a mythical underworld beneath our feet. And if this is so, the story of Christ's descent into hell and of his ascension into heaven is done with."[2] But how is Bultmann oversimplifying? And what is the permanent content in our profession of the Lord's Ascension in an age in which the idea of a heaven localized above the clouds has in fact been eliminated for good?

If our answer is to be more than an arbitrary rationalization, we must find it by listening more attentively to the Scriptures. These are the original proclamation of our faith, and we must look to them to discover what is really signified by the event that the liturgy speaks of as "the Lord's going up" or "being exalted" and that we usually call "the ascension of Christ into heaven".

A first point to be made emerges directly from what I have just said: the liturgy and the Bible make only incidental use of the term

---

Translated by Matthew J. O'Connell.

[1] In R. Bultmann and others, *Kerygma and Myth: A Theological Debate*, ed. H. W. Bartsch, trans. R. Fuller (London, 1953; rev. trans., New York, 1961), 4.

[2] Ibid.

Himmelfahrt, "journey to heaven". This is the term to which popular usage has assigned a content that from the beginning was thought of with far greater discrimination and in far less imaginative terms than the German word by itself would suggest.

In speaking of "going up" and "being lifted up", the liturgy is relying primarily on the terminology of the Gospel of John, which uses this language to describe the event being celebrated in today's feast and which has given us what is probably our deepest insight into it. We shall have to come back to this point; for the moment it is important to note that we shall find the answer to our question about the meaning of the "ascension into heaven", not in a single text or even in a single book of the New Testament, but only by listening to the entire New Testament. Moreover, since the content of the word is utterly beyond our powers of representation, it cannot be expressed in a single formula; we can only give intimations of it by approaching it from many angles and thus making it accessible to our understanding.

As a matter of fact, we must even go back beyond the New Testament and realize that the term "raise up" or "exalt" originates in the Old Testament, where it refers to enthronement. To say this is immediately to have an initial answer to our question about the meaning of "ascension into heaven". As the feast of Christ's exaltation, the Ascension tells us that the crucified man Jesus now exercises God's kingship over the world.

In the Acts of the Apostles, from which the [first] reading in today's Mass is taken, the whole event may well seem to be viewed very concretely and externally. And yet if we examine the text more carefully, it becomes clear that even here there is a much greater depth than appears at first glance. What happens in the "ascension into heaven" is described by passive verbs; we are told that Jesus is "lifted up" (v. 9) and, a moment later, that he is "taken up" (v. 11). In other words, the event is described as a mighty act of God, who brings Jesus to himself, and not as a kind of aerial journey into the sky.

Furthermore, the image of the cloud, which seems to indicate such a journey, is in fact a very ancient image from Old Testament cultic theology. In this latter context, it is a sign of the hiddenness of God, who, in his very hiddenness, is close to us and exercises his power for us; who is always beyond our reach and yet always in our midst; who eludes our every attempt to lay hold of him and manipulate him, but by that very fact exercises a providential rule over us all.

Through this image of the cloud, the Ascension narrative is thus integrated into the whole history of God's dealings with Israel, from the cloud on Sinai and over the tent of meeting in the wilderness down to the radiant cloud that shows the nearness of God on the mountain of the Transfiguration. The Lord present in the hiddenness of the cloud —the image that is at the center of today's reading—is thus saying the same thing, in the last analysis, as the metaphorical language of "sitting at the right hand of the Father". Regarding the latter, John Damascene, the great Father of the Eastern Church, observes that the Father's right hand is not a place but an image of his power and glory. "Sitting at the Father's right hand means, therefore, that even in his human nature Christ shares in God's world-encompassing power" (*De fide orthodoxa* 4, 2).

What, then, is the meaning of Christ's "ascension into heaven"? It expresses our belief that in Christ human nature, the humanity in which we all share, has entered into the inner life of God in a new and hitherto unheard-of way. It means that man has found an everlasting place in God. Heaven is not a place beyond the stars; rather, it is something much greater, something that requires far more audacity to assert: heaven means that man now has a place in God.

The basis for this assertion is the interpenetration of humanity and divinity in the crucified and exalted man Jesus. Christ, the man who is in God and eternally one with God, is at the same time God's abiding openness to all men. Thus Jesus himself is what we call "heaven"; heaven is not a place, but a person, the person of him in whom God and man are forever and inseparably one. And we go to heaven and enter into heaven to the extent that we go to Jesus Christ and enter into him. In this sense, "ascension into heaven" can be something that happens in our everyday lives.

Only in the light of these various connections can we understand why Luke should tell us, at the end of his Gospel, that after the Ascension the disciples returned to Jerusalem "with great joy" (Lk 24:52). They knew that what had occurred was not a departure; if it had been, they would hardly have experienced "great joy". No, in their eyes the Ascension and the Resurrection were one and the same event. This event gave them the certainty that the crucified Jesus was alive; that he had overcome death, which cuts man off from God, the Living One; and that the door to eternal life was henceforth forever open.

For the disciples, then, the "Ascension" was not what we usually misinterpret it as being: the temporary absence of Christ from the world. It meant, rather, his new, definitive, and irrevocable presence by participation in God's royal power. This is why Johannine theology for practical purposes identifies the Resurrection and the return of Christ (for example, 14:18ff.); with the Resurrection of Jesus, by reason of which he is now with his disciples forevermore, his return has already begun.

That Luke did not have an essentially different understanding of the situation is again clear from today's reading. In it Christ rebuffs the disciples' question about the restoration of the kingdom and instead tells them that they will receive the Holy Spirit and be his witnesses to the ends of the earth. Therefore, they are not to remain staring into the future or to wait broodingly for the time of his return. No, they are to realize that he is ceaselessly present and even that he desires to become ever more present through their activity, inasmuch as the gift of the Spirit and the commission to bear witness, preach, and be missionaries are the way in which Christ is now already present. On the basis of this passage, we may say that the proclamation of the Good News everywhere in the world is the way in which the Lord, during the period between the Resurrection and the Second Coming, gives expression to his kingship over all the world, as he exercises his dominion in the humble form of the word.

Christ exercises his power through the powerlessness of the word by which he calls man to faith. This fact reminds us once again of the image of the cloud, in which the Lord's hiddenness and nearness are combined in a unique way. John the Evangelist has depicted this fusion even more comprehensively by the new meaning he has poured into the Old Testament term "raise up", or "exalt". This word, which had hitherto expressed only the idea of elevation to royal dignity, also refers in John to the crucifixion, in which Christ is "lifted up" from the earth. For John, then, the mystery of Good Friday, of Easter, and of Christ's Ascension form but a single mystery. The Cross has a second, mysterious dimension: it is the royal throne from which Christ exercises his kingship and draws mankind to himself and into his wide-open arms (cf. Jn 3:14; 8:28; 12:32–33). Christ's royal throne is the Cross; his exaltation takes the form of what seems to the outsider the extreme of disgrace and humiliation.

This final New Testament explanation of the "Ascension into heaven" implies at the same time the claim that faith makes on man and the promise that faith offers him. For, the Christ who became king of the world through complete self-surrender and radical self-despoliation on the Cross and whose embrace is big enough to include everyone is the counterpart of the first Adam, that is, of all of us—that first Adam who sought in arrogant independence to exalt and divinize himself but thereby only destroyed and lost himself. Thus the exaltation of Christ, which makes its appearance in this eon only under the sign of the Cross, expresses the law of the grain of wheat, a law that holds good for all of us: "Unless a grain of wheat falls into the earth and dies, it remains alone; but if it dies, it bears much fruit" (Jn 12:24).

The feast of Christ's exaltation, which we are celebrating today, is evidently marked by great seriousness, and yet its fundamental feature is hope and joy. God has a place for man! Should we not react to this Good News as the disciples did who returned home from the Mount of Olives "with great joy"? Today there are only too many people trying to convince us that it is absurd to imagine that God, who encompasses the world, can spare a thought for man or be bothered with him at all. How petty their conception of God must be, since they think of him as being like us, who are forced to choose because we cannot survey everything at once! How far superior an understanding of God that unknown thinker had to whom we owe the splendid sentence that the poet Hölderlin took as a motto for his *Hyperion*: "Not to be contained by even the greatest reality, and yet to contain even the smallest— *that* is divine." In God there is a place for us! The confident words with which the African ecclesiastical writer Tertullian summed up the meaning of Christ's Ascension over fifteen hundred years ago are no more outdated today than when they were written: "Be consoled, flesh and blood, for in Christ you have taken possession of heaven and of God's kingdom" (*De carne Christi* 17).

31. Mind, Spirit, and Love

A Meditation on Pentecost

Is it really worth our while on feast days to pause for a moment and reflect on their meaning and, in the process, on the meaning of our own life, with its restlessness, hopes, and anxieties? Or is such a practice just a bourgeois custom, a desire for a bit of tinsel, a pious attempt to use earlier times as a means of "transfiguring" our own lives, and an attempt that we really ought to abandon once and for all?

For many people Pentecost is undoubtedly just a name for a long weekend on which they shift gears from everyday routine to leisure. They may spend the weekend endangering life and limb; in any case, it is just as hectic and agitated for them as their typical weekday, but at least it offers the advantage of change, perhaps an illusion of freedom, perhaps even moments of real relaxation and satisfaction.

It would be foolish, of course, to look with condescending irony on weekends and the leisure they afford. Every one of us, after all, is happy about the chance for freedom that a weekend brings, even if views on how best to use the time surely differ greatly. And yet anyone who lives a truly conscious life will be unable to settle for being passively driven from work to leisure and from leisure back to work again; now and then such a person must pause and ask where his life is leading and where mankind and the world as a whole are heading. He will have to accept his small share of responsibility for all this activity and its direction and not simply enjoy access to an ever wider selection of consumer goods without asking where it comes from and where it is leading them.

Consequently, the person who is living with some degree of self-awareness will surely not regard reflection on a feast as so incredibly outmoded and purposeless as it might seem at first glance. When Pentecost comes around, he can remind himself, first of all, that in one

Translated by Matthew J. O'Connell.

form or another this feast has to do with what we call "spirit". Even a person for whom access to the Christian faith has become difficult will be moved to various reflections by this reminder.

What, then, is really meant by "spirit"? Today we encounter "spirit" chiefly as the rational mind that calculates and deals with the kind of stored-up knowledge that the computer can collect and manipulate; the mind that plans and, in the process, turns us into parts of a gigantic apparatus that no one can grasp in its entirety any longer but that moves forward and makes men both now and in their future an increasingly calculable element in an all-embracing whole.

When we hear this kind of talk and see the prospect opening before us of a mathematized world in which the last traces of romanticism have been swept away, then, despite all our hopes and expectations, we may well feel dismayed. For, even though we cannot deny the advantages, the comfort, the hopes, and everything great and liberating that the rationalization of the world has produced, yet we spontaneously understand statements like those of Jean Rostand: "I am so afraid of the natural sciences precisely because my faith is in them alone",[1] or of Henri Bergson, who in contemplating the vast technological development that the twentieth century has witnessed came to the conclusion that mankind today "has too big a body for its soul".[2]

But the question then arises: Is the reality of "spirit" really coextensive with what we have been describing, or does it reach farther? Is spirit to be found only in the "positivistic" form of the computer, or does it also take the form of what Bergson calls "soul"? In fact, do we perhaps encounter the real meaning and phenomenon of spirit, the element that is decisive and liberating, only when we move beyond the kind of "spirit" that can be stored in computers? Here we approach once again the threshold of decision that Pentecost challenges us to cross. It takes a decision to move from weekend to feast, from the simple use of the machinery of consumerism to reflection on it. It takes a further decision to pass from the calculating spirit at work in the science of planning to something greater that is admittedly more hidden as well.

Pierre-Henri Simon suggests that in dealing with all we have been describing thus far, we should speak about "mind" rather than about

---

[1] Quoted from P.-H. Simon, *Woran ich glaube* (Tübingen, 1967), 176; to this important book I owe the initial ideas for the present meditation.

[2] Cited in Simon, *Woran ich glaube*, 180.

"spirit". Mind, then, is the sum of the receptive, logical, and pragmatic powers of consciousness. Spirit, on the other hand, discovers the order of values that lies beyond facts, the freedom that transcends law, the kind of existence in which justice has priority over self-interest.[3] Spirit, thus understood, is not the object of calculation and computer storage; it is correlated precisely with what is incalculable. It is a name for an attitude "that brings fulfillment and happiness to the self by bursting through the limitations of self-centeredness"; an attitude, in other words, that requires a decision of the heart, of the whole person.

When one reaches this threshold, he has, of course, not yet reached the Christian message of Pentecost. The decision, as I have been describing it, for "spirit" over against positivism is one that even non-Christians can make; it is within the power of all mankind. At the same time, however, the decision does represent the point at which people today will become capable of understanding once again what is meant by Christian faith in the Creator Spirit who renews the earth.

To most of our contemporaries and often even to those of them who mean to be believing Christians, the Pentecost message of the Bible and of those who preach it sounds like the stammering of a drunkard or the unintelligible babbling of dreamers who have not yet noticed that we have emerged into the daylight of the modern era, in which such talk is no longer acceptable. The people who react in this way hardly realize that in the confrontation between the "positive" and the "spiritual", between individuals who serve only the great machine and those who despite everything believe in contemplation and love, in truth and the abiding values that it yields—that in this confrontation they are, in the last analysis, face to face with the reality of Pentecost. When all is said and done, the urgent question of our time is whether mankind is to be saved by the perfecting of the "apparatus" or whether, on the contrary, Pascal's words still hold true: "All bodies together and all minds together and all their works are of less worth than the smallest act of charity."[4]

But let us come at last to the main question. What is the real Christian message of Pentecost? What is this "Holy Spirit" of which it speaks? The Acts of the Apostles gives us an answer in the form of an image;

---

[3] Ibid., 175–83.

[4] Pascal, *Pensées*, fragment 829, in *Oeuvres completes*, ed. J. Chevalier (Paris: Bibliothèque de la Pléiade, 1954), 1341f. Cf. the thorough analysis of this passage in R. Guardini, *Christliches Bewußtsein: Versuche über Pascal*, 2nd ed. (Munich, 1950), 40ff. and 101ff.

perhaps there is no other way of expressing it, since the reality of the Spirit largely escapes our grasp. It relates that the disciples were touched by fiery tongues and found themselves speaking in a manner that some (the "positivists") regarded as drunken stammering, a meaningless, useless babbling, while others, people from all parts of the then known world, each heard the disciples speaking in his own tongue.

In the background of this text is the Old Testament story of the tower of Babel; taken together with this, the Acts of the Apostles provides us with a penetrating insight into the theology of history. The Old Testament account tells us that men, their sense of independence augmented by the progress they had made, attempted to build a tower that would reach heaven. That is, they believed that by their own powers of planning and constructing they could even build a bridge to heaven, make heaven accessible to themselves by their own efforts, and turn man into a deity. The result of their effort was the confusion of tongues. Mankind, which seeks only itself and looks for salvation in the satisfaction of a ruthless egoism by means of economic power, suffers instead the consequence of egoism, which is the radical opposition of each to his fellows, so that no one understands the other any longer and, consequently, even egoism remains unfulfilled.

The New Testament account of Pentecost takes up these same ideas. It is also convinced that contemporary mankind is characterized by disunity, by a superficial coexistence and a hostility that are based on self-divinization. As a result, everything is seen in a false perspective; man ends up understanding neither God nor the world nor his fellowman nor himself. The "Holy Spirit" creates such an understanding because he is the Love that flows from the Cross, from the self-renunciation of Jesus Christ.

We need not attempt here to reflect in detail on the various dogmatic connections that are implied in such a description. For our purpose, it is enough to recall the way Augustine tried to sum up the essential point of the Pentecost narrative. World history, he says, is a struggle between two kinds of love: self-love to the point of hatred for God, and love of God to the point of self-renunciation. This second love brings the redemption of the world and the self.[5]

In my opinion, it would already be a giant step forward if during

---

[5] Concerning Augustine's evaluation of the opposition between Babylon and Pentecost, see J. Ratzinger, *Die Einheit der Nationen* (Salzburg and Munich, 1971), 71–106.

the days of Pentecost we were to turn from the thoughtless use of our leisure to a reflection on our responsibility; if these days were to become the occasion for moving beyond purely rational thinking, beyond the kind of knowledge that is used in planning and can be stored up, to a discovery of "spirit", of the responsibility that truth brings, and of the values of conscience and love. Even if for the moment we did not find our way to Christianity, strictly speaking, we would already be touching the hem of Christ and his Spirit. In the long run, after all, "truth" and "love" cannot subsist in a vacuum, without relation to other things. If they are the timeless measure and the real hope of man, then they are not simply a part of the ever-changing historical scene but, rather, the point of reference for the movement of history. They are not remote ideas but have a face and a name. They issue a call to us. For they are "Love", that is to say, a person.

The Holy Spirit is truly "spirit" in the fullest possible sense of the word. In all probability, we must make our stumbling way to him anew from the midst of a profoundly changed world. Many perhaps will think it impossible to travel that way to the end, that is, to the "sober drunkenness" of Pentecost faith. But the urgent question raised by Pentecost, a question that disturbs that terrible "sleep of conscience" of which Pierre-Henri Simon speaks,[6] is one that should and could apply to us all. The mighty wind of Pentecost blows on all of us, even today, especially today.

[6] Ibid., 190.

32. The Meaning of Advent

Confronted with the externalism and distortion to which Advent and the Christmas season are increasingly subject, the Church has experienced the awakening of a lively desire for an authentic Advent based on faith. The unsatisfactory nature of all mere moods, of all mere feelings, however exquisite, has become evident, and we yearn again for the heart of the matter, for that strong solid nourishment for the spirit of which only a glimmer is left for us now in the pious, exalted sentiments we have during the "blessed and joyous Christmas season". What, then, is the real heart of the Advent experience?

We may start with the word itself. "Advent" does not, for example, mean "expectation", as some may think. It is a translation of the Greek word *parousia*, which means "presence" or, more accurately, "arrival", that is, the beginning of a presence. In antiquity the word was a technical term for the presence of a king or ruler and also of the god being worshipped, who bestows upon his devotees the time of his *parousia*. "Advent", then, means the presence begun—the presence of God himself.

Advent reminds us, therefore, of two things: first, that God's presence in the world has already begun, that he is present, albeit in a hidden manner; second, that his presence has only *begun* and is not yet full and complete, that it is in a state of development, of becoming, and maturing toward its full form. His presence has already begun, and we, the faithful, are the ones through whom he wishes to be present in the world. Through our faith, hope, and love, he wants his light to shine over and over again into the night of the world.

The lamps we light on the dark nights of this winter season are both a comfort and a warning. They are a comforting assurance that "the Light of the world" has already begun to shine in the dark night of

Translated by Matthew J. O'Connell.

Bethlehem and that the unholy night of man's sin has been transformed into the holy night of God's forgiveness. They are also a warning: this Light wants to keep shining and will do so only if it shines in those who as Christians carry on Christ's work through the ages. Christ seeks to illumine the night of the world with his light by having us be lights in our turn. His initial presence is to grow through us.

Therefore, during the holy night of Christmas, when we hear again and again the words resound: "Hodie Christus natus est": Today Christ is born, it should remind us that what was begun at Bethlehem is meant to increase through our constant new beginnings and that the holy night truly can be, and is, "today" whenever man allows the light of goodness within him to shine through his self-centeredness and egoism. That night is "today" whenever the "Word" again becomes "flesh", the reality of deeds. "The Christ Child comes" in a real sense whenever men act out of authentic love for the Lord and do not settle for a mere exchange of "gifts".

Advent means the arrival of the Lord that has *already* begun but has *only just* begun. This also means that the Christian looks not only to the past and what has been but also to what is coming. Amid all the catastrophes of this world, he has a transcendent certainty that the seed of the Light is growing in secret, until one day the good will achieve a definitive victory and all else will be made subject to it. On that day, Christ will come again. The Christian knows that the presence of God that has now only begun will someday be a full and complete presence. This knowledge sets him free and gives him an ultimate security.

With that, basically, the decisive point about Advent has now been made. But the Church realizes that man does not live on abstract truths but on concrete images. Therefore, she sets the meaning of Advent before us in lively pictures. It may be said that the liturgy of Advent paints a kind of triptych. On one panel of the tripartite altar stands John the Baptist, the great figure that dominates Advent. The other side panel shows Mary, the Mother of the Lord. They both point to the central panel and to Christ himself. John the Baptist and Mary are the two great types of Advent existence. Therefore, they dominate the liturgy of Advent.

Let us look first at JOHN THE BAPTIST. Challenging and active, he stands before us, a type of the masculine mission in life. He is the stern herald who summons the people to *metanoia:* to a change of heart or conversion. Anyone who wants to be a Christian must be constantly "changing his thinking or outlook". By nature, we are inclined to be always asserting ourselves, repaying in kind, making ourselves the center of attention. If we want to find God, we must be constantly undergoing an interior conversion, turning around and moving in the opposite direction, and this even in the way we understand life as a whole.

Day in and day out, we are confronted with the world of visible things. So strongly and insistently does it impinge on us through billboards, the radio, commerce, and every incident of daily life that we are tempted to think nothing else exists. But in fact the invisible is greater and more valuable than all visible reality. According to a marvelous saying of Pascal, a single soul is worth more than the entire visible universe. But if we are to grasp this truth in a vivid way, we must be converted; we must, as it were, do an interior about-face, overcome the spell that visible reality casts over us, and acquire a sensitive touch, ear, and eye for the invisible. We must treat the invisible as more important than all the things that thrust themselves upon us with such force day after day. "Be converted": change your thinking, your outlook, so that you perceive God's presence in the world; change your thinking so that God may become present in you and, through you, in the world.

John himself was not spared this difficult process of changing his mind-set, of having to convert, of undergoing what de Lubac calls "the alchemy of being". It already begins with his having to proclaim, as one crying in the wilderness, a man whom he himself does not know. Is it not the fate of the priest and of every Christian who proclaims Christ that we, too, know him and yet do not know him, that we, too, despite the darkness of our ignorance, must bear witness to him whom unfortunately we still know, and will always know, only too imperfectly?

But the real passion of John, the real crucible in which his whole being was melted down and recast for God, began in earnest with the activity of Christ during the time when John was in prison. The darkness of the prison cell was not the most terrible darkness John had to endure. His real darkness was what Martin Buber has called "the eclipse of God": the abrupt uncertainty John experienced regarding his own mission and the identity of the one for whom he had sought to prepare the way.

In words of burning power, John had prophesied the coming of the judge and had painted in fiery colors the great day of the Lord. He had portrayed the Messiah as the judge with the winnowing fan in his hand that would separate the chaff from the grain and throw the chaff once and for all into the eternal fire. He had portrayed him as one who would cast out this adulterous generation and, if need be, raise up children of Abraham from the very stones to replace the faithless people who called themselves the children of Abraham; as the one who had already laid the axe to the root so as to cut down the tree. Above all, amid the terrible ambivalence of this world where we are constantly waiting and hoping in darkness, John had expected and proclaimed a clear message: that the day would finally come and dispel the hopeless darkness in which men are tossed to and fro so that they know not where they are going. The ambiguity would disappear, and men would no longer have to grope their way in the endless mist but would know for certain that this and no other is God's unequivocal claim on them, that this and no other is their situation in relation to God.

Meanwhile the One had come, and, at God's command, John's prophetic finger pointed him out. "Behold the Lamb of God, who takes away the sin of the world!" (Jn 1:29). God's presence had begun . . . but what a difference from what John had imagined! No fire fell from heaven to consume sinners and bear definitive witness to the just; in fact, nothing changed at all in the present world. Jesus went about preaching and doing good in the land, but the ambiguity remained. Human life continued to be an obscure mystery that man has to pursue with faith and hope into the world's darkness.

Clearly it was this utterly different character of Jesus that most tormented John during the long nights in prison: the eclipse of God continued—and the imperturbable advance of a world history that is so often a slap in the face to believers. In his distress, John sent messengers to the Lord: "Are you he who is to come, or shall we look for another?" (Mt 11:3). It is a question all of us could have asked during the nighttime bombings of the Second World War and are inclined to ask over and over again in all the distresses of our own lives: "Are you really he: the world's redemption? Are you really the Redeemer? Was that really all that God had to say to us?"

In answer, Jesus reminds John's messengers of what the prophet Isaiah had said in foretelling precisely this kind of peaceful, merciful

Messiah who "will not cry or lift up his voice, or make it heard in the street" (Is 42:2), but will go about preaching and doing good. Jesus adds the significant words: "Blessed is he who takes no offense at me." Blessed is he who ceases to ask for signs and absolute certainty. Blessed is he who is able, even in this darkness, to go his way in faith and love.

This was probably the final task assigned to the Baptist in prison: to become blessed by this unquestioning acceptance of God's obscure will; to reach the point of no longer demanding external, visible, unequivocal clarity but, instead, of discovering God precisely in the darkness of this world and of his own life and, thus, becoming profoundly blessed. In point of fact, we cannot see God as we see an apple tree or a neon sign, that is, in a purely external way that requires no interior commitment. We can see him only by becoming like him, by reaching the level of reality on which God exists; in other words, by being liberated from what is anti-divine: the quest for pleasure, enjoyment, possessions, gain, or, in a word, from ourselves. In the final analysis, it is usually the self that stands between us and God. We can see God only if we turn around, stop looking for him as we might look for street signs and dollar bills, and begin looking away from the visible to the invisible.

John, then, even in his prison cell had to respond once again and anew to his own call for *metanoia* or a change of heart, in order that he might recognize his God in the night in which all earthly things exist. "Blessed is he who takes no offense at me."

No other way of reaching an understanding with God can be shown to the Christian of today, either: he must stop looking for external clarity and begin to turn from the visible to the invisible and, thus, truly find the Lord who is the real foundation and support of our existence. When we do so, another and doubtless the greatest saying of the Baptist acquires its full significance: "He must increase, but I must decrease" (Jn 3:30). We will know God to the extent that we are set free from ourselves. This brings us back to the main theme of Advent: We will know God to the extent that we give him room to be present in us. A person can spend his life seeking God in vain if he does not allow God to continue in his life the presence begun.

The second panel in the Advent triptych shows MARY, the pure handmaid of the Lord. At first her message is of quite a different sort: she is a model, not of masculine activity, but of feminine receptivity.

Among us Germans, the Gospel of the Annunciation to Mary and the miraculous conception of the Son of God is read daily in the *Rorate* Masses.[1] "The angel Gabriel was sent from God to a city of Galilee named Nazareth, to a virgin betrothed to a man whose name was Joseph, of the house of David, and the virgin's name was Mary. And he came in to her and said, 'Hail, full of grace . . .'" (Lk 1:27–28).

This scene is one of the fateful moments of world history, for at this moment and in this place the presence of God—in the full sense of the term—truly began among men. Here there was a real "Advent". But we must observe that this fateful moment of world history was also one of history's most silent and hidden moments. It was a forgotten moment that no newspaper recorded and no illustrated magazine mentioned or would have mentioned, had such a thing existed at the time. What is proclaimed to us here, then, is first and foremost a mystery of silence.

That which is truly great grows unnoticed, and silence at the right moment is more fruitful than the constant busyness that all too easily degenerates into spiritual idling. In the present age, when [European] public life is being Americanized, we are all possessed by a strange restlessness that suspects any silence of being a waste of time and any tranquility of being negligence. Every bit of time is weighed and measured, and in the process we forget the real mystery of time, the real mystery present in growth and activity. That mystery involves silence and stillness.

Even in the religious sphere we tend to expect and hope for everything from our own activity. We use all kinds of exercises and initiatives to sidestep the real mystery of interior growth before God. And yet in the religious sphere, receptivity is at least as important as activity.

This brings us to a second point: the mystery of the Annunciation to Mary is not only a mystery of silence; it is also, and even more, a mystery of grace. We must ask ourselves: What is the real reason why Christ decided to be born of a virgin? It would have been quite possible for him to be born of a normal marriage; that would not have detracted from his Divine Sonship, which of course is independent of

---

[1] In older liturgical practice the *Rorate* Masses—originally votive Masses celebrated in honor of the Mother of God on the Saturdays of Advent—were celebrated on the weekdays of Advent and were quite popular. In the reformed liturgy in Germany, these Masses can still be celebrated on the weekdays of Advent until December 16 inclusively.—Trans.

the Virgin Birth and would be not at all unthinkable even under other circumstances. The Virgin Birth did not signify any depreciation of marriage and conjugal union, nor was it required in order to safeguard the Divine Sonship of Jesus. Why, then, did it occur?

We find the reason when we open the Old Testament and see how the way was already prepared for the mystery of Mary at decisive points in the history of salvation. The process begins with Sarah, the mother of Isaac, a women who was barren; only when she is well on in years and her vitality has withered does she become by God's power the mother of Isaac and, thus, of the chosen people. The preparation continues with Hannah, the mother of Samuel, who is likewise barren but eventually gives birth; with the mother of Samson; and again with Elizabeth, the mother of John the Baptist.

The point of what happens is the same in all these instances: they show that salvation comes, not from men and their own powers, but solely from God and his gracious action. That is why God intervenes where there is a complete vacuum; he starts at the point where, humanly speaking, nothing can be done. He gives life to the bearer of the promise in the dead womb of Sarah and follows the same pattern through history down to the Lord's birth from the Virgin. The law he follows is spelled out in Isaiah 54:1 (Gal 4:27): "Sing, O barren one, who did not bear; break forth into singing and cry aloud, you who have not had labor pains! For the children of the desolate one will be more than the children of her that is married, says the LORD."

The meaning—let us repeat it (it is already brought out in Romans 4)—is that the salvation of the world is exclusively God's doing and therefore occurs in the midst of human weakness and powerlessness. From the viewpoint of the Bible, the Virgin Birth is in the last analysis a sign that what occurs is a pure act of grace on God's part. It is a symbol of grace, the most fully real verification of Mary's words: "He has put down the mighty from their thrones, and exalted those of low degree" (Lk 1:52).

And yet the mystery of grace that takes place in Mary does not create a distance between us and her and make her unapproachable, turning her into an object of mere (and therefore empty, meaningless) wonder. On the contrary, she becomes a consoling sign of grace, for she proclaims the God whose light shone on the ignorant shepherds and whose mercy raised up the lowly in Israel and the world. She proclaims the

God who is "greater than our hearts" (1 Jn 3:20) and whose grace is stronger than all our weakness and, indeed, has already outstripped and overcome this weakness. If John the Baptist represents the unsettling seriousness of the divine summons, Mary represents the hidden but profound joy that this summons brings: "Rejoice in the Lord always; again I will say, Rejoice" (Phil 4:4).

Joy is a basic element in Christianity, for by its very nature Christianity is and ought to be "Gospel", or good news. Yet precisely here the world is mistaken about the Gospel and Christ; people leave the Church in the name of the joy of which (they say) Christianity with all its countless demands and prohibitions deprives men! Admittedly, the joy of Christ is not as easy to see as the trivial pleasure deriving from this or that satisfaction. On the other hand, it would be incorrect to interpret the words "Rejoice in the Lord" as though they read "Rejoice, *but* in the Lord" and as though the added clause really took back what is said in the opening verb. No, the sentence reads simply, "Rejoice in the Lord", because the Apostle quite evidently believes that all genuine joy is connected with the Lord and that apart from him there can be no genuine joy.

And the fact remains that all joy that arises independently of Christ or contrary to his will proves insufficient and only thrusts the person back down into a turmoil in which, when all is said and done, he can find no lasting joy. So the Scripture verse is telling us that authentic joy has made its appearance only with Christ and that ultimately nothing matters in our lives except to learn to see and know Christ, the God of grace, the Light and Joy of the world. Our joy will be genuine only when it no longer depends on things that can be snatched away from us and destroyed and when it has its basis rather in those innermost depths of our existence which no worldly power can take from us. Every external loss should turn us back to these innermost depths and better dispose us for our true life.

So it is that the two side panels of the Advent triptych, John and Mary, both point and refer to the central panel, to CHRIST, their source and destiny, who alone makes them intelligible. To celebrate Advent means—let us say it again—to bring to life within ourselves the hidden presence of God. John and Mary show us how this awakening takes place. It takes place to the extent that we travel the path of conversion and of a change of heart by turning from the visible to the invisible. As we travel this path, we learn to see the miracle of grace; we learn that there can be no more luminous source of joy for men and the world than the grace that has appeared in Christ.

The world is not a futile commotion of drudgery and pain, for all the world's distress is supported in the arms of merciful love; it is caught up and surpassed by the forgiving and saving graciousness of our God. The person who celebrates Advent in this spirit will legitimately be able to speak of "the joyous, blessed, and grace-filled season of Christmas". He will know that there is much more truth to these words than is believable or imaginable to those people for whom Christmas is just a time for picturesque sentimentality or merely a sort of simplified carnival celebration.

33. Three Meditations on Christmas

1. God Has Crossed Over to Us

Today it is practically obligatory for a theologian or preacher to direct more or less withering criticism at the conventional way in which we celebrate Christmas and to contrast the placid comfort of our festivities with the hard reality of the first Christmas. Christmas—they tell us—has been commercialized irredeemably; it has degenerated into a meaningless commercial bustle. Its piety has been sentimentalized; the celebration of the unfathomable mystery of God's Incarnation has turned into a cheap melodrama that is focused on a pretty, curly-haired baby, mixed with a little romanticism about the family and much emphasis on bourgeois contentment. In fact, in most instances all that survives of religion is a whiff of sentimentality; people find it comforting once a year, on this night when all the lights blaze out, to be touched by a feeling that stirs reveries of childhood and an idealized time now long past.

The criticism is undoubtedly justified in large measure, even though it has not sufficiently borne in mind the fact that, behind the façade of commercialism and sentimentality, the yearning for the original greatness has not wholly disappeared. Indeed, the sentimentality acts as a screen behind which a profound and pure feeling hides, too shy to reveal itself to the gaze of others. Nevertheless, we have no trouble in admitting that the criticism is justified in the main. In the long run, however, it begins to prove somewhat suspect inasmuch as the idealized picture it presents of the Christmas celebration and Christmas piety seems quite incapable of being turned into a reality. Finally, the critics themselves cannot escape the conditions of our time and would even feel somewhat deprived and outcast if they unexpectedly managed to do it.

Translated by Matthew J. O'Connell.

All this suggests that we should try in a different way to find a meaningful idea of Christmas. It must be possible to reflect on and retain the main points of the criticism but also to discover the solid, uncorrupted core of the sort of celebration being criticized, that is, the original significance and meaning that lie hidden in it and that became the point of departure for the exaggerations and abuses. If we adopted this approach, we would at the same time—within our own limits, as it were, in the context of the reality that is ours—find the starting point for a meaningful interpretation of these days of Christmas. Then we would not have to throw ourselves directly into the magnificent but all too unfamiliar realm of that spirituality which (we rightly suspect) contains the source of a more authentic and purer piety.

Let us start, then, with the fact that our celebration has become commercialized. What is behind the feverish concentration on business that rightly repels us and is actually the condition least suited for reminding us of the unobtrusive mystery of Bethlehem, the mystery of the God who became a beggar for our sakes (2 Cor 8:9)? Does all this incongruous activity not still start from the idea of giving, that is, from the impulse that is at the heart of love and forces it to communicate itself and share what it has with the other? And does the idea of giving, in turn, not take us to the very heart of the mystery of Christmas?

The Offertory prayer for the Mass of December 24 asks that we may receive with joy the eternal gifts that come to us through the celebration of Christ's birth.[1] The prayer shows that the idea of giving is anchored in the Church's liturgy. At the same time, it reminds us of the original Christmas gift: God determined that on this holy night he would give his very self as a gift to man, and in fact he did give himself over to us. The real Christmas gift to mankind, to human history, and to each of us is Jesus Christ himself. Even someone who does not believe that he is God incarnate will have to admit that through generation after generation Jesus Christ has made man interiorly rich and

[1] This meditation of Cardinal Ratzinger, previously unpublished, was written before the revision of the Missal after the Second Vatican Council. At this point and in subsequent paragraphs (cf. nn. 2 and 3), he is using texts that in the Ordinary Form of the Roman Rite no longer occur in the precise place he indicates. They are, however, still to be found either on December 24 (with its two Masses) or on days shortly before Christmas.

The prayer that in the traditional Missal was the prayer over the gifts in the Vigil Mass is now the Post-Communion Prayer for the morning Mass (as distinct from the Vigil Mass) on December 24.—Trans.

fulfilled and that, independently of belief or unbelief, he is among the greatest treasures of mankind. Every Christmas gift, therefore, ought to reflect that gesture of divine love which in the final analysis could and would give nothing less than itself. Whether a gift is expensive or cheap matters little: if we have not given a bit of ourselves along with it, any gift we give is too small.

This brings us back to our present-day situation. Are we not in fact attempting to make money a substitute for our hearts? To buy our way out of the real challenge of giving? Has not commercialism long since ruined the gesture of giving? Above all, if we look at our Christmas giving from this vantage point, will we not be stirred to reflection by these words of Jesus: "If you love those who love you, what reward have you? Do not even the tax collectors do the same? And if you salute only your brethren, what more are you doing than others? Do not even the Gentiles do the same?" (Mt 5:46–47).

As a matter of fact, Christmas giving has largely degenerated into a kind of calculated exchange and has thus lost its soul. The Christmas liturgy does, of course, speak of a holy exchange of gifts initiated by God, but this exchange consists of God taking upon himself our human existence in order to bestow his divine existence on us, of his choosing our nothingness in order to give us his plenitude. If we learned to see this exchange as the model for our gift giving, we would practice a more human form of giving and would be concerned chiefly with a generosity that looks for no gift in return.

But let us get back to the main line of our reflections: we were considering the conventional criticism of our Christmas celebration with a view to criticizing it in turn. The criticism goes on to say that in the consciousness of devout people today, Christmas has lost its magnificent content and been turned into an innocuous idyll centered on a divine infant. Here again we must admit that the criticism is salutary and needed. We have only to look at the texts of the Christmas liturgy to see how far removed they are from such a belittling approach.

One of the threads running through the Vigil Mass is the singing of Psalm 24 [23], which celebrates Yahweh as the king who is entering the temple: "Lift up your gates, O princes, and be lifted up, O eternal gates, and the King of glory shall come in" (Ps 24 [23]:7, Offertory, according to the Latin text in the old Missal).[2] Originally this psalm

---

[2] Again, Cardinal Ratzinger is referring to the Extraordinary Form of the Roman Rite.

was probably sung during the entry of the sacred ark into the Temple at Jerusalem; perhaps it was part of a "gate liturgy" in which the Temple gates were personified and summoned to make way for God the King. In the Christmas liturgy, then, the event at Bethlehem is regarded as the festive entry of the king; the world, the whole earth, is his sanctuary, which is summoned to open its gates wide and give entry to the Creator.

The Entrance Antiphon and the chant after the Epistle repeat the mighty promise with which Moses announces to the complaining people the miracle of the manna in the wilderness: "Today you shall know that the Lord will come and save us, and in the morning you shall see his glory" (Ex 16:6–7). Christ is thus presented as the true manna, as the real, royally magnificent and bold answer God gives to the complaints of men, for whom any venture with God is too much a plunge into darkness and who would prefer to sink into the comfort of a well-supplied existence as slave who does not have to take responsibility for his own future. Finally, the Communion Antiphon uses the words of the prophet Isaiah (40:5) to depict the event of Bethlehem as the revelation of God's glory.

Only in the perspective provided by these various Old Testament texts do we see Bethlehem aright. The scene that takes place there is not a touching little domestic idyll, but a reversal that encompasses heaven and earth. God is no longer separated from us by the iron curtain of his inaccessible otherworldliness; he has crossed the dividing line to become one of us. From this point on, he himself comes to meet me in my neighbor, and any worship oblivious to my fellowmen would also miss the God who has taken on a human face.

At the same time, however, if we think this idea through to its logical conclusion, we will realize that behind the trivialized rapture about a God who becomes a child stands a powerful Christian idea that in fact leads us to the innermost core of the Christmas mystery. For at the heart of the mystery is the paradox that the glory of God decided to manifest himself, not in the triumphal advance of a Caesar subduing the world by force, but in the helplessness of a child who is overlooked by

---

In the Ordinary Form, Psalm 24 is used as a Responsorial Psalm on December 20 and on the Fourth Sunday of Advent (A), but verse 7 is not one of the verses recited. Exodus 16:6–7 and Isaiah 40:5, however, are still used for the Entrance Antiphon and Communion Antiphon, respectively, in the Vigil Mass; the Latin text in the revised Missal is the same as in the traditional Missal.—Trans.

adult society and comes into the world in a stable. The powerlessness of a child has become the proper expression of God's omnipotence, for the only force he employs is the silent force of truth and love.

It was, then, in the defenseless weakness of a child that God wanted us to have our first encounter with saving mercy. And, in fact, how comforting it is, amid all the self-assertiveness of this world's powers, to see the peaceful tranquility of God and, thus, to experience the security emanating from a power that in the end will be stronger than any other force and will outlast all the loud triumphal cries of the world. What freedom proceeds from such knowledge, and what loving kindness it contains!

A great deal more could be thought and said on the point I have just made, but we shall turn instead to consider a final criticism leveled against our contemporary way of celebrating Christmas. I am referring to the assertion that in this celebration the truly religious spirit has been diluted into nice but meaningless feelings.

Once again, it is unfortunately all too true that for many people religion has been transmuted into a sentiment that is no longer supported by reality, because the faith that formerly gave rise to the feelings has now disappeared. Yet in many respects another attitude is perhaps even more dangerous: the attitude of those who regard themselves as religious but limit religion to the realm of feeling and allow it no contact with the sober rationalism of their daily life in which they seek nothing but personal gain. It is clear that such behavior is only a caricature of authentic faith. The unparalleled realism of the divine love of which Christmas speaks and the action of the God who is not satisfied with words but takes on himself the wretched burden of human life—these should challenge us anew, year after year, to examine the realism of our faith and to strive for something more than the sentimentality of mere feeling.

But, while recognizing this need, we must at the same time avoid any undue condemnation of feeling. Once again, the Vigil Mass says something that offers food for reflection. In the Post-Communion prayer of this Mass, the faithful ask God to let them "catch their breath" by means of the celebration of his Son's birth.[3] How they are to breathe is not specified, and consequently we are free to take the word in the

---

[3] The Post-Communion Prayer for December 24 in the traditional Missal is, in the Ordinary Form of the Roman Rite, used as the Post-Communion Prayer of the Vigil Mass (as distinct from morning Mass on the 24th), but the verb *respirare*, "to breathe", has been

simply and properly human sense it has at first sight. In other words, the feast is meant to let us catch our breath again. The hustle and bustle with which we have cluttered the feast nowadays causes us to be short of breath and smothers us in a rush to meet deadlines. But then, according to this prayer, it can be said with all the more assurance that the feast is given to us so that we can have a little peace and quiet; that we should unhesitatingly accept as God's gift the good feeling of festivity that the day brings us.

In thus catching our breath, we may even be touched by the breath of that divine love and holy peace which the holy feast of Christmas bestows. For this reason we should not try to take away, from those who think they can no longer believe, the feeling that perhaps comes to them as a final echo of their faith and gives them some share in the "catching of breath" proper to this holy night that is so filled with the breath of divine peace. Rather, we should be grateful if they still enjoy this last little bit of God's Christmas gift, and we should try to be one with them all in celebrating a blessed Christmas.

2. Light in the Darkness

Over the fields of Bethlehem, on the night on which Jesus was born, according to the account given by Luke the Evangelist, an angelic song of praise resounded: "Glory to God in the highest, and on earth peace among men with whom he is pleased" (Lk 2:14).

In all probability, Luke here is deliberately setting up an alternative to the political philosophy current in the Roman Empire, which was put into words when Emperor Augustus took "Peace on Earth" as the motto for his reign and allowed Virgil to exalt him as "Son of God and Bringer of the Golden Age". The Evangelist is saying that the salvation of the world comes ultimately, not from Roman arms, but from the love—powerless in human terms—of the God who appeared at Bethlehem as a child.[4]

Today, two thousand years later, both of these promises sound almost ironical to us. The Roman Empire was in fact unable to secure a

---

replaced by *vegetari*, "to be enlivened, invigorated", or "strengthened", as it is translated in the English Missal of the Ordinary Form.—Trans.

[4] See A. A. J. Ehrhardt, *Politische Metaphysik von Solon bis Augustin* (Tübingen, 1959), 1:295, 303; 2:27; A. Stöger, *The Gospel according to St. Luke*, trans. B. Fahy (New York, 1969), 1:45–47.

lasting peace and managed to continue in existence only at the cost of repeated military conflicts, until finally it broke down itself under the pressure of stronger powers. But—and this distresses us much more— even faith in Jesus Christ was evidently not capable of bringing peace to the world. It even became a constant occasion for conflict and bloody battles. The post-Christian world in which we live today is not only overshadowed by fear of threats of annihilation that are far more terrible than anything previously known, but repeatedly and in ever new ways experiences the lack of peace in human life as an inescapable curse that no efforts on behalf of peace can remove.

The bright promises of Christmas now have a strongly melancholic ring to them. The "salvation of the world" of which they speak seems nowhere to be found. One half of mankind is starving and freezing; the ever-increasing masses of the deprived and forgotten groan under the burden of social inequality and suffer the lack of even the simplest prerequisites for a decent life; the pictures we see of them disturb us, but we do not know how we can effectively help them. The other half lives in affluence, but their satiety has become a scourge to them. Not only do we destroy what others lack, under the strange compulsion of economic laws that seem to subjugate man against his will; in addition, wealth itself torments modern man and makes his life unbearably empty even though it seems to bring fulfillment. The wealthy have everything and have enjoyed everything, yet everything is still too little to bring peace and fulfillment. On the contrary, it leaves behind it only disgust and a consciousness that nothing but disaster lies ahead.

The person who has everything he wants feels just as manipulated, abused, and mocked, in his own way, as the person who lacks everything. There is, then, a revolution against poverty, but there is also a revolution against enslavement to riches and consumerism; the satiated and the starving are strangely united by a common lack of peace.

In this situation, it is only with difficulty and hesitation that the Christian utters the Christmas message of peace. To the have-nots and the hungry, whose lot the message does not change, will it not seem like mockery from those who have, for whom such talk is easy? Is not the message really an empty consolation, an evasion hiding a bad conscience that seeks reassurance from it? And among those who have, is not the message just an empty sentiment with which they artfully contrive to conjure up a dim sacral radiance for their secular lives, even though the sacred has long since ceased to be a reality to them? Should we not, therefore, just skip the pious words and simply set about changing the world?

Or, on the contrary, does the Child of Bethlehem, who cannot make any direct show of earthly power, perhaps really matter to us? R. Raffalt recently put a question to Christians who are all too worldly in their concerns, and it is a question that should make us think: "In the final analysis, does not the person who is exploited, oppressed, and abused really want the same thing as his brother who has been devastated by comfort, sex, and drugs—to be able to believe?"[5]

Such a question should at least force us to ask ourselves seriously, once again, why we really celebrate Christmas, why we dare to celebrate it, despite the wretchedness, turmoil, and isolation that are still man's lot and, if anything, are intensifying rather than lessening. What is the real point of Christmas?

We might begin with an answer that is very human and does not yet bring us into the realm of faith proper. We might say: "Christmas is the birthday of a man, Jesus of Nazareth, who lived an irreproachable human life, that is, a life for others, and who sealed the authenticity of his life, his preaching, and his service by a death for others."

If someone should give this answer, a further question immediately arises: "Amid all the darkness that is mankind's lot, must not such a man be like a brilliant light that gives others hope?" Hope that the prospects for mankind cannot really be so bleak. Hope that in other men, too, the power of the pure and the holy may be able to work effectively. Such a hope then encourages others to make the message and the way of this man their own. We may not be able to turn darkness into light, but like him we can at least post the signs of hope along the road of history: signs of hope that are connected each with the others like a chain of lights and form islands of peace, understanding, and relief in the midst of the inhumane laws of material progress.

Is it not consoling to see how, despite all the misunderstandings, his message is heard? It is not only conflict that the message has produced, but also and even more the miracle of understanding, so that across ages and cultures, and even across the boundaries between religions, men find one another in his name. Distance vanishes, and people are

---

[5] R. Raffalt, *Das Ende des römischen Prinzips* (Munich, 1970), 21.

drawn together when this name is spoken. Is all that to be regarded as nothing? Are we to reject the tiny light because we want only the blazing flame?

Faith, of course, has more to offer, a deeper message: This man Jesus, who looms over history like a quiet light of peace and reconciliation and casts his rays across the millennia into even the prisons and ghettos of the world—this man is God come into our world. He is Light from Light, Son of God and very God. God is like Jesus. God is such that he can become and has in fact become a child; he is such that he can suffer and love as a man among men. Because our poor eyes simply could not see God as he is in himself, he has shown himself to us by the light of a man; it is really *his* light, but a light meant for us.

All that we said previously from a merely human perspective remains true, but in the context of faith it acquires an entirely new and truly redeeming depth. For Christmas says to us, amid all our doubts and bewilderment: God exists. Not as an infinitely distant power that can at best terrify us; not as being's ultimate ground that is not conscious of itself. Rather, he exists as One who is able to be concerned about us; he is such that everything we are and do lies open to his gaze. But that gaze is the gaze of love.

For anyone who accepts this in faith and knows it by faith, there is no longer any ultimate isolation. *He* is here. The light that one man became in history and for history is not a feeble accident, but Light from Light. The hope and encouragement that emanate from this light thus acquire a wholly new depth. But precisely because it is an entirely divine hope, we can and should accept it as an entirely human hope also and pass it on to others.

Viewed from this perspective, celebrating Christmas means accepting a feast we have not created for ourselves but have received from God as a gift. This fact radically differentiates the Church's feasts from mere leisure and from any entertainment we provide for ourselves. The reality of Christmas exists even if we do not perceive it, even if we do not look for it. It has been given to us once and for all in the birth of the Child in whom God decided to become one of us. At Christmas we are already recipients before we give any gifts to one another.

This is what makes such a day redemptive when properly understood: to us has been given something that none of us has made or devised; we know that Someone has already been mindful of us in advance, and we need only enter into the unfiltered light of a feast that awaits us and assures us there is more to reality than the little world of our own activity. Let us not hesitate to take pleasure in all this, to relax and rejoice and so be able to pass on to others what mankind needs above all else: the interior joy that liberates and redeems and imparts to all other gifts their meaning and proper context.

3. Christ the Savior Is Born

The lights of Christmas are shining again in our streets; Christmas shopping is in full swing. For a moment the Church is allowed, as it were, to share in the economic upturn, for on Christmas Eve the churches are packed with people who for a long time afterward will once again pass by the church door as though it led to something quite distant and alien and that is no concern of theirs. But on this night the Church and the world seem reconciled for a moment.

Everything is almost too beautiful: the lights, the incense, the music, the look in the eyes of those who are still able to believe, and finally the mysterious, ancient message about this Child who was born long ago in Bethlehem and is called Redeemer of the world: "Christ the Savior is born!" It still moves us—and yet the words we hear: "redemption", "sin", "salvation", sound like words from a bygone world. It may have been a beautiful world, but, no matter, it is no longer ours.

Or is it? The world in which the feast of Christmas came into existence was dominated by a mood very similar to ours today. It was a world in which the "twilight of the gods" was not a slogan but a real event. The old gods had suddenly become unreal; they no longer existed. People could no longer believe in what had for generations given life its meaning and support. And yet man cannot live without meaning; he needs it as he needs his daily bread. Therefore, when the old stars have burned out, he must look for new sources of light. But where were these to be found?

A widespread trend saw the solution in the worship of the "unconquered light", that is, the sun, which day after day journeys across the earth, strong and victorious, like a visible god of this world. December 25, during the days of the winter solstice, was to be celebrated as the annual birthday of the light that is born anew out of every decline, as the splendid guarantee that, amid the settings of all transient lights, the world's light is never extinguished, nor its hope for a way leading from every decline to a new beginning.

The liturgies of the sun religion thus made very skillful use of one of man's primordial fears and primordial hopes. Primitive man, experiencing the onset of winter in the lengthening nights of autumn and the diminishing intensity of the sun's warmth, had each year grown fearful once again and had asked: "Is the golden sun really dying this time? Will it return? Or will it be overcome someday by the evil powers of darkness, perhaps this year, perhaps next year, and never return again?" The realization that the winter solstice was an annual occurrence gave assurance at last that the sun would indeed conquer and that its return each year was certain. The winter solstice was the feast that summed up the hope, indeed, the certainty, that the luminaries of our world are indestructible.

The period of history in which the Roman emperors, through the cult of the unconquered sun, sought to give new faith, new hope, new meaning to their subjects amid the irreversible decline of the ancient gods coincided with the period when the Christian faith was striving to win the heart of Greco-Roman man. This faith saw in the worship of the sun one of its most dangerous foes. For this great symbol, the sun, was only too visibly present to the eyes of men—far more visible and attractive than the sign of the cross with which the preachers of Christianity came. And yet the Christian faith won out. Its invisible light proved stronger than the visible message with which the paganism of antiquity sought to maintain its position.

Christians soon laid claim to December 25, the birthday of the unconquered light, and celebrated it as the birthday of Christ, in whom they had found the true light of the world. They told the pagans: "The sun is good, and we rejoice in its ever-recurring victory no less than you do. But the sun has no power of its own. It exists and has power only because God created it. Therefore, it tells us of the true light that is God. It is this God, the fountainhead of all light, that we should be celebrating, and not his work, which would be powerless without him. But that is not all, nor is it even the most important thing. Have you not perhaps discovered that there is a darkness and a cold against which even the sun is powerless? It is the darkness and cold that emanate from the darkened hearts of men: hatred, injustice, the cynical manipulation of truth, cruelty, the dishonoring of man."

Here we suddenly realize how startlingly contemporary all this is; how the conversation of a Christian with a Roman sun-worshipper is at the same time the dialogue of today's believer with his unbelieving brother, the ceaseless dialogue of faith with the world. True enough, the primitive fear that the sun may one day die ceased to haunt us long ago; physics dissipated such fears with the cool breath of its clear formulas. The primitive fear is gone, but has all fear vanished? Or is man not still a being agitated by fears, so that modern philosophy can speak of *angst* as the "basic existential possibility" [*Grundexistenzial*] of man? What period of human history has felt a greater fear of its own future than ours does? Perhaps man today concentrates so much on the present simply because he cannot bear to look the future in the eye; merely to think of the future gives him nightmares.

I repeat: we no longer fear that the sun may be overcome by the darkness and not return again. But we do fear the darkness that emanates from man. We have at last discovered true darkness, and it is a far more fearful thing in this century of man's inhumanity to man than the generations before us could possibly imagine. We are afraid that what is good in the world may become utterly impotent; that the effort to live in truth, purity, justice, and love is gradually becoming completely meaningless, because it is now the stronger fist that rules the world, and the ways of the world agree with the brutal and the unscrupulous, not with the saints. Money rules, as do the atom bomb and the cynicism of those to whom nothing is sacred.

How often we catch ourselves fearing that in the last analysis there is no meaning in the chaotic course of this world and that world history divides all men into the stupid and the strong. The prevailing sense is that dark forces are on the increase and that goodness is impotent. When we look at the world, we are struck by a feeling quite similar to the one that men must have had long ago when the sun appeared to be in its death throes as fall drew on into winter. Will the sun survive? Will goodness continue to have any meaning, any power in our world?

In the stable at Bethlehem a sign has been given to us that bids us answer joyfully, "Yes!" This Child, God's only begotten Son, is set before us as a sign and pledge that God has the final say about world history; and God is truth and love. This is the true meaning of Christmas: it is the "birthday of the unconquered light"; it is the winter solstice of world history and, amid all the advances and declines of this history, gives us the assurance that, here again, the light will not die but already has the final victory in its possession. Christmas rids us of the second and greater fear that no physics can dispel: the fear about man, the fear of man himself. We have a divine certainty that the light has already conquered in the hidden depths of history and that no advance, however great, of evil in the world can change this fact. The winter solstice of history has come to pass irrevocably in the birth of the Child at Bethlehem.

Of course, on this birthday of the light, at this entry of goodness into the world, there is a question that occurs to us and may cause us to feel an anxious uncertainty once again. It is this: Did the great event of which we have been speaking really take place in the stable at Bethlehem? The sun, after all, is great and glorious and powerful; no one can fail to see its annual triumphal procession. Now must not the sun's creator be even mightier and more unmistakable in his coming? Would not this real sunrise of history inevitably flood the face of the earth with ineffable glory? Instead, how poor and shabby everything is that we hear in the Gospels!

But may not this very paltriness, this insignificance (as the world measures insignificance), be the sign by which the Creator makes his presence known? This seems, at first, an incomprehensible notion. And yet, if we reflect on the mystery of God's providence, especially as manifested in the writings of the Old and New Covenants, it becomes increasingly clear to us that there are two kinds of signs pointing to God. First, there is the sign of creation, the greatness and splendor of which give us a glimpse of him who is even greater and more glorious still. But alongside this sign, there is increasing emphasis on another kind of sign: that which is small in the world's terms. By means of this second kind of sign, God testifies to all the world that he is the Wholly Other and thus lets us see that he cannot be measured by this world's standards but transcends all its orders of magnitude.

The strange contradiction between the two kinds of sign in which God bears witness to himself and the nature of the second sign, that of lowliness, are perhaps best understood by looking at the contrast between the messianic preaching of John the Baptist and the messianic reality of Jesus himself. John described the coming Messiah in grandiose Old Testament terms as the one who lays the axe to mankind's roots, as a judge filled with holy anger and divine power. But how different the reality was when he came! He is the Messiah who does not cry out or raise his voice in the streets and who does not break the bruised reed or quench the smoldering wick (Is 42:2–3; Mt 12:18–21).

John knew that the Messiah would be greater than he, but he did not know the new form that this greatness would take: that it consists of humility, love, the Cross. It is to be found in the values of hiddenness and silence that Jesus would establish as that greater something and, indeed, as the greatest thing in this world. When all is said and done, true greatness lies, not in the magnitude of physical dimensions, but in something that can no longer be measured in those terms. Actually, anything great by material standards represents only a very provisional, tentative kind of greatness. Real values of the highest kind make their appearance in this world under the sign of lowliness, hiddenness, and silence. That which is decisively great in this world, that on which the world's history and destiny depend, is something that seems insignificant in our eyes.

At Bethlehem, the God who had chosen the small, forgotten nation of Israel as his people definitively made the sign of littleness the decisive sign of his presence in the world. The decision we make on Christmas night, the decision of faith, is to accept him in this sign and to trust in him without grumbling. To accept him: that is, to place ourselves under this same sign and under the truth and love that are at once the highest, most godly values and the most forgotten and unobtrusive of all.

Let me close with a story from Indian mythology in which there is an astoundingly magnificent anticipation of this mystery of the divinely small. One of the stories that has become intertwined with the figure of Vishnu tells how the gods were overcome by demons and forced to look on while these demons divided the world among themselves. Then the gods thought of a way out of their plight: they asked the demons to give them only so much territory on earth as the tiny dwarf body of Vishnu could cover. The fiends agreed, but they failed to realize one thing: Vishnu, the dwarf, was the sacrifice that fills the entire world. As a result, through him the gods regained possession of the world.

When we hear this, it sounds like a dream that, through the confused perspective of dreaming, suggests the shape of reality. For in fact, it is the tiny reality of sacrifice, of vicarious love, that proves in the end to be stronger than all the might of the strong and that in its helpless littleness finally permeates and transforms the world. In the Child at Bethlehem, this unconquerable power of divine love has entered our world. This Child is the only true hope of the world. We, however, are called to throw in our lot with him, to entrust ourselves to the God who has taken the small and lowly as his sign. On this night, our hearts should be filled with a great joy, for, despite all appearances, it is and will remain true: Christ the Savior is born.

34. Do We Have Reason to Celebrate?

In a world in which men are starving to death every minute; in a world in which cruel wars torment men in a merciless and seemingly senseless way; in a world in which men are oppressed, tortured, and murdered for their convictions; in a world in which, despite all its progress, injustice and affliction are perhaps more than ever before exercising their fearful reign in many forms: in such a world it must seem like a gesture of contempt when those who are able to do so escape into the happy forgetfulness or expensive pomp of a festive celebration.

Well, if celebration means simply a self-satisfied enjoyment of one's own affluence and security, then there is really no place for that kind of celebration today. But is this really the meaning of celebration? It is certainly not the original meaning of a Christian feast. A Christian feast—the birth of the Lord, for example—means something entirely different. It means that man leaves the world of calculation and determinisms in which everyday life ensnares him and that he focuses his being on the primal source of his existence. It means that for the moment he is freed from the stern logic of the struggle for existence and looks beyond his own narrow world to the totality of things. It means that he allows himself to be comforted, allows his conscience to be moved by the love he finds in the God who has become a child, and that in doing so he becomes freer, richer, purer.

If we were to try celebrating in this fashion, would not a sigh of relief pass across the world? Would such a feast not bring hope to the oppressed and be a clarion call to the forgetful ones who are aware only of themselves?

Translated by Matthew J. O'Connell.

35. Meditation for New Year's Eve

A year is coming to an end. This means, as always, that we spend an hour in reflection. We draw up balance-sheets and try to anticipate what the future may bring. For a moment we become conscious of the strange thing called "time", which otherwise we simply use without thinking about it. We feel both the melancholy and the consolation of our own transiency. Much that caused us distress, much that weighed us down and seemed to make it impossible to go on, has now passed and become quite unimportant. Difficult days, in retrospect, are transfigured, and the now almost forgotten distress leaves us more peaceful and confident, more composed in the face of present threats, for *these too* will pass.

The consolation of transiency: nothing lasts, no matter how important it claims to be. But this consoling thought, which gives patience its character of promise, also has its discouraging and saddening aspect. Nothing lasts, and therefore along with the old year not only difficulties but much that is beautiful has passed away, and the more a person moves beyond the midpoint of life, the more poignantly he feels this transformation of what was once future and then present into something past. We cannot say to any moment: "Stay awhile! You are so lovely!" Anything that is within time comes and likewise passes away.

Our feelings toward the new year show the same ambivalence as our feelings toward the old year. A new beginning is something precious; it brings hope and possibilities as yet undisclosed. "Every beginning has a magic about it that protects us and helps us live" are the words Hermann Hesse puts in the mouth of the Master of the Game in his novel *Magister Ludi* (*The Glass Bead Game*) at the moment when the now elderly character breaks out of his accustomed world of intellectual play and feels once again the spacious promise and intense excitement

Translated by Matthew J. O'Connell.

of a new beginning. At the same time, however, we fear a future whose paths we do not know and the ceaseless dwindling of our own share in that future.

What can we as Christians say at this moment of transition? First of all, we can do the very human thing the moment urges upon us: we can use the time of reflection in order to step aside and survey, thus gaining inner freedom and a patient readiness to move on again. One of the ancient philosophers once remarked that man differs from the beasts essentially because he can, as it were, raise his head above the waters of time. The beasts are like fish swimming in the water; they are simply carried along by the stream of time. Man alone can raise his sights above the water and so become master of time. But do we really do that? Are we not, too, mere fish in the sea of time, carried along by its currents without a clear view of whence time comes and whither it goes? Do we not become so completely absorbed in the details of daily life, with its constant demands and troubles, moving from deadline to deadline, duty to duty, that we are no longer able to perceive ourselves?

This should be an hour, then, for emerging from the water and trying for a moment to look beyond the sea of time to heaven above and its stars, so that in the process we may lay hold of ourselves as well. We should try to reflect on the road we have traveled and make some value judgments. We should try to see what went wrong, what blocked the way to ourselves and to our neighbor. We should gain this knowledge in order interiorly to turn away from these obstacles, so that our journey in the new year may truly be progress, a forward movement for us.

Once when Augustine's contemporaries complained about the bad times, he told them: "We ourselves are the times!" And in fact when we talk about the Biedermeier period or the Baroque age or the French Revolution, we are really referring to the people who together turned those years into a particular kind of era. Human beings with their changing ways make up the times.

But can time really advance when men do not? Do men make progress when they enjoy greater comfort but their hearts stand still or even shrivel up? And can a man make progress when he does not even know himself? When he has time only for what he owns and not for what he is? When he himself, therefore, remains outside of, disengaged from time? How can he learn to distinguish the valuable from the worthless and to preserve the one and abandon the other, and how can he find his way, when he continues to be simply a fish in the waters of time and does not really become a man with head uplifted?

We men are the times. We ought to reflect further on this surprising statement. When we do, we stumble upon the fact that man lives through quite different periods: childhood, youth, adulthood, old age. But today more than ever these stages of life become separated from one another. It is as though the elderly and the young were living in different times, and the two groups compete with each other for the time. If we look more closely, the picture becomes even more confusing. On the one hand, human life-expectancy has increased; people have more time than in the past, or, more precisely, the span of time given them for living has become longer. On the other hand, human life changes ever more rapidly: it is used up sooner, so that the difference between past and present becomes steadily greater, the present moments become ever shorter, and the past recedes faster and faster and ends up at an increasing distance from the present.

This, however, means that man is thrust into the past at an increasingly earlier point and belongs to it longer. It also means that increasingly divergent times must coexist within a single time and that increasingly sharp tensions must be endured within one and the same time, which in fact consists of a stratification of contradictory times. People, therefore, find themselves increasingly difficult to deal with. They find it more and more difficult to accept their temporality because they inevitably experience this more intensely as transiency, as slipping into the past, and, therefore, as hopelessness.

This results not only in the conflict between the generations that we encounter every day. Another result is that people deny the time in which they actually live and are willing to acknowledge and accept only one stage of life: youth. In an era that derived its inner strength and organizing power from tradition, the most revered stage of life was old age. This experience is still reflected, in ecclesiastical language, in the word "priest", which is derived from the Greek work *presbyteros* and means "an elder". People who have experienced the coherence of time —the interconnection of the stages of life—are the ones who carry the times. Today, however, people try to stop the clock and remain fixed in a particular moment of time; makeup artists help them, with varying degrees of success, to remain thus disguised from themselves and others. But in both cases—the emphasis on age and the emphasis on youth—people deny the wholeness of life, resist time, and deceive themselves.

Should this hour not cause us to reflect for a moment along those lines as well? Should we not recognize and acknowledge to one another that people need not be ashamed of any stage of life, provided they accept it from the heart and live it accordingly? As we ring out the old year and ring in the new, should we not realize once again that, in order to be fully himself, man needs the whole of his allotted time, from childhood to old age? Should we not try to accept again more fully the entire span given to man and to develop tolerance and even appreciation for the stage of life through which each person is living, with the realization that all of us have something to offer one another?

Let us put the matter more concretely. What would the world and the Church be like without the cheerful, innocent, unfeigned faith of children, whose childhood should not vanish into a premature puberty, as so often happens today? What would the world and the Church be like without the urgent restlessness and questioning of the young as they press on into the future? What would they be like without the energy and decisiveness of those who are at the height of their powers? What would they be like without the maturity of experience, without the quiet patience, the resigned serenity of the elderly? And what would we all be like without trust in one another, without the readiness to see and accept one another as we really are? In this period of history, when the future is the predominant concern and people therefore seek to stop the clock at a certain point, perhaps by far the most important thing we can learn is to say a wholehearted "Yes!" to older people and to our own growing old and, in so doing, to accept time and the future.

We men are the times. In making this point, Augustine was not simply reacting against the pessimism of the malcontent; he was taking a stand first and foremost against a very ancient tradition in pagan religion. According to the Greeks, *Chronos*, or Time, is the primordial divinity who ferociously devours his own children. There is a similar idea in the mythology of India, which therein expresses its pessimistic interpretation of the sensible world: time is identical with death; it brings forth all things, then swallows them up; life is in reality only a game death plays with itself. The divinization of time begets desperation, not hope.

It is only at a superficial level that such myths are alien to our way of thinking. We must agree with C. G. Jung that they reveal archetypes or permanent potentialities of the human soul. They exert their influence in varying ways, of course, and can disguise themselves to the point of being unrecognizable, but they do not therefore lose their identity.

Helmut Kuhn, a philosopher at Munich, observes in his book on the State that the triumph of Hegelianism in Germany meant that the philosophy of history replaced ethics, and what is modern or up-to-date was equated with the good.[1] Regardless of the extent to which Hegel himself was or was not responsible for this development, Kuhn is, in my opinion, describing very accurately the consequences of the current of thought that Hegel originated. The modern is the good: Is this not the opinion held today even in the Church and among churchmen? And must we not regard this view as evidence that after the widely proclaimed death of the Christian God, old Chronos has regained his place as the supreme deity?

Chronos is a cruel god, now as in the past. Just think of all the things that those who worship the modern as the good have had to adore and then, a short time later, cast into the fire! Only the oblivion that Chronos bestows on his worshippers prevents them from seeing through his cruel game with all its contradictions. How cruel a game it really is becomes clear to anyone who turns the pages of twentieth-century history and sees all that men have done to themselves in the name of modernity. When time becomes master of man, man becomes a slave, even if Chronos makes his appearance under the alias of Progress or the Future.

In the church of Saint Cunibert at Cologne there is a strange altar cloth that dates back to the ninth century. On it the god Chronos is depicted under the Latin name *Annus*, "Year"; he is surrounded by the symbols of time: day and night, seasons, the twelve signs of the zodiac. But present, too, are Christian symbols: Alpha and Omega, or Beginning and End, and *Annus* is set in parallel to Jesus Christ as a pontifex, or bridge builder and priest.[2]

This parallelism can be taken as a dangerous sign of an all too up-to-date Christianity that interprets Christ according to the age, identifies him with time, and thus makes Chronos the real god. As a matter of

---

[1] H. Kuhn, *Der Staat: Eine philosophische Darstellung* (Munich, 1967), 29.

[2] I owe this reference to the *Annus* altar cloth and its significance to W. Nyssen of Cologne.

fact, now is not the first time in the history of the Church that this danger has threatened. Submission to the dictatorship of the modern has always been a temptation for Christians, beginning with Constantine's notion of an imperial Church and coming down to the German Christians of 1933.

But the Cologne altar cloth can also be interpreted as pointing to the victory over Chronos that Jesus Christ embodies. He is a man who had time for God, and thereby he freed us from the dictatorship of time. There is a great deal more to be said here and food for further reflection.

But this evening must not end with neat formulas. Its purpose is rather to stimulate reflection. It is more appropriate, therefore, to let this image suggest some questions that are especially relevant to us at this hour. We said earlier that medical science has lengthened the human life span. People have more time. But do we really have time—or does time have us? In any case, most people do not have time for God; they use their time for themselves, or so they think. But do we really have time for ourselves? Or is this rather the very thing we lack? Do we not live in such a way that we pass ourselves by? And is it perhaps the case that man's true time is the time he has for God?

Jesus Christ had time for God, and in him God now has time. Should we not try once again to make time for God, to make time *his* time? For there are all too many indications that time that is no longer open to God becomes Chronos that swallows us up and that only having time for God gives us time for man and frees us from the dictatorship of Chronos. Let us all wish one another this kind of freedom and, in this sense, a happy New Year.

36. The Visitation

The angel of the Annunciation told Mary about Elizabeth, who like-wise became an instrument in the fulfillment of the promise. Now Mary goes forth to this sign God has given her. She enters Elizabeth's house and greets her cousin. Her face bears the mark of profound joy and of the mysterious new mission that has broken into her life and now gives meaning and substance to her entire existence.

With a woman's intuition, Elizabeth evidently senses the new and special atmosphere in which her young cousin is now moving. She senses that Mary, too, has been drawn into the mystery of God that has recently touched Elizabeth herself. The Spirit of God opens Elizabeth's heart fully. The eternal God is near; the presence of the Creator stands like a holy power between her and this young woman, permeates the life that is developing in Elizabeth's womb, and inspires her to speak words that subsequent generations of Christians have repeated after her: "Blessed are you among women, and blessed is the fruit of your womb."

Yet she adds the reason why Mary is blessed among women: "Blessed is she who believed. . . ." The words are not simply an allusion to Elizabeth's own doubting husband, who has been struck dumb and imprisoned in the silent space of his own self because he was not ready to abandon and surrender himself and to dare take the hand God was offering him. Elizabeth's words are also a prophetic anticipation of a later conversation the Lord himself would have. One day, a woman, moved by one of the Lord's sermons, cries out to him: "Blessed is the womb that bore you, and the breasts that you sucked!" He corrects her and says, "Blessed rather are those who hear the word of God and keep it!" (Lk 11:27–28).

Translated by Matthew J. O'Connell.

It is not blood kinship with the Lord that makes a person blessed —not flesh and blood, not race and descent, not blood and soil, not nation and class—but the spiritual kinship of faith. The blessed person is not the one who is a blood relative of the Lord, but the one who has ears to hear: the one who is not locked into the narrow world of flesh and blood, the narrow world of the self-centered and earthly; the one who knows how to listen to God's Word. Elizabeth's greeting to Mary tells us in advance that the Lord's later correction of the woman in the crowd does not deny Mary the praise that is due her but simply points out the real basis for such praise.

Mary is the great believer who humbly offered herself to God as an empty vessel for him to use in his mysterious plan. Without complaint, she surrendered control of her life; she did not try to live according to human calculation but put herself completely at the disposal of God's mysterious, incomprehensible design. All she wanted to be was the handmaid of the Lord, the instrument and servant of the Word. Therein lies her true fame: that she remained a believer despite all the darkness and all the inexplicable demands God made on her. She believed even in the face of certain incomprehensible expectations: that she should carry her Creator in her womb; that the child growing there should be the Lord; that he who was the source of Israel's salvation should be regarded by his fellows as deranged; that, first as a twelve-year-old and again at the beginning of his public life he should brush her aside; that he who was to bring salvation and healing to Israel should be executed by that same Israel.

Today God is still mysterious; indeed, he seems to have a special kind of obscurity in store for each person's life. But could he ever render any life as dark and incomprehensible as he did Mary's? "Blessed is she who believed", even when this faith became a sword that pierced her heart. This is the real reason for her greatness and her being called blessed: she is the great believer. Consequently, she is represented to us, not as a distant haloed figure, but as though still the young girl who entered Elizabeth's house with the shining light of mystery on her brow and surrounded by the radiance of purity and holy hope: "Blessed is she who believed."

But, like Elizabeth, Mary cannot remain silent at this moment. It is said that even today, under the influence of a great joy, simple Arabian women will improvise a song in which they pour forth the hidden poetry a simple heart composes when moved by a powerful joy. "My soul magnifies the Lord, and my spirit rejoices in God my Savior." Mary deflects Elizabeth's praise from herself to God the Lord. It is he who deserves all praise. In so acting, Mary has shown the way for all future Marian devotion: it is to be praise of God as he is mirrored in his graciousness to men.

In uttering her Magnificat, Mary did not compose an original poem. Her song resembles a tapestry whose threads are phrases from the Old Testament; the entire sacred history recorded there is woven here into a single song of praise to the gracious and faithful God. Almost every word of the Magnificat is taken from the Old Testament, as the scriptural praises of God the Father come to the lips of this young woman in the moment of joy and exaltation she experiences when she enters Elizabeth's house. Evidently, she was thoroughly imbued with, permeated by, the Word of God; her life was wholly lived under the influence of this Word, and it came spontaneously to her lips in her moment of joy.

It is this very point that may put us in a reflective mood as we contemplate Mary's canticle. Where are the quiet folk to be found in the land today: the people who, without causing a stir or being highly educated, really live by the Word of God, breathe it, think it, and are thoroughly at home in it? We have only too many people today who can talk and show that they are clever and have something to say— preferably something critical, something to make it clear that while they do not know everything, they are nonetheless wiser than anyone else. But we have too few people who still know how to listen in silence, to return again and again to God's Word, and to let that Word permeate and fill them so that it truly becomes their bread.

Who among us can say that for him the Sacred Scriptures, the Psalms, the praises of God throughout the Holy Bible have really become the self-evident language of the heart? That they come spontaneously to his lips when he ceases to examine and reflect and begins to let the mouth speak from the heart's fullness? For the most part, we live on lentil soup [cf. Gen 25:34] and water, even though the delicious wine of God's Word is offered to us in Sacred Scripture. The humble handmaid of the Lord puts our proud race to shame in this matter and should stir us once again to a livelier love of the marvelous gift we have in God's book. She should inspire us to become people who have ears to hear God's Word, even amid the noises of the present age that admittedly are often capable of deafening our very souls.

In a few moments we shall join in uttering the Eucharistic Prayer of thanksgiving and praise as we proceed with the liturgy of the Mass. Today let us praise God for his Word; for Mary, the sign of his grace and benevolence; for the quiet ones still to be found in the land, who live by the Word; for all the favors he has bestowed on us in our lifetime. And as we thank and praise him, let us try to open our hearts ever more fully to the marvelous gift of his Word. With it he consoles us in the night of this world; with it he helps us rejoice in this world's joys, for these, too, are from him, the Father of all lights.

37. The Assumption of Mary

On November 1 it will be eighteen years since Pius XII declared the statement that Mary, Mother of God, was taken body and soul into heavenly glory to be a dogma of the Catholic Church. Since that day in 1950, much has changed. Our basic mood is different today, so that we can hardly comprehend the enthusiasm and joy that prevailed then throughout large sectors of the Catholic Church.

At that time we—that is, people who were trying to live by faith and to think with the Catholic Church—were delighted that in an age that has rediscovered in a new and at times disturbingly passionate way the human body with its beauty, greatness, and dignity, the Church did not respond by condemning the body or even try to play down and blunt the edge of the rediscovery by drawing cautious distinctions. Instead, the Church responded with a hymn to the human body, with praise of the body that was bolder and more far-reaching than anything people outside the faith would have dared to say.

We were delighted that in an age that has rediscovered matter (corporeal things) and this earth of ours and does not want to hear about a flight into a world beyond, but loves the earth, cleaves to it, seeks to acquire its treasures, and wants to live by and for the earth, the Church again did not respond with an anathema. Instead, she intoned a hymn to the earth and its permanence. Once again, she spoke more magnanimously and more forcefully of the earth's glory than we ourselves would have dared.

We were delighted that in an age that has rediscovered the future and is filled with faith in progress; an age that refuses to be tied to the past or measured by the past; an age that is unwilling to look back as though everything decisive lay behind us; an age in which man seems to be a being of the future and one whose possibilities are far from

Translated by Matthew J. O'Connell.

exhausted: we were delighted that in such an age the Church was not calling us to turn our gaze to the past, as might have been expected of her. Instead, she herself was turning us to the future by interpreting man, on the basis of her faith, as a being who is yet to come, a being with an endless future, a being who can attain full stature only by advancing.

Finally, we were delighted that in an age in which something like a revolution of the proletariat, the forgotten, and the despised is going on even outside the Marxist world; an age in which we refuse to acknowledge any more castes; an age in which we are no longer willing to accept the old distinctions of classes and social strata, but want to see every person valued simply as a person—that in such an age the Church, once again, agreed in a loud and emphatic voice by pointing to the woman who called herself a lowly handmaid of the Lord. The Church proclaims that the entire greatness possible to man is embodied and fulfilled in this woman, quite independently of descent or class.

Since that day in 1950 a great deal has changed, and the dogma that caused such exultation then is rather a hindrance now. We wonder whether by proclaiming this dogma we might have put unnecessary obstacles in the way of reunion with our fellow Christians; whether it would not be much easier if the road were clear of this particular stumbling block that we ourselves set up in the not-so-distant past. We also ask ourselves whether this dogma perhaps threatens to turn Christian piety away from its proper object. Instead of looking to God the Lord and the one Mediator Jesus Christ, who as man is our brother but is at the same time so much one with God that he himself is God, are we not letting our attention be turned aside to the saints? These may seem to be closer to us, but in fact no one can be closer to us than he who created us and whose very thoughts we all are!

Finally, in addition to these objections that originate within the faith itself, the character of modern thought and of the age we live in suggests a further, very ordinary human question. The expression "Journey of Mary to Heaven" (German: *Himmelfahrt Mariens*)—which admittedly coarsens the Latin term that lies behind it: *Assumptio Mariae in coelum*—practically challenges us to raise objections. We instinctively ask whether it is not really nonsensical, foolish, and a provocation to claim that a human being can be taken bodily into heaven. We are inclined to say that such a statement might have made good sense two thousand years ago or even two hundred years ago, but the situation is entirely different now. We know with incontestable clarity that the heavens we can see are really part of the world and are subject to the same conditions as our world here on earth. In addition, we know that constant change is going on throughout the entire corporeal, material world. Given all this, it seems arrogant to claim that a human being was taken bodily into heaven. Where is that supposed to be? How can it be? Is it not utterly naïve to say such a thing?

Now there is undoubtedly a legitimate insight behind all these questions that have piled up in the eighteen years separating us from November 1, 1950. They can help us realize that the great things of this world, including the things of faith, have their limitations and that they will give rise to a sense of dissatisfaction if we think of them in a one-sided way and not in their relation to the whole of reality. The questions can help us realize, too, that every period of history looks at things differently and, therefore, sees and fails to see different things. We can also gain a clear understanding of a further point that is extremely important for the whole of our faith: if, in connection with this particular matter of the Assumption, we see that no age is capable of having the whole of reality or the whole of the faith clearly before its eyes and that each age will understand some things better, other things less well, then we will also see the true nature of faith. To believe always means, in the final analysis, that we focus our attention on the whole and on the decisive thing, which is God's call to us, and that, with the confidence we derive from this whole, we accept what may be remote from us or perhaps even utterly inaccessible to us for one reason or another.

The liturgy we are celebrating today is not the time for detailed reflections on all of the questions we have just mentioned. But some points seem self-evident. First of all, we are probably all aware today that the word "heaven", as used in connection with the Assumption, is not a place somewhere beyond the stars, but something far greater and also far more difficult to put into words. "Heaven" means that God has a place for man and gives him an eternal existence.

We know from personal experience that the dead live on somehow in the memory of those who knew and loved them. A bit of them remains alive in those who remember them. But it is only a bit of them, a shadow, so to speak, and the day comes when those who remember them likewise die, and the continued existence that love gave them comes to an end. But God never forgets, and we all have being because he loves us and because he has thought of us creatively, so that we exist. Our eternity is based on his love. Anyone whom God loves never ceases to be. In him, in his thinking and loving, it is not just a shadow of us that continues in being; rather, in him and in his creative love, we ourselves, totally and authentically, are preserved and immortal.

His love is what makes us immortal. This love guarantees our immortality, and it is this love that we call "heaven". Heaven is simply the fact that God is great enough to have room even for us minuscule beings. And the man Jesus, who is also God, is our everlasting pledge that man and God can forever exist and live in each other. If we grasp this truth, then, I think, we will also have some insight into what the odd expression "bodily assumption into heavenly glory" means.

The Assumption cannot mean, of course, that some bones and corpuscles of blood are forever preserved somewhere. It means something much more important and profound. To wit: that what continues to exist is not just a part of man—the part that we call the soul and that is separated out from the whole—while so much else is annihilated. It means, rather, that God knows and loves the entire person that we now are. The immortal is that which is now growing and developing in our present life. The immortal is that which is developing in this body of ours wherein we hope and rejoice, feel sadness, and move forward through time; that which is developing *now* in our present life with its present conditions. In other words, what is imperishable is whatever we have become in our present bodily state; whatever has developed and grown in us, in our present life, among and by means of the things of this world. It is this "whole man", as he has existed and lived and suffered in this world, that will one day be transformed by God's eternity and be eternal in God himself.

All this should fill us with profound joy today. Christianity does not promise a salvation of the soul alone in some kind of otherworldly existence in which all that has been precious and valuable to us in this world will vanish like a pageant that is staged for a single occasion and then has no further meaning. No, Christianity promises that what has transpired on this earth will be eternal.

Nothing of what is precious and valuable to us will be lost. Christ said on one occasion that "the hairs of your head are all numbered"

(Mt 10:30). The final and abiding world will be the fulfillment of this earth of ours. Thus, the point we noted at the beginning is once again made clear: that Christianity is not a religion focused on the past, a religion forever chaining us to something that took place once upon a time, but a religion of hope in what is to come. It is a religion that opens the way for us into the future, into the definitive and abiding creation. Precisely as Christians, we are called upon to build our world and to work for its future, so that it may become God's world, a world far transcending anything that we ourselves could ever build.

If we reflect on all this, we will ask the Lord today to make us ever more alert to the way he meets us in the realities of our world. We will ask him to make us believers a people of hope who do not look to the past but build for today and tomorrow a world that is open to God. We will ask him to turn us believers into a joyous people who, amid the distresses of daily life, glimpse the beauty of the world to come and, with this certainty as our foundation, live our lives in faith and hope.

38. Sermon for the Feast of Saint Augustine

In our Baroque churches of Bavaria, the paintings over the main altar at the end of the nave are designed in such a way that they resemble doors. That is to say, they act, not as a terminus, a wall that turns the church into an enclosure, but rather as a new entryway that gives access to something greater. They open upon what is essential, just as the Eucharist that we celebrate on our altars is not focused upon itself but is, so to speak, the threshold over which the Church, during her existence in this world, may cross into God's world.

Similarly, the saints who are represented in these paintings are not self-sufficient beings. They are not what a historian of religion once described them as being: the successors of the gods, independent helpers in time of need, to whom people turn because they must think that the eternal God has no time for their concerns or would not understand them. No, the saints are not self-sufficient; like the paintings, they too are windows that look into God's eternity. In the world of the saints, with which we come in contact during the liturgical year, the simple, invisible light of God is refracted, as it were, through the prism of our human history so that we can encounter the eternal glory and light of God right here in our human world and in our human brothers and sisters. The saints are, so to speak, our older brothers and sisters in the family of God. They want to take us by the hand and lead us, and their lives tell us: "If this person or that could do it, why can't I?"

These are the words that Augustine, the saint of today's liturgy, thought he heard at the time of his conversion. They helped give him

---

Translated by Matthew J. O'Connell.

For biographical data, see especially F. van der Meer, *Augustine the Bishop*, trans. B. Battershaw and G. R. Lamb (New York, 1961; corrected edition in Harper Torchbooks, 1965). For Augustine's exegesis of the Song of Songs (second conversion!), see J. Ratzinger, "Die Kirche in der Frömmigkeit des hlg. Augustinus", in *Sentire Ecclesiam*, ed. J. Daniélou and H. Vorgrimler (Freiburg, 1961), 152–75, esp. 168f.

the final encouragement he needed to risk the leap into faith and into God's love. Despite the intervening centuries, there is hardly a saint who has remained so close to us, so understandable, as Saint Augustine, for in his writings we encounter all the heights and depths of the human condition, all the questioning and seeking and exploring that are still ours today. He has not inaccurately been called the first modern man. He was born in an age of crisis and transition that was only too like our own, an age in which faith was not something taken for granted but had to be sought and found through all the abysses of the human condition.

Augustine became a Christian, not by *birth*, but solely through *conversion*. And in the two great conversions that divide his life into its main periods, we can still discern clearly today the real mission and meaning of Christianity. For it is a permanently valid principle that a man can become a Christian, not by birth, but only by conversion. Just as the waters of the earth, obeying the law of gravity, naturally flow downward but can be controlled by man's mind and technology and be made to flow in another direction, so the waters of human existence flow downward of themselves, and only by a conversion to faith, hope, and love can they follow that new course that leads man to his authentic humanity.

1. The First Conversion

Augustine became a Christian by conversion. We shall take a brief look here at the two conversions in his life and try to get some new insight into the mandate that is ours as Christians.

Most people are familiar with the story of his first conversion, at least in outline. In keeping with the custom of the time, Augustine was not baptized as a child but only received the salt given to catechumens. As a result, he was accepted into the Church, but in a provisional way. But he had learned to know and love the name of Jesus Christ, and he had prayed to him in the difficulties, major or minor, that children have. When we read his *Confessions*, we are still moved by his account of how in the early morning he often prayed to his God with passionate fervor that he might be spared the rod in school that day.

But then he becomes an older student. He comes into contact with the higher learning of his day, and in comparison with the extensive erudition of antiquity, the Bible seems to him like a foolish storybook that is no longer worthy of an enlightened, educated man. He slips into rationalism, first as a Manichean, then as a follower of the skepticism of the Academy. But his heart remains empty. The result was the interior strife that led him at last to his conversion in the garden: the interior conflict between his heart's yearning for eternity and the restraints that his passions and his academic skepticism imposed on him.

He tells us that one day he tears himself away from his friend Alypius in order to be alone in the garden with his distress, his temptations, his inner conflict. In this moment of extreme agitation, he thinks he hears a child crying repeatedly, "*Tolle, lege!* Take and read!" He asks himself whether this can be part of a children's game. He can think of no such game and feels that the words are meant for him, that they are the summons that is to turn his life around. He rises, finds a Bible, opens it, and reads the words: "Put on the Lord Jesus."

This was indeed the turning point in this life. Whatever historical explanation we give to the child's words, "*Tolle, lege!* Take and read", Augustine truly made them a program for his life. At this moment, he really discovered the Word of God and henceforth remained a hearer of the Word, constantly turning to it in order to gain light and direction for his life. At this moment, then, he experienced anew in his own person the situation of decision, the primal situation of Adam in the garden. And in this primal situation of Adam in the garden of decision, he found in God's Word the tree of life that brought him the closeness to God and the communion with God that Adam had lost because he had attempted by his own powers to become like God and actually divine.

In his later years, as Augustine wrote the story of his life, the child's voice chanting "*Tolle, lege!* Take and read!" may have reminded him of the voices of his assistants at the liturgy as they stood near him, the bishop, at the lectern and read to the assembled faithful the passage on which he was to preach. It is as though in describing the scene in the garden, he wished to tell the faithful: "The voices of the lectors who proclaim God's Word to you echo the cry of that child, '*Tolle, lege!* Take and read!' For all of you are likewise at the moment of decision; you are in the garden of decision. No man can evade the primal situation in which Adam found himself. Each person must face it, endure it, and emerge victorious. The child's voice is addressed to all of you; it tells you where the tree of life is: in God's Word.''

At that moment of conversion, Augustine discovered the Word of God. Now, if we reflect on ourselves, to whom all this likewise applies, we must confess how shamefully limited our own discovery of that Word has been; how much time we spend patiently reading second- and third-rate magazines and God knows what else, and how little we trouble ourselves about the Word of God. If we had never heard of this Word and then by chance had learned that there was a book somewhere in which God himself speaks to us, what would we not do to get our hands on that book? Yet it is right in our midst, and we do not bother about it!

And so this celebration of the liturgy should be a summons to us: "*Tolle, lege!* Take and read!" It should be a summons to rediscover God's Word as light for our days and as the tree of life for us, too. To Augustine, the discovery of God's Word, which was the decisive event of his life, was also a decision in favor of the invisible. Until then, visible reality with all its power and allure had so fully dominated him that he dared not make the leap into the invisible. But at this moment, he realized that the invisible is the true reality that sustains all else.

And again, I think, it is just the same with us. In our time the pressure of audio-visual stimuli has, if anything, increased. The loudspeakers and the shouting voices of this world have reached such a volume that now we are hardly able to perceive the silence of God. We often fancy that we have grown wiser and more clever because we take visible reality more seriously, but at the same time we must admit that our hearts have lost their keenness of vision, for we are no longer able to see beyond the visible to the invisible and eternal realities apart from which the visible has no being or subsistence. This liturgical celebration should therefore challenge us to put our trust in the invisible and to acknowledge that it is the truly foundational reality.

2. The Second Conversion

After his conversion, Augustine returned to Africa with his family and friends. Years of undisturbed joy followed, during which the group established a kind of monastic community and began to live wholly in accordance with God's Word and the beauty of truth. From now on, truth alone and the hearing of God's Word were to give substance to their lives and to be the source of their happiness.

But once again things turned out differently. Augustine's plans were completely derailed one day when he came to visit Hippo, the great seaport of North Africa. He entered the church and listened to the elderly bishop, Valerius, preaching. The bishop said, among other things, that he was on in years and that, being Greek by birth, he found preaching very difficult; he had long been looking for a suitable priest to assist him. At this moment, a tumultuous cry ran through the church: "Let Augustine be our bishop!" The people laid hold of him; his refusals and tears and resistance were unavailing, and they dragged him to the front of the church. Bishop Valerius reaffirmed the invitation. As a result, Augustine was ordained a priest entirely against his own wishes.

Augustine has left us a profoundly moving testimony from this period. It is a letter he wrote to Bishop Valerius, shortly after his ordination, asking once again for time to prepare himself for his new pastoral work. In the letter he writes: "In my own eyes I am like a man who has never learned to row a boat yet is suddenly forced to become the pilot of a large ship. That is why I was quietly weeping at my ordination to the priesthood."

That seems quite odd to us: a man who is made a priest against his will and who weeps at his ordination. But it is precisely here that we see Augustine's greatness: in the fact that out of obedience he accepted this new direction for his life and devoted himself completely to the new task now laid upon him. For from this moment forward, there was no more time for tranquil study of the Word and for the stillness of contemplation that he had chosen as his lot in life. From early morning to late evening, he was constantly up against the whole panorama of human life. The doorbell of his house rang all day long, and he had to reconcile enemies, comfort mourners, and do everything that a priest has to do. Moreover, according to the legal system of the time, he was judge in all the civil disputes of the town and was drawn into all the human dealings of its citizens.

In his writings there is a passage that gives us a glimpse of how he came to grips spiritually with this entirely new situation. He is reflecting on verses from the Song of Songs that say that the bridegroom knocks at the bride's door late at night; she refuses to open it, saying:

I do not want to get up again and dirty my feet; I have just gone to bed and have no time for you. Augustine comments: The bridegroom and the bride symbolize Christ and his Church; but how can the bride get her feet dirty by opening the door to Christ, and how can the Church have no desire to open the door to him? Then Augustine goes on to say: The Church that has gone to rest and refuses to be disturbed is an image of those believers who live their Christianity in a purely self-centered way, seeking only to taste the joy of God's Word, and are unwilling to let their lives be touched by the dirt of this world.

But Christ will not leave us in this kind of repose. In all who are searching, erring, or needy, Christ knocks at the door of our life and calls out: "Aperi mihi et praedica me!—Open to me and proclaim me!" And for the sake of Christ who comes to us in men with their needs, their ordinariness, their triviality, who waits for us and knocks on our door in their person—for his sake we must constantly risk getting our feet soiled with the dirt of this world. For his sake we must be always ready to set aside our joy in the Word, our satisfaction with the purely individual dimension of Christianity, and go out to others so that the Word of the Lord may reach them as well.

Nietzsche once said that he could not stand Saint Augustine: the man seemed so plebeian and ordinary. Nietzsche is making a valid point about Augustine, but it is precisely here that we find the saint's real Christian greatness. He could have been an aristocrat of the mind, but for the sake of Christ and for the sake of his fellowmen, in whom he saw Christ approaching him, he abandoned the ivory tower of the intellectual in order to be wholly a man among men, a servant of the servants of God. For the sake of Christ, who was not ashamed to lay aside his divine glory and become a man like us, Augustine relinquished all his higher education and learned to speak God's Word ever more simply and plainly to his people. For the sake of Christ, he became increasingly an ordinary man among ordinary men and the servant of all. In the process, he became truly a saint.

Christian holiness does not consist in being somehow superhuman or in having outstanding talents or a stature that someone else does not have. Christian holiness is simply the obedience that makes us available where God calls us to be, the obedience that does not rely on our own greatness but allows our God to bestow his greatness on us and knows that only in service and self-surrender can we truly find ourselves.

3. The Restless Heart

The basic attitude that lies behind the two conversions and changes in Augustine's life, that is, behind his turning to the Word and later to the selfless service of others, is what he himself once called his restlessness of heart. He means the attitude that will not let man be at peace with himself and his present state but keeps him journeying toward the eternal reality in which alone he can find repose and fulfillment.

Augustine himself has given us an unforgettable description of this restlessness of heart that reaches beyond all things earthly to take what is eternal. The description is connected with an experience he had shortly after his conversion. With his family and friends, he had come to Ostia, the great seaport at the mouth of the Tiber, in order to take ship there for Africa. One evening he was standing with his mother at a window of his house and looking out over the wide sea that in the endless distance melted into the blue sky. As they reflected, peacefully and with profound submission to God, on what had taken place in their lives and what still lay ahead and as they gazed out into the endless vista, mother and son spoke together about the eternal God. They talked of what it will be like on the day when earth and sea vanish from sight and past and future are no more, when the only thing left is the one eternal Today of God. Augustine then adds: At this moment it was granted us to touch for an instant the mystery of eternity, and we left there the first fruits of our spirits.

Five days later, his mother fell ill with malaria, the disease that not too long after would turn Ostia into a dying city. Nine days after that, she closed her eyes forever. But that picture of peace, of their shared contemplation of the wide sea and, beyond it, of the eternity of God himself, remained before his soul's eye as a picture of the promised permanence that can never be taken from us.

For us, Augustine himself has become, as it were, a window through which we gaze on eternity. We should ask God the Lord that he would allow us, too, to touch at least for an instant this eternity of God and to leave our love there, so that henceforth our hearts may be restless in their desire for God's eternity wherein alone they can find rest. Amen.

39. Meditation on the Day of a First Mass

It is still cause for celebration when a young man has the privilege
for the first time of changing earthly bread into the Lord's Body. We
still regard the first blessing he gives with anointed hands as a precious
gift. The priesthood is still a gift that we hope will be bestowed and
for which we give joyous thanks. But we also know that nowadays the
festive joy of this occasion has a somber backdrop: the seminaries we
enlarged and expanded only a short time ago are now almost empty.
Fewer and fewer risk the final step to the altar; more and more numerous are those who later doubt the meaning of their vocation and look
for another way.

The shadows are lengthening, the solitude is deepening, and those
who remain are asking with heavy hearts what future lies ahead of
them. Is there still any point to being a priest in a world that prizes
only technological and social progress? Has faith any future? Is it worthwhile to stake one's whole life on this one card? Is not the priesthood
an outdated holdover from the past, something no one needs any more,
while all energies should be devoted to getting rid of poverty and fos-
tering progress?

But is all this a true picture? Or, as mankind gets the machine of
progress moving ever faster, is it not at the same time driving itself
deeper into suicidal madness? The famous French aviator Antoine de
Saint-Exupéry once wrote in a letter to a general: "There is only one
real problem in this world: how to give men once again a spiritual meaning and a spiritual restlessness; how to make something like a Grego-
rian chant drop its gentle dew upon them. Do you not see: people can
no longer live on refrigerators, politics, balance-sheets, and crossword
puzzles. They simply cannot do it." And in his book *The Little Prince*,
he says: "How foolish the world of grown-ups, the clever people, is!

Translated by Matthew J. O'Connell.

We understand only machines, geography, and politics. But the things that matter—the light, the clouds, the heavens with their stars—these we no longer understand."

In a similar vein, the Russian novelist Solzhenitsyn tells of the cry of distress uttered by a Communist who had ended up in Stalin's jails: "We need cathedrals once again in Russia, and men whose purity of life turns these cathedrals into living spaces for the soul!" And in point of fact, man does not live solely on refrigerators and balance-sheets. The more he attempts to do so, the more he despairs and the emptier his life becomes. Today—today more than ever—we need men who do not sell luxuries or turn out political propaganda but who instead are solicitous for the human soul and seek to help men not to lose their souls in the turmoil of everyday life. We need priests, and the more alien they become to the world of business and politics, the more we need them.

But what is a priest's real task? For what purpose is he ordained? Each of the two New Testament passages we have just heard read (1 Pet 5:1–4; Mt 20:25–28) describes the priest's role in a single word: he is to be a "shepherd", he is to be a "servant".

A shepherd: in the background here is the picture of Jesus as the Good Shepherd. In the ancient Orient, "shepherd" was a title for kings. But in this title, kings expressed the complete contempt they had for their peoples as well as the claim to total power that drove them: the people were but sheep in their eyes, and they disposed of them like sheep, in whatever way they pleased.

Jesus, the Son of God, is the true shepherd, to whom the sheep belong because they are his creatures. And because they belong to him, he loves them and wants the best for them. He even offers them his own life as their food. In non-metaphorical terms: By his Word he shows them how to live. He shows them the truth that men need just as much as they need their daily bread in order not to waste away. He gives them the love they need just as they need water each day in order not to die of thirst. And since his Word is not enough, he gives them himself, backing the currency of his Word with his own precious blood that is shed for them.

Like Christ, the priest is to be a shepherd. But how can he be a shepherd? It means, first, that the priest is not primarily an executive who keeps records and makes administrative decisions. He will, of course, have to do this kind of thing repeatedly, but it ought to be peripheral in his life. It is not his real business; others can and should be of assistance to him in that area. To be a shepherd in the service of Christ means something more. It means leading men to Jesus Christ and, thus, to the truth and love and meaning they still need today. For today as in the past, man does not live on bread and money alone. The priest leads them to Jesus Christ and to the truth that gives meaning; he does this by transmitting the Word of Jesus Christ and administering the sacraments in which the Lord continues to give us his life.

Word and sacrament: the two main tasks of the priest. This sounds very prosaic, very ordinary, but the terms contain wealth enough to bring authentic fulfillment to a man's life.

Let us begin with the *Word*. We may be inclined to say: "The Word? What is that? Only facts matter; words are nothing." But if you reflect a bit, you come to realize that words have power to create facts. Thus a single lying word can destroy a whole life and sully a person's name irreparably. A single word of kindness can transform a person when nothing else is of any use. It should be clear to us, therefore, how important it is for mankind that there be talk about more than money and war, power and profit, that beyond the babble of everyday life someone should speak about God and about us and about what makes a person human.

A world that lacks such words becomes infinitely boring and empty. It becomes cheerless. It becomes a trackless waste. We are seeing today how life can become monotonous and absurd to people even though they have all the possessions they could ever desire. They no longer know what to do with their lives, or what a man should do and avoid doing. Man is turning into a meaningless being who finds his very self intolerable. People must first invent themselves, but this is a process that continually overtaxes them; at best they manage to find in themselves only something boring and mean.

And so we can begin to understand anew how important it is that our children should learn not only to calculate and count but also to live. All the arithmetic and writing is useless if they do not know the purpose of their lives; if they do not learn why we are on earth; and if this knowledge does not produce freedom, serenity, and goodness.

The Word of God is not transmitted solely through preaching. It is also mediated through instruction in school. It is mediated through conversation with the elderly, the abandoned, the sick, the people for whom no one has time and for whom life has become gloomy and burdensome. What a great need we have today of people who know how to listen, to be there with someone who is struggling with doubts, to talk with the sick in the evening of their lives and be able to give them hope and meaning as this world's lights grow dim! The Word of God—indeed, we need it as truly as we need our daily bread! We also need men who are servants of this Word, precisely because it is a word that has become so alien to us.

We should keep all this in mind when we are tempted to grumble at a sermon we find too boring or trifling. It is difficult to proclaim God's Word today in a world that is sated with every kind of sensation. It is difficult to proclaim God's Word today in a world in which the priest himself must grope his way with difficulty through the darkness and must choose between saying what no one will understand or, in a hesitant and inadequate way, translating for our world what is so far removed from our everyday experience.

The service of the Word has become difficult. Today's priest may feel on many occasions like the prophet Jeremiah, who roused only anger by his prophesying and who often rebelled passionately against his prophetic task: "You deceived me, God!" he cried out in despair; "Leave me in peace!" He would have liked to cast away the word that had turned him into a solitary, a fool, a marked man with whom no one wanted to have any dealings. But he had to carry the burden of the word. And precisely by doing so, he served the very people who refused to understand him.

We should keep all this in mind when we are tempted to bemoan the inadequacy of the preaching we hear. Instead of grumbling, let us pray together that God may grant to hearers the gift of hearing aright, to preachers the grace of eloquence, and to all of us much patience with one another. Let us pray, too, that through it all his Word may sustain us: the bread of truth for which our soul hungers even when we do not understand it.

With service to the Word goes service to the *sacraments*, which embrace the whole of human life and are meant to place this life in a visible way into the hands of Mother Church and the hands of our Lord himself. In nostalgic, almost melancholic tones, Goethe once spoke of how the sacraments of the Church take possession of and transform all the important moments of life, from birth to the difficult moment of final farewell. By his sacramental ministry, the priest is present throughout the entire journey of life and at all the great fundamental decisions men make; in the final analysis these decisions will be made correctly only if God gives us a hand.

Let us consider here only the two sacraments that above all else shape the priest's everyday life and work: the sacrament of penance and the sacrament of the altar. People receive the sacrament of penance less frequently nowadays. But this does not change the fact that guilt is a reality even today and that we, too, are in need of forgiveness. How important it is to know that a man can repent; that at times each year he is forced to stop shifting the guilt to others and to think of his own sinfulness; that he is forced to accuse himself, to see and admit his guilt, to acknowledge that he is a sinner and has failed! And how important it is to know that forgiveness is to be had; that there can be a new beginning; that there is an authority that can say: "Go, your sins are forgiven you!"

But we ourselves must follow God's example and repeatedly learn to forgive others, for a world without forgiveness can only be a world of mutual destruction. One of the most difficult and most rewarding tasks a priest has is to speak that word of forgiveness. Often it is burdensome to be the place where mankind deposits all the filth it has accumulated. And yet it is a hope-filled activity, for he knows that everything is capable of being transformed and that men do allow themselves to be changed.

The high point of a priest's daily life is the sacrament of the altar and the intimate though mysterious union of heaven and earth that this sacrament brings about. God invites us to his table; he wants us to be his guests. At this table he gives us himself, for God's gift is God himself. The Eucharist is the holy feast God provides for us, and even though the outward circumstances of the feast be ever so shabby, here we cross the threshold leading from everyday life, and God keeps festival with us. This feast of God is something far greater than any leisure time, which turns empty in the absence of the feast that we ourselves cannot provide.

But there is a further point on which we ought to reflect here. The feast is produced by the sacrifice. Only the grain of wheat that has died produces fruit. The center of a priest's life, therefore, is the sacrifice of Jesus Christ. But it is a sacrifice that cannot be celebrated without our participation, without our sacrificing together with Christ. For the priest, this means that, without a sacrifice of his own, without the drudgery of slowly learned self-denial, he cannot authentically carry out his service of Christ. That is the point we just heard made in the Gospel: To follow Christ means to follow him who came to serve and to give himself.

Here we can see both the greatness and the difficulty of the priestly calling. The priest will never fully succeed in his task, for the servant is not greater than his master. Moreover, he can succeed at all only when the support and faith and prayers of others sustain him. Even and especially as Christians, all of us live with the help of one another, and every celebration of the Eucharist is a new summons to this mutual dependence.

In conclusion, let us listen once again to God's Word as it has come to us in the Old Testament reading of this first Mass (1 Sam 3:1–10). It is night. Eli, the high priest, is quite elderly and beginning to go blind. All these details give us at the same time a picture of the historical moment in which Samuel receives his calling. Israel is living in the night, like a man blind to God. Life has become routine; the days pass, and God seems far away. The ordinariness of life hides him; it is as if he no longer existed, and in a period of peace and comfort no one bothers to ask about him.

And yet the lamp of God has not gone out, and the voice of the Lord calls to this boy whose heart is pure and whose soul is open. God once again makes himself heard in the midst of man's indifference. He pursues his people even when they seem ready to forget him. He remains with them. But he can call only because in the midst of Israel's night there is one person who is able to hear and whose life is not crammed full of the rubbish of his own cares and interests.

Samuel hears. From the hearing a vocation emerges, and from the vocation a burden that he must carry through the toil and hardships of a long life. But the burden yields the fruit of grace: for himself, who finds fulfillment in his difficult service, and for his fellowmen, who slowly find God once again and, in so doing, find themselves as well. How moving this story is for us in the dark hour, the hour of blindness, in which we are now living! Let us ask God that his lamp may not go out in our time! Let us ask him to call men today as in the past and to raise up men who are able to hear. And let us thank him at this moment for again sending a young man forth with his Word. Let us commend to the Lord's kind solicitude the journey that is beginning today. Lord Jesus Christ, Good Shepherd, bless this beginning! Complete what you have begun! Amen.

EPILOGUE

40. Ten Years after the Beginning of the Council
—Where Do We Stand?

Recently while leafing through some old papers, I came across an issue of the *Ruhrwort* dated October 13, 1962. It reports that the French historian and author Daniel-Rops observed that the Council that had just begun would have little or nothing at all of the character of a dogmatic council. When asked, then, whether it was a matter of overcoming a crisis, whether the Church urgently needed "reform", as she did, for instance, in the fifteenth century, he replied: Certainly not. He approvingly cited the following statement of then-Cardinal Montini of Milan: "Unlike many other councils, Vatican II is convening at a peaceful, religiously zealous moment in the life of the Church." Anyone who reads that today and compares Montini's statement then with what the same man is preaching tirelessly now as Paul VI will realize with something of a shock how long ten years are. Back then, basically, no one maintained that the Church was in a crisis; today, no one denies it, even though there are widely divergent opinions about its nature and the reasons for it.

What happened? Could it be that the Council created the crisis, since it did not have one to overcome? Not a few hold this opinion. It is, to be sure, not entirely false, but then again it tells only one part of the truth. In order to evaluate what has happened since and what may help the situation along today, such an interpretation is certainly inadequate. Here I must deny myself the luxury of sketching the conflicting intellectual currents that had developed in Catholic theology before the Council while confronting the problems of a fast-changing world and that had united at first under the common banner of progressivism.

Translated by Michael J. Miller.

Gradually it became obvious that they could not, at a deeper level, be unified; this was one of the processes that started in slow motion toward the end of the Council, especially after the discussion of the Pastoral Constitution on the Church in the Modern World, only to accelerate as time went on. The most important thing, however, it seems to me, was that the end of the Council coalesced with a generational change of decisive importance in the overall intellectual situation of mankind and especially of the Western world: with the transition from the first to the second postwar generation. To the extent that this is being accomplished, the defining factor of today's mind-set is no longer the urgency of rebuilding a world from nothing but rather the oppressive force of a world that is already completely built, in which everything has already been done but offers no meaning. Postwar theology, too, was at least partly responsible for this meaning-vacuum. Under the guidance of existentialist thought, it had retreated to the position that faith and meaning cannot be made objective, thus leaving the world to pure objectivity. During the reconstruction phase, this release of the world to run itself by its own laws had been perceived as useful; now, however, the value-free objectivity of business and politics seemed dubious; it increasingly appeared to be a curtain concealing behind it special interests that had to be brought into the light of day. Thus at the moment when it seems that a high point in the reconstruction has been reached, a revolt breaks out against a world that is complete and, in that very completeness, meaningless: it is necessary to destroy in order to be able to build again. In a promotional book about Canada, I happened to find a poem by a young man who describes his encounter with the world of knowledge, symbolized by an atlas, in which every path, every crossing, every body of water and every hill is already recorded; there is nothing more to discover, and he finally burns the atlas so as to find the paths through the world himself. This seems to me to be a fitting image for this feeling of asphyxiation in a world that offers everything except a reason why.

After the initial fierce shocks, two opposing models for mastering reality crystallized: the neo-positivistic model, in which the decisive thing is the concept of rational reform, the further development of specialized knowledge, and the neo-Marxist model, which is not unfairly reprimanded by the positivists for being crypto-theological; whereas that very positivistic objectivity is despised as a cloak for ideologies and special interests, and so politics is deliberately conducted, not objectively, but according to Marxist tenets. Here, in our attempt to trace the postconciliar development of the Catholic Church and describe her current position, we cannot pursue further the political and economical problems associated with these points of departure but rather must try to see how the generations on which they made such an impression found points of contact between their own feeling for life, on the one hand, and faith and theology, on the other. Two slogans, I think, characterize this problem: the new movement means a farewell to history and a farewell to metaphysics.

Farewell to history: history to this way of thinking is the ready-made world, which in its secular form is referred to by the title "establishment" and in its ecclesiastical form, by the title "ministerial church" and which appears as the oppressor, the impediment to what is new and the cause of all that is wrong with the present world system. Thus history is regarded as an obstacle; being the power of what has been, it stands in the way of what is to come; it is not possible to find models of progress in it. Citing history appears to such a mind-set to be an expression of reactionary thinking and hence baseless, indeed, false. Only against the background of such intellectual presuppositions can one explain how swiftly the actual statements and intentions of Vatican II could be consigned to oblivion and be replaced at first by the utopia of an impending Vatican III and, then, by synods that may make much of the "spirit" of Vatican II but ignore the documents. The "spirit" here means turning to the future as the field of unlimited possibilities. History, furthermore, admittedly plays a role in two other forms as well, although in a way that just goes to underscore what has been said thus far:

1. History becomes significant insofar as it has been "seen through" or scrutinized along Marxist-Hegelian lines. In this scrutiny, however, the one who scrutinizes positions himself outside of history, which he takes in hand so as to bring it to its destination.

2. History can be evoked as the "dangerous memory" of mankind: the reservoir of antihistorical elements that have become pent up in history is discovered as a potentially revolutionary force that it is worth arousing. Ernst Bloch challenged leftists to understand the Bible in a new way from this perspective: From the serpent in Paradise on, in his opinion, there is a series of figures who contradict currently accepted

truths and stand up to those in power; this revolutionary leaven that has accumulated in world history makes the Bible and history important after all. This offers a new guideline for interpreting Scripture and tradition, which also affects contemporary readings of the Second Vatican Council; for those who from their reading of the past are already attuned to hearing little else but the voices of conflict, contradiction, and struggle, it seems relatively easy to read everything in that way and to be assured that they are following the spirit of the Council by the fact that they set out from its teachings to make even bolder breaks with what has been.

Farewell to history, however, also and necessarily means farewell to Being as a constant reality of man and turning to the pragmatism of what is yet to be created at any moment. Eschatology, the expectation of the world to come, is no longer seen within the theology of creation but, rather, replaces creation: the real world worth living in is yet to be created, namely, by man himself, contrary to what he finds already in place. This also means, then, that the *pragma* of human work is no longer situated within the *Logos* of the creation that has taken place but, rather, abolishes the *Logos*. Man himself is the eschatological creator, whom *Logos* does not precede but only follows: in the beginning is not "the Word" but "the deed".

If we return to the starting point of our reflections, we can sum up our discussion thus far by saying: Today's situation in the Church and the world can be explained to a great extent by the meshing of the spiritual and intellectual shocks experienced in the transition to the second postwar generation with ideological and theological movements that played into each other's hands. This means that the debate about the true heritage of Vatican II today cannot be conducted in terms of the documents alone. A decisive factor in its progress will be whether an intellectual defense can be found not only for an antihistorical-utopian interpretation of the Council, but also for a creative-spiritual understanding of it in living union with the true tradition. It also depends, however, on whether theology and Church in the long run will still have anything at all to say to mankind. Thus it all comes down to the question: What forces, if any, can the Catholic Church and her theology count on at present? I see three:

First of all, we should mention the postconciliar progressivism that is fusing more and more with neo-Marxist ideas and, thereby, becoming increasingly narrow; this movement is distancing itself ever more rapidly from its starting points. Its initial approach was found in the theology of the world that J. B. Metz developed by fusing Karl Rahner's reinterpretation of Thomism in terms of transcendental philosophy with the interpretation of the world inspired by Luther and elaborated by Friedrich Gogarten. In its encounter with Ernst Bloch, this theology of the world turned, first, into the theology of hope and, then, with logical consistency into political theology. Today this trend has developed far beyond the teachings of its founders into a general reform pragmatism having various currents; more and more it has come to be a movement without any big names. Precisely in its anonymity, this movement presents itself as the power of the one true modernity, which increasingly fuses with the general neo-Marxist trend and for that reason is not really a critical force in society that could produce some hope, however much it tries to recommend itself through the slogans of "hope" and "criticism". Such trends spread chiefly in student unions and, of course in a more muted form, in individual groups of priests; anyone who reads the papers of the German Catholic Student Union [*Katholische Deutsche Studenten-Einigung*], the umbrella organization of student unions, senses that he has been transported to a Marxist branch office in which politico-economic and theological vocabulary mingle in a way that is sometimes quite amazing. They understand themselves as a "*sine qua non* for a new Church" and, conscious of this mission, seek to engineer events that are supposed to overcome history and bring about a classless society and their earthly paradise in the Church, too, through their revolutionary exploitation of the Church.

Secondly, we should mention the position that sees the only possible salvation in precise adherence to Scholastic theology and philosophy: this is a continuation of what had made its appearance during the Council as the force of conservatism. In the realm of theology, this approach scarcely plays any role at all; on the contrary, it is striking how quickly the very same proponents of a homemade Scholastic theology not infrequently lay down their weapons and went over to vague forms of Modernism. Much more important is a devotional movement that feels betrayed and abandoned by theology and now is determined to find its own way without theology or, indeed, in opposition to it. Having grasped instinctively the threat of a total falsification and an unavoidable collapse of the values that until now were fundamental, people embark on a flight into that which they consider especially Catholic: into a Marian devotion that is fueled by visions and miracles, into a narrow-minded battle for the letter of the old liturgy, and so on—only in this way, they believe, can they preserve their Catholic identity. We should not underestimate the extent of genuine religious forces that are at work here as well. Yet there is likewise a danger of formalistic narrowness that leads to sectarianism; this is clearly discernible where people suspect Vatican II itself of heresy and thereby leave the path of association with the universal Church.

In third place, we should point out those forces that actually made Vatican II possible and shaped it but very soon afterward were steam-rollered by a wave of modernity for which it had been possible to mistake them only by a fundamental error. We are talking about a theology and a piety that developed essentially on the basis of Sacred Scripture, the Fathers of the Church, and the great liturgical heritage of the universal Church. At the Council, the proponents of this theology had been concerned about nourishing the faith, not only on the thinking of the last hundred years, but on the great stream of tradition as a whole, so as to make it richer and livelier but, at the same time, simpler and more accessible. For the time being, this attempt seems to have failed; it had little effect in comparison with the more compre-hensible programs that have replaced it since. Nevertheless, there are more and more indications that the impulse of this theology was not spent in a vacuum. There is much reason to expect its reestablishment, and in this I see the hope of the present situation. After all the flirting with self-concocted liturgies, we are experiencing the dawning of a new desire for a deep personal encounter with God and for worship that really allows believers to recognize the presence of the Eternal. We are experiencing the longing of people for Jesus Christ and that simple gesture which unpretentiously opens itself to the action of the Holy Spirit, not in order to flee the world, but precisely so as to have more to give it than new problems. It seems to me that more and more people are beginning to recognize after all that the mere pragmatism of reforming ecclesiastical structures neglects precisely what ought to be given to the people: in reality, the fanatical reform of structures is a new clericalism and a clerical egotism that overlooks people and cares primarily for one's own interests. The forces counterbalancing this il-lusory progress are still weak, but they are developing, and so perhaps the formless ferment in which we find ourselves at the moment, ten years after the Council, will slowly give rise to a renewal that deserves the name.

In conclusion, allow me to explain in somewhat greater detail this hope and the goal to which it is directed. One of the characteristic demands of that neo-clerical progressivism mentioned earlier is the demand for an end to sacred spaces, for the end to liturgy that leads worshippers out of their everyday routine: according to this theory, liturgy can only be a concentration of daily life; the Liturgy of the Word must be presented as a discussion, while the celebration of the Sacrament must take the form of ordinary table fellowship. Related to this is the demand for a "functional" ministry, as they put it: the priest is supposed to coordinate the assembly's discussion and meal and normally will lead them, too, but his vocation should be as secular as any other; whenever he is not actually leading a congregation, he is not a priest. I think that such seemingly modern demands do not come from people who are really contemporaries of our world today and of its distress. They come from people who are still stuck deep in yesterday and suffer from an "outdated" complex. They feel tangibly constricted by the sturdy armor of ecclesiality or "churchiness" in which they were raised, and they try in vain to get rid of it. They are rebelling against *their* world, which, however, for most people today has long ceased to exist. Their outcry stems in large measure from the fact that they have not kept up at all with the present age. For the problem of people today is not that they are constrained by so-called sacral taboos; their problem is that they live in a hopelessly profane world that relentlessly pursues its programs even into their leisure time. The real threat that is breathing down our necks is no longer the ecclesiastical order but rather the all-encompassing management that, for all our bourgeois freedoms, increasingly degrades us and makes us functionaries of an anonymous, suffocating system and nearly drives one to despair. And then a multi-purpose hall, functional ministry, and profane liturgy besides? No. That is certainly not what can ensure a future for the faith.

Only someone who lives half his life in yesterday feels that the faith is oppressive or dangerous. Only someone who lives half his life in yesterday has to compete with faith for the future. Anyone who sloughs off yesterday and finds himself exposed to the unadorned today discovers that the world needs holiness. Its dark nights ask for God. And he knows that faith has a future. Not the future of functionaries and of neo-clerical management, but God's future. The future of mystery, of faith, of prayer, of true liturgy, with its poetry that comes from eternity. The heritage of Vatican II has not yet been awakened. But it is awaiting its hour. And it will come; of that I am certain.[1]

[1] On this question, see also my book *Faith and the Future*, trans. Ronald Walls (Chicago: Franciscan Herald Press, 1971), especially the section: "What Will the Church Look Like in 2000", 89–106.

41. What Good Is Christianity Now?

Our ears ring with the assertion that is gradually becoming self-evident: It is no longer possible today to deal with the faith of the Church. Meanwhile, in many quarters, describing something as traditional is already equivalent to dismissing it as outmoded and irrelevant. The Church, however, is vitally dependent on the tradition of what she received from the beginning and thus seems to have no chance whatsoever, at least in her present form. Such arguments and ideas would not wield such force if they were not based on an experience that hardly anyone can avoid: on the one hand, the perception that everything in the world is different now; it seems to be changing faster and faster and so radically that none of the familiar standards holds and only entirely new ways can help an entirely altered mankind. This is accompanied, on the other hand, by the experience of the ineffectiveness of Christian culture, which cannot tear man away from his misery and, thus, for many people ends up being a mere consolation, a pseudo-redemption that passes reality by. Indeed, someone who does not share in the Christian experience can hardly arrive at a different judgment; the result, though, is that people begin to be ashamed of the Christian message and want to serve up more tangible successes: social and economic accomplishments that no one can dispute, which tangibly liberate people and save them from their misery. Meanwhile, the need grows faster than the assistance that is offered, and with this swerve into material aid, which shamefully attempts to obliterate tradition and to redefine Christianity as part of the modern human development project, comes increased division in the Church, which thus becomes that much more joyless, hopeless, and problematic for everybody. Little remains, it seems, of the Good News; instead, there is conflict and embarrassment. A long time ago Cardinal Döpfner compared the Church of today with a

---

Translated by Michael J. Miller.

construction site in order to explain the unease that is widespread within her; a critical voice added that she appears to be a construction site where the blueprint has been lost and each one of the bricklayers and carpenters keeps working as he pleases: the result looks like it.

What good is Christianity now? Christian redemption by faith has been replaced today by two new ways in which people try to redeem themselves: the political-economic-social way and the psychological way. On the one hand, more and more often the affluent society seeks out those secular father-confessors whose scientific knowledge of the human soul is supposed to restore order to its shattered, empty existence: supposedly we have yet to discover what love is, what honor is, and all that is primordially human. But do these doctors really help? They may be able to say *how* the individual faculties of the human soul function, but not *why*. Meanwhile, the disintegration of the human soul is caused precisely by the fact that its faculties are idling. As we look at its efforts, we can see quite clearly that the human soul is so constructed that it does not provide an explanation for itself. It is not assembled like a clock, a self-enclosed whole that functions when you know in what place each piece belongs. Rather, the soul lives in an open-ended circular course, or, better, in an open parabola, and without its center or focus, which lies outside of it, it cannot be healed. An image from Augustine comes to mind: he said that human life is constructed in such a way that God forms the keystone: when this highest part is locked in place, the other parts hold together in a meaningful arrangement; if it is loosened, however, then everything else falls apart and only pieces are left.

But we must not get ahead of ourselves. Alongside psychological redemption stands the socio-economic version, the way of all-encompassing politics. Everything is political, we hear today; therefore, only the deliberate politicization of Church, faith, and liturgy can blaze the trail into the future and "redeem" mankind. Anyone who sees the terrible poverty of the people in India and Indochina, in the slums of the major cities in North and South America, anyone who discerns how the process of industrialization increasingly programs man and threatens to take away his soul, will certainly not underestimate the importance of politics for the salvation of mankind. He will understand why the Church from the very beginning—together with the synagogue—through her prayers for world leaders recognized the political realm as a partial realm of human salvation. In this respect, Christians have a political obligation, and if they do not fulfill it, they deprive the faith of its realism. The honesty and seriousness of the faith is demonstrated precisely in its ability to undertake positive political activity as well as political resistance when that is called for.

Political concerns are part of human salvation. But *all-encompassing* politics would surely be a human disaster. Whereas man does need bread in order to be saved, he is not redeemed by bread alone; a just distribution of power is pertinent to his salvation, but the redistribution of power cannot be his redemption. There is a politico-economic interpretation of the Old Testament that claims that salvation consists in the establishment of welfare and security. The account of the temptation of Jesus characterizes this notion of salvation as Satan's concept of salvation. Very real currents of Jesus' time are behind the story that Satan suggested that he turn stones into bread and offered him dominion over all the kingdoms of the world: the Messiah, it was thought, would prove himself by giving plenty of bread to all and by establishing an earthly kingdom of peace under the banner of his political power. That is precisely why Jesus, who neither put an end to world hunger nor changed the balance of power, could not be the Messiah. . . . You redeem mankind only if you redeem it politically and socially; everything else is meaningless. In contrast to that view, the Gospel declares: Such a redemption would hand mankind over to Satan, that is, completely enslave it.

That seems to be a very stern judgment. But perhaps the experience of our generation can give us a new understanding of this assertion. In Solzhenitsyn's great novel *The First Circle*, there is a remarkable parallel to this biblical statement. First of all, inasmuch as the entire book takes place in "the first circle of hell", and this hell is found where totalitarian politics has set up its paradise: this paradise *is* hell, in which man destroys man—terrifyingly portrayed in the concluding scene, where prisoners are hidden from the public and crammed into food wagons that bear the lettering: "MEAT". The correspondent of the French newspaper *Libération* sees these delivery wagons again and again and jots in his notebook: "One can only conclude that the provisioning of the capital is excellent."

There is one scene in the book in which, it seems to me, this connection seems to be heightened to unmistakable clarity. The author places on the lips of the old, idealistic Marxist Rubin a moving interpretation of Goethe's *Faust*. It is well known that Goethe's tragedy does not conclude tragically but, rather, with an optimism that admittedly is based on a remarkable contradiction. Faust was supposed to lose his soul if he said to some moment in his life: "Stay a while, you are so fair." In all the seductive pleasures with which Satan attempts to bewitch him, Faust does not let that word slip out. At the end of his life, he organizes multitudes of workers to reclaim land from the sea, and now, to the clanking of the shovels that seem in fact to be creating a new earth, he pronounces the words:

> This now is wisdom's ultimate conclusion:
> The only man deserving life and freedom
> Is he who has to conquer them each day.
> And so, despite encircling dangers here,
> Child, man, and old man spend their active year.
> Such an industrious throng I wish to see:
> To stand on free soil with a people free.
> To such a moment I could surely say:
> You are so lovely, do not pass, but stay!

Faust returns to its beginning. The protagonist had translated the Prologue to the Gospel of John: "In the beginning was the Deed", replacing Word with Deed; he saw the redemption of the world, not in the Logos or meaning that supports it in advance and is Word to each individual, but rather in the Deed whereby man creates his own meaning for himself. He dies in the hope of the redemption that his deed will accomplish for him: political-social action that creates a free people on free soil—that is what lasts; that is salvation. Solzhenitsyn's character Rubin comments: "But if one analyzes it, was Goethe not laughing at the illusions that underlie human happiness? In actual fact, there was not any service to mankind at all. Faust pronounces the long-awaited phrase one step from the grave, utterly deceived and perhaps truly crazy. And the lemurs immediately shove him into the pit. . . ." Indeed, when you reflect on it, the whole thing seems to be pure irony. The clanking shovels that prompted Faust to exclaim belong to the *lemures*, the ghostly servants of the devil; they are not shaping a new world but are digging his grave, and only a blind man or one who has been blinded can hear in them the music of redemption, not suspecting that he is mocking himself. Given the context of the whole book, it seems quite clear to me that Solzhenitsyn is thereby giving his interpretation of Stalinism (and, in fact, of Marxism in general): "Stay awhile, you are so fair", he says now to a world of work, to a self-made world to be built up by man himself, which in reality is a world of evil spirits, in which man's grave is being dug—the devil's mockery of man, who is blind, blinded, and wizened and no longer notices that he is praising hell as his redemption.

Let us try to say what is meant without metaphor: Man needs politics, social and economic planning and activity. But when that becomes all-encompassing, when politics purports to be the redemption of man, it is trying to play the role of theology or of faith and then becomes the total enslavement of man. Without a meaning that goes deeper than the ordering of the economy, man perishes. Perhaps in the history of man's self-emancipation during the last 150 years there really have been moments that gave the impression that man could walk away from the God question without suffering any harm. That he could put it aside as something dispensable. Perhaps it might even have seemed as though the God question were really hindering him from becoming free of the past and devoting himself emphatically to his own concerns. But anyone who looks at the historical configuration today will at least have to give that a lot more thought. The situation today is defined by the opposition between positivism (as the new form of liberalism) and Marxism as a political prophecy of salvation: between the two runs the dispute about man, in philosophical terms as a dispute between Popper's neo-positivism and the Frankfurt School. Whereas positivism can prove to all Marxist philosophies that they are secretly theologies that cannot be verified by the facts, Marxism can prove to positivism that its objectivity lacks a standard and a goal. In neither camp, however, does one cross the real threshold at which man asks about himself, about why he exists and where he is going. Ultimately they both have nothing to say about anything except power and consumer goods. But that leaves man's unique nature empty. The oppressive thing about many forms of modern Christianity is that they, too, seem to have become blind to anything that is not power or consumer goods. That they, too, can understand the Church only in terms of power or gratification.

That is certainly not the way to salvage Christianity. Its greatness lies in the fact that it gives humanity to man. A way, first of all. Guidance as to how he should act and live. Perhaps ten years ago that still seemed to us like mere moralism that we would prefer to do without. Today we know that the man who has no essence (in Sartre's sense), who must always invent himself first, is by that very fact ruined physically and psychologically, and we can appreciate again the gift of the way. Admittedly: a way is only a direction and, hence, to be followed only if it offers hope of a destination. If it leads forward. Hope, however, for man is ultimately just love. For the one who believes in Jesus Christ, however, it has become visible and certain as the foundation of the world. And the Christian way leads to him. Indeed, he himself is the way. Thus one could formulate the basic Christian principle as follows, a bit theoretically perhaps: Love that has been believed and has become visible in Jesus Christ is man's hope as the way.

Allow me to conclude with a more practical remark. In his prison notebooks, Bonhoeffer once remarked that today even the Christian must live *quasi Deus non daretur*—as though God did not exist. He must keep God out of everyday entanglements and shape his earthly life on his own. In contrast, I would prefer to put it precisely the other way around: Today even someone for whom the existence of God and the world of faith have become obscure should live practically *quasi Deus esset*—as though God really did exist. He should live as a subject to the reality of the truth, which is not something we produce but is, rather, our master. Live by the standard of righteousness, which we do not merely devise but which is a power that measures us. Live mindful of our responsibility toward Love, which waits for us and loves us. Live according to the claim of the Eternal. Anyone who is alert to current developments will see that this is the only way man can be rescued. God —he alone—is man's salvation; this unheard-of truth, which seemed to us until now to be a scarcely attainable ideal, has become the most practical formula for our present hour in history. And anyone who entrusts himself, although perhaps hesitantly at first, to this demanding and yet ineluctable As-If—to live as if God existed—will become increasingly aware of the fact that this As-If is the genuine reality. He will perceive, along with its responsibility, its redemptive power. And he will know profoundly and ineradicably why even today Christianity is still necessary as the truly Good News that redeems mankind.

Sources

1. "Kirche als Ort der Verkündigung", previously unpublished.

2. "Maßstäbe der Evangeliumsverkündigung heute", previously unpublished.

3. "Christozentrik in der Verkündigung?" *Trierer Theologische Zeitschrift* 70 (1961): 1–14.

4. "Theologie und Verkündigung im Holländischen Katechismus" was published under the title "Der Holländische Katechismus: Versuch einer theologischen Würdigung", *Hochland* 62 (1970): 301–13; in Swedish, in *Katolsk informationsjänst*, 1970: 363–68 and 390–93.

5. "Der heutige Mensch vor der Gottesfrage", previously unpublished.

6. "Verkündigung von Gott heute", previously unpublished.

7. "Beten in unserer Zeit", previously unpublished.

8. "Thesen zur Christologie", previously unpublished.

9. "Was bedeutet Jesus Christus für mich?" in *Wer ist Jesus von Nazaret —für mich? 100 zeitgenössische Antworten*, edited by H. Spaemann, 23–26. Munich, 1973.

10. "Nachfolge", *Klerusblatt* (Munich) 45 (1965): 140f., and in *Die Funkpostille, ein Querschnitt durch das Programm des Saarlünd: Rundfunks* (1964/1965): 99–104.

11. "Schöpfungsglaube und Evolutionstheorie", in *Wer ist das eigentlich —Gott?* edited by H.J. Schultz, 232–45. Munich, 1968.

12. "Gratia praesupponit naturam", in *Einsicht und Glaube*, Festschrift for G. Söhngen, edited by J. Ratzinger and H. Fries, 135–49. Freiburg, 1962.

13. "Christliches Weltverständnis" was published under the title "Angesichts der Welt von heute: Überlegungen zur Konfrontation mit der Kirche im Schema XIII", *Wort und Wahrheit* 20 (1965): 493–504; expanded under the title: "Der Christ und die Welt von heute: Überlegungen zum sog. Schema XIII des Zweiten Vatikanischen Konzils", in *Weltverständnis im Glauben*, edited by J.B. Metz, 143–160. Mainz, 1965.

14. "Zum Personbegriff in der Theologie" was published under the title "Zum Personverständnis in der Dogmatik", in *Das Personverständnis in der Pädagogik und ihren Nachbarwissenschaften*, edited by J. Speck, 157–71. Münster, 1966.

15. "Abschied vom Teufel?" was published in various diocesan papers, spring 1973 (Regensburg, Munich, Passau, Bamberg, Rottenburg, Würzburg, Aachen, Speyer).

16. "Vom Geist der Brüderlichkeit", *Horizonte* 1 (1962): 1–2.

17. "Die anthropologischen Grundlagen der Bruderliebe", *Caritasdienst* 23 (1970): 45–49.

18. "Kirche als Ort des Dienstes am Glauben", in *Offene Horizonte*, edited by E. Späth, 119–24. Freiburg, 1970.

19. "Bischof und Kirche" was published under the title "Wo der Bischof da die Kirche", *Regensburger Bistumsblatt* 41, no. 22 (1972): 3–4.

20. "Vom Sinn des Kirchbaus", previously published only privately.

21. "Zur Theologie des Todes", in "Tod und Auferstehung: Erwägungen zum christlichen Verständnis des Todes", Klerusblatt (Munich) 39 (1959): 366–69.

22. "Was kommt nach dem Tod?" in *Dialog mit dem Zweifel*, edited by G. Rein, 108–13. Stuttgart, 1969.

23. "Auferstehung und ewiges Leben", in *Tod und Leben: Von den letzten Dingen*. Liturgie und Mönchtum, edited by T. Bogler, vol. 25, 92–103. Maria Laach, 1959.

24. "Der Stammbaum Jesu", *Bibel und Leben* 3 (1962): 275–78.

25. "Die Zeit der vierzig Tage", *Klerusblatt* (Munich) 50 (1970): 75ff.

26. "Karfreitag", previously unpublished.

27. "Das Geheimnis der Osternacht", *Klerusblatt* (Munich) 39 (1959): 101–2.

28. "Auferstehung als Sendung" was published in daily newspapers.

29. "Ostern heute" was published in daily newspapers.

30. "Christi Himmelfahrt", *Geist und Leben* 40 (1967): 81–85.

31. "Der Verstand, der Geist und die Liebe: Eine Pfingstbetrachtung", *Die Rheinische Post*, Düsseldorf, 1969.

32. "Vom Sinn des Advents", *Klerusblatt* (Munich) 38 (1958): 418–20.

33. "Drei Weihnachtsbetrachtungen": the section "Das unbesiegte Licht" appeared in *Hochland* 52 (1959/1960): 97–100; otherwise unpublished.

34. "Haben wir Grund zu feiern?" previously unpublished.

35. "Betrachtung am Silvesterabend", previously unpublished.

36. "Mariä Heimsuchung", *Bibel und Leben* 3 (1962): 138–40.

37. "Mariä Himmelfahrt", previously unpublished.

38. "Predigt am Fest des heiligen Augustinus", *Cor unum: Mitteilungen an die deutsche Augustinerfamilie* 22 (1965): 177–81.

39. "Betrachtung am Primiztag", previously unpublished.

40. "Zehn Jahre nach Konzilsbeginn—wo stehen wir?" previously unpublished.

41. "Wozu noch Christentum?" *Lebendige Kirche: Mitteilungen des Diözesanrates im Erzbistum Köln*, 1972, 6–9. Reprinted in *L'Osservatore Romano: Wochenausgabe in deutscher Sprache* 2, no. 23 (1972): 10. Excerpts were circulated by KNA in several weekly publications.

Index of Names

Index of Biblical References